TAMATA and the ALLIANCE

Also by Bernard Moitessier

Sailing to the Reefs

Cape Horn: The Logical Route

The Long Way

Bernard Moitessier
TAMATA
and the
ALLIANCE

A MEMOIR

Translated by William Rodarmor

WATERLINE

Copyright © 1993 by Arthaud
Translation Copyright © 1995 by William Rodarmor

First published in the UK in 1995
by Waterline Books, an imprint of Airlife Publishing Ltd

First published in France under the title
Tamata et l'Alliance by Editions Arthaud

British Library Cataloguing-in-Publication Data
A catalogue record for this book
is available from the British Library

ISBN 1 85310 738 7

Printed in the United States of America

Waterline Books
an imprint of Airlife Publishing Ltd
101 Longden Road, Shrewsbury SY3 9EB

The Indochinese Peninsula

CHAPTER 1

In the days when Vietnam was still called Indochina, my parents left France as newlyweds, drawn by the lure of distant lands. My father had a business degree from the Hautes Etudes Commerciales, my mother her palette and brushes from the Beaux-Arts. She also had me—an embryo nestled in her womb.

They sailed first to Madagascar, but Madagascar didn't appeal to them. They wanted to go farther, to that land of rice paddies and reed-covered plains that stretch as far as the eye can see, and a river so wide it looks like the sea—a river that gives life to the earth every year during the floods of the rainy season.

A land of hills and mountains, with forests so vast that you can walk in them for weeks on end, beyond time, with only the sounds of the jungle speaking to your senses, awash in a smell of humus that comes from the oldest part of life and works its way into the deepest part of your being.

A fairy-tale land, with dragons and gods, pagodas everywhere, and an enormous city of gigantic temples swallowed by the jungle. A land virgin in its essence, but pregnant with its people's past and present. A dreamland where East and West might blend into a wider, deeper, richer life.

So my parents traveled on to Indochina, where I was born a few weeks later, in April 1925. My mother and my Chinese *amah* sang me lullabies from their native countries, and each of those profoundly different cultures had dragons buried deep in its roots. But the dragons were the same, and you had to learn to fight them.

Soon after arriving in Indochina, my father took over a small importing business in Saigon. Françou was born the following year, Jacky a year later. Then came Babette, nine years younger than me, and finally my brother Gilbert, a few years later. Our *amah* Assam, who was practically our second mother, stayed with us until we left Indochina twenty-seven years later. So did Minh, the cook, who joined our household shortly after Jacky was born.

Every year we spent our three months of summer vacation in a village on the Gulf of Siam close to the Cambodian border. There, my brothers and I lived in almost limitless freedom, a freedom of the senses and the body so intense we practically turned into little jungle animals. The rest of the year meant the city, school, the swimming pool, our house, and a few escapades in the streets of Saigon.

With its sounds and smells, Saigon was a dense swarming of people, a world echoing with the clatter of thousands of wooden sandals clicking along the sidewalks, a world balanced on shoulders, pulled in carts and pedicabs, and carried on bicycles amid a carillon of ringing bells.

The streets were criss-crossed by *tac-tacs*, carts that looked like matchboxes mounted on big iron-rimmed wooden wheels, drawn by little horses with bells on their collars, whose drivers pounded their wooden seat-boxes to clear the way through traffic.

Everything moved by muscle power. There were few cars and you rarely heard the sound of a motor, either on the streets or in the craftsmen's shops. Yet the city echoed with a deep murmur laced with the thousands of smells from peddlers' wares: dried fish from the great Cambodian lake, shrimp paste from the Ca Mau region, *nuoc mam* from Phu Quoc and Phan Thiet, the fragrance of Chinese noodle soup, spices, ginger, mint, camphor, durian fruits, pastries fried in coconut oil or dusted with chili powder, and the bland smell of live fish being picked over in big woven-bamboo baskets waterproofed with a mixture of pitch and cow manure.

My brothers and I often walked home from school by way of the market. In front of a stand, an old woman was sticking her thumbnail into a guava to see if it was to her liking. She returned the fruit to the pile, took another, jabbed her nail into the pulp, once, twice, three times, sniffed, spat a stream of betel-nut juice, haggled endlessly, smelled a fourth guava before lancing it with her nail, decided to take it . . . no, she was choosing yet another one, again sticking a thumbnail into the soft pulp and arguing about the price in her high-pitched voice. Along the fruit stands, all this was multiplied a hundred times in a gabble that drowned everything out, with splotches of betel-nut juice dotting the ground like bloody stars.

Crouched in front of his patient, a sidewalk dentist rubbed black paste into the man's jaw. Then, with his thumb and forefinger, he seized the molar deep in the patient's mouth, braced the man's head with his other hand, arched his whole body . . . and yanked out the tooth. He dropped it into a little basket full of other stumps extracted the same way, using nothing but his magic paste and iron fingers. He dabbed at the gum with a bit of cloth hanging from his belt, chopped up a pinch of leaves he took from a little chest, rolled it into a miraculous little ball and applied it to the gum. The patient stood up, paid a piaster, and walked away, feeling no pain.

Françou and Jacky shouted for me to come. On the way, I passed rows of chickens with their wings twisted behind their backs in a kind of hammerlock. The French thought this cruel, but I wasn't so sure. The chickens stayed calm and didn't seem to be in pain. They couldn't stand up, but they must have preferred having their wings locked to having their feet trussed with string. And it was a lot better than the fate of chickens in Africa, where live chickens are apparently sold in the market already plucked.

I came to where my brothers were calling me. A noisy crowd was watching a duel between a pair of Siamese fighting fish in a large bowl. Neither one bigger than your pinky, the two were attacking each other furiously. With their huge fins like fiery rainbows ranging from red to violet, they looked like tiny fans for dolls. The ground around the bowl was covered with the piasters people had bet. After a few minutes of fierce battle, one fish turned grey and sank to the bottom. Its owner plucked the victim from the bowl and paid out piasters to the winners.

Outside the market, we lingered to watch a scene that never failed to delight us. An old man was crouching in front of a cage that held a crested red-spotted bird. Near the cage stood a board covered with slots labeled with Chinese characters. When enough bets had been stuck in the slots, the man made a whistling noise with his tongue. The bird hopped through a hole in a box at the

XXV. — Scènes de la rue : Marchand de Soupe, Panier au bébé

Il s'en va, toujours courant à petits pas, et s'annonçant par une claquette de bambou. « Qui veut un bol de koutiou fumant ? »

Sketch by Marthe Moitessier

Street Scenes

back of its cage, to emerge a few seconds later holding in its beak a tiny sliver of bamboo bearing a Chinese character. Then it hopped across the cage and laid the sliver on the finger of its owner, who rewarded it with a grain of rice. Three times in a row, the bird went to find a bamboo sliver in the mysterious box and was rewarded with a grain of rice. The person who guessed the right combination of characters got four or five times his original bet and had his horoscope told. The old man put the other bets away in a buttoned pouch he wore next to his skin.

A little further down the sidewalk, a fat woman was fanning a fire under a clay oven, boiling eggs in a pot. Three coolies were crouched around it, eating a local delicacy. The eggs had embryos inside, more or less mature, depending on your taste, and were supposedly delicious with a little salt and pepper; chicken eggs cost twice as much as duck eggs.

Day and night, the streets rang with the cries of peddlers and artisans, each distinct from all the others. A "click-clack" as piercing as a grasshopper's song would precisely locate a noodle-soup seller banging his bamboo clappers on a street corner. The blind masseurs had their own special call, as did the fishmongers, tooth-pullers, fortune-tellers, public scribes, even the children who sold those tiny clay good-luck turtles, no bigger than a fingernail, whose bamboo feet were moved by a live fly trapped inside.

Thus, even in the midst of all that hubbub, everyone could tell by sound alone what everyone else was up to in the teeming anthill called Saigon.

Though I risked a whipping for it, I sometimes used to wander the river banks during school hours, watching the junks.

The most unusual ones came from the Annam coast. Only their gunwales, bow, and sternpost were wood. The rest of the hull was made of woven bamboo sealed with a mixture of cow manure, pitch, and wood oil, like the fish baskets in the market. During the northeast monsoon, these junks arrived from Phan Thiet loaded with *nuoc mam*, then headed back north at the start of the southwest monsoon loaded with rice for Tonkin. Once I found myself chatting with the *tai cong* of one of these junks, who was astonished to meet a French boy who could speak

Vietnamese. Seeing how badly I wanted to go on board, he ferried me over in a kind of huge floating basket which I learned could carry up to ten two-hundred-pound bags of rice. He sculled the boat with a short, very wide paddle—but by pulling, instead of pushing. I was amazed at his skill; the basket boat was completely round, yet he could paddle it in a perfectly straight line. Once we were aboard, my new friend showed me around the junk. Surprised that it could so interest a child, he kindly answered all my questions. He said his boat could carry fifty tons of rice and sail closer to the wind than any other kind of junk. He showed me how the huge rudder slid in the grooved transom, and could be lowered well below the bottom of the boat to serve as an aft leeboard. A kind of daggerboard slid in a slot near the bow, acting as a forward leeboard to compensate for the boat's shallow draft. With these two fully adjustable leeboards, you could achieve a perfectly neutral helm under sail. When approaching a beach or a river mouth, you raised the daggerboard and rudder, and the boat then drew very little water . . . *I would give anything to sail away aboard this junk, far from school.* But when I told the *tai cong* this, he stroked my cheek and said he couldn't afford any trouble with the police. He gave me a model of an Annam coastal junk carved out of a coconut and brought me back to shore.

The junks were loaded and unloaded by lines of coolies with sweaty, glistening chests, who wore those wide conical palm-frond hats that protected you so well from the sun, and even from rain. The coming and going never stopped. With huge loads hanging from limber bamboo slats tucked on their shoulders, the coolies practically ran up the narrow gangplank in a dance punctuated by insults when the man ahead didn't move fast enough.

On deck, women in black turbans, their mouths red from chewing betel nut, stowed the loads each man shrugged off his pole. The coolie then ran down the other plank, took the bamboo counter the boss handed him and stuck it in his belt without slowing his smooth pace, his bare toes gripping the sweat-slippery gangplank like suction cups.

Sampans glided from one junk to the next like the small tan hawks that soared in the sky, looking for fish in the brown river. Watching the coolies work, the shallow-draft sampans hoped to be called to speed the loading of the junks when the tide began to ebb. It would mean more bamboo counters in the belts, more pay to be spent at night in the streets.

When the house was asleep, my brothers and I sometimes tip-toed down the wooden staircase and stepped outside into the great freedom of Saigon's powerful life after dark.

Around the market, little groups of men and women squatted in circles betting on card games or playing games of chance involving squares with genies, strange animals, Chinese characters, crosses, and lozenges, all drawn right on the sidewalk.

Everywhere, dice were being thrown, cards shuffled, bamboo sticks bearing black, red, blue, and yellow symbols moved. The little piles of piasters on the ground changed hands, arguments erupted, insults flew. Even as a child, I could sense a kind of violence that ran like a thread through the breath of the city at night.

Then came Tet, the lunar new year festival, and Saigon became delirious for a week. Great fireworks went off all night long above an enormous throng that overflowed the revelling city's streets. It was the week of the new-moon dragon, the luminous dragon that danced and danced to the sound of drums, bronze cymbals, and the thousands of firecrackers exploding everywhere. There were dragons for the poor and also dragons for the rich, thirty or forty yards long, with tiny bells all along their bodies. Opening their huge jaws beneath some prosperous merchant's balcony, they swallowed strings of firecrackers and a package of piasters that Assam told us were supposed to bring good luck.

This was the French colonial period; our house was big and the servants numerous. In addition to Assam and Minh the cook, who were part of the family, there was the boy who waited at table and cleaned the living quarters; Chu the chauffeur-mechanic who looked after the car and the delivery wagons; a maid, who was often replaced; and the rickshaw driver.

We were raised in fairly Spartan fashion, however, because my parents worried that their children would grow soft in the general climate of ease. Papa hated to see us slouch. "Stand up straight!" was a phrase I heard often, accompanied by a slap on my shoulder blades.

No mattresses for the children. We slept the way the Vietnamese did, wrapped in a sarong, with only a mat between our bodies and the wooden pallet. And we got whipped, too, especially on Saturdays when we came home with zeros on our report cards. My father couldn't understand how his children could be such dunces. "Three generations of intellectuals," he would say, "and this is all they produced?"

He hated lying, especially bluffing and cheating, which he considered the most contemptible kinds of lies. But if we didn't lie a little from time to time, the whippings would never end.

Very early, my father taught us to defend ourselves. "Faster! Faster! Harder! Harder!" he would shout, as our little fists punched his open hand. Laughing, Papa corrected our form and we laughed with him, happy and proud of our progress. He reminded us to always keep one fundamental rule in mind: never seek a quarrel and always try to work things out, but strike first once it was clear a fight was inevitable. When one of us happened to come home from school covered with bruises, Maman, half-laughing, half-serious, would ask the ritual question: "Did you bring the teeth?" She meant the other guy's teeth, of course.

Papa's temper scared us, but we admired his strength. No one in Saigon ever beat him swimming underwater; on one breath, he could swim two and a half times the length of the 33-meter pool. He could rise to a handstand by the strength of his arms alone, and walk on his hands for a ways. Françou became excellent at that, and could walk on his hands the entire length of the pool. I could never cover more than twenty yards. Jacky was the worst, but became the best shot with his air rifle. I remained faithful to my slingshot, and Françou concentrated on swimming.

My mother wanted us to grow up into handsome little animals full of life and health, with sharp eyes and agile feet, steeped in the wonderful stories of *The Jungle Book*, which she read to us in the evenings before we went to sleep.

While in the elementary grades, we rode to school obediently seated in the family rickshaw—or so our parents thought. Actually, once around the first corner the three satchels rode in the rickshaw while we covered the remaining mile at a jog. We wanted to become as strong as Papa and have his wind and endurance so we could play rugby and water polo like him when we grew up. It felt good to run, to listen to your body come happily alive, to make friends with it again, and to arrive at school all sweaty.

Running along Saigon's houses was like crossing an enormous

orchard. Almost every street was lined with fruit trees, mangoes and especially tamarinds. They were everywhere, the city was covered with them; you could walk for hours, always shaded by a tamarind tree. They are tall trees with tiny leaves like those of acacias or mimosas, that give a soft shade and close up at night as if to sleep. Their pods are used to make jams and other ingredients in Asian cooking. Gangs of people came with hand-carts and sacks and raised bamboo ladders to the lowest crotches in the trees. The coolies climbed the trees to shake the branches and the dry pods fell clattering to the sidewalk and the street, to be swept up, bagged, and piled on the carts by the women.

It was a feast for the birds, which darted and chirped around the pickers, hunting the insects driven from their hiding places. A feast, too, for the street children with their slingshots, who shot at the birds distracted by their pursuit of food.

There were also big parks where we used to go for slingshot practice, aiming at the stems of ripe mangoes to bring them down without bruising the fruit. And a zoo where egrets and teals roamed freely around ponds carpeted with water lilies, whose seeds were used in delicately flavored cakes. We sometimes passed through the zoo at the end of the day, running as usual alongside the rickshaw that carried our satchels.

More often than not, though, we ran toward the pool, where Papa was waiting for our swimming lessons. Once, one evening when I was seven or eight, he had to force me out of the pool. I had already done the crawl for three miles nonstop, and Papa was afraid I would have an attack. I protested that I wanted to go on, but he dragged me out of the water and kissed me, his eyes full of love.

Our house was enormous. It was actually two houses, with two roofs, separated by a small patio where we did gymnastics in the sunshine with our father before lunch.

The offices and storerooms of my father's business were on the ground floor, with courtyards crowded with barrels and crates of cans. Working at tubs, the women washed bottles, which, refilled with wine, were then delivered to the Chinese shopkeepers in the house's bicycle carts. You could hear the pounding of hammers as crates were nailed up, dull thuds as the coolies stacked merchandise to the ceiling, the squeak of packing straw, the clink of bottles, the rumble of barrels being rolled and the pounding of mallets as their bungs were knocked out, the fore-man's orders and reprimands. It was the life of the house, and it never ceased.

A circular staircase led to the first floor, where we lived with some of the servants. The rooms were huge, and the ceilings so high that our paper airplanes could loop the loop and glide to a landing without ever touching the walls. The building was so large that several upper rooms were used to temporarily house mer-chandise that overflowed the downstairs storerooms; we used to play cowboys and Indians in them during nap time.

From the first floor, another staircase led up to the terrace where a cistern supplied our water. Papa was careful to see that a thin film of kerosene always floated on the surface of the water, to kill the larvae of the dreaded malaria mosquitoes.

Beneath the roofs on either side of the terrace were attics, which you could only enter through two small, cobweb-covered openings next to the rain gutters. There we slipped into a secret world, in the company of bats hanging from the rafters like the kapok pods in our village, their large wings folded around their bodies, their eyes waiting for darkness.

Far above were the rooftops, level with the tops of the tamarind trees which muffled the sounds of the city like a leafy blanket. There, nobody ever came to bother us children. Under the sky, the roofs really belonged to us. I would bring my har-monica, Jacky his flute, on which he could play Ravel's *Boléro* all the way through without missing a note, and Françou the sketch-book he always carried with him.

Up there on the roofs, we escaped toward our village on the Gulf of Siam.

Jacky was sewing a sail for his outrigger canoe, using an old flour sack he had begged and pestered Assam into giving him. Among a jumble of old crates, I had helped him find a board wide enough for a rudder, and we spent days shaping it with our pocket knives. My own canoe was already fully rigged; so was Françou's.

Since returning from our last vacation, Françou had been drawing a map of the village. Every hut was in its exact place along the road, labeled with the name of the friend who lived there. Beyond the village lay the beach, the sea, the islands, the forest.

Looking at the picture, which was so real we could already imagine our return "home," Jacky and I argued over a detail.

"You know the old wasp nest? Well, it was closer to the tombs behind Derk's hut."

Françou wasn't convinced, but he moved the nest a bit anyway. We had burned it down, using torches made out of woven palm fronds, practically without getting stung by the hairy yellow and black wasps, whose backs bore a red spot that looked like an angry eye.

"Your green is a little too dark here. It should be lighter next to the big wild jackfruit tree at the bottom of the hill. And there, along the stream where the squirrels climb down the pistachio-tree vines to drink, the green should be darker. Don't you remember?"

Françou was a bit concerned, but didn't quite agree. He decided to hold off on correcting the green; we would wait until we were back in the village to be really sure.

Obediently bent over a notebook covered with drawings of boats, a boy in the very back row of the classroom sits looking out the window. He doesn't hear a word the teacher is saying, but immediately recognizes the song of the red-throated shrike, which is always so alert and cautious. And that of the fork-tailed widow, which gets distracted when it spends too much time smoothing its feathers.

A slight change in the trill tells him that the bird will move to another branch, and the boy strokes the slingshot hidden in his pocket. He knows that one trill means, "I'm just changing branches," and another, "I'm going to fly away."

And the boy flies off with the bird. He flies very, very high beyond the vast sweep of the rice paddies dotted with white egrets, beyond the bridges, the streams, and the branches of the Mekong River, far beyond the horizon, as far as the hills from which he can see his village. Before him stretches the great curving black sand beach, which is full of clams at low tide, and its two rocky points. Where the path to the temple makes a bend near the left-hand point, we could swim out to our magic island, noisy with the rattling of kingfishers, its miniature beach covered with perfect slingshot stones. And there, farther off but still within canoe range, the second island, strange and a little mysterious, which Françou had dubbed "Deadly Sin Island." And on the horizon, all the other islands. Behind the village lies the forest where birds call, with tiny plots of green pepper trees hidden on the brushy hillsides, the nests of the big hairy wasps we hated so much, the hives of wild bees that could be smoked out without too much trouble, and the green snakes you had to watch for along the barely visible trails made by the hills' wildlife. Then the boy returns to the village beach, lined with coconut trees, where his and his brothers' slim Cambodian outriggers wait. A beach hemmed with white, where he follows the little sandpipers with his eyes as they zigzag like flecks of foam in front of the waves so as not to get their feet wet. They're almost impossible to hit with a slingshot; they never stop moving, and you never know where they will be from one moment to the next.

Saigon had neither sea nor forest, but we brought back the forest of our vacations in the shape of tiny squirrels, no bigger than our hands, that had survived our slingshots. They traveled back with us between our skin and our shirts, knowing our smell. They came with us from the forest where they were born, the forest behind the village.

And so in the evenings, instead of doing their homework, three little boys quietly watched the squirrels playing on the rough walls of the nursery. They were treasures of life and beauty, with yellow bellies and three black stripes running along their backs, which were a pale gray that reminded you of the forest at dawn. Before going to sleep, each of us held his squirrel in his hands, palms joined in a nest of love, brushing it with our lips so he would be warm and always recognize its friend.

Then one morning I found mine stiff and cold on my wooden pallet, smothered between the mat and the warm, sleepy body he had come to nestle against, close to me, his friend. Great sobs racked my child's chest, and my mother tried to console me, but I still didn't feel like going to school that day. Our three squirrels, which were such soft, warm little balls of fur in the evening, all died the same way, amid many tears.

At school, I was in an almost total fog. Only chemistry drew me partway out of my stupor: you mixed powdered charcoal with sulfur and saltpeter in the right proportions, and bang! went the fireworks, and off went the rockets. Hit potassium chlorate a

*Il porte dans sa barbiche la sagesse de la
vieillesse ; dans ses lunettes la connaissance du
lettré ; dans son ombrelle, la dignité et le respect
que l'on doit aux gens bien nés.*

XXI. — Scènes de la rue : Malabar,
Pousse, Lettré,

Sketch by Marthe Moitessier   Street Scenes

sharp blow, and bang! Chemistry, at least, served a purpose, it might come in handy someday.

A history essay on "Napoleon's Egyptian Campaign." I handed in a sheet with a dozen lines that told of a distant country somewhere in Asia, watered by the Nile and strewn with pyramids. Not a single word about Napoleon. My father was speechless. If he had asked me about the Russian campaign, I would probably have answered that it was very cold there in winter and hot in summer, with steppes and sleds and a bridge called the Berezina . . .

On another occasion, the subject in French composition was, "A rolling stone gathers no moss." There, the gods finally flew in the window to warm my agile little fingers. In a wonderful essay, I rambled on, developing the obvious theme that the more you move, the more you travel, the more different things you do in life, the less you risk getting gummed up with bad habits and other disgusting things sticking to your skin. And yet another zero came to join my string of other zeros. The teacher's comments: "You are not only a lazy dunce, but a cretin and an incorrigible. Boys like you never amount to anything in life. Given to anarchy."

It was the same with Françou and Jacky. Sitting at our lifeless desks, we dreamed of the village and held contests to see which of us could shoot out the most streetlight bulbs in a week. We even briefly turned to shit-bombs, tossing them from our roof into our neighbors' yards. They could thank the Lord that this latest discovery was quickly suppressed by a whipping, with a double dose for me, the eldest.

We were dunces and delinquents, my brothers and I, dreaming of the sea and the forest, and of freedom, while stuck in a kind of torpor broken only by crises in which despair and rebellion went hand in hand. And we would take out our slingshots and shoot at anything, blowing away a city we wouldn't open our hearts to.

So Saigon became the sum of the endless, boring months that kept us from the village. Saigon for us was like walking under a leaden sun on an endless, stony path, a path without a drop of water as far as the eye could see, a hundred thousand miles in every direction.

Soon afterward, I entered the most troubled period of my adolescence, and started shoplifting. More out of bravado, to show what I could do, than from any real inclination, because it would never have occurred to me to steal a penny from my mother's purse. And then one day I stole a harmonica I really wanted . . .

"I've had my eye on you for some time. Put that back where you took it and come over here."

It was a plainclothes policeman. I went white as death, paralyzed with shame and fear. My father and mother would never understand something as unthinkable as this.

He led me to one of those little Chinese bistros around the market, pointed to a stool, sat down across from me, and ordered two cafés au lait.

"I was at the corner when you got into that fight as school was letting out last week. You fought well; he was bigger and stronger than you."

I felt very small, huddled on my stool. I was afraid. What was he getting at, talking about a fight I hadn't gone looking for? In my distress, everything was getting mixed up.

"I've seen you play water polo a few times, too. You always play fair, even if the other guy cheats a little under water, when the referee can't see him. So why do you steal things?"

My throat was so tight, I couldn't answer. In any case, there was nothing to say, it was all I could do to keep from crying. Birds were singing in a nearby tamarind tree, and I remembered the beautiful blackbird with white spots on its wing tips which I had watched for several days on the terrace before managing to shoot it down with my slingshot.

Without raising his voice, the policeman repeated his question: "Why do you steal?" His eyes were boring into mine, but I could feel his warmth as he tried to understand. And my fear disappeared. "We'll keep this between us. I'm taking a big sponge and wiping everything out, just this once. I'd hate to think of you in a reform school someday, with a bunch of juvenile delinquents for friends."

My heart felt huge, and my eyes were rimmed with tears. I was barely able to murmur "Thank you, monsieur." He waved it away as if he were brushing off a fly.

"Thank your lucky stars instead. Say your real thanks in what you do, not just in words."

He got up and left. I stayed sitting there for a long while. I drank my café au lait in little sips, then finished his.

The market's noise and shouts, its colors and intense life, all rushed into me like waves of light.

I listened to the birds telling each other stories in the tamarind tree. The blackbird I had hit the other day on the terrace had woken up in my hand with nothing broken. I opened my hand to let it go and watched as it flew away, with the beautiful white spots on its wing tips.

CHAPTER 2

My father's business was thriving and his office buzzed like a beehive, but his real passion was agriculture. Whatever he earned from his Ovaltine, barrels of wine, and crates of canned food, he invested in land.

Shortly after arriving in Indochina, my father received a land grant of 370 acres in the Terres Rouges part of the Djiring Plateau, between Saigon and Da Lat, to plant coffee trees. Then he received another one, 740 acres of wetlands near a small fishing village on the Gulf of Siam, for a rice plantation.

This was the village where we spent our summer vacations, three months each year between the sea and the jungle, since . . . well, since forever!

In a routine that never varied, our departure from Saigon for the village began the night before, with loading our enormous dust-colored Hotchkiss. Unbelievable, all the stuff that could be crammed into it; and what didn't fit inside was tied to the roof. The entire load was held down with inner-tube straps to keep the ropes from working loose in the hundred thousand bumps along the road.

Wakeup came at three in the morning, but we jumped up as if we were mounted on springs. We quickly ate an omelet with rice soup while Chu the chauffeur, who had driven the car out to the street, slowly warmed up the engine. Once the last-minute items were stowed, the tribe climbed aboard: first Papa, then Chu, Maman, Minh the cook, Assam, and finally a maid—one of the skinny ones.

Then it was the kids' turn to be jammed into the tangle of legs and packages. When territorial disputes erupted between brothers,

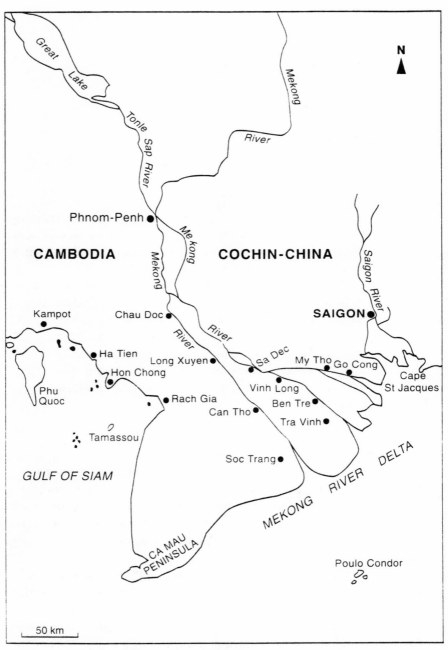

Cochin-China

they sometimes drew a round of slaps which you couldn't see coming because the bulb in the streetlight in front of our house was always smashed. We closed the doors, being careful not to slam them (Papa was irritated enough by then), and the car finally took off on what would be a three-day trip.

First Saigon disappeared in the quiet night. Then Cholon, its twin city, stretched out, still yawning in the darkness. And soon we were driving along rice paddies as far as you could see that were just beginning to stir.

Papa drove, Chu kept an ear cocked, listening to the engine, Maman held Babette in her arms, and Assam prepared Gilbert's baby bottle. Minh had fallen asleep, his head leaning on the shoulder of the equally sleeping maid. Jacky stroked his air rifle, which he had managed to pull from the trunk just before we left. Françou scribbled a poem on his knees. The quiet Cochin-Chinese plain rolled by in the first glimmer of dawn, a backdrop for the delicate fronds of betel palms among the bamboo thickets.

Betel palms, just like the ones our dead squirrels used to play in . . . But we would bring new squirrels back from the village: one for me, one for Françou, one for Jacky. And I would be the one to get all three of them with my slingshot. Because Françou didn't shoot that well and Jacky didn't use anything but his air rifle; when he shot a squirrel, he would find it half-dead with its guts hanging out, or else the squirrel would run away with a broken paw. Me, with my slingshot, I always got one alive out of every three I hit.

Once I got mine, I would trade the next one to Françou for a hundred clay balls for my slingshot; that wasn't a bad deal. For Jacky, it would be four flying lizards for one squirrel, that wasn't bad either. But maybe from now on I should say two hundred clay balls for Françou and six flying lizards for Jacky; it's pretty hard to get a squirrel in good shape.

The sun climbed in the sky, its reflection gleaming on the wet paddies, the water in the streams, the irrigation ditches, the still ponds where black water buffaloes rolled in the mud to escape the heat, guarded by little naked children, almost babies. The water buffalo is the rice paddies' engine; it pulls the little wooden plow and it never breaks down. The buffalo is slow, say the peasants, but the earth is patient.

From time to time, we would see a buffalo getting ready to cross the road, and the car slowed down a safe distance away. Tugging on a rope tied to the ring forged through the buffalo's nostrils, a child would pull the enormous beast like a toy. The buffalo would hesitate, take a few steps on the road. The child tugged on the rope and the buffalo would shake its great curving horns, strong enough to gore an elephant, advance a bit, turn back to the others still in the pond, think things over, hesitate again, take forever to cross.

It was best to stop a good distance away and let the buffaloes take their time, because they didn't like cars. We would get out to stretch our legs, pour more water into the radiator, breathe in the silence and the peace of the paddies. Maman used these frequent stops to make sketches on her drawing pad.

Our tribe reached My Tho at morning's end, after a detour to visit Go Cong, where Papa had to see some customers. The hundreds of miles spent on the road were part of his job, and he took advantage of the trip to take orders from the local merchants.

We ate lunch and went on. A big ferry beyond My Tho, the road, the little town of Ben Tre, a quick departure, the road, another ferry-ride in the company of a bus crammed with people, a mountain of bamboo cages filled with chickens on its roof, the road, a left turn into Tra Vinh before continuing.

Except for Papa's brief business stops, we barely had time to see what those country towns were like. With their streets lined with tamarind trees, they reminded me of little Saigons. The village was still far, far away. The road, full of humps and dips, stretched out forever in front of the car—and we had to stop every ten or fifteen miles to fill the radiator when it heated up. Chu would take the occasion to open the hood and check this or that. He would slip a washer under a rattling bolt, tighten the fan belt a little, putter about with pliers and a bit of wire while the engine cooled. Lucky Chu was along; Papa and he took turns driving, but without Chu the car wouldn't have kept running for long.

I liked Chu. He had been with the household since we were all little, and he liked us too. When we asked him for a bit of wire, he would always lend us his pliers too. He gave Françou and Jacky oil to lubricate their air rifles, and me good inner tubes for my slingshot.

Clumps of trees punctuated the somewhat monotonous countryside. We were driving at twenty-five miles an hour in a car with big recapped tires, a motor that coughed when it was tired, patched inner tubes, a rubber band to keep the gas pedal up, and curved springs that went "kerblang-kerblang" on a rutted dirt road that was as bumpy as corrugated iron. The Mekong had flooded a few weeks before, sending water over the dikes and damaging the delta roads, but in exchange it left a lot of good things to make the rice shoot up in the fields that stretched on to infinity.

Another of Papa's stops in Vinh Long, then we were on the road again, the road, the road, chickens zigzagging in front of the car and short-haired yellow dogs running behind it when we passed a village, the sun and its reflection everywhere, water buffaloes gleaming with mud in the paddies, white egrets flying in long triangles across the sky, solitary silver herons, betel palms, clumps of bamboo, junks and sampans on the *rach*, square nets stretched on bamboo crosses, people fishing in every conceivable way in brown water that teemed with fish, right down to the tiniest pond.

Once in a great while, we would pass a mango or tamarind tree. The maid said the mangoes weren't very good, but they were a lot better than no mangoes at all for people traveling on foot or by oxcart. Whoever could have planted them here along the road, so far from any village? Assam and Maman thought it must have been the monks; Minh said it was by accident. But nobody knew for sure except the people who planted them for everyone to enjoy.

The car rattled along this horizon of rice paddies and flooded plains stretching from Saigon to the sea along dikes and canals, streams, ferries, and branches of the Mekong that were so broad you couldn't see the other side.

And within us, time stretched out like the river water flowing through the immensity of these Cochin-Chinese plains, dotted here and there with groves of trees and the occasional villages.

Did these roadside villages also have flying lizards in their betel palms? I wondered. The ones in our village were full of them. Problem was, they were very wary. In fact, they were so wary they could see the stone coming and sometimes had time to leap to safety behind the trunk. With their air rifles, Françou and especially Jacky were a lot better at hitting them than I was. But I still brought down quite a few with my slingshot.

In the village, Kieu's father paid ten *sous* for each flying lizard you brought him, but the head had to be intact, untouched by the stone or pellet. Kieu's father was the village healer and everybody liked him. Besides, he was really nice and he knew lots of things, and he was the only one there who could read Chinese characters.

He crushed the flying lizards with his black stone and then squeezed them into a bottle, except for the head, which had to go in whole. Kieu told us his father used them to make remedies that cured all kinds of illnesses, even tuberculosis, but that was as much as we knew.

We got our second flat tire of the day, so we got out, stretched, listened to the silence of the plain. Not far from the car, near his three buffaloes, a boy was catching catfish using a kind of big funnel made of laced bamboo strips. He would plant it at random in the paddy, stick his hand in through the opening at the top, and feel around in the mud with his fingers. Then he would pull out a catfish with its long poisonous spines and put it in a bamboo weir he dragged behind him.

Once the tire was fixed, the trip continued. Near a village of a dozen huts, two peasant women were raising water from the ditch by pedaling inside a water wheel made entirely of bamboo. The buckets around the huge wheel scooped up the brown water and poured it into an irrigation pipe—also made of bamboo—which carried it to water a field of manioc on a hillock.

It was unbelievable, all the things that were made of bamboo in Indochina: lashings as strong as wire, wall sections, wheelbarrows, carts, scaffolds that rose four stories high in town, beautiful little bridges that could carry trucks and were marvels of ingenuity, and a hundred things beside. But the most amazing were the big Annam coast junks made of woven bamboo, which could haul fifty tons of rice between Cochin-China and Tonkin. You didn't see any around here. Papa said that Annam had very few forests with big trees, but plenty of large bamboos, more beautiful than the ones here. That was why the people there built all their boats out of bamboo.

Sketch by Marthe Moitessier   In the rice paddies

After spending the night in a Chinese hotel in Sa Dec, we hit the road again, first along the Mekong toward Long Xuyen, then finally toward Rach Gia and the Gulf of Siam.

As we got farther from the Mekong, the road improved a little. The ground had had time to absorb most of the recent flooding, and the water hadn't reached the level of the road, as it had in the rest of the delta. Tonight, if all went well, we would sleep at Rach Gia and smell the sea. Then, the last stretch to the village, as if in a dream.

A bus was approaching in a cloud of dust, so we pulled over. It stopped as well, right at the edge of the ditch, and waved us on. We crept by, close enough to scratch its paint. The bus was full to bursting, as usual. On its roof lay a row of cylindrical bamboo baskets, each holding a fat live pig, its legs trussed along its body. On top of the pigs' baskets stood a dozen wide-mesh cages—made of bamboo, of course—full of chickens sticking their heads out for a breath of air.

We didn't meet too many ox-carts, luckily; passing them was always a nuisance. On the roads across the jungle of the high Cambodian plateaus, they went in convoys of a dozen, one behind the other, so as to be safe from tigers. It was all you could do to get around them, because they would clump up in the middle of the road. Besides, the carts dropped nails on the road, something cars didn't like at all.

Here, there were canals everywhere and goods moved almost entirely by junk. Even in the driest part of the dry season, the powerful Mekong kept rolling along. It came from a great distance, gathering water along the way before carrying it here, to bring life to the earth and fill every canal in the farthest corner of this land of plains.

In the old days, long before the French came, the area near Sa Dec belonged to Cambodia. The former inhabitants had been driven out by the Cochin-Chinese, but many Cambodian pagodas remained, with roofs that curved up toward the sky at the ends like the trunks of royal elephants in salute. This magical architecture, Assam told us, forced the evil *ma qui* spirits that landed on the roof to go back where they came from without being able to come to earth to torment people. It was simple: the pagoda was very beautiful, so the *ma qui* landed on it instead of some hut. Then, when the monk on duty saw the spirit up on the roof looking over the plain and preparing a dirty trick, he would strike the bronze gong very hard. The terrified *ma qui* would run full speed along the ridge, reach the end where it curved up, and zoom! was sent flying back up to the clouds. Françou asked how the monk could see the *ma qui*. Assam answered that monks can see many things that are invisible to other people.

Papa announced that after spending two months of our vacation in the village, we would come back by way of Cambodia, with a stop at Phnom Penh to see the Water Festival. We were beside ourselves with joy. Phnom Penh was a beautiful city built on the shores of an amazing river, the Tonle Sap, which flowed one way for six months, then the other way for the other six. During the rainy season, the Tonle Sap's current flowed toward the Great Lake of Cambodia, which would rise about thirty feet, to the point of tripling the surface of this veritable inland sea, which was huge—90 miles long by 20 wide—even at low water. Its millions of tons of fish were then free to go feed in the huge area of flooded jungle. They found the choicest food, grew quickly and multiplied, and returned to swarm in the Great Lake as the water level began to fall. Then the fishing produced miraculous catches, with nets full to bursting and catfish up to eight feet long.

When the blue skies of the dry northeast monsoon returned, the water level all over the country dropped, and the Great Lake gradually shrank to its usual shoreline. The Cambodians treated as divine their river that first flowed six months in one direction to fill the Great Lake and spread its riches, then six months the other way, carrying junks loaded with dried fish.

The current's change of direction toward the Mekong also signaled the upcoming dry season harvests. Then the head monk would cut a rope stretched across the river, signaling the start of the Water Festival with its canoe races and the sacred dances along the Tonle Sap before the king, in front of the Silver Pagoda where the sun glinted on walls covered with thin sheets hammered from the precious metal. There was gold there as well, cast in a statue of Buddha, but it stayed inside the pagoda. We would be seeing all that in two months, on our way home from vacation.

I daydreamed as I watched water buffaloes plowing the paddies, and amused myself by counting the junks and sampans on the canal beside the road we were bumping along toward the Gulf of Siam. Here, all the boats were made of wood, not woven bamboo as on the Annam coast. That's because there was a lot of forest in Cochin-China, and when you come right down to it, wood is stronger than bamboo.

The biggest junks I saw cruising the canal could carry at least a hundred tons of rice or limestone in their great round bellies, with water lapping at their decks. I wondered how the ones carrying wood could be loaded so high without tipping over.

The small junks carried clay or wood to the brick- and pottery-yards whose smoke you could see near the villages. They returned loaded with tiles, jars, cauldrons, ovens, and bowls. In this part of lower Cochin-China, with its silt and clay, household utensils were made of fired pottery.

When the monsoon was favorable, all those junks traveled by sail. When it wasn't, the crew towed them while walking along the bank. Some of the boats came from as far as the Great Lake of Cambodia, and their trips lasted weeks, sometimes months. Ducks, pigs, and chickens were penned in a corner of the deck and the whole family hauled the towline when there was no wind or it was blowing the wrong way.

The tide helped as well, since the current in the river and canals changed direction at regular intervals, even very far from the sea. Phnom Penh, 185 miles upstream from the mouth of the Mekong, had an eighteen-inch tide. Saigon, which was near the delta, had more than three feet.

The trip had been going well so far, but then we had another flat. For some reason they always happened to the rear wheels, never in front, and we wondered why. Papa enlightened us. "The nail is lying on the road in the dust, waiting for its chance. When the front wheel goes over it, nothing happens, but the nail is thrown into the air like a bit of gravel. And if the nail happens to be sticking up when the rear wheel goes over it . . . well, you get the idea. Same thing with snakes. If the three of you are running down a jungle trail and the first one steps on a dozing snake, the next will be the one to get bitten."

So that was why Chu had rigged a rubber flap under the fenders, right behind the wheels, to deflect nails off to the side once the front wheel had passed over them and snapped them to attention. But it didn't always work, because we got another flat. Jacky wondered why we couldn't fasten a big magnet behind Chu's deflectors; that way, the nails would stick to it instead of flying every which way. Laughing, Papa patted his head and gave us a treat before we went on: a shooting contest with his .22 caliber rifle. He won, Jacky was second, Françou third, and I was last, by an eyelash. So I challenged all three of them to shooting with slingshots at a tin can ten yards away; I was sure I could beat them. Papa laughed again and made us get back into the car; it was time to get going.

I really liked the way my father was when we were driving to the village. He was cheerful, played and joked with us, and didn't ask nosy questions about what we were doing in class. School and Saigon were too much like the Hundred Years' War, whereas vacations were a real, lasting truce.

The engine was purring and Rach Gia wasn't far, but the sun was hot and everyone was sleepy. Suddenly Françou started to scream, "The ducks! The ducks!" We squirmed while Chu pulled the car over to the side of the road. The ducks were a big event and we always stopped when we saw them.

The entire paddy on our left seemed to be moving, as tens of thousands of ducks paddled along. The huge flock, which covered several acres, was moving toward the road. In front of them, a herder was pulling his canoe across the muddy paddy. On the rear thwart, he had a bundle wrapped in a scarf and a clay oven the size of a large, somewhat oval plate, the kind you saw in all the markets. Far behind him, also pulling his canoe, walked the flock's second herder, waving a long, flexible pole.

Within moments, the tide of ducks reached the road, crossed it, and went on its way toward Long Xuyen, like a river flowing down the furrows. They weren't walking so much as leaping forward, probing the mud with their bills, in a deafening "flap-flap" and "quack-quack" concert. The ones in back shoved the ones ahead, tried to climb over them to get in front, where there was more to eat. It looked like a rolling wave. After they passed, there couldn't have been a single fish, frog, toad, or insect left. But the droppings they left behind were the joy of the earth!

The ducks had begun their trip while still very young, barely hatched, and run along, finding food on the way, reaching the country markets as adults. Minh said the biggest flocks came from the Plain of Reeds west of Saigon, and fed the huge urban Saigon-Cholon area.

Outside of Rach Gia, we saw an island on the horizon that for some reason the locals called Hon Tre (Bamboo Island). We called it Turtle Island, since that was what it really looked like, with its humped back, long neck, and tiny head at the end. The car got here a bit late, but Papa still had time to see a few customers before the stores closed. He would finish his work tomorrow morning, and we would leave right afterward.

Rach Gia was my favorite town along the trip. Its market bustled with activity, life, and color. And the people were more handsome, more peaceful, and friendlier than in any other city. Maman said it was because of the mixture of races here.

It was a pretty town that stretched along the coast at the mouth of a delta full of junks from every corner of the Gulf of Siam. They traded their goods with those on the river junks, which sailed into the interior. At Rach Gia, you could see real ocean-going junks, so different one from another and so beautiful beneath their huge sails, smelling of seaweed and salt and far-away places.

Rach Gia was our last stop before the village. We would sleep here tonight. Tomorrow, we would be in the village.

Though it was only dawn, we could hardly contain ourselves. At last, Papa came back from seeing customers and the car started on the third and final day of the trip.

The road here was long and empty, baked by the sun and studded with ruts and potholes. It was less a road than one long clay dike built along the bank of the canal that stretched from Rach Gia to the port of Ha Tien on the Cambodian border. Sixty miles in a straight line, straight as straight, all the way, without a single tree; a real sweat-box of heat and boredom.

"Those sails on the canal are only part of the great work that is gradually bringing the land to life around here," Papa told us. "Watch the countryside on either side of the road for a half hour, and then you can tell me what you notice."

He pulled out his watch and checked it. My parents enjoyed playing this kind of game with us, but I think it was partly to keep us from chattering all the time.

To the left, toward the Gulf of Siam which the car was following a few miles away, the land looked desolate and swampy, with a lot of mangroves. Their roots could stand salt water, and grew half-way into the air; they looked like octopus tentacles. This place must be full of walking catfish! They could breathe both in and out of water, and hopped like sparrows among the mangrove roots to find a sunny spot. Their large globe-like eyes were always alert, making them very hard to hit with a slingshot.

On the other side of the canal, the plain was dense with *cai tram* trees. They were about as thick as your arm, and could live in brackish or alum water. There were also long stretches of reeds and a few sparse rice paddies. We would often see little canals, just wide enough for two canoes to pass, that flowed into the big one. An occasional hut stood on their banks.

At last, Papa announced that the half hour was up. I hadn't noticed anything special. Neither had Françou or Jacky. We really didn't see the great work that was supposed to be bringing the land to life. The junks on the canal, sure, that we could understand, they carried cargo. And the big canal was probably very handy during the southwest monsoon when you couldn't sail between Ha Tien and Rach Gia. As for the rest, it was pretty much a desert, except maybe for those few rice paddies here and there, which must produce pretty runty plants. All that I had noticed were some water buffaloes, about fifteen of them, a while back. But we couldn't see any miracle.

Maman asked us to try again just for another fifteen minutes, and to use our inner eyes and to look both at the past and the future.

Well now, that was getting pretty complicated! The past, all right, that was in books and a little in what you saw around you. But the future? How could you see that?

"Can you, Maman? And our 'inner eyes,' what's that?"

"If I put a marble on a table, and I tilt the table, can you tell me in advance what's going to happen?"

"The marble's going to roll."

"Well, you big sillies, that's what's meant by 'looking into the future.' Some people can see very far into the future, but we can all see a little way. The people who decided to dig this canal were looking much further ahead than just a channel for junks."

So Papa told us the story of the land that was coming to life.

When Françou was still in diapers, he said, this whole area was nothing but a huge two-thousand-square-mile basin of stagnant, brackish water. No rice could grow here. The only solution was to drain the basin into the sea.

The government brought in people from all over to clear the way for the future canal. Fifty miles of machete work for the trees, then spade work to clear the stumps. People camped on the marshy ground. It was mosquitoes, malaria, and loneliness.

Two huge dredges followed them, one out of Ha Tien, the other from Rach Gia. They advanced at a snail's pace because of the ancient *cai tram* and mangrove forests buried in the mud. The stump clearers constantly had to retrace their steps to clear the way, hauling out trunks with block and tackle.

The dredges met four years later, having dug this 85-foot-wide canal. Meanwhile, other dredges dug perpendicular canals that emptied into this one.

"The stagnant water is draining out," said Papa. "The land is waking up, the rice is beginning to grow. Before the French came, there were 1.2 million acres of rice paddies in Cochin-China. Since then, nearly two thousand miles of canals have been dug and the paddy surface has increased five-fold."

"The people who did this knew how to look far ahead," added Maman. "They also knew that nothing big ever happens without an alliance between thought, sweat, and faith. All three are needed to bring earth and sky together in the hearts of man."

It was funny; when Papa explained something to us, we always understood at least a little; but when Maman spoke, either we understood right away or we didn't get it at all.

The trip was unfolding in a dream; no one was talking any more. The countryside had changed a lot, with hills beginning to appear on the left. The car left the main canal to follow another one heading for the sea. Then the hills quickly grew higher and higher. We turned right at the sea, four more miles of very flat road, up a hill, down the other side, a left turn onto a road with grass growing in the middle, barely wide enough for the big Hotchkiss, our hearts began to pound, and we were there—at the village!

 CHAPTER 3

Long before dawn began to lighten the sky, we were already running through the darkness to find our friends and make plans for the day. In the village, we went to bed with the chickens, rose at cock-crow, and our days were full to overflowing.

On the big wooden platforms under the huts' overhanging eaves, the first meal of the morning was being eaten by the light of palm-oil candles: rice soup flavored with spicy *nuoc mam*, with a few pieces of dried fish cooked in a savory herb broth. The birds were still asleep, but families were already gathered around the clay cooking pots in the middle of the platforms.

The village stretched for nearly a mile along a road rutted by cart wheels and generations of bare feet. It consisted of about twenty huts with mud walls and thatched roofs, set between clumps of betel palms. Windbreaks against the monsoon, high walls of stakes and woven branches covered with palm fronds hid the huts' bare yards. Mounted on a post to the left of each hut stood a little altar no bigger than a pigeon coop, to honor the ancestors and the gods that watched over the peace of the village.

An com roi chua? (Have you eaten?)

The call rang out in the darkness to passers-by, whether friends or strangers, adults or children.

An com roi, cam on. (I have eaten, thank you.)

Françou was at his best friend Phuoc's hut, right next to ours. He and Phuoc planned to paddle out to the second island, which Françou was beginning to map. He wanted to leave early, because the island was a long way past Monkey Point. Before we went to bed last night, Assam prepared their usual *ban terc*, a cake of sticky rice and sweet soy sauce wrapped in a banana leaf.

Jacky went over to Kieu's hut, not far from Phuoc's. Kieu's father needed flying lizards, and Jacky was going to hunt them in the betel palms with his good friends Kieu and Hao. I had agreed to let Hao use my air rifle in exchange for a flying lizard; Kieu was taking Françou's for the same price.

I continued alone along the path, my bare feet, after so many summers, able to recognize its most subtle nuances. In the dust by the sides of the road were lots of little craters dug by ant-lions. We would often amuse ourselves by feeding them orange ants, watching the ant-lions pelt them with grains of sand to make them tumble down the crater. But if you gave them dead ants, they would briskly toss them out.

Dawn was near. I passed Xian's hut beyond the big leaning termite mound, then Sung's, with its new windbreak. The week before, Sung had slipped while climbing down a coconut tree, scraping the skin on his chest into one terrible sore. Maman treated him with Cadum cream, and it was nearly scabbed over. She treated the villagers for everything from little cuts and bruises to dysentery and malaria.

A gong struck in the distant temple and I walked fast, in a hurry to see my pal Xai. When we grew up, we would sail together to Siam in a junk even handsomer than Papa's. Maybe we would go as far as Singapore. We had talked this over while setting our bird traps in the forest. But we didn't tell anyone else; it was just between the two of us.

An com roi chua?

Xai made room for me on the platform, and I huddled against him for warmth. A lot of people could fit on one of those platforms. It was the family hearth, where all the meals were eaten. We would sometimes sleep there on calm nights, rest after lunch, or play cards when rain put a stop to everything. The platform was where the neighbor women would gather to chew betel nut and tell stories. Xai's grandfather spent his days there, waiting for sunset to smoke his two pipes of opium. Under the platform lay a coffin of smooth black wood; it was for him, and he often stroked it with his foot. At our last vacation, there had been two coffins. Now grandmother was gone, waiting for him with their ancestors in her tomb behind the hut, beyond the little manioc field close to the forest.

Xai's mother handed me the soup bowl. She had kept it warm, knowing that I would be coming as usual, and of course without having eaten yet.

In the yard, Xai's father was tending a fire of coconut beans under a cauldron half full of water. He then threw the ashes into the pot, stirred it with a stick, and added warm water. The water foamed just like soap, and he untied and washed his hair in it.

Squatting beneath the big *badamier* tree by the beach, Xai and I helped Phuoc tend the fire we had built in a pit in the sand. Phuoc was feeling glum. He was supposed to have gone canoeing with Françou, but his father needed him today, and he looked sad. The end of a large iron bar glowed gaily in the fire. Soon it would be used to enlarge the holes that Phuoc's father would drill to pin the large pieces of a wooden anchor together.

Phuoc was blowing on the base of the fire using a bamboo tube long enough so you didn't burn your face; its inner joints had been pierced with an iron rod. Xai and I often took turns with him. First, because he was our pal, but also because unless you spelled each other, blowing into the pipe too hard and too long made you dizzy.

The clear flames rose and danced around the iron rod, giving off a smell of pitch that blended with that of the joss sticks planted in a triangle in the sand. His father had told Phuoc to re-place them before they burned down, so the good spirits hover-ing nearby would come join us, to watch the work and give us advice.

A few paces from the fire, Phuoc's father was making an an-chor for his boat. It was actually Papa's boat, but you could say it was Phuoc's father's boat, since he used it to go fishing all the time and kept it in perfect shape.

Phuoc's father also took care of "Cabriette," our house, when we were in Saigon. And he looked after the kitchen garden, plant-ing green beans a week or two before our arrival. He and his fam-ily lived in a hut on the property adjoining ours. The hut had four mango trees around it, with five clumps of banana trees to the right, plus ten betel palms and an old jackfruit tree near the wind-break by the road.

I never knew my friends' parents' real names. Assam ex-plained that in the country, an adult's name had to be forgotten so that the *ma qui*, the nastiest of all the evil spirits, couldn't steal it. The only person in the village who could use his name openly was Bai Ma, because he came from a family of mandarins.

Phuoc's father had been working on his anchor for the past three days. Like all the anchors in the village, and in the Gulf of

Siam generally, it was made of hardwood, including the stock, with long, wide flukes that held both in mud and sand. He shaped it with his little hatchet, which had a long strip of light-colored wood fastened opposite the cutting edge like the feathers on an arrow, to guide it through the air. Shavings flew, looking like fish scales. I watched, fascinated by the arabesques made by a tool that was light as a bird and sharp as a razor; it reminded me of a green crested woodpecker.

With both flukes and the shank completed, Phuoc's father smoothed them with his machete as precisely as if he were using a plane, and temporarily tied the parts together with a length of inner tube. Then he started drilling two holes as thick as a finger through the assembly. The red-hot iron would enlarge the holes to take the big wooden pins that held everything together.

He used a drill bit fabricated from a piece of reinforcing bar flattened at one end and filed into a diamond shape. Phuoc's father spun the bit very rapidly using a bow made from a length of bamboo and a leather cord that he wrapped around the bit.

Hao's father walked over, wiping his forehead with a checkered scarf he wore on his head to hold his top-knot. My ear had caught the crunch of his steps in the fine sand behind me. He was repairing his own boat's rudder on the beach, and I had been listening to the blows of his mallet. I was dying to come crouch nearby and watch him work, but I didn't dare, because of the shadow between us—a shadow as dark as a monsoon cloud.

Hao's father answered Phuoc's greeting, but only favored Xai and me with a distracted grunt and a vague glance that bore right through us. He suspected us of having stolen his big brown hen, the pride and envy of the village. He was close to the truth, but close isn't quite the same as truth.

The bit and bow belonged to him. He had loaned them to Phuoc's father and had come by to see how the drilling was going. In the village, Hao's father was considered a master at anything having to do with boats and woodworking. He suggested that the second hole not be drilled parallel to the first. That way, when the connection loosened with time and strain, the flukes and shank would stay connected.

Hao's father rearranged his top-knot, replaced his scarf, and squatted on the beach. He smoothed the sand with his palm, took a mouthful of water and sprayed it out to harden the sand's surface. Then, with a coconut-frond twig, he drew two sketches. The first showed the hooks and the shaft connected with parallel pins. On the other sketch, the pins were driven at an angle.

"That way, the anchor will last, for Phuoc's sons to use. Maybe his grandsons."

It was luminous . . . the sketches came alive! And I finally understood why our foreman in Saigon, when the coolies were nailing up crates to be shipped to the countryside on the boat, always made them drive the nails at an angle.

The massive pieces of dark red wood strewn around us gradually became a first-class anchor, simple and strong, with reinforced bamboo lashings over the pins and at the joint with the stock. As Hao's father worked with us, I could sometimes feel his gaze on my neck as clearly as if I had eyes in the back of my head. But he would never know the real truth about his hen; that would remain an absolute secret between Xai and me.

We had come across the hen by accident on the path that led to our bird traps. It was a barely visible path that ran beneath the trees at the bottom of the hill and behind Hao's hut, at the edge of the tombs. That morning, a *con chom* (a kind of large spotted marten) had beaten us to the traps and left a neat little semicircle of feathers around one of them, as if to taunt us. It had robbed us of a nice magpie, which are very hard to catch. Then, right afterwards, as we were building a trap for the *con chom*, Xai and I had been stung by big hairy wasps.

On the way back, rage was still thundering in our hearts. And the Evil Eye, which had been following us since dawn, put Hao's father's chickens on our path.

Without meaning any harm, without even aiming, Xai fired his slingshot into the flock—and the big brown hen took the stone right in the head. She had been in the bushes with her chicks; we didn't even know she was there. It was an incredible stroke of bad luck, a kind of miracle gone wrong. I quickly finished her off before her flapping in the dry leaves roused the whole neighborhood. Xai hit her again to make sure she stopped moving, and we ran off through the creepers carrying the hen, feeling really worried. But what else could we have done?

After all, we couldn't have strolled over to see Hao's father with our slingshots draped around our necks, holding his hen, and told him we had just found her behind the hut that way, with her head crushed. And we couldn't have left her there, because the *con chom* would have gotten her.

So it was a bad day for Hao's father and for his hen. But for Xai and me, it felt good to eat the hen together, crouched side by side near a fire deep in the forest under the tall wild pistachio tree on top of the hill, with a little pile of well-gnawed bones at our feet. A mosquito buzzed at my ear, and I brushed it away. We watched as it zigzagged off to go land on Xai's foot. Slowly, its swelling belly turned pink, then red. Just as it pulled out its thin probe, ready to fly away, full of life, Xai crushed it with his index finger, then sucked his bloody fingertip.

From the village, waves of sounds reached us in our refuge. Despite the distance, we could make out the regular squeaking of the millstone as Xian's big sister hulled the paddy, turning it into sweat-scented brown rice. She accompanied the millstone's gravelly song with one of her own, which rose clearly to the top of the hill. Another millstone was singing farther on, and the two songs played a duet across the village. Everywhere, you could hear the dull thuds of the big wooden mortars as the girls punctuated the strokes of their pestles while kicking aside the chickens drawn to the grain. And the rice turned white as its ground husk fell away, to be mixed with thin slices of banana tree stems and fed to the black pigs, whose bellies dragged along the ground.

Sated, we went looking for *lam nuoc* vines to drink. You slashed them, then sucked out as much pure water as you could swallow. Then we walked back to our fire to finish the hen, which was enormous.

With eyes along its body and its ears everywhere, the *con chom* would probably come to see what was going on tonight, attracted by the remains of the chicken. To catch it, we would use the same kind of trap as for birds, but much stronger.

With our jackknives, we trimmed the branches from a small tree about ten feet tall. The sapling was as limber as a fishing pole, and I bent it down and held it while Xai cut the top, notched it, and tied a line to it. The line ended in a noose halfway up the rod.

With this kind of trap, the trickiest thing to build is the trigger mechanism. We drove a small, strong stake into the ground, notched it, and tied a twig no bigger than a match stick to the line just before the noose. Held against the notch in the stake by a half-turn in the line, the twig had to rest gently against a stick laid horizontally on top of the bait. Getting it set just right took a lot of patience, many attempts, and much trimming of the twig's point.

At last, it worked perfectly. If the *con chom* so much as

brushed the bait in the center of the noose, the bent sapling would straighten up in a flash. If it got caught by the neck there wasn't the slightest chance of its getting free, and we would soon be eating roast *con chom*. If it got caught by the paw it would probably be able to bite through the line, even while dangling from the tree. In that case, maybe the damned bird thief would learn never to mess with our traps again.

We also rolled clay balls for our slingshots and dried them in the shade. You could aim them much more accurately than stones, whose shape and weight always varied a little even if you chose them carefully. We gathered white clay in a secret vein only the two of us knew about, where the stream flowed past the frog pond. We then mixed it with brown clay we got by kicking in a termite mound. The termites knew where to find good clay, the same clay the villagers used for the mud walls of their huts. But as slingshot ammunition, it became even better when you mixed it with white clay.

Each time we broke into a termite mound, we stuck an ant nest into it, which the big orange ants made by binding a bunch of fresh leaves together with their saliva. Huge soldier-termites would then destroy the ants, chopping them in half one after the other, down to the last one, including their damned eggs. It served them right. Xai and I hated the big stupid ants, which were mean and always angry, their stingers full of fiery juice. They were forever dropping onto our backs for no reason when we had to crawl under one of their nests, heading toward the call of a bird.

In general, I preferred to hunt alone. Jacky liked his air rifle, and Françou would drift off into his own world, where the forest, the islands, and his canoe got all mixed up. He and Jacky had slingshots too, but it wasn't a religion with them, the way it was for me.

So I hunted alone. I sometimes went with Xai, so as not to leave my friend in the lurch, but he preferred trapping, and I, hunting. What I liked best about Xai was that we could spend whole days in the forest together without saying a word. And yet we were always telling each other lots of things. It was inside that we talked, as if we were the same person, maybe a little like being twins. When I went back to school in Saigon, we would write each other at least once a month. He would write about his traps, I about the teals at the botanical garden and the streetlight bulbs.

In addition to a few pepper trees planted on the hillsides, all the villagers owned rice-paddy plots in the plain beyond the hills. They sold pepper during the rainy season, when the southwest monsoon kicked up big waves and you couldn't go fishing, except during the rare calms. But pepper didn't bring in much, because of blights and the birds that came to eat it. So the little rice-paddy plots allowed the villagers to more or less fill their clay cooking pots during the rest of the year.

The season of the great rains was almost over. Dark, water-swollen clouds full of wind still rushed by overhead, but less often, leaving room for blue sky, from which the sun would shine down and hasten the harvest.

On the other side of the village, beyond the hills, the rice was slowly turning golden brown, rustled by a wind that was lighter and drier by the day. The surface of the mud was beginning to harden, and the first cracks appeared. Soon the ponds, which teemed with catfish, would dry up, and the fish would burrow deep in the mud to hibernate and wait for the next rainy season.

Then the cracks became numberless, meeting in a tracery of thousands of cells welded together that made the earth look like a gigantic slab of wild honey.

Water still hid in the ditches along the little dikes, but the water that covered the fields was gone now, soaked up by the earth and burned off by the sun. And the rice stems bent under the weight of their ears, heavy with golden grains.

The harvest was finished in less than a week. The rice stems were beaten in place and the sacks of paddy moved along the road to the huts. The villagers also carried bales of straw to thatch their roofs later on. I heard heated discussions about Bai Ma. Derk's and Chon's mothers were furious at him, and for two days, I heard them complaining. From what I could understand, Bai Ma loaned the money to buy seed grain, then demanded too big a share of the harvest.

And the village turned again toward the sea, toward fishing and the islands far off on the horizon.

The land breeze would start blowing soon. The sea grew calmer with the approach of the northeast monsoon, which would bring fair weather. On the beach, you could hear mallet blows on hulls; the junks were being caulked.

Hauled up, the junks had been waiting for months, shaded from the sun by a thin layer of palm fronds spread on their decks. That way, air could circulate between the leaves, letting the boats slowly dry out without any play developing between the planks. Each week during the rainy season the hulls had been sprinkled with seawater, so the salt—the basic protection against rot here— would protect their pitch-scented wood.

The beach was alive with intense activity around the boats. With the twin eyes painted on their prows, the junks watched a new season coming and their owners busily at work. Phuoc's father told me that the *yin-yang* symbol near the bow where the anchor hung was carved there to bring balance.

In the village, the few available tools passed from one person to another. The villagers helped each other, one loaned this, another borrowed that, it was cheaper and everything went better that way. Only the heavy machetes were really personal. Each villager felt it was a point of honor to have a machete that could as easily trim a toothpick as fell a tree.

The village had created a kind of fishing cooperative; the five little junks grouped under the palm trees belonged to all twenty huts. By custom, you said, "Chon's father's boat" (or Derk's father's, etc.) giving the name of the most experienced sailor on board. But the boat itself belonged to several families bound by ties that extended to the entire village on important matters involving the community. At that moment, the only important questions concerned fishing and the preparation of the boats. Hao's father was often consulted on particularly tricky repairs and the toughest caulking problems.

A few days before, Xai and I had brought him the *con chom*'s skin.

"This is for you."

And, along with the carefully scraped hide, a big bundle of *cai tram* bark.

"This is for you too."

He hesitated a little. But Hao's mother saw how handsome the hide was, and Hao's father could immediately tell that the bark was exceptional, perfectly selected by choosing only the best of the best, stripped into lengths that were as soft as silk. All this, he took in at a glance.

"We went out to gather it for you."

It had taken us all of a very long day, leaving before dawn, walking beyond the hills, beyond the rice paddies, very far, deep into the flooded forest which went on and on, to where the most beautiful *cai tram* grew, where no one went because it was so far and full of leeches and very dangerous striped watersnakes.

We had come home at nightfall, dying of hunger, fear, and exhaustion. But our bark was a thousand times more beautiful than Bai Ma's, who took his horse and carriage to buy *cai tram* fiber from the Chinese shopkeepers in Ha Tien, and resold it here at a big profit. Ours was so soft, warm, and light; it was like having a bird in your hand.

His eyes closed, Hao's father rolled a handful between his palms. He lit a piece and sniffed the smoke, which danced like that of a joss stick, and smelled almost as sweet.

Then he smiled at us for the first time in a long time. He knocked our heads together, but not too hard, just enough to give each of us a bump. And his eyes said that the big brown hen was buried at last.

From that day on I followed Hao's father around the beach like his shadow, hypnotized by his magician's hands as they pounded *cai tram* fiber between the planks, using wooden tools that looked like chisels. He had made them himself and soaked them in *cai dau* oil. With his machete, he would occasionally trim their edges or change their curve, depending on the shape of the cracks to be filled. As I watched him working, his eyes almost closed, I knew that the water wouldn't leak in.

From time to time, Hao's father would stop pounding with his mallet and prepare some betel nut to chew. It was almost like praying; he would lay the betel leaf flat on his hand, spread it with a little reddish lime paste, slice off a piece of betel nut with his machete, fold it all into a nice tight package and pop it into his mouth. Then he would talk for a while, with a faraway look in his eyes.

"To really caulk properly," he said, "you have to enter the

crack along with the fiber, become the *cai tram* fiber itself, with its eyes. If you're able to do that, you'll see how the water will try to get in, because you'll be seeing with the same eyes as the water."

Françou and Phuoc made fun of me behind his back, saying I reminded them of a monkey. I felt like beating them up, but actually, I didn't care what they thought. I just rolled the bark exactly the way Hao's father wanted it, not too tight and not too loose, neatly combing the strands with my fingers. And I tried to enter the crack with him.

Hao's father said he knew old people who had caulked all their lives, and still didn't know how to keep the water from getting in. It was because they had never learned how to enter the crack themselves, so they couldn't see what they were doing.

Françou and Phuoc said I looked like a novice monk, holding his yellow-robed master's begging bowl. But I *knew* that Hao's father wasn't talking foolishness. When I swam in the Saigon pool for a very long time without stopping, I could sometimes see myself from above, watching myself swimming. And a couple of times I went inside my lungs and my muscles, as if I were inside and outside at the same time. If I could do that while swimming, someday I should be able to enter the crack, the way Hao's father did. So what if I looked like a novice monk with his master? But I really felt like giving the two of them a licking just the same.

Except for the old people, who stayed in the quiet of their huts, the whole village seemed to have gathered under the tall twin jackfruit trees by the road at the edge of the beach. It was almost as noisy as the Saigon market, but the noise was completely different, full of laughter, gossip, and children's cries.

On their thighs, the women rolled the fiber of a plant that grew near Ha Tien which was used to make the fishing nets and lines. They sat in a circle the better to gossip while watching the babies who played among them with stones, pieces of wood, and bits of string.

For the past two weeks, they had been meeting every day at the same place under the jackfruit trees, where they pulled up their wide trousers to roll strands of fiber against their thighs. They held the spindles with their toes to keep the babies from tangling the huge skeins that slowly grew as they twisted the string.

Next to them, the men were making barbless hooks out of

heavy wire that they flattened with a hammer, then sharpened with a file. In Saigon, when you needed something, you bought it at the Chinese store; here, you made it with your hands. The men worked unbelievably quickly, in teams of three or four. The heavy wire was threaded between nails driven into a template board; the first man twisted it into shape with a flick of his wrist; the next snipped it off with a chisel; the third sharpened it and tossed it into a flat basket. Xai and I were on a team headed by Xian's father, working with Xai's father and Phuoc's older brother. Our job was to arrange the hooks in a kind of big bamboo shuttle open on one side. You had to put exactly forty-nine hooks in each shuttle. Neither Xai nor anyone else, not even Kieu's father, though he was the village healer, could tell me why we didn't put in fifty hooks instead of forty-nine. It certainly would have made them easier to count.

Once the work was done, we would have thousands of hooks to rig on the lines, which were more than half a mile long. Stretched about five feet above the bottom, with an unbaited hook rigged every three hands-breadths, they would make a huge curtain that snagged rays and flat-headed blue sharks as they burrowed in the mud for crabs and shellfish.

On the road, where children played with tops fashioned from the wire bobbins, Derk's older brother turned a vertical wooden wheel mounted on a pointed stick, which in turn spun three smaller wheels at top speed. Each had a hook at its center; tied to it was one of the strings the women's group had twisted. The other end was anchored to a coconut tree a hundred yards away.

In that way, the fiber brought from Ha Tien in Bai Ma's carriage was transformed day after day into miles of strong, heavy lines. Kieu's father soaked them in a clay jar on a fire, filled with salt water mixed with pig's blood and three flying lizards. To my surprise, he dropped a coin into the jar. It was a very ancient coin stamped with Chinese characters, with a square hole in the middle. I asked what it was for.

"It was in my grandfather's ancestor's belt when his boat capsized," Kieu's father said. "A porpoise came along as he was drowning, took him on its back, and brought him to shore."

When I repeated this story to Xai in a joking tone, he told me it was no laughing matter. He said that a year later, on the same lunar day, they had found the porpoise dead, at Monkey Point right between the two rocks where Kieu's father's ancestor had walked ashore. It was to honor the porpoise that the monks had built the little wooden altar there. Xai told me that the monks of the temple had kept the coin ever since, and every year, it was used in the fishing line jar. That way, the porpoises would know that the hooks weren't meant for them, and that no one in the village wished them harm. Xai also told me that except for the oldest monk in the temple, only Kieu's father was allowed to touch the coin. And when Kieu's father died, Kieu would be the one to soak the lines in the jar with his ancestor's coin.

Great outings in the wind of the open sea, with these fishermen who were my teachers, who faced the dragons of the sea and the dragons of the sky empty-handed. Camping on desert islands with huge rays and blue sharks cut into strips and drying on sticks. Xai being poisoned from eating turtle-meat, though he had been told not to. My terrible fear for my friend who was dying, and whom Kieu's father saved by feeding him seven almost transparent sand crabs, which he had mashed into a paste with his black stone.

Year after year, fishing with long lines that needed no bait; hooks that popped out of the shuttles, gleaming in the sun, as the boat sailed along; a little junk, its palm-frond sails rolled onto the gaff, resting at anchor near the magic island. Light breezes and strong winds, reefs in the squalls as I admired Phuoc's father, his boat drunk with wind, sea, and sun, flying across the waves, flying toward the islands, toward the village and toward the forest.

The sea and the forest . . . Ever since I was little, I had felt the terrific pull of those two poles, binding me to the village forever. If I were to live a thousand years, the village would be in my blood, in my very roots.

I can still hear the distant temple gong, Xian's older sister singing on the road, the children's laughter, the frequent quarrels, the gentle friendliness of *an com roi chua*, and the stories about Asia the mothers used to tell us while chewing betel nut on the wooden platforms, and—all around us—the gods, spirits, dragons, and the silent prayers to bring us peace.

Behind the huts, I can see again the tombs of those who had left us, honored by the scent of the slim joss sticks at the edge of the creepers and the green.

That was where the other world began, the one that enchanted me. That world, equally full of gods and dragons, where I can see the Child with his slingshot slip into the whispering forest behind the village. Every sense alert to the slightest quiver that might carry a message, he listens as the trees speak to him in the language of the birds high in the tall branches. And little by little, in a silent dance, he changes into a forest god, walking on bare feet that have eyes of their own.

He freezes, the dance having flowed into the core of his being like the breath of the trees. He is listening through his skin now, a transparent shadow playing among the patches of light scattered by the sun in the darkness of the forest where he seeks that something which has the shape of the absolute.

I can see him very slowly raising his slingshot to his lips in a sacred gesture, for a sacred act . . . and the slingshot becomes magical through the light breath that comes from the deepest part of the human soul. And then he silently kills with love the bird he loves, and the more beautiful the bird, the more the love of the boy for the bird.

Then the boy takes out his knife and very carefully cuts a new notch in the fork of his guava-wood slingshot. And when he comes home at night, his eyes all luminous with the mysteries he has seen, to show the bird to his father, his mother reminds him not to forget the little fire under the mango tree, in deference to the Great Law which declares that the Bird that is killed must be eaten, so that no life is taken for the sole pleasure and reason that a bird was beautiful.

Later, much later in my life, my mother told me that all this pained her deeply, but that she hadn't wanted to interfere with my quest for the Enchanted Bird which would one day free me from that love.

I found it many years later, on a desert island in the Pacific. I had been hunting rock crabs with my slingshot, since they were too quick to catch enough of them by hand. The bird was fishing out in the bay near the edge of the beach, standing in the water, out of range. Completely absorbed by its fishing, it hadn't seen me. I had enough crabs to eat for two days and was getting ready to go back on board my boat.

But seeing how beautiful the bird was, the Child gently came out of my heart and sat down close to me on the rocks. And together we contemplated the Enchanted Bird—because that was what it was, no doubt about it. From time to time the bird bent down on its long legs, spreading its wings and holding them level with the water, as if to make a shadow, the better to see the bottom through the surface reflections. The feathers of its wings sparkled with silver, ocher, and blue, making pearls of fire that mixed with the diamonds the sun had scattered on the water.

We sat a long time side by side, the Child and I, watching the Bird and remembering the forest behind the village, where we had never, ever seen, or even imagined, a bird so beautiful.

I wanted to go back aboard to fix my dinner then, since the time had passed when I would take a life without needing to. In any case, the bird was too far away and we were out in the open. There was only one chance in a thousand of hitting it, even if I had wanted to further disturb the peace of that anchorage where I had already caught fish and sea turtles and caused a small massacre among the crabs. It was time to head out to sea again, to renew my friendship with my soul.

But the Child smiled at me and said that we had to try to find the Magic Stone. And his gaze told me that if we found it, the stone would make the choice.

We looked for it together. "Just one stone," I said. Taking his time, he spotted it first, hidden among thousands of others in a crack in a rock, rolled for centuries, just the right weight. As I held it in my hand, the Child said again that the stone would choose. And he reminded me to moisten it with a little spit, as in the old days, so that it wouldn't slip on the leather.

The sun was behind us, the air so still you could see two birds, the real one and its reflection in the motionless water in front of the distant beach. And the gods of the forest behind the village watched also, motionless, so as not to influence the choice, not to interfere.

The Child then let out the breath whose secret he had kept in the depths of his soul. The stone traced a great arc across the sky, hiding in the sun, and the Bird fell on its reflection in the water, its neck broken, its wings of light spread on the sea.

And the Child gave me a sad little smile before returning all warm to my heart, where there would never be slingshot hunts in the forests or on the beaches, ever again.

CHAPTER 4

The gong rang out in the powerful breath of the jungle at night. Seven strokes close together, followed by a pause of a few seconds. Another seven, another pause. Then the final seven strokes. In the first days after my arrival here, the servant boy had had to wake me up. Within a week, I started opening my eyes even before the first sound of the gong.

Lying on my mat, I savored the calm of the night for a moment longer. Then I got up, splashed cold water on my face, and went to drink my café au lait on the veranda of the little cabin where I had been living for the past few months. It was four o'clock, long before sunrise.

By the dozens, coolies began to emerge from the darkness. Soon, nearly three hundred men and women were crowded around for roll call. The day's work at Long Than plantation was beginning.

I was fresh out of agriculture school, and felt a kind of vertigo whenever I faced the attentive, respectful mass of humanity crouched before me in silence under the watchful eye of the fierce *cais*. To keep discipline during roll call, the *cais* didn't talk; they didn't even shout. Instead, at the slightest crackle of a toe on a dry leaf, they screamed.

Arms crossed on his chest, each *cai* carried a *ca dui* (a whip or club) at his belt. Using it during roll call was forbidden, and at the job sites, only in exceptional cases.

They were waiting for my orders. I was eighteen years old.

Around us stood 1,500 acres of tapped rubber trees, plus another 370 acres of trees too young to be productive yet. To this you had to add many thousands of acres of virgin forest, where tigers sometimes roamed. And this estate was just one parcel of the properties owned by my employer, the Indochinese Rubber

Plantation Company (IRPC), spread across the gray and red soils of southern Indochina.

Roll call was over. Led by their *cais*, the teams headed for their respective plots. Everything was in order: only five people were ill, of malaria. While the Indochinese nurse gave them quinine, I watched to see that they didn't spit the bitter medicine out. A dozen cut feet. I checked the bandages; nothing too serious. Only one coolie, who had arrived from Tonkin the week before, remained in the infirmary, with a large oozing sore on his ankle that went nearly to the bone. We didn't have any sulfa drugs because of shortages caused by the war in Europe, so he was being treated by maggot therapy.

This amazing technique had saved many wounded men from gangrene during the Sino-Japanese war, when no medicine of any kind was to be had. You let flies lay their eggs on the wound, then carefully bandaged it. The maggots multiplied beneath the bandage and fed on the rotting tissue, right to the last scrap, without ever attacking healthy flesh. In less than two weeks, an absolutely horrible wound would be as clean as a whistle. But as far as I knew, only one variety of fly, *Lucilia sericata*, produced those magic maggots.

Day hadn't yet broken. I strode along under the rubber trees. They rose sixty feet high, making a canopy so thick you couldn't see the stars through it; underneath, it was pitch black. But the ground was cleared and covered with a thin layer of leguminous plants which provided nitrogen to enrich the soil. It was carefully tended, and I could walk quickly, guided by the lights of the little kerosene lamps carried by the rubber tappers scattered around the plantation.

The rubber trees had to be tapped in the cool of the day, between night's end and dawn. That way, the latex had time to flow down the spiral gouged into the trunk without thickening too soon. This part of the job usually took me about two hours. It was a sort of routine, like my breathing and warm-up exercises before breakfast. I was there mainly to be seen, so the workers would realize I was around, ready to appear at any moment to check that the chisel wasn't cutting too deeply into the bark or not deeply enough. Too deep, and it hurt the tree; not deep enough, and the latex wouldn't flow freely. But I had little reason for concern; the tappers knew what they were doing, though the women seemed to have the steadier hands.

Some of the young girls among them were very pretty. But I

was the Boss, the *Ong Quang*, the "Grand M'sieur," despite being only eighteen. If the *Ong Quang* had a romance with one of the girls, the *cais* and the coolies would laugh up their sleeves, discipline would collapse, and the work would slow down. All I could do then would be to pack my bags and leave.

My own boss, my *Ong Chanh* ("Très Grand M'sieur") had warned me about this the very first day: "Here, you either beat off or you beat it." And to make things perfectly clear, he added, "And not too much beating off, either. There's work to be done, and jerking off doesn't get it finished."

I was very fond of my *Ong Chanh*. He was a compact, husky man, gruff and taciturn. When he opened his mouth he got right to the point without wasting words. The other day, he had seen me limping a little, with a bandage on one knee and a six-inch scrape on my forearm.

"What happened to you?"

"I skidded in a turn near the charcoal ovens. Luckily nothing happened to the bicycle."

"That was smart!"

"My mother always used to say that skin wasn't too serious, because it grew back all by itself. Whereas ripping your pants was more of a nuisance, because you had to sew them up."

"What about your father? Didn't he ever advise you to look where you were going? Your father never told you that accidents almost always happen to people who are either nasty or stupid, did he? That's what my father told me, and it's helped keep me on my toes all my life."

Yes, I did like him. And I sensed he liked me too, though I suspect he had had his doubts in the beginning. He must have thought that I would never be able to manage all the work at my age, what with having to be everywhere at once, seeing both the big picture and the details, and going right to the heart of any problem.

Now he trusted me. We would meet for an hour at the end of each day, after the crews came in from work. Then I would climb into his battered little old car with his dog, and we toured the empty job sites, where the air bore the healthy smell of sweat left by the coolies, mixed with the scent of the earth breathing in the twilight calm. He checked to see how the work was going, and sometimes yelled at me a little, for appearances' sake, to make sure I was wide awake.

The rest of the time, I was alone with my eighteen years, my *cais*, and my three hundred coolies. I was responsible for their work in an area so vast that I covered more than twenty miles a day on my bike each day seeing, feeling, sensing, and understanding it all.

I had to send two crews to protect the seedlings in plot 26 against a sneaky invasion of *tranh*, a nasty weed as dense as horsehair, whose runners had to be dug up and burned. Then I had to cross plots 43, 44, and 45 to see how the weeding by the three crews of women under *cai* Nhgi was going, and also to make sure they were hoeing at the same time, to slow evaporation. It made sense to kill two birds with one stone, and hoeing was hardly any extra effort. But *cai* Nhgi always pretended not to understand; he needed to be shaken up a little, that one.

On my way, I would stop off briefly at the workshop, where that lazy fellow Thai was supposed to have finished repairing the axle of the cart that brought the latex to the factory. While I was at it, I would check the temperature of the rubber smokers and the supply of green wood. Then go take a look at the two crews working to maintain the erosion walls, a trip of a couple of miles that would also allow me to see if Hoi had looked after the diseased rubber trees we had noticed in plot 37.

From there, I would zip up the charcoal ovens road to see how the wood cutters under *cai* Sui were doing, clearing the newest plot in the forest. I couldn't stay out in the forest with them for too long, though. The jungle worked a kind of enchantment on me, and I tended to daydream there. I had to tear myself away, and to head instead for the sweaty Tonkinese crews under *cai* Tha, who were digging holes for new plantings out in the full sun. *Cai* Tha was a hell of a good crew boss. *Cai* Sui was, too. Tha did everything with power, Sui did everything with grace. Too bad all my other *cais* weren't like those two! I had the impression that *cai* Tha and *cai* Sui couldn't stand each other, that they would get into a fight at the first opportunity. Behind their mask of icy politeness, I could always sense a little tension between the Tonkinese who came from the north to work under their three-year contracts and the local Cochin-Chinese. In the north, people were dying of hunger and stomachs were empty. In the south, rice grew thick and fish was plentiful. That was the whole story.

As for me, I was lucky to be there at all. The large plantations tried to avoid hiring young Frenchmen who had grown up in

Indochina. We were regarded (perhaps with a touch of envy) as "locals," layabouts who had never seen the hard times back in France, had never experienced snow or cold, poor little rich kids used to the easy colonial life, so spoiled by their servants they couldn't even make their own beds.

But the outbreak of war had cut the sea link with France and the big companies had no choice but to hire locally. Besides, my bed was a woven mat, and I didn't need anyone's help to roll it up in the morning.

Having been kicked out of all the local *lycées*, I had wound up at fifteen at Saigon's vocational high school with my father's resigned blessing: "Since you won't do anything with your head, work with your hands. Maybe it will help you understand something."

Welding, boiler-work, carpentry, metal working. A good overview which would surely come in handy some day. Over each work bench hung the same sign: "A good worker has good tools." Just the same, I found myself kicked out as usual even before the end of the year.

By a miracle, a small agriculture school had just opened at Ben Cat. Located at the edge of the jungle thirty miles from Saigon—and a few minutes from a reform school—my new school looked like heaven.

There weren't good grades for the good students and bad grades for the poor ones. There weren't any grades at all, period. So we all became good students, since we didn't have fear or resentment in our guts.

Shovels, picks, a lake, a tennis court, a 25-meter swimming pool, a sports field which we laid out in a month, a classroom with new desks that didn't reek of boredom, a cafeteria, and a dormitory where we were left in peace. And above all—above everything—there was agronomist Jean Bouillère, our director. Jean Bouillère, the soul of that school for reformed dunces.

He led us straight to the basics by ways of his own choosing. In his general agriculture course, the mysterious phenomenon by which primary nitrogen is transformed into nitrogen which plants can assimilate took the shape of a fairy tale whose images were so vivid, we could feel the slow metamorphosis of nitrogen in the earth within our bodies, as if the earth was becoming us. He would re-create in our minds a magic garden of microorganisms that loved roots and tiny beasts that teemed underfoot when the earth was happy. We didn't need a microscope to see them, and I could sense Hao's father at my side, who had come to help all of us enter the crack. Bouillère joined the sky and the earth, binding them together into a sheaf that became light. And he drove all of that home to us, right to our very core, with his eyes. Dancing before me, I could see the Chinese character that Assam used to paint with her brush to show me that heart and spirit were the same, and were represented by the same symbol.

The evening before he handed out our diplomas, Bouillère put this question to us:

"Now that you know everything, tell me what the best kind of irrigation is."

All hands went up. Some called out, "Rain!" Others, "The Mekong!"

"Those aren't bad answers," he said, "but the very best irrigation for the earth is Man's sweat; it's better by far than all the rain and all the rivers of the world."

There was no lack of sweat at Long Than plantation, and only one law: Action. Nothing else counted. I was caught up in the terrific intensity of being young and leading people. Everything came down to three points: organization, efficiency, output. Those three pivotal points sparkled before my eyes like diamonds.

The holes dug for the new seedlings were three feet wide and three feet deep. I would always dig one myself, in average soil, as the work progressed. That let me estimate the time and effort the coolies would require. I did the same thing for hoeing and weeding, building erosion walls, and clearing brush.

That way, I could set daily tasks that were reasonable, neither too much nor too little. With vocational school three years behind me, I now understood that filing a piece of steel, swimming two thousand meters, and digging a hole in the ground all had something in common. They all gave you the same sense of completion, of balance between body and spirit, if you turned them into a game in which you aimed for perfection.

I had practically reached balance and perfection, especially between my Tonkinese hole diggers and my Cochin-Chinese woodcutters. But during my first months at the plantation, before

I got the hang of things, I had a tendency to aim too high in esti-mating the day's jobs. I would say, "Let's go!" and assume every-one would start running with me. Result: I barely avoided a revolt by the hole diggers.

Thank God, *cai* Tha liked me! Taking his *ca dui*, he promptly slashed at the biggest complainer, then restored order by yelling at the others that they were nothing but a bunch of *con khi* (mon-keys) and a swarm of shit-fly larva. *Cai* Tha wasn't very big, but his eyes blazed when he was angry. He came to talk with me later, after dinner, with his *ca dui* at his belt. Nobody had ever seen *cai* Tha without his *ca dui*. If he went to mass on Sundays, I believe he would keep it within arm's reach.

His eyes still shooting flames, he told me that I was going too far by setting unrealistic tasks. That the crews of women doing the weeding and hoeing would soon revolt. That the erosion wall builders would get fed up too. And that the tappers would stop when the others did, so as not to be beaten up by everyone else.

And that no *ca dui* could change anything, unless I started changing a little myself . . .

A general strike in an IRPC plantation would entail a hopeless loss of face, a very serious matter which would certainly have led to the firing of the *Ong Quang*. I had to take a good hard look around me, wake up to reality. It was a near thing, but thanks to the warning and advice from my ally *cai* Tha, I managed to adjust the work quotas without looking ridiculous in the coolies' eyes.

Now the work was humming along. I even offered a bonus to the hole diggers who exceeded their daily quota. And suddenly, they started digging faster than before, even racing each other during the last big push of the day. They started to catch up with the woodcutters who in turn started hurrying to prove they weren't lazier than the Tonkinese. And deep in my heart, a fan-tastic joy was boiling, a terrific feeling of belonging to a gigantic human adventure: the Rubber Empire.

It was an empire to which I belonged with every fiber of my body, every thought in my mind. An empire which had already established 7.4 million acres of rubber trees in Southeast Asia and 320,000 acres in Indochina. And those immense plantations, carved out of the jungle with tanker-loads of sweat, those rubber trees now so numerous that it would take more than a lifetime to touch them all with my hand as I walked among them . . . all were born of a single handful of seeds!

Those seeds had been brought out from the depths of the

Brazilian jungle sixty years before, by a man who was prepared to risk his neck to change the world.

He had gone up the Amazon alone in a canoe, borne by his faith, led by his vision into the forbidden heart of the huge jungle where dragons watched, to seek the seeds of the fabulous tree that grew only there.

He had found them, and selected only the heaviest ones, the ones that looked like agates. He hid them in his bamboo cane and slipped past the crocodiles of high finance who refused to let their riches fly free and spread. And he came out of the jungle in one piece, with his cane and his vision, to share the seeds with others.

Just like that, all alone, he had broken the absolute power of the first rubber kings, defeated the dragons that guarded the treasure, and allowed that treasure to spread to other lands.

When Jean Bouillère told us about the origins of the rubber trees, someone asked the name of the man who had set out to find the seeds that would change the world.

"His name isn't important," he answered. "It belongs to our collective memory, the common stock of humanity. What is important for you to remember is that a man tried."

The handful of seeds from Amazonia reached Ceylon. There, only three or four sprouted, producing plants.

Having seen the proof, another man left for Amazonia in turn, but with more efficient means. He brought back 70,000 seeds hidden in a shipment of bamboo. Barely four percent sprouted. That isn't much, but four percent of 70,000 seeds meant at least a thousand trees, taking early deaths into account. And those trees grew and yielded their own seeds, which were better adapted to their new climate. Millions of seeds. The liberation had succeeded.

Then it took off like wildfire, like those Chinese fireworks that shoot up into the sky, showering sparks everywhere: Ceylon, Malaysia, India, Burma, the Sunda Islands, Siam and Indochina; millions of acres of forest were set ablaze.

But the forests of Asia stretch on forever, and the fire scars soon healed, covered with rubber trees. And it wasn't finished yet, we had to plant, plant, plant . . .

Collecting the latex was a routine, a peaceful breathing that kept the plantation alive while we expanded the empire. Because the great task was to clear the uncultivated jungle where only rain fell, to bring new rows of rubber trees to life.

Hatchet, machete, fire . . . seventy-five acres had been wrested from the forest since my arrival. Picks and shovels followed close behind: 160 holes per acre, 12,000 holes already. And then the women arrived, planting, planting, planting, dancing around the young shoots, their bare feet tamping down the sweat-drenched earth in which the trees would grow tall and beautiful.

The pick and the shovel were still advancing, pushing the woodcutters deeper into the forest. But I wouldn't be there for the planting when the next rainy season returned. I was pedaling toward Saigon with my mat and my bundle, looking at the sky.

The night before, *cai* Tha had come to see me to find out why I was leaving. His eyes full of fire, hands crossed on his *ca dui* hanging at his belt, he wanted the truth.

So I told him the truth—but not all of it. I told him that my father needed me in his business in Saigon and also for his rice paddies, which was true.

But I didn't tell him about the tree I had found in the forest while hunting one Sunday with *cai* Sui. The tree that climbed to the sky as I looked at it . . . and which became planks . . . which became a junk . . . and which was telling me that the world is limitless.

We talked late into the night, *cai* Tha and I. He told me about the rice paddies of Tonkin, where life is hard, with typhoons and floods. He spoke of the land here where the rows of holes were marching on so well, where he wanted to eventually settle with his family.

I told him that I would never forget the earth, even if I had to work for a while in Saigon, even if I went far away someday. And I also told him I would never forget *cai* Tha, my friend. And he knew that was the truth.

When we parted, he put his *ca dui* on the ground in front of him and kneeled down, touching his forehead to the ground. That meant, "I greet the god within you."

With my old mat tied to the bike frame and my little bundle on the baggage rack, I was pedaling toward Saigon. The jungle gave way to forested clearings, then rice paddies, small dikes, and streams. Little hawks soared in the blue sky, their eyes watching all that existed, their wings trembling when they saw a fish. And my heart, a bit heavy when I thought of *cai* Tha, was bursting with joy as I watched the sky.

I was nineteen years old, and I knew the world belonged to me.

CHAPTER 5

So there I was, back in Saigon under my father's thumb, working in his import business. Well, so be it! The world might belong to me—but not just yet.

Among the Chinese, the eldest son always follows his father into business. They wouldn't have understood my doing anything else, even before my adolescence. And my father wouldn't have had it any other way. From the time I was ten or eleven, I had accompanied him when he called on his customers during our vacation trips to the village. That was the rule; following the country's ancient custom, I was under his wing, being trained. I resisted a bit, for show, but felt a certain pride in translating Vietnamese for my father, a language I had spoken since childhood, while he chewed watermelon seeds and took orders.

In the eyes of the Chinese, I was gradually becoming the "son of the bat." In a brilliant move, our business had chosen a good-luck animal—a bat, or *chauve-souris*—to decorate the label of the wine we bottled and sold. And *Chauve-Souris* wine was drunk in thousands of huts across the Indochinese countryside. A magic potion designed to avert the Evil Eye, it made my father's fortune.

The "son of the bat" was now nineteen. Instead of a classroom desk that stank of boredom, I had a well-organized office, with bills to check, an inventory book to maintain, and merchandise to tally. But I still had a tendency to daydream as I listened to the sparrows playing in the tamarind trees nearby. And I couldn't quite understand what had happened to me the night before.

A Child I had long known came and squatted close to me on my pallet. He held my hand, as if to console me, while telling me stories full of light, stories about freedom. I heard midnight strike, and the Child left, leaving me alone. And my heart became heavy with loneliness.

I got dressed, took my slingshot, and went out for a walk through the streets, intending no harm. Feeling the slingshot in my pocket comforted me. Maybe I hoped it would help put the Child on my path that night.

I walked for a long time under the tamarind trees, not going anywhere special. When I heard the clock on the cathedral on Catinat Street strike two, I turned back toward home. A policeman was leaning against a streetlight. He was facing away from me, and I was pretty sure he was dozing. I came a bit closer, walking soundlessly on my rubber-soled shoes. The streetlight went "pop!" and the policeman jumped, as shards of glass rained down on the sidewalk in a tinkling that was music to my ears. A real master-stroke—and the slingshot was already back in my pocket. The policeman looked about. The street was empty. He and I were the only people for a hundred yards around. But he couldn't see the Child, who accompanied me like my shadow. Whereas I saw everything that was going on in the policeman's head, exactly as if I were inside it. "He did it . . . No, he didn't . . . Sure he did . . . No, he couldn't have. . . . A beetle must have smashed into the bulb and broken it . . ." And I calmly went on my way home, holding the Child's warm hand in mine.

Saigon . . . it was a beautiful city, day or night, full of tamarind and mango trees, parks and birds. I wonder who laid Saigon out, and especially who decided to plant those thousands of fruit trees. A missionary with a generous vision, come from some cold country early in the century? A noble-born mandarin who could see further than ordinary people? One of the council of wise men? Or some collective conscience? In any case, it must have taken a powerful vision and a clear grasp of things to come, to have created this orchard-city with its innumerable fruit trees, a gift to its working people. And yet I couldn't bring myself to love Saigon, because of the greed and harshness that suffused its daily life. I could too often make out the image of money etched into the heart of its bustling streets. They were full of color, sounds, and smells, but in what could have been a Garden of Eden, money had become God. If I hadn't headed for the swimming pool and water polo after each day in the office, I wouldn't have lasted long there.

Lord, how far away the Long Than plantation seemed! The heroic days of *cai* Tha and *cai* Sui were but a memory. Those two may have hated each other, but they were linked by the sweat they gave the earth, and we had worked together in an act of creation. Still, I didn't regret returning to the big city, which had its own rules. Out on the plantation, surrounded by jungle, I had lived in almost complete isolation, cut off from the outside world. And I knew that the life of a planter would have meant a larger and larger gap between what I was and what I hoped to become—which was still unclear, but whose fabric was woven of space and freedom. I needed to escape from that trap, so when my father asked me to come work with him, I didn't hesitate.

A few serious clashes had already set us against each other. He had been running his business for nearly twenty years, with habits that time had turned into routines. In his eyes, I was still his little boy, to be shaped in his own image.

Sure, I knew the world belonged to me . . . but not right away. And patience wasn't my strongest suit. I had to learn to cultivate it, as we all did, in our precariously balanced country.

My father was a reserve officer, and had been mobilized when war broke out in Europe. When I was fifteen, I saw him cry. I never imagined that a man that strong could cry. It happened the day Guderian's panzers overran the French army at Sedan.

As Hitler's tanks rolled toward Moscow, the Japanese air force destroyed the American Pacific fleet at Pearl Harbor in a matter of hours. Three days later, it sank the PRINCE OF WALES and the RE-PULSE, the British warships that held the Strait of Malacca, the key to Malaysia and the Dutch islands. With that gateway opened, the Japanese army swept over Southeast Asia and Micronesia: Guam, Wake Island, the Gilbert Islands, Malaysia, the Philippines, Java and Sumatra, Siam and Burma. Just eight months after Pearl Harbor, Japan was master of the Pacific, controlling immense reserves of oil and nearly all the world's rubber. The Allied forces had either been driven back or shipped off to prisoner-of-war camps.

"Allied forces" . . . that was an expression to be used only in private, far from indiscreet ears—because the Japanese army had also occupied Indochina since August 1940. It was a "peaceful" occupation, part of a "collaboration in the Empire of the Rising Sun's war effort." The way I understood it, the June 1940 armistice between Germany and France had made Indochina a country officially under the orders of the Vichy government, which in turn was more or less allied with Germany, an ally of Japan. Since allies don't fight among themselves, Indochina had so far been spared the butchery that was bloodying Europe, China, the Pacific, and Southeast Asia.

Assam felt a visceral hatred of the "Japs." She often told us of the atrocities they committed in her native China, where the Sino-Japanese war had already lasted more than ten years. The Japanese soldiers threw train engineers alive into locomotive fire-boxes, she said. It was so staggering, we couldn't believe it. But she assured us it was true, she had received letters from her family; all the Chinese knew that the Japanese were worse than rabid dogs.

When the Nipponese troops first arrived, my parents had feared that the Vietnamese would forsake them for the new slant-eyed occupiers with their shaved heads and tiny caps. They called themselves "liberators from colonial oppression," but despite active propaganda for the "New Order" that the Mikado's empire wanted to establish in Asia, the Indochinese masses quickly became disenchanted. The Japanese in turn showed their contempt for ordinary Vietnamese. They were brutal and quick to slap people around; their swords would occasionally chop off a hand for some minor theft. By comparison, the French colonists were *tu té lam*—very nice.

Everything was calm, yet it would have only taken a spark, a "misunderstanding," for Japan to swallow our little colonial army in one bite, turning that surface calm into a sea of blood and tears. Within the French colony, orders were clear: hold your tongue, no stupid provocations, no sly smiles in front of the Japanese.

As the years went by, the winds changed for Japan as they had for Germany. Russia didn't fall. Neither did England or America. Germany's defeat at Stalingrad was followed by the Normandy landings. The radio told us lies, as did the newspapers, but news filtered through anyway. Clandestine radio stations existed, tracked by the Japanese secret services. While working at the Long Than plantation a few months before, I learned that the Americans had landed in the Philippines after retaking Guadalcanal and the Gilberts. Two years before the Philippines, the Japanese fleet had been crushed in the naval battle at Midway.

I was still at the Ben Cat agriculture school when the news about Midway was broadcast, presented in the usual guise of a "strategic withdrawal." Neither I nor any of my schoolmates knew where Midway was, but we sensed immediately that the war in the Pacific had taken a major turn that day.

From then on, right down to the poorest hut in the remotest part of the Plain of Reeds, the whole Indochinese people knew that the Japanese army, spread across Asia and the islands of the Pacific, was being pushed gradually into the sea by American might. In movie theaters, you could see propaganda newsreels showing fierce naval engagements, with aircraft carriers sunk by kamikazes and Flying Fortresses in flames. From time to time, the Vietnamese spectators applauded. But we all knew that those images were out of date. Despite their incredible courage, the kamikazes were powerless to change events. The Mikado's fleet had been swept from the sea, and for every Flying Fortress that was shot down, twenty or thirty more rolled out of America's factories.

Since being mobilized at the start of the war, my father divided his time between his office and the 11th Colonial Infantry Regiment barracks in Saigon. He would disappear for a few days or a week to go on maneuvers with his regiment. I envied him. He was going on vacation while I stayed behind, stuck in an office tallying figures I didn't really understand.

Papa, on the other hand, could stay in his office for days on end, completely absorbed. He made money with money, the way you grow trees from seeds, but without the sweat. In his eyes, honesty was by far the most important quality required to succeed in business. I think it was innate in him, as it was among the Chinese. With them, no contract or signature was needed; your word was worth more than a stack of papers, and it was kept whatever happened. Otherwise, you would be shamed. And in a country where *buon-ban* (buying and selling) revolved around the Chinese, no commercial enterprise survived shame.

Of course mere honesty and keeping your word wasn't enough. "Don't ever yield to the temptation to fart higher than your ass," my father used to say. Also: "Just go your own way without worrying what others think."

During the economic crisis of the Thirties, Papa had survived the terrible depression without going broke. Cutting costs to the bone, he had traveled by bus to see his customers in the countryside, staying in cheap, flea-ridden Chinese hotels. Up on blocks, the big Hotchkiss patiently awaited the end of the storm.

My mother still talked of those black days, when meat almost disappeared from our meals, replaced by rice, fresh-water fish, and home-grown vegetables. Most of the French who came out to the colonies tried to maintain their habits from home, in food as in other matters. But my parents chose to adopt the local lifestyle, which was in many ways both healthier and cheaper.

With an instinct that amazed me, my father bought apparently worthless pieces of land cheaply in areas he felt Saigon might expand into. He then soon resold those pieces of swampland at top prices.

Sniffing the winds of history, his ear cocked for distant noises, my father had caught the sinister rumblings of a new economic collapse as war approached. So he invested all his money in merchandise he ordered from France. It arrived in the last ships to get through. He filled the ground floor storeroom to the ceiling, part of the offices, and every available room on the first floor. Even the big room between the dining room and the kitchen was crammed with crates of Ovaltine, *Chauve-Souris* wine, and condensed milk. A narrow corridor between walls of stores led to Minh's stoves and Assam's room.

It was double or nothing, and he didn't have a penny left in the bank after taking the plunge. Our home, on the other hand, looked like a biblical pharaoh's storehouse. And if my father had guessed right, the lean cows would soon become fat ones.

Five years later, the first floor of the house was nearly cleared out. We still had a substantial stock of French products, but from the time rationing began, my father had doled them out piecemeal, and always linked to local products. To get a dozen boxes of our precious Ovaltine, unavailable elsewhere, or a half-case of condensed milk, which had become very scarce, the Chinese shopkeepers had to also order a dozen boxes of local merchandise. It was up to them to retail it in the Saigon-Cholon markets or among the humble people in the countryside and little backwater towns, where we were particularly well established.

The big Saigon import houses would send their Chinese agents into the countryside looking for orders. But those contacts were fairly neutral, even impersonal, in a way. Whereas our business was small-to-medium size, and my father had been visiting his provincial customers for twenty years. Together, they had survived the great trials of the Thirties, when the sky was falling.

Commercial and emotional ties had thus been formed between their families and ours. During our trips to the village two or three times a year, customers would feel my arms and congratulate my father: "He's growing, he's growing!" I was fascinated by the nimbleness of their fingers as they counted wads of one-piaster bills. I was also fascinated by the Chinese characters carved on their shop signs. They enjoyed translating them for me, and I tried to remember them.

"He's growing, he's growing!"

Then I took to the road myself, delivering our goods to the Chinese merchants in the countryside. My father stayed behind in Saigon, busy with his office and barracks. He gave me the car to use, under the loving care of Chu, who had been looking after it for a long time by then, sticking parts back together and fiddling around in the motor. In the old days, it ran on gasoline. When the Japanese army requisitioned that, it ran on rice alcohol lubricated with castor oil. Then, as the war dragged on, petroleum supplies became scarce and the Japanese requisitioned alcohol. So our good old Hotchkiss was now powered by a *gazogène* conversion unit, with a large burner full of glowing charcoal bolted to the left fender and three spare bags tied to the roof.

About 35,000 Japanese were based in Indochina, stationed around the country in roadside camps. Once when leaving Cholon, Chu and I watched one of the most impressive rounds of slaps we had ever seen. Some thirty soldiers were standing at attention, and an officer barked at them as he gave each man two terrific slaps. In the French army, if you screwed up, you got your head shaved and were sent to the stockade. The Japanese were more expedient: slam-blam!

But the war would end, and they would soon go home. In six months? Perhaps a year? No, certainly not a year! For all the slaps and iron discipline, it was clear that the invincible Japanese army wouldn't last much longer.

My Tho, Ben Tre, Tra Vinh, Sa Dec, Rach Gia . . . the road, rivers, hawks in the sky above, white egrets perched on black buffaloes' backs, villages, betel palms buffeted by the wind . . . I had traveled that road so often since I was a child, I knew its smallest details, and never tired of it. It was simply beautiful, a bare line crossing the countryside as the dry-season wind hurried along, bringing the plain to life in waves, a golden sea of rice growing as far as you could see.

What a joy it was to get back on the road in Chu's company. With his broad shoulders and muscular body, spare gestures and lively eyes, Chu reminded me of a bodyguard, like the ones you saw in the movies. His hair had started to go gray, but he hadn't changed in fifteen years, and his little mustache was as carefully trimmed as ever. When I was little, Chu helped me make sling-shots. It was he who taught me to cut the inner tubes crosswise instead of lengthwise, so they wouldn't snap, even when you pulled with all your might. I didn't see that it made any difference, since it was the same rubber, cut from the same inner tube. So he had me try it both ways.

"Learn to see things for yourself," he said, "and not just through other people's eyes."

I would be twenty soon, but at the end of the road with Chu there would be Saigon again, as in the old days when I was still in school.

Saigon: the office, boredom, a kind of sticky suffocation I tried to shake off at the swimming pool by pushing my body to the limit. And at night on my mat, the Child would come nestle against me and talk about all the things we had yet to discover together. Brilliant images would race through my head then, images of Indochina, so vast and mysterious. I was born here, yet knew almost nothing about the country. I was wasting away, doing work that didn't interest me, imprisoned in a city I liked less and less. The trips with Chu were too infrequent; anyway, they no longer gave me anything except quickly forgotten scraps of space and freedom. In Saigon, my life was dripping away like tepid water from a faucet.

Things couldn't go on like this, sitting behind a sterile desk which only generated images of merchandise to be bought cheap and sold dear. I was learning how to make money by using other people's money, while caught in a trap that was slowly closing in on me.

I would watch my father sitting at his desk, completely absorbed in adding up a long column of figures. His pencil would run down the page without hesitating or pausing. He would write down the figure at the foot of the column, and the pencil point would immediately move to the top of the page to resume its steady, rapid progress toward the bottom. He would check his addition, from the bottom up this time, but he always got the total right the first time, whereas I couldn't add without counting on my fingers, at a snail's pace; and when I checked the total, it was nearly always wrong.

It was long past closing time; I was alone with my father. He wrote down the total, carried it to the top of the next page, stretched, raised his eyes, and became aware of my presence.

"Aren't you going to water-polo practice?"

"Not tonight. I have to talk to you."

"Don't bother me with that business again! I've already told you that I won't give you a raise until you've spent at least three months in each department, including accounting, where you're hopeless. To get a raise, you have to deserve it."

That wasn't what I wanted to talk to him about. But how to broach the real question? I wasn't interested in a raise anymore, I had finally realized. I was counting my piasters already; with a raise, I would just count them all the more. I stared at the wall, my eyes far away, and cleared my throat, about to speak. But my father had become engrossed in adding up another column. He was once again enclosed in his own world, a thousand light-years from mine.

I had to take a stand, try to explain myself, at least hint at what he would almost certainly refuse to understand. But I understood it, because it had to do with me. The world is full of people who dream while counting their piasters without looking to see what lies beyond them. They wait for more, and more, and still more—and they don't see the trap closing slowly on them and their piasters. Having spent all their time fearing the lean cows, they wind up being devoured by the fat ones.

Suddenly, the flood-gates burst. And what came pouring out was all my anxiety at the prospect of a life on a treadmill, spent scurrying like an ant over tons of merchandise and barrels of wine stacked to the ceiling. Before the rushing flood that was sweeping away any hope of having his oldest son someday take his place, my father was speechless. He closed his ledger, started to listen at last. The flood continued to spread, calmer now, but much more vast, covering the plains and forests of Asia, swallowing villages, stretching as far as the sea. And I told him the story of Kim, the boy in Kipling's story.

Disguised as a Hindu beggar and living like one, Kim had set out to wander alone on the roads and paths of India. He was searching for something new, wanted to touch other minds with his, to understand the world and become a man. I said I wanted to wander the roads and trails of Indochina in turn, the way Kim had in his native land.

"It's impossible," Papa said, "absolutely impossible! The Japanese will take you for a spy, and you'll disappear, pure and simple."

"I'll be barefoot, wearing only a sarong, and I'll dye my skin with betel-nut juice. I'll look like a kind of Hindu monk. And I'll speak only in gestures, as if I were dumb. Don't worry, I've figured it all out. I've been thinking it over for a long time, ever since my days working at Long Than."

My father went pale. He could hardly get the words out.

"Jacky isn't doing a damned thing in school," he said. "Françou spends his time writing poems instead of working. And now you've gone crazy. Your idea is insane. You wouldn't last three weeks before disappearing for good, without leaving a trace. Don't you know yet what the Japanese are like? Don't kid yourself, we're at war."

I pulled up a chair and sat down near him. He was very pale. For the first time, I saw fear in his face. No anger, just fear. And I also saw love in his eyes, like the night he dragged me out of the pool when I was seven or eight.

The color slowly returned to his cheeks. He looked at me intently, as if seeing me for the first time. I couldn't say why, but he reminded me of that policeman, the one who caught me red-handed stealing the harmonica when I was fourteen. His eyes had the same look, as they bored into mine.

"Listen, son, I'm going to tell you a very serious secret, it will help you understand. The tall thin man you saw in my office last week was your uncle André. That was our second meeting in four months. Nobody knows about it, except you, now. I don't know when I will see him again. Or even if I ever will."

Uncle André! My father's brother . . . After a brief stay in Indochina, he had settled in Morocco. I had seen old, yellowed photos of him in our family album. In one of them, he was holding me by the hand. I had been three or four years old.

"He's with the Free French forces, parachuted in by the

English on an intelligence mission. If the Japanese catch him, it'll be torture first, then a bullet in the head. So you understand, son, your stories about Kim are all very well, but the way things are now, with the Japanese hunting spies everywhere, you'll soon wind up at the bottom of a hole. And before they kill you in some part of the forest, they'll make you dig the hole yourself."

We stayed together in his office for another long moment. My father had always intimidated me, except when I was very small, a little boy he used to bounce on his knees with my brothers. The charm disappeared as we grew up, to be replaced by his terrible rages at our report cards and our misbehavior at school. But that night, for the first time in ages, I felt an immense wave of tenderness for him. For the first time in an eternity, we were really talking, and a current flowed between us, simple and warm. And in his eyes, I saw a kind of respect.

"Keep on working with me until your military service. Be patient for another six months. That isn't too long, is it?"

"No, it isn't. But I need to think it over some more first. After my military service, maybe . . . we'll see. In the meantime, I'm going to the village to go fishing with Xai. But don't worry about Kim anymore. I understand."

I had a rainbow in my heart that evening, as I went to the pool with Françou after dinner. We sometimes used to go swimming together in the middle of the night, climbing the fence while the guard looked the other way. Françou was the junior 100-meter champion of Cochin-China and Cambodia. Until I was sixteen, I used to beat him with ease. Then, in a few months, he overtook me.

A thousand meters . . . we kept up the tempo, and I began to see the crack. I knew that Françou was in it already, he was in it even before we covered the first thousand meters. He swam like a god, swam like his poems, blending his breath with the water that flowed along his body. When I entered it in turn, time would cease to exist and my entire being would float in the absolute, the way his was, right then.

Two thousand meters . . . the crack was there all right, but I was struggling in vain to enter it. Yet I was still close to Françou, reaching far in front and pulling the water as far as possible behind me. Watch the attack of your left hand, it isn't quite synchronized with the exact instant when your mouth goes underwater . . . watch your breathing, take only as much air as you need . . . pull with your arms, stretch all the way, but without straining, above all without straining . . . suppleness, muscles . . . don't work your legs too much, forget about your kicking for the moment . . . come back to your left hand . . . that's good . . . now forget about your left hand . . . forget about the fatigue . . . forget about everything . . . just swim in that cloud where your body turns into the water's dance.

Three thousand meters . . . and I finally slipped into the crack! Françou picked up the pace a little then, knowing I would follow. Because where we were, we knew everything, and I could clearly see the essence of what had taken place between my father and me: I finally had to decide to cut the umbilical cord, choose between the security of the leafy tree in which I was starting to fall asleep, like a frightened monkey, or swinging out into space toward that other tree, more beautiful, larger, farther away. To choose between staying on my comfortable branch, at the risk of never daring again, or overcoming my fear once again and letting go, jumping into the awakening unknown.

Five thousand meters, soon . . . For the final laps, Françou speeded up some more. But I was in the deepest part of the crack, swimming body to body with my brother, wrapped in a rainbow that was now telling me that it was true, that the world really did belong to me and that in just a few days I would be in the village, with my life in my own hands.

CHAPTER 6

I recovered that life in a flash of clarity, and it lent me wings. I thought of the story they tell about the frog. You take a frog and put it in a pot of warm water, without a lid. Set it on a low flame; the temperature will rise, but the frog won't jump out. When the water is boiling, the frog will be perfectly cooked, still floating calmly in the pot. I had jumped out in time, but it had been a near thing.

A few days after saying goodbye to my father's business, his crates of merchandise, and his *Chauve-Souris* wine, I reached the village. My head was full of plans, and everything there happened at breakneck speed. With the help of Phuoc's father, Xai and I located our future fishing junk near Ha Tien. Her owner was asking too much but would eventually lower his price, tempted by the idea of being paid in cash. A little patience.

A week later, Xai and I took the bus for Rach Gia with a list of things to buy. We planned to return on the boat with the goods we ordered, to set up a cooperative before launching our fishing project.

Under the mango tree in front of the junk docks, Xai and I talked a little, recalling the events that had led us here to Rach Gia. Xai drew circles, crosses, and squares in the dust, then wiped everything out with his hand, only to start again. That meant he was happy. This was his first big escapade so far from the hut where he was born.

For my part, I was incredibly happy. Though in setting up this cooperative, I suspected I had made myself an enemy in the village—Bai Ma. He took advantage of the fact that he was rich and owned a carriage and the only horse for ten miles around to

charge unfair prices for materials that were essential to other
people's existence. Bai Ma would sell wire for hooks, bulk fiber for
fishing line, rolls of woven latania for sails, and *cai tram* bark for
caulking for fifty or seventy-five percent more than he should
have.

From my business trips with Chu, I knew that the Chinese
shopkeepers at Rach Gia charged much lower prices, so I had suggested to the villagers the logical idea that we form a cooperative.
A ten percent surcharge over wholesale would cover my travel
and shipping expenses for the sixty miles by canal as far as Ha
Tien. From there, Derk's father's ox-cart could bring everything
back in half a day. It was simplicity itself.

Yet my project encountered incredible resistance. As the
only person with ready cash, Bai Ma was powerful, and almost all
the villagers were in debt to him. He charged a shameful twenty
percent interest *per month*, yet people went along, thinking they
had to.

All they had to do was say "no" once and for all, tighten their
belts for a few seasons, and stop gambling their money away on
cards. But age-old habits run deep. So the debts never stopped
mounting and the interest piled up hand over fist. If the villagers
weren't careful, they would wind up naked as worms under Bai
Ma's heel, scratching the earth for that bastard during the rainy
season and fishing for him during the northeast monsoon. I had
tried to make them understand that, but it was like talking to the
mud walls of their huts. Things hadn't much changed from the old
days of slavery.

I had beaten the drum of rebellion against Bai Ma. And now,
because of me—or thanks to me—the village was split into two
camps. On one side, a large majority of the villagers judged it prudent to continue crawling beneath the pirate's sword, for fear of
future reprisals. The bravest ones chose to run the risk, but were
only a handful: Kieu's father, Xai's father, Hao's father, Chon's father, Derk's father, and Phuoc's father.

Xai was still drawing his circles and squares as the mango
tree's shadow lengthened across the dust. We had finished buying
supplies for the cooperative and were watching the life of the
boats.

In the Rach Gia harbor, criss-crossed by boats whose crews
shouted stories to each other, you could smell the *nuoc mam* jars

being unloaded from the big Phu Quoc Island junks; they would set sail full of sacks of rice. Others arrived from Ca Mau Point to the south loaded with shrimp paste, which smelled much, much stronger than *nuoc mam*. The largest junks came in hugging the coast, sailing in short stages from the Siamese border far to the northwest, under Chinese rigs that looked like huge bat wings. They carried teak logs and would return home with pottery brought by the river junks, or lime, charcoal, rice, or five-gallon jars of liquid palm sugar. Sometimes even pigs stuffed in bamboo cages; they must have wondered what they were going to eat and drink during the long voyage.

I always marveled at the variety of boats gathered here. The only thing they had in common were sails of woven latania leaves, sewn with long stitches of coconut-fiber thread. In a few hours, a sail for a five-ton junk could be sewn, seamed, and laced on, all set to go. But everything else about them was different. By traveling just ten or twenty miles along the coast, you went from one type of junk to a completely new one. Hulls and constructions methods seemed adapted to minute nuances of geography which were impossible to perceive. Shaped by the Mekong's alluvium, the shores of Cochin-China and the Gulf of Siam were shallow and muddy, built up by the huge mass deposited by innumerable river branches flowing into the sea. Except for the islands, nothing in the appearance of the coast seemed to change for hundreds of miles, so you would expect the boats to all be pretty much alike. But the logic of the East isn't that of the West; eyes here don't see like eyes there. So in one coastal village, the junks would be slim, lean as panthers, with bows that stretched far forward over the water. Yet in the neighboring town, boats that did exactly the same work looked like placid, somewhat lazy buffaloes. It was baffling, but true. Trying to see through the eyes of my native land, I think I grasped that the numberless spirits that populate the skies of Asia were orchestrating all this, each one putting its stamp on the boats within its zone of influence.

In three days, Xai and I gathered most of the material our future village cooperative would need except wire for hooks. The local Japanese army camp had snapped up the entire available supply. In a week, Chin Sang would get a shipment on the boat from Saigon and would set aside the ten rolls we needed.

Stopping by his store earlier to pick up raw fiber for the fishing lines, I had found Chin Sang having a lively, silent discussion with a Japanese sergeant. Neither knew the other's language; they were conversing by using Chinese characters, which are common to both languages. They concluded their business by brush strokes on a sheet of paper, without a word being spoken. When they were done, the sergeant had his merchandise loaded onto a truck.

When I was a child, Assam told us that many dialects are spoken in China. And that a long time ago, people in different regions of that vast country couldn't understand each other, since their languages were different. They were as different as Vietnamese is from Cambodian, Thai, or French, as different as Cantonese from Mandarin or Taiwanese.

So people thought hard—and Assam closed her eyes a little, without moving her lips, to show us how to think. And by thinking long and hard, the Chinese invented a magical way of writing. It was magic because it didn't need the sounds made by your mouth to overcome the wall between languages. Its characters represented the meaning of the words, not their sounds. It was like a crack in the wall, Assam said, which allowed all the languages to become one.

Ever since those days, when a Chinese from Peking wanted to communicate with a Chinese from Hong Kong or anywhere else, he could take a brush and a piece of paper and say anything he wanted. If they met on a street corner or out in the countryside, and didn't have brush and paper, they used their fingers to draw messages on their palms that could be read as plainly as if written with pen and ink.

I now understood that those ideograms not only united all of China, they also allowed China and Japan to communicate. It really was a crack in the wall, just as Assam had said. I realized all this while Xai and I were checking the material for our cooperative. Tomorrow, he would bring it to Ha Tien by boat. I had to wait for the wire to arrive before returning to the village.

Not that I minded the delay. Abadie was getting his little junk TITETTE ready, and suggested I sail with him to Tamassou Island, some forty miles away. We would spend about a week there, and by then, Chin Sang would have received the merchandise Xai and I needed.

Alyette, Abadie's wife, was spending her vacation at Tamassou with a couple of friends. She ran the Rach Gia Bungalow, a kind of hotel-restaurant that was subsidized by the government. All the provincial towns had such bungalows, which offered inexpensive food and lodging to travelers passing through.

To my eyes, Abadie represented adventure, both simple and fantastic. In the Thirties, he and a journalist friend had driven a little Citroën all the way from Indochina to France. They cut their way by machete through the bamboo forests between Cambodia and Siam, then made the impossible crossing over the Tenaserrim mountain ranges between Siam and Burma, taking the car apart so it could be loaded on the backs of a dozen elephants. They ended their trip in Paris with a car stripped to a motor, four wheels, a chassis, and a seat—and the two rifles they had used to hunt for food along the way.

Rach Gia was a stopover which we never missed on our vacation trips to the village, so I had known Abadie for years. Like Chu, he hadn't changed with time, except for his hair, which was beginning to thin. At one end of the scale stood my natural father, a sportsman and man of action whom I both admired and feared, who frightened me at times. At the other stood Abadie, a kind of guide or spiritual father with whom I had felt comfortable since I was a child. Now that I was nearly twenty, and could perhaps see things a little more clearly, I realized that my father never liked Abadie much, though he respected him. In my father's eyes, he must have contained the seeds of dreams that were dangerously attractive to Françou, Jacky, and me, his uncontrollable offspring. My father's feet were firmly planted on the ground, he looked straight ahead, and played his life like chess, a game at which he excelled. Abadie's feet ran across the sky and his head was in the clouds.

Born on Reunion Island, Abadie had come to Indochina very young and spoke Vietnamese perfectly. He survived the butchery at Verdun, where many of his comrades died; his specialty was throwing hand grenades into machine-gun nests. Later, he spent a few years in Egypt, hanging around the pyramids and colossal temples. He then returned to Indochina, working at all sorts of jobs. In front of my somewhat embarrassed father, he called the teacher who had given me a zero for my essay on "A rolling stone gathers no moss" a fool. I loved the man, and it was thanks to him that I had overcome a feeling of inferiority brought on by my awful school work when I was fourteen or fifteen and everything felt black inside.

"There's a school where you wear out the seat of your pants learning things that are often useless nonsense," Abadie told me one day, "not to mention the lies that are fed to generations of children. And there's a school of life which helps you more or less figure out how things work, provided you open your eyes, which isn't always easy. You'll be in that school until you're about forty. After that, you may find another school on your path, but I can't really say what it will be like; I can't quite make it out myself."

The low Rach Gia coast was disappearing in TITETTE's wake. To the right, Turtle Island was pulling its head into its shell. Abadie had given me the tiller and gone to stretch out on the foredeck, leaving me alone with the boat and the sea, alone with my huge joy. "After that, you may find another school on your path, but I can't really say what it will be like." Could that be the school that the old monk at the Cave of Coins had told me about?

I had first met him with Xai, thanks to Bai Ma. We were ten or eleven, and had been hunting green pigeons with slingshots along the road to the rice paddies behind the village hills. It was terribly hot and we were empty-handed after three hours of hunting.

Bai Ma came along with his horse and carriage and suggested we take a little ride. We both liked him in those days, and he liked us too. He was going to Hon Chong, fifteen miles in the opposite direction from Ha Tien, to buy sprouted coconuts and a bag of lime. On the way, he dropped us off at the Cave of Coins, near the sea. He said he would pick us up on the way back, after he did his shopping.

There were lots of walking catfish along the path, lazing in the sun among the mangrove roots. Flying lizards could see a slingshot stone coming, but walking catfish were even more clever; they could read your thoughts and jump aside in a flash. Still, we had managed to hit one apiece when the old monk came out of the cave. He almost seemed transparent, he was so old. He didn't appear to be angry; he just looked at us as if to say, "They didn't do you any harm, and they're too small to eat." Then he said there was good water in the cave, and asked if we were thirsty.

It was very dark inside, and I couldn't see anything at first. But I recognized the smell of bat droppings right away, then saw the swarms of bats blanketing the cave's ceiling. And then, very gradually, I began to make out the big reclining stone Buddha half-way up the left-hand wall, near the little oil lamp and the incense sticks.

We were very thirsty. The water the old monk had promised us flowed from a crack in the rock at the foot of the large Buddha, in a thin trickle that filled a hole cut into the stone; from there, the rest must have disappeared into another crack, since none of it overflowed.

I knew the taste of water in the paddies that you drank when there was nothing better to be had, and the water that fell from the sky onto the tile or thatch roofs and ran off into cement cisterns and ceramic jars. I also knew the taste of water in the forest streams and the ponds on the plains where birds came to drink. But we never tasted water as good as that from the great Buddha in the Cave of Coins.

After that, Xai and I came back to visit the old monk every year. We would bring him joss sticks for the Buddha and rice cakes wrapped in banana leaves which Assam fixed. On my last visit, Xai hadn't been able to come, and I had gone alone. I was pretty sure the old monk was close to dying, and it must have been the school Abadie mentioned that he told me about that day. He said it was called the school of "transmitting," but before entering it, you had to go to the school of "seeing" and to the school of "doing." He ended by saying some very strange things, that the three schools were the same and that they had to work together, otherwise none of them could really exist.

Turtle Island was now far astern and you could see the outline of Tamassou Island, clearly visible in the twilight before TITETTE's bow. I thought about the old monk, and didn't know what he really wanted to tell me. It was as if he had hidden a secret in a tiny, extremely precious jar, and had given it to me well sealed, so I wouldn't lose what he had put in it. I didn't have the key, and didn't know if I would ever find it. To be honest, though, that was the least of my concerns. I had all the time in the world; my whole life was ahead of me. For now, the only thing I knew for sure was that I was on my way to a school that people hadn't often told me about. It was called the school of "making the best of life," and I knew for sure that I planned to stay there as long as possible.

Abadie went below to cook our rice on the wood-fired clay stove. I held the tiller with my foot, listening to the gurgling of the wake. I wanted it all to last forever. The sea was very calm and a

light northeast monsoon breeze whispered through the thousands of holes in the woven latania leaves. I used to think that
Indochinese sails weren't very efficient, but Abadie set me
straight. By passing through those tiny holes, the wind created a
low-pressure area in the lee of the sail. So with a following wind,
the sail was both pushed by the wind and pulled from the other
side.

This was my first long sailing trip, and I didn't have anything
to do except take it easy, seemingly forever. Take it easy, and let
myself be caressed by the warm wind, carried and rocked in the
whispering of the water and the air. Night had fallen, cloaking the
boat and the sea, with me on the boat and on the sea.

Abadie was resting below; he trusted me. I had picked a star
that was closest to my heading to steer by. As it gradually slipped
to the left across the sky, I adjusted my course a finger's-breadth
to the right from time to time. That was what Phuoc's father had
taught me, when I went out with him during the fishing season.

With Phuoc's father, you had to work hard in the sun, store
the hundreds of fishhooks in their shuttles as the boat returned
to the island, then labor until nightfall cutting the rays and sharks
into strips and drying them on the stones of the beach. And then
you had to set out again before dawn to put out the lines, with
your eyelids still sticky with sleep. I used to think constantly
about Alain Gerbault's trip around the world, about Eric de
Bisschop on KAIMILOA, and especially about Henri de Monfreid,
sailing the Red Sea among smugglers and fishermen on their Arab
dhows. All of them, even Monfreid, used a compass. And one day
I brought a compass to show Phuoc's father. It was the first time
he ever saw such an extraordinary thing, a needle that never
changed direction. It was the greatest gift I could have given him.

Crouched on the beach, Phuoc's father spent the whole morning with that marvelous device, turning it in his hand, fascinated
by the trembling finger that always pointed the same way, as if
showing something hidden far beyond the horizon.

He didn't say a word for the rest of the day, and I could tell
that his entire mind was on the compass. He thought of nothing
else as he prepared the lines and checked to see that I had correctly put forty-nine hooks in each shuttle. But the next day, be-

fore taking me fishing with Jacky and Xai, he was his old self again, and he gave the compass back to me.

"You need light to use this thing at night," he said, "and that blinds you. But with the stars or the direction of the waves or the wind, you can always tell where you're going, and your ears stay open to hear what the sea is saying."

Sailing by night in that apparent darkness, while knowing where the island was . . . it was a magic that renewed within me my alliance with the universe. The stars were speaking, as were the sea, the wind, and the island cloaked by night. And in their way, they were all saying the same thing. Still, I would probably never understand why nobody in the village wanted to know that the Big Dipper, Cassiopeia, and Orion all show where north is. I had tried to explain it, but in vain; it was as if I were talking about the *ma qui*. Yet everybody there knew these three constellations, they didn't have anything to do with the *ma qui*, and they hadn't changed in a hundred generations of fishermen.

I hitched a line around the tiller and TITETTE continued on a nice straight course next to my chosen star, responding to tiny adjustments and half-spoken conversations between me and her. Though I was alone on deck, Phuoc's father was near me, and I could hear him clearly say: "I don't regret the pains I took to teach you all this. And one day, when you have a compass, the dragons of the sea will have had time to become your allies."

In the course of the night, the sky and its stars slowly turned. I didn't wake Abadie; he needed to rest and I wanted to be alone and have the whole boat to myself, alone with the sea. And then the island was ahead of me, like my life, standing out clearly in the dawn.

I dreamed of sailing away someday on my own boat, very far and perhaps alone, like Gerbault, all the way to those islands you see on old maps. Sail away on a beautiful junk, just big enough to shelter me from the sun and spray, but which would ride easily, of course. It would have all I needed aboard, a clay stove to boil rice on and *nuoc mam* from Phu Quoc, which was the best in the world. And hooks, so I would have some fish to cook with the rice. There would also be a big water jar tied aft of the cabin top, which would be made of woven bamboo covered with thatch, and an extra barrel below, on the ballast stones.

Then my boat would encompass the open ocean, all the way to infinity. And it would be at sea that I would attend the school of "making the best of life."

In the meantime, the only thing I asked of heaven was that I should never forget this light on the horizon of the Gulf of Siam, or this breeze flowing so softly into me, its power carrying the perfume of immensity.

CHAPTER 7

Abadie had his hands up. It was all happening so fast . . . things had gone a hundred miles an hour since yesterday noon. I just stood there, my brains turned to mush.

"Get your hands up, for God's sake. He's going to shoot you!"

Abadie's hoarse voice cut through the now-deadly silence, and my stupor immediately vanished. I raised my hands, blinded by the reality of the Japanese soldier a hundred feet away who continued to aim at me for a few more seconds. He lowered his rifle a little. I started to breathe again. But he kept it pointed at my belly, and I felt a chill creeping over me.

On the bank of the *rach* in front of the hut, the bullfrogs had fallen silent. On the alert, an egret stood very straight, its delicate feet poised at the water's edge. I looked at it. Two beings seemed to inhabit me, both of them very real. One, motionless, his hands in the air, was a child frightened by a world turned upside down. The other had gone to join the white egret on the opposite bank. From there, he could hear the silence, could see and feel it like the hawk wheeling and playing with the sky above the calm stream. And the cold slowly left my gut.

A second Japanese soldier came running. Alarmed, the egret raised its head and the chill gripped me again. The Japanese always scream when they attack, to give themselves courage and to terrify the enemy. I could see his bayonet glittering in the dawn and the egret, both at the same time. Maybe he felt I hadn't raised my hands fast enough, that I was rebelling against the New Order. He was still running toward us, still screaming, holding his rifle barrel level, and as I watched the bayonet, my stomach turned to ice.

The soldier who was aiming at us gave a bark sharp enough

to freeze your blood. The other one stopped in his tracks, pointed his weapon at the ground, and slowly walked over on his bowed legs. My heart started beating again, and I managed not to smile as I remembered one of Jacky's cracks: "The Japanese spend their childhood riding barrels to develop their sense of balance; that's why they're bowlegged." The soldier's comrade shouldered his weapon; he approached, handed his rifle to the first one, and tied our hands. They lit a cigarette, blew smoke in our faces; they were in conquered territory. They barked between every puff. You would think the Japanese couldn't talk without barking, even among themselves, even to ask for a light. The Vietnamese say a dog that barks never bites. That may not always be true, but for the moment, the rifles were shouldered and the white egret on the other shore had gone back to fishing; taut as a bow, I could see it practically turning into a fish, and zip! a silvery flash was flapping at the end of its beak. The bullfrogs had resumed their drumming, answering each other among the clumps of reeds. Death had gone to prowl somewhere else.

Over the years, I had grown up surrounded by the war. But it was far away and didn't really concern Indochina, which by a miracle had been spared the bloodshed caused by men's madness. Just the day before, in the middle of what seemed like peace, Alyette and I had been scaling fish for lunch near our camp on the beach at Tamassou. I watched as a little fishing junk approached, heeling prettily in the wind under a beautiful sky. It looked like the one I wanted to buy with Xai to go shark fishing. The junk folded its sails in the lee of the island and dropped its wooden anchor near TITETTE, where Abadie was puttering with something. I could hear very animated exchanges between the two boats, and several times caught the word *Nuoc-Buom*—Japanese. Alyette was tending the fire in silence, pausing at times before snapping a twig to feed it. The sun was already shining less strongly, and I could sense a kind of anxiety spreading great dark wings across the sky. Then Abadie joined us on the beach, looking terribly pale.

"They've attacked. It was bound to happen sooner or later."

We immediately set sail aboard TITETTE, leaving Alyette and her two friends on the island. We planned to go to the house of an old friend of Abadie's, a rich Vietnamese rice grower who lived near Rach Gia at the mouth of a little *rach*. He had a radio, and we hoped to find out what was happening. The wind was fair and we reached the place at about two in the morning. The man seemed very frightened by our arrival and confirmed what the fishermen had reported.

"The Japanese neutralized the entire French army in Indochina the night before last. It happened all at once, without warning. They're the ones broadcasting on Radio Saigon."

He told us that by now all the French soldiers were either captured or dead. The slightest resistance had been crushed. The administrators and the few colonials in the countryside around Rach Gia had been rounded up at dawn and taken to the bungalow. Leperson, the police chief, had been executed for sabotaging police headquarters before he surrendered. And Faucillon had apparently been shot when the Japanese went to his rice plantation to pick him up.

The tide had already dropped, and TITETTE was sitting in the mud, high and dry. It was too late to leave. Anyway, where would we go? Pick up Alyette and the couple at Tamassou, race to the village and get my mother and my younger brother and sister— and then what? Sail in circles in the Gulf of Siam until the end of the war, a month or a year from now? We would be kidding ourselves. The Japanese hadn't lost the war yet, the country was crawling with them, we would all wind up facing a firing squad as rebels or spies. In any case, the tide wouldn't be coming up for hours and hours, it would be broad daylight, everybody would know what was going on, we wouldn't get far . . . "Go get some rest, you're exhausted. We'll decide what to do later."

And in the gray dawn, the two soldiers had come to get us in front of our host's house, tipped off by the informers who had long been multiplying among the local populace.

They pushed us toward a sampan, on which we crossed the *rach.* Then they marched us a couple of miles along the rice-paddy dikes to Rach Gia. That pretty, lively town, which we had left the week before, looked dead today, its shops closed, its market deserted. In the harbor, even the junks had fallen silent; sails folded, they seemed to be waiting to sense which way the wind would be blowing. But the wind wasn't likely to change for a long time. Japanese flags arrogantly flew on the police headquarters staff, in front of the administrator's residence, and on all the public buildings. My heart sank when I saw the swarm of smaller Japanese flags decorating the Chinese storefronts and the eaves of the Vietnamese huts along the river. They had all blossomed during a single night, speaking of fear and proclaiming the arrival of the New Order.

Escorted by our guards, we walked in silence through the paralyzed town. A group of five or six Vietnamese crouched at the edge of the sidewalk glanced at us, full of contempt, and muttered a word I didn't know.

"What does *doc lap* mean?" I whispered to Abadie.

The Japanese immediately barked at us. Abadie waited a while for him to calm down, then whispered, without moving his lips:

"Independence."

I remembered what my father had told me a few months earlier: "Very serious things could happen before the end of the war. The Japanese are determined to overthrow the colonial regime. They know that Germany will be defeated and that their turn will come. It'll probably lead to a hell of a mess, *even before the war ends.*" I couldn't imagine what my father was worried about. Granted, he was pretty sharp in business matters, but here, he was really imagining things . . . And then the mess hit in a single night, like a terrific thunderclap in Indochina's peaceful sky.

The two guards shoved us into the grounds of the former police station, which was now the Japanese command post. We were interrogated, without being slapped or barked at, by an officer who was only about thirty.   We had expected to be turned over to some kind of brute, but he ordered the guard to untie our hands and politely asked Abadie to sit down. His look was straightforward, yet his gestures were a bit awkward, almost shy. He said he would send a junk to Tamassou to pick up Alyette and the couple left behind. My eyes were drawn to a photo on a corner of his desk showing a woman in a kimono holding hands with a young man who resembled the officer. After a few discreet glances, I decided it must be his mother. I told him that my own mother was at the village near Ha Tien with my younger brother and sister, aged seven and eleven. That my father, an officer in Saigon, might be dead. And that I had to return to the village to look after my mother and her two children. Lying across the desk, the Japanese officer's long sword was a powerful reminder to behave and tell the truth.

But the officer had known the truth before he even saw us. I wasn't aware that Abadie had been wounded at Verdun, though we had been friends for years. Yet the officer could tell us everything about ourselves; all he had to do was check his files. He knew I wanted to buy a junk to go fishing near Ha Tien. He knew I was a swimmer. He knew my father belonged to the 11th Colonial Infantry Regiment—and told me not to worry, that the casualties in Saigon had been insignificant. He also reassured Abadie, saying that one of his men would accompany the junk to Tamassou, to avoid any possible trouble with the crew. And that I could take a boat to go join my mother in a few days. I would even be authorized to stay at the village while waiting to be evacuated to Saigon. I couldn't believe my ears. I would see Xai again, and Bai Ma, too. There were some very important things I absolutely had to tell Bai Ma. Life is a hell of an adventure. This morning, I thought I was going to die, and then I was sure we were going to be tortured. An enormous wave of joy filed my chest. The officer looked me straight in the eyes and gave me a brief smile. No, he wasn't shy. And the Japanese weren't necessarily brutes.

We were sent to join the other Frenchmen at the bungalow, which was guarded by an easygoing Japanese soldier. There, we learned that nobody in the Rach Gia province had died. The French authorities had had time to give the order not to resist, the only way to avoid a pointless massacre. But Faucillon had a close call. Accompanied by a Vietnamese interpreter, the soldiers who came to get him had first arrested police chief Leperson at dawn, and the interpreter had discreetly stolen a revolver from the station. A little while later, when they were picking up Faucillon on his plantation, the interpreter had pulled the trigger at point-blank range . . . but the revolver hadn't fired. While waiting for the Japanese, Leperson had spent the night removing the powder from all the cartridges. He came within an inch of being executed for this "sabotage," but his Eurasian wife managed to get the Japanese commander to change his mind. Leperson came through with a nasty beating: two black eyes and a badly battered arm.

CHAPTER 8

In less than a week, the little town came back to life. Traffic on the Rach Gia–Ha Tien canal picked up again and the junks came and went as usual. Only the new uniforms showed that power had changed hands. We were allowed to leave the bungalow by day, but not at night. And we were warned never to wander far from the Japanese guards who were responsible for keeping order.

Japan had proclaimed Indochina's independence, but its army was maintaining strict order, thank God. Thank God too, the Vietnamese had a holy terror of the military which had "liberated" them. So order reigned—at least for the time being. But I was starting to worry about getting back to the village. I didn't see how my mother would be able to return to Saigon safely with two small children, even with Chu and Minh's protection. And it was rumored that the French at the bungalow would soon be evacuated to Saigon. We were all aware that rebellion had been brewing since the independence proclamation, but Abadie was sure the countryside would stay quiet for a while yet. I didn't know what to think. I was in a sweat about my mother, isolated in our village sixty miles away.

Then one morning the guard came to rouse me out at dawn, accompanied by the same Vietnamese interpreter who had tried to kill Faucillon. "Hurry up!" Outside, a soldier took charge of escorting me to the boat for Ha Tien. I felt grateful to the garrison commander for keeping his word. When I told my companions at the bungalow how decent he had been during our interrogation, several called me naive: "He just wants to cover his rear. He knows the war will be over soon and that there will be scores to settle once France has the country back in hand." But I think there are bastards and decent people everywhere. Still, Leperson had barely escaped a firing squad. But would they really have shot him? I doubted it.

As we walked along, I stuck to the guard like a leech. I was safe next to him, whereas you didn't have to be a genius to realize what a danger the interpreter represented. He was walking on my left, a revolver on his hip, his ugly anti-French face full of hate. He reeked of hate from every pore. I wish I knew what humiliations he had endured at French hands; maybe also at the hands of the Japanese who employed him now.

The guard climbed aboard the boat. As I understood it, he would accompany me to the village, where I would await instructions from the garrison commander at Ha Tien about returning to Saigon with my mother and the two little ones. I was relieved to see the interpreter stay behind on the dock. He could easily have shot me in cold blood during the trip and later claimed that I had tried to steal his weapon in order to kill him.

The boat chugged along low in the water, crammed with Vietnamese peasants, the lively women and children calling to one another in high-pitched voices from bow to stern. The boat stopped here and there, putting off passengers and taking on new ones. There were chickens, ducks, bundles of dried fish, jars of shrimp paste and palm sugar, baskets of betel nuts, and many scents among which my delighted nostrils recognized mint, ginger, and cinnamon. All of Indochina's subtle aromas were mixed with the acrid smell of the charcoal that sustained the regular throbbing of the boat's *gazogène* motor. At times, though, a dull ache stabbed at my chest and I felt the dark wings that had hovered in the sky above Tamassou stirring deep within me.

An old woman swiped a handful of charcoal to fry her pepper beignets, which led to a noisy argument between her and the skipper. They traded a flurry of insults involving several generations of ancestors whose mothers apparently had been nothing but a bunch of whores and bitches in heat. But everybody knew that this was just an oratorical battle. The old woman kept the charcoal and the skipper waited for his share of beignets fried in coconut oil. It was the unchanging way of Indochina.

In the beginning, these simple country people watched me with curiosity, perhaps mixed with contempt. They probably wondered how a Frenchman could still be free to travel the way I was in spite of the New Order, even accompanied by the Japanese soldier dozing in a corner. But their attitude wasn't hostile. Abadie had guessed right; the rice paddies were calm. My anxiety faded and the countryside smiled at me.

When she had sold her beignets, the old woman took some more charcoal, fed it into the clay stove she had propped in the lee of the transom, scooped up water from the canal, and started washing rice for her family's meal. Other stoves were glowing here and there. The skipper might get in trouble over the amount of charcoal his *gazogène* burned, but he had no worries where lunch was concerned. I had barely had time to gulp down a bowl of café au lait before embarking, and had stupidly passed up a chance to buy one of the old woman's beignets. So I held out a piaster and asked her if she could put a helping of rice for me into the pot. She stared at me, astonished. I gave her a smile, and she smiled back. I had addressed her in a form that was exactly suited to her age, her role in the family, and her place in society.

Now people started looking at me with real interest. The looks took me in, sized me up, weighed pros and cons. I overheard one man tell his neighbor: *Ong nai tien Annam kha lam* (That gentleman sure speaks Vietnamese well). He had spoken quietly enough to show respect, loudly enough so I would hear. And the tone he used clearly said that I had my place among these humble country folk. Only by living for a long time among the people can someone learn their difficult language (which is both monosyllabic and polytonic) in which *co co co co co* means, "The policeman's wife has a neck like a heron." But if each *co* isn't pronounced with just the right accent in just the right place, the sentence is meaningless. With a few rare exceptions, such as Abadie, a French person had to have played as a child with local children to really speak Vietnamese. On the boat, the doors had swung open, and the old woman sent her son-in-law to say that the meal was ready and they would be honored if I would share it with them.

Some doors had opened, but one of the passengers kept his firmly shut. He was a few years older than I, and his clothes and manner suggested he came from a family of educated Vietnamese.

Leaning on the gunwale forward, he seemed to want to keep his distance. I was pretty sure he was Tonkinese*.

Having washed my bowl in the canal and thanked my hosts for the meal, I made my way forward and went to lean on the gunwale next to the man. He didn't pay me the slightest attention. A kind of shyness held me back, and the silence soon became oppressive.

The children were sleeping, their parents resting, the boat chugging along at five knots. We were already halfway there. The countryside had certainly changed since those days not that long ago when my father had made us notice how the land was beginning to come alive. New villages had sprung up along the canal, and I was surprised to see how tall the betel palms were, where huts once lacked for shade. I had driven every mile of this area— but without looking around me.

"What a beautiful country . . ."

I had muttered the words, both to myself and to try to break the silent barrier the man seemed to want to maintain between us. He had heard, but didn't show any inclination to become better acquainted. His gaze was lost in the distance, watching the countryside along the canal slowly drift by. The silence fell again, even heavier than before.

The man intrigued me. Before lunch, he had been conversing in Chinese characters with my guardian angel. It had surprised me to see an ordinary Japanese soldier, with his broad peasant's face, handling such a difficult written language. But I had been even more surprised to see a Vietnamese of my generation doing the same. A few old Vietnamese scholars had preserved the ideograms of their ancient culture, like relics, but our Western alphabet had long since replaced them. Without that alphabet, there would have been no letters exchanged between Françou and Phuoc, between Kieu and Jacky, between Xai and me, ties of

---

*Before independence, Vietnam was divided into three countries: Cochin-China in the south, Annam in the middle, and Tonkin in the north. Its inhabitants were called Annamese. They shared a common language, and physically closely resembled each other. It takes years in the country to tell a Cochin-Chinese from a Tonkinese. Cambodia and Laos are two other neighboring countries, with different languages and physical types. Together, Cochin-China, Annam, Tonkin, Cambodia, and Laos formed what used to be called Indochina.

Saïgon le 6 Novembre 1.943

Phước ôi

Trước kính lời thăm, Gardien, Sáo, lành
, cái, ngỗi, Niên cho đặng mạnh giỏi
ở Saïgon mưa ít, mùa Hôm qua đi 3
ngày giời mưa nhiều. tôi sợ tết Tây
những cô đi Đường Hoa

Mẹ tôi mường hết đây. tôi đi xe ôtô
Bernard ở nhà nó (Long-Thành) Nó làm
ông chép có một tháng 3.oo #!!
Chiếng nào mầy gửi thơ cho tôi, mầy
để ở bao thơ, một cái ở tôi. vô mầy
nói mầy làm ở đâu. Mầy để cái là
tết, tôi cảm ơn mầy. Siot map ít và
me call đi bên Amérique. tôi mường
lại Đường Hoa nhiều lắm.
ở bao thơ mầy để F. rancois Montenier
24 B° Charner Saigon

ở nhà cả hai con mèo nhỏ lắm
mầy để mươi mùi lớn chỉ hộ tôi
cảm ơn mầy nhiều lắm

gởi thơ mèo mèo   Francois

ở Saïgon có một xe mùi nhỏ lắm

friendship that leapt across the distance. Thanks to *quoc ngu,** which French missionaries popularized early in the century, anyone could learn to read by age ten, and thus get an education. The entire Vietnamese people, from intellectuals to peasants, had immediately embraced the new kind of writing, which was so much easier to learn than Chinese characters. It was one of France's greatest gifts to the country.

"It really is a beautiful country . . ."

I knew that the man had heard me perfectly well, and could feel him briefly hesitate. Then he answered, speaking French practically without an accent:

"Yes, a beautiful country. But is it also your country? Perhaps it would become truly beautiful again if the French weren't here to impose their law on us with rifles and policemen. The law of the strongest."

He had spoken in a calm voice, without anger or apparent passion, and his mastery of French took me aback. He continued in the same tone:

"When I think that France once stirred the peoples of Europe with her great Revolution . . . But what has she done since then? Do you even know your beautiful Declaration of the Rights of Man and of the Citizen? I can recite its seventeen articles by heart."

And he slowly recited them one after another in his clear voice, carefully enunciating each syllable. I didn't even know the Declaration's first line. I was just barely aware that it dated from 1789, and that mountains of heads had rolled in those days, first those of the nobility, then many others.

"You summarized that solemn text in three words: *Liberté, Egalité, Fraternité*, three words that burn like beacons for the rest of us. But for you French, they have lost their meaning; they belong to a past you have turned your back on."

On the threshold of her canal-side hut, a woman was pounding rice in a wooden mortar. In a field, a naked boy astride a water buffalo followed as his father plowed. Nui Trao Hill could already be seen on the horizon before the bow. The rice paddies stretched

---

Quoc ngu: a system of phonetic transcription of Vietnamese, using the Roman alphabet. The language's different tones are indicated by diacritical marks: acute, grave, and circumflex accents, vertical and horizontal question marks, or by a dot written beneath the word, depending on the tone used to pronounce each syllable.

Dường Hoa le 21 — 11 — 1943.44)

Francou oi may ngu

francou diên làm sau may gỏ thỏ cho tôi may
dễ giày ở trong cái thỏ nặng lắm, nhà gơ dày
thép nó phát tôi ở hết 00ᵈ18. nó gỏ giày lên
Dường hoà cho tôi, tôi lên vatien tôi cho,
nó hết 00ᵈ18. tôi lãy cái thỏ di về tôi mở
coi thãy giày nhiều quá có 2 cái bao thỏ
có 4 con cỏ có 3 tãm giày người ta cho,
sau một cái cho sài một cái tôi một cái
nhỏ làm sau tết tay mãy không có lại mãy
hỏi cha với mẹ coi tỏ tết tay lại không
Dường Hoà không chung cha mẹ lại mãy ro
việt thỏ cho gardien biết ở Dường ở II mua
ở Dường hoà lúa chưa chính mãy dứng dễ
dỏ ở l trong bao thỏ mua coi chung nhà dày
thép nó phat tôi mãy dược cái thỏ này của
tôi mãy phải gỏ thỏ mao mao cho tôi
biết thời it lời cho françous mành giỏi
chung nào lại mua một sợi dây vừa làm
reo ghe kêu cha mãy mua ;) phướ
gardien kêu mua

into the distance, each parcel protected by neat, carefully maintained dikes, with wooden dams to control the drainage of what was once a wasteland. The rice I had eaten had been cooked in the canal water, which was hardly brackish any more. The earth was coming alive everywhere, and France certainly had something to do with it. But what would be the point of reminding him of that? Best keep quiet for the time being.

"You see that boy on the buffalo over there? When he grows up, he will find it hard to believe that before the Japanese took over, Vietnamese didn't even have the basic right to travel across the borders within their own country.* In a Frenchman's mouth, 'liberty' is nothing but a word."

I spent a long time mulling over what he had just told me. I knew something about the Indochina of old; I had read about it in old books, and been told about it by settlers who had come here long before my parents.

With the French gone, the Vietnamese might have the right to travel freely—but they could never do so. They would still be enslaved by their debts, just as they were today. Ten percent interest a month was the minimum among Vietnamese, a scourge that France had struggled in vain to end. *Ca lon an ca nho; ca nho an ca nho nua*—Big fish eat little fish; little fish eat smaller fish. My father didn't charge interest, and neither did the other French rice growers, who owned four or five percent of the delta's arable land. The rest belonged to big Vietnamese landowners who squeezed the common people, stealing their little plots by driving them to ruin, the way Bai Ma did in the village. If there were big fish among the French, they seemed less voracious than the big Vietnamese fish, and in any case much less cruel.

Moreover, my traveling companion seemed to have forgotten that if the borders between north and south were opened, his Tonkinese compatriots would sweep down to Cochin-China to settle the rich Mekong lands one way or another. The land had once belonged to Cambodia, but the Cochin-Chinese had driven the Cambodians out at sword-point and seized this rich rice-bowl for themselves. All of the countries that now formed Indochina had been at each other's throats for centuries before the French

---

*A reference to the borders between Cochin-China, Annam, and Tonkin, which after independence became Vietnam.

regime. Around the time I was born, bands of pirates still lurked in the Plain of Reeds, terrorizing the countryside, robbing and often killing. France may have pacified the country by force of arms, but what else could it do? The missionaries had tried the Bible, and that hadn't worked. Granted, the law of the strongest isn't especially admirable, but when it's the one thing that lets a people live in peace . . .

"Liberty, Equality, Fraternity," he went on. "Three words united in one generous breath. But what actually happens? All the responsible positions go to the French and we get the subordinate ones, like crumbs—regardless of our educational level. I myself have a law degree and am studying for a doctorate while working in the administration. My immediate superior is a lazy drunk. If he were Vietnamese, he wouldn't even be hired as an orderly. But he's French, he earns a salary that is astronomical compared to mine, and he barely has a grade-school education."

Lord, the countryside was beautiful, warmed by the breath of the water buffaloes patiently pulling the little wooden plows, led by hard-working, tenacious peasants. I didn't doubt that the man next to me was sincere, but he was kidding himself. He was ignoring the fact that the smallest scraps of power given to the Vietnamese immediately become piasters squeezed out of the common people. *Ca lon an ca nho; ca nho an ca nho nua* was the other breath of Indochina, a stinking breath where the corruption of the local bureaucrats was beyond belief.

The man had used the word "generous," a word that didn't exist in Vietnamese, as far as I knew. I knew *tôt* (good), I knew *tu té* (nice), but how would you translate "generous"? Probably by *ngu* (stupid). Nor did I know the translation of the word "liberty." *Doc lap* meant "independence," as I had learned the week before. But how did you say "liberty" in Vietnamese? I knew it didn't translate into Chinese. Abadie had once told me about a friend of his, an old Sinologist, who had set out to find a Chinese character that meant "liberty." He couldn't find one. So he asked his Cantonese friends, and they couldn't find one either. The closest ideogram they could find translated as "disorder," "confusion," and "anarchy."

Kipling had been sure that East and West would never meet. But I didn't think the gap between us was insurmountable. Patience and mutual effort would bridge it; and making that effort wasn't just worthwhile, it was essential. If the words "generosity" and "freedom" didn't exist in Asian vocabularies, it was because these concepts hadn't yet been born in Asia. Before being born in Europe, they hadn't existed for us, either. It took time for them to begin to touch our consciences, then slowly grow and come to life in our actions. Come to life only to a certain point, of course . . .

"For a Frenchman, you don't talk much."

"I was listening to you. And thinking. In spite of all appearances, I'm sure that Vietnamese and French can and must come together."

"That's what I thought before I joined the administration. Now I don't know what to think. France has committed so many serious mistakes in Indochina, so many unforgivable blunders."

"It turned nearly half a million acres of virgin forest into rubber plantations. It built six thousand miles of roads and some splendid bridges. It dug thousands of miles of canals like this one, and turned huge areas of wasteland into fertile rice paddies. Were those mistakes, or blunders?"

"France did that for the sole purpose of getting rich. What has it done on the moral plane?"

"Hospitals and free health care for the poor. And above all, it ended your wars, your pirates, your lack of personal safety. Don't you think that's moral?"

"France came to impose order among us with no other goal than its own profit. Open your eyes a little. Even your hospitals are part of it: healthy people work better than sick ones. Morality doesn't have much sway in a situation where one people's sweat serves to enrich another."

"I was watching you write Chinese characters with that Japanese soldier," I said. "Fortunately, the Vietnamese have long had an alphabet that anyone can learn. Did France do that for profit too?"

"So that's your unbeatable argument! Without realizing it, you've hit on an essential point. There's the rub, and it's a painful one. I'll be happy to tell you about it if you'll first try to put aside the fact that you're French, which may not be easy. And I'll forget that I'm Vietnamese. We'll just talk like two human beings trying to communicate, with completely open minds. It will require careful attention on your part. Are we agreed?"

He took a notebook out of his pocket and drew an ideogram.

"This Chinese character, which I'm sure you know, is pronounced *homme* in French, *nhôi ta* in Vietnamese, *monus* in Cambodian, *man* in English, and *hombre* in Spanish—yet it's the same ideogram. It is pronounced a thousand different ways in all the languages in the world, without ever changing its shape. That's because Chinese is the only living language which is universal in its written form. Now I'm going to try to give you an idea of what follows.

人 man becomes 从 humanity.
大 big, and 小 small, become 大小 size.
宀 roof and 女 woman, become 安 peace.
女 woman, and 子 child, become 好 good, well.
心 heart-spirit, and 小 small become 心小 attention.
日 sun, and 月 moon, become 日月 brilliant. Separately, those two characters also express a notion of time: day for sun, month for moon."

He again drew the character for sun 日 , but added a little comma on the upper left: 白 whole. Then he put it below the sun-moon pair 日月 (brilliant), and the three together became 白日月 , to understand.

"These ten ideograms—man, big, small, roof, woman, child, heart-spirit, sun, moon, whole—further let you express nine *concepts:* humanity, size, peace, good, attention, day, month, brilliant, understand. Whereas ten words written in an alphabet can never express anything more than those ten words."

Fascinated, I looked at the symbols drawn on the pages of the notebook. I could feel them coming alive and dancing within me. I began to understand the roots of a country where I had lived for twenty years without opening my eyes to what it contained. My gaze had only touched the surface, without penetrating or seeing further.

"You're probably thinking that I'm very knowledgeable, right? Not at all. At my elementary, basic level, Chinese characters are easy to learn. Does that surprise you?"

He explained this mystery. His grandfather, a Tonkin mandarin, had selected the hundred and fifty most useful ideograms from among the thousands available. And had taught them to him, between the ages of seven and twenty, at the rate of ten or twelve a year. Barely one a month. Without effort and without distracting him from his studies at the Hanoi *lycée*.

"All of us, French as well as Vietnamese, could do the same. A hundred and fifty Chinese characters studied over a dozen years, from kindergarten through the end of high school. With that, you could get by very well. But more important, it would open a door between our two peoples. I'm not sure you see what I mean. French and Vietnamese would reach out to each other, each culture penetrating the other, each giving the best it has to offer, instead of the one-way intellectual street your laws have established."

It was a fantastic idea, and it slowly made its way in my mind. I could feel it flowing toward my heart, as clear as a forest stream, and then it exploded, the way sun and moon together meant "brilliant," and then became "understand" when you added a little something extra . . .

"There's no doubt that the *quoc ngu* represents a great contribution to this country," my companion went on. "But France committed a real murder, ripping out the very roots of our culture, by her radical suppression of Chinese characters in the schools. It was a crime of pride and contempt. Those hundred and fifty characters were all it would have taken to keep the door open. But France decided it would be much more profitable to lock and bolt it. And it destroyed the *ong gia* [old man, symbolizing the transmission of customs] and the *ong bai da* [allegorical form representing the old man wearing the seven robes of wisdom] in the process.

"It replaced them with her own henchmen, an army of functionaries trained in her schools, docile, covered with medals, hunchbacked little vultures walking with their eyes to the ground, concerned only with protecting their rackets and privileges. The rule of Shame."

I looked the man right in the eye. The only time I had seen such fire was in *cai* Tha's eyes, when we were digging holes to transform the jungle. Real mandarin blood flowed in the veins of this *anh hai*, this older brother. And I knew that someday, he would be an *ong bai da*. If more Vietnamese could be like him—if we French could be like him—what a terrific country we could build together!

"I've never spoken to a Frenchman the way I have today," he said. "Until very recently, you had to be very careful with what you said, even among my own people. You know what your Sûreté Générale is like, with its cruelty, its eyes and ears all over the country where so many people betray their own for money, or favors, or privileges. I would have ended up in the Poulo Condor penal colony with the other hot-heads. Maybe even been shot, like many who dared demand the truth. It's so much easier to kill people who ask questions than to answer them. The Japanese will leave when the war is over and the French will want everything to be the way it was. That will be their final mistake. I think you understand that."

We stayed there, leaning side by side, for a long time. I was struck dumb by his powerful indictment of our colonial system. I knew he was grateful for my having let him talk without interruption, listening all the way through without arguing about the evidence. And I was grateful to him for everything he had told me, for teaching me what I hadn't known.

Nui Trao Hill was very close by then, shining in the setting sun, looking like the water buffalo it was named for. A huge buffalo, standing on land the Mekong had created for people who wanted to work it. Not far to the left of the canal stood the gentle hills of my village, where I would sleep that night.

Now I knew what to say to Bai Ma and to the others in the village. I was born in this country, I had spent twenty years growing up here, and I wanted it to remain mine as well as theirs. But it had taken the Japanese attack to open my eyes to something other than my own pleasure, the junk I wanted to buy with Xai, my plans, my personal affairs. Today, I was discovering my own unchanging Indochina, thanks to this Older Brother standing beside me and showing me the way.

CHAPTER 9

We left the village at dawn. I had spent two whole months there with my mother and the two little ones without seeing a single Japanese. Phuoc's father had heard about a very big battle on one of Japan's islands, and this time I was sure the war was ending. Then a Japanese sergeant came from Ha Tien to tell us to get the car ready. It was time to return to Saigon, but we would be going by way of Cambodia—a three-hundred-mile trip—because the bridges in the Mekong delta had been destroyed by American bombing. We left before sun-up, escorted by the sergeant sitting between Chu and Minh.

We crossed Phnom Penh in the late morning. The huge Khmer city was as calm and relaxed as ever, devoted to its venerated king. A peaceful city stretched out in the shade of its tamarind trees, Phnom Penh always seemed to be just waking up from a long nap, and the recent events that had rocked Indochina hadn't changed the Cambodians' attitude toward us in the least. During a brief stop near the Silver Pagoda along the Tonle Sap River, a woman dressed in a traditional sarong and carrying a basket on her head gave us a handful of dried bananas, and wouldn't accept anything in exchange. A friend of my father's who had visited Tahiti before the war said that the Polynesians and the Khmer people had many common traits, including the same friendliness, the same hospitality, and the same gentle gaze.

As the car drove toward Saigon, my mind kept drifting back to the village. Something in the air there had changed, and I felt worried about the future. As soon as I returned from Rach Gia on the boat, Xai signaled me to meet him at our old pistachio tree on top of the hill, where only birds and squirrels could hear what he had to tell me.

The sapling we had used for the *con chom* trap had grown into a handsome young tree with a fork where we had notched it to anchor the trip-line. By scuffing the humus under the dead leaves, we found the charred wood we had burned to cook Hao's father's hen; it lay intact on the fire-hardened ground between the three mossy stones of our fire pit. But the sounds coming from the village had changed in the last month. The songs that used to float up to us from all directions were missing, and the wooden pestles that hulled the rice no longer echoed across the village. Crouched side by side at our usual spot on the big root, we let our memories from days past wash over us.

After a long silence, Xai leaned toward me a little. I felt as if I were hearing the sudden silence of the forest, in which all sounds cease when a vague danger is sensed and fear approaches. He whispered that Bai Ma had a rifle hidden in his hut. Where had it come from? He couldn't say. A few weeks before, under the old regime, the weapon would have sent Bai Ma straight to the Poulo Condor penal colony. But the law was on his side now. When Bai Ma spoke, the village bowed its head in submission. People looked at him the way you look at a tiger: with cautious respect.

My big plan to free the villagers from Bai Ma's tyranny had gone up in smoke. Yet I had to say that, right to the end, he had remained polite, even friendly. Too many ties bound him to my family for him to be able to shrug them off. Bai Ma couldn't help but remember that my mother had saved his oldest son from dysentery when he was a boy. Or that my father had gotten him out of a nasty jam involving the Ha Tien police. He still wore the good sunglasses I had brought him from Saigon for his inflamed eyes, five years before. Not to mention all the small favors we had done each other, which created a feeling of closeness in spite of our differences.

But I hadn't been able to talk to Bai Ma the way I thought I could after my meeting with the mandarin's son on the boat. And now my heart ached when I looked to the future.

As we drove along, the big kites that watched over the harvest gradually vanished from the sky, and the elegant ox-carts of Khmer country disappeared. Cambodian stilt houses, built of massive wooden planks, with their wide doorways, gave way to

Vietnamese huts squatting on the ground, with mud walls and windows so tiny they barely let in any light. The sugar palms started to thin out as we entered the lowlands of the Plain of Reeds. The road ran straight to the horizon. Peaceful Cambodia lay far behind us.

After the calm expanse of the countryside, Saigon came as a shock; the face of the city had completely changed. When I left a few months before, Saigon had been at peace. Now it was criss-crossed by deep trenches dug along the main roads, with the sunken hulks of bombed ships showing their bows here and there along the river. But the most painful change could be read on the often closed, sometimes contemptuous faces of some Vietnamese. Right after the Japanese takeover on March 9 that ended French rule, a number of Frenchmen were attacked by coolies, and several killed. The new Japanese administration immediately put a stop to the outbursts: independence, yes, but no settling of scores, and above all, no disorder. Through the press, the Japanese informed the population that whoever was found guilty of acts of revenge would be beheaded. Since then, the city had become calm again. Nonetheless, Minh and Chu warned us to be extremely careful. Assam kept Babette and Gilbert under her wing; they rarely went outside, and never far from the house.

For the time being, the Japanese were keeping a lid on things, imposing a discipline that was tinged with terror. Frenchmen suspected of having taken part in the resistance were tortured to death by the Kenpeitai, the terrible Japanese secret police. It was answerable to no one, and its authority, which brought tears and screams of terror in its wake, couldn't be questioned even by the most senior regular army officers. The Kenpeitai was clearly warning the French that the war was total. Abadie and Alyette, and Leperson and his wife, were all living with us. The French brought in from the provinces were sent to live with those in Saigon. The Japanese controlled everything. Possessing a firearm was punishable by instant death. My father was still being held prisoner with his regiment, and we had no news of him.

I saw bombing raids by American Flying Fortresses. They were the first ones for me, but not for Françou and Jacky, who had been here during my stay in the relative calm of the Gulf of Siam.

The high-altitude carpet bombing was intended for the Japanese defenses, but often fell on the clusters of Vietnamese huts along the river. The pages of Françou's diary were full of bodies torn to pieces, arms and legs ripped off, brains ground into the mud, screams arising from blazing huts that reeked of the horrible smell of burning human flesh. I will long remember the image in Françou's journal of a woman staggering toward him, a bloody ghost tripping on her own intestines, clutching a headless baby in her arms.

At the other side of the world, bombed into ruin, Germany surrendered. A few weeks before Germany, the island of Okinawa fell after terrible fighting. This was the great battle that Phuoc's father had told me about in the village. That tiny island, that lump of Japanese soil, was now a huge American aircraft carrier, an unsinkable, impregnable fortress a few minutes from the great nerve centers of the mother island.

The dream of defeating America had given way to the reality of arms, but the Japanese were fighting with all their might. And America knew that the Empire of the Rising Sun wasn't afraid to fight; that it had never been afraid, and never would be. Whatever the cost in bravery. Whatever the cost in blood.

After Okinawa, America knew that the Japanese would fight all the way along their chain of islands, bunker by bunker, beach by beach, village by village. They would fight in the cemeteries, they would fight in the ruins of cities pounded by bombs, they would fight every inch of the way, they would fight to the death. Japan had loudly declared that every square foot of its soil would be another Okinawa for the Americans. And when too many of its people had died, the dead of the Land of Samurai would rise again a thousand times over to transmit to the living the Great Wind that commanded the Sacred Land never to yield.

A rumor was making the rounds in the streets of Saigon. When hope and fear go hand in hand, when screaming sirens send you flat on your belly on the ground, when death strikes blindly and the world is mad, all rumors are worth heeding. This one had it that America was beginning to fear seeing the blood of its youth flowing on Japanese beaches bristling with guns. That peace talks were under way to stop the massacre. America, it seemed, had decided to deal with the Mikado as an equal, was discussing an honorable compromise that would let each side go home peacefully.

But the Flying Fortresses continued to drop their thousand-pound bombs on Saigon, without listening to the rumors.

One morning, a new rumor started. At first we just shrugged our shoulders, weary of all the false talk. Yet the Flying Fortresses hadn't come for the past few days, and we couldn't help but give the newest rumor some credence.

Toward noon, the rumor had swelled like a mosquito whose belly turns pink, then red. And by nightfall, the mosquito of this morning had taken on the appearance of the great Chinese dragon of the Tet festival, the fire-colored dragon, full of lights and flames, that snaked along for hours before raising its huge mouth to the sky, where it swallowed the millions of sparks shooting from the strings of firecrackers men lit to appease the gods. And the dragon was so fantastic, so unbelievable, so colossal, that the whole city froze, holding its breath, like a hut in the path of a typhoon but hoping for a miracle.

That evening, I met a Japanese officer in the street who was dead drunk. I had never seen such an unthinkable thing.

For three days, Saigon held its breath as it watched the dancing dragon. Whether it was the dragon of all-out war or the dragon of peace, no one knew. But hope was boundless.

For three days, Saigon and all the cities of Indochina watched the dragon dancing. So did all the cities of America and all the cities of Japan . . . except one, which, the rumor said, no longer existed, swallowed by the dragon.

At the end of the third day, the monstrous beast took to the air and changed into the *bom viên tua** in a gigantic sunburst.

Bom viên tua, a new phrase in the Vietnamese language, a new phrase that buzzed along the sidewalks, at every street corner, around all the little round tables, sticky with condensed milk, where rickshaw drivers crouched on the stools of Chinese bars, on the terraces of all the bistros where you no longer saw a single Japanese. They had all returned to their barracks, to hear what the Mikado had to tell them.

Bom: flower, or bomb. *Bom viên tua:* bomb (or flower) that kills everything.

CHAPTER 10

Once, when I was thirteen, Phuoc's father and I were leaving Hon Mon Tai Island to sail back to the village. It was at the end of a period of very bad weather that had kept us anchored in the lee of the island for almost a week. During the short crossing, an enormous wave nearly swamped our boat. The rogue wave was completely unexpected, since the monsoon weather had settled and the sea had calmed a bit. After we had bailed for a solid hour, my teacher said:

"It's right after a storm, when you think everything is fine, that you tend to let your guard down. Just then, one final, huge wave can come out of nowhere and sink your boat in a moment. That's how Kieu's ancestor got caught. If the porpoise hadn't come along that day, it would have been all over for him, just as it was nearly all over for us today."

Today, I was twenty years old and I was going to die.

I was going to die because I forgot about the wave that hit Phuoc's father and me. I let my guard down. The rogue wave was about to break, and no porpoise in the world could save me.

His hand on his holster, the Japanese officer was about to kill me. In the tradition of the Japanese army, a single life is of no importance. Discipline must be respected above all. I hadn't respected it. So he had to kill me, to set an example.

He was standing above me, his legs spread. I was on the cement floor, where he had thrown me with a powerful judo move. I was fully conscious, and I could tell that he was giving me a brief respite so I could leave the world without making a sound.

My mother was kneeling in a corner of the cell near Alyette, who was holding her by the arm. My two brothers, Abadie, and

Leperson stood motionless next to the two women. A vision of the old monk from the Cave of Coins came to me. In his hand, he was holding the little jar and the key he had wanted to give me. But I was too young then, and it was too late now.

I heard the click of the safety catch. The soldier's eyes were two icy slits. His fingers curled around the handle of his revolver. In a fraction of a second he would draw, steady his fist against his hip, and pull the trigger. Everything would end in the sound of a shot.

A moment later, I stood up, feeling as if I were in a dream. My being had turned to water and cloud. As the Japanese soldier's steps faded away down the hallway, two immense, luminous wings hovered above my head. Around me, the cell was in total silence. I could see my mother, still kneeling next to Alyette. The others hadn't moved either. They were still right where I left them just a moment before, incomprehension in their eyes. They were like phantoms around me. They were looking at me the way you look at a ghost.

Abadie was the first to move, to come over to me. Abadie was more than a father to me, he was the man whose son I would have wanted to be. He touched my shoulder, but I gently brushed his hand away. I wanted to be alone. I didn't want anyone talking to me. I didn't want to speak, and even if I could, I wouldn't have been able to tell them what I had seen, over there. I couldn't tell them. They would think I had gone crazy.

At the instant when he had been about to draw, my eyes met those of the Japanese soldier. There was no fear left in me, no hate, no prayers. We gazed deep into each other, seeing all the way back to humanity's very beginnings. I saw that he and I were the same, born of the same origins we all share, the common essence of humanity. If he killed me, he would be killing himself as well. But beyond that, he would be wiping humanity from the face of the earth.

I now know this was true, because we both glimpsed it in the same instant. Maybe I would be able to talk to Françou about it some day. He was always in both worlds at once, sometimes here, sometimes there; you never knew where he was. But today I wanted to be left alone in my corner to think. I wanted to go over everything carefully in my head while the others prepared for yet another night in jail.

It had all begun with something I did, something as smart as teasing a sleeping crocodile, its belly empty after being defeated in some terrific battle, battered in body and pride. After lunch on the day following the second *bom viên tua*, Françou, Jacky, and I had raised the French flag on the flagpole on our balcony. By the time Abadie and Leperson noticed, the deed was done.

Less than an hour after this idiotic bit of bravado, the Kenpeitai arrived. They rounded up everyone in the household, slapped and punched us with all their might, then threw us into a cage in their sinister building. They didn't take Babette or Gilbert, who were too young to be responsible, or Leperson's wife; she was dressed Vietnamese-style, and they mistook her for the maid.

Our cage was three yards square, with heavy wooden bars and a toilet in the corner. We were forbidden to talk or to lie down, except at night, after one last round of slaps. Next day, a Vietnamese interpreter with cruel eyes announced that the Japanese colonel would soon give us his decision, and that it would be "very severe." We had insulted Japan with our flag, he said; we had also insulted the people of Vietnam, who were independent and had their own flag.

After three days spent fearing the worst, we emerged from the hole to be marched to the central prison on Lagrandière Street with a dozen other Frenchmen guilty of minor political offenses committed during the recent events. Our lives had been spared. No more Kenpeitai, no more gut-twisting fear. And no more of that thirst that had so parched our throats. In the cage, our jailer used to thrust a pot of boiling water under our noses for a few seconds. We couldn't even wet our lips, so we weren't really thirsty, were we? We were lying, right? Maybe we wanted another good beating? A real sadist.

Our new cell was huge, with a squat toilet where we could drink all we wanted. Nothing could be simpler: you just stuck your coconut shell under the spray and flushed. There wasn't any toilet paper, but you could wash your behind with your hands; millions of Indians and Arabs did it every day.

Our guard was a Japanese soldier we called "Four-Eyes." He was pretty decent and didn't carry a gun. He let us talk, walk around the cell, lie down during the day, even play cards. All that he asked was that we not make any noise.

But we got a little rowdy, raised our voices a bit, laughed in a way that rubbed the usually easygoing guard the wrong way, and suddenly a spark was fanned into an inferno—all because I had forgotten the lesson of the past and let my guard down. Furious, Four-Eyes kicked the door open and started slapping people right and left. I'll never understand what went through my mind, but I dodged his blow. He stared at me, incredulous. Then he grabbed my elbow and slipped his foot behind my heel, intending to trip me with a judo move. If I had simply let myself fall, I think the incident would have ended there. But again, I was crazy enough to resist, to stand up to the iron Japanese law. He turned very pale and left the cell without even closing the door. A few seconds later he returned with the officer. And the rogue wave nearly crashed down on me.

I could hear sparrows chirping on the tamarind tree outside the cell window. It was dawn already. My soul was still filled with all of eternity. My cellmates stirred in their sleep. Spending the night under a light bulb burning in the ceiling isn't much fun, but you soon get used to it. Sleeping on cement isn't especially pleasant either, but it feels like heaven when you have your whole life ahead of you.

A week passed, then two. Ours was a one-way cell: you came in, but you didn't leave. From the beginning of our incarceration, new lodgers arrived almost daily. There were already about thirty of us, mostly men but also a few women, all French except for one Vietnamese who somehow wound up in with us. Leperson thought he must be a snitch, but what did he have to snitch about? He must have been asking himself the same questions we were. Was the war over? Was it true that two big Japanese cities had been leveled by a single bomb apiece? Apparently so. One thing was certain, though: the Japanese really tightened the screws right after the second *bom viên tua*. And the war wasn't over, in spite of the certainty that had filled my heart and made me act like an idiot when I was outside and free.

A new shipment of French prisoners arrived. We squeezed a little tighter, shared as best we could the ten coconut shells we used as bowls for our daily rations. Soon there were forty of us, despite my mother and the other women having been moved to Phu My prison yesterday morning, to ease the crowding in our cell.

A round of shelling, not far off. No buzz of planes, no rumble of bombs, so it wasn't antiaircraft fire. What was going on? Then bursts of machine-gun fire, very close. Was the war taking a new turn? Next day, people in the street in front of the prison started to roar, shouting anti-French slogans; the communists had called a huge demonstration. The prisoners in the other cells yelled back, and the whole prison started screaming. With fixed bayonets, the Japanese restored order in the cells that held Vietnamese prisoners.

Another batch arrived. There were now nearly fifty of us, jammed together in a hundred square yards of cement. The toilet flushed constantly, as people drank. But the biggest thirst you can experience in prison must be the thirst for news, the craving to know what was happening outside. Losing your physical freedom didn't seem as painful. I could always escape in my mind, roam the streets in my thoughts. But I remained a ghost among the living, seeing without hearing.

Our cell was becoming more livable. Yesterday half of our companions were released, Françou among them. This morning, ten more were let go; this afternoon, another six.

A big storm was approaching quickly. Just as a huge thunderclap hit, Jacky rushed to the window and glimpsed an American Flying Fortress buzzing the rooftops in front of the prison. No anti-aircraft fire. Clouds of confetti were falling from the sky. The plane circled over Saigon for another hour, dropping leaflets. The anti-aircraft batteries still hadn't fired. Swept by a wave of emotion, we spent a sleepless night talking about what was going on.

And then, just like that, the last of us were out in the sunshine, free to go home. We raced off like a shot, hugging the walls.

The Japanese empire had surrendered on August 15, 1945, one week after the second *bom viên tua*. In Indochina, the Japanese hadn't told anyone. That's what the Flying Fortress had been doing two weeks later, blanketing the city with leaflets while we were still in prison.

CHAPTER 11

Emerging

from my three weeks in jail, I barely recognized the city I had lived in for so many years. Saigon was like a snake coiled on itself, with hundreds of would-be Bai Mas and little interpreters like the one in Rach Gia in its scales, who would have loved to start killing the French right away. All the other scales, hundreds of thousands of them, were the mass of undecided people, who both feared and were drawn to the unknown. They were the downtrodden, marginal ones, people once so peaceful who, in just a few weeks, had become as menacing as a water buffalo about to charge.

Independence flags, with a yellow star on a red background, hung everywhere. Parades marched through the city. The phrase *doc lap*, which I had first heard muttered at Rach Gia, now erupted from a thousand throats. The snake was uncoiling, the buffalo sniffing the wind and pawing the ground, and we could feel hatred for the French growing.

My father's old purchasing agent told me about an even more rampant hatred, that of the communist Viet Minh for the vast majority of the intelligentsia and for the remaining pro-French Vietnamese. Both the intelligentsia and the working people feared an independence that was too hasty and ill-prepared, as they would cholera. It was synonymous with *long som*—anarchy. But the Viet Minh was recruiting fanatics who would stop at nothing, who could goad the ordinary people, and who knew how to crush their opponents.

The Viet Minh didn't speak for the people; it spoke only for the Viet Minh, a tiny minority determined to apply the golden rule of any budding dictatorship: all-out terrorism and brainwashing. With that, it was sure to raise troops and set them marching in lock-step.

At the time, Leperson was reading a book on crowd psychology, whose author made the point that, taken one by one, people are willing to listen to reason, but when a mass of them is manipulated by a handful of well-organized agitators, it can turn into a wild beast. You don't even need leaders for that to happen, added Abadie. A branch cracking in the bushes, a moonbeam glinting on a dew-drop, or a strange smell carried by the wind can panic a herd and whip it into an uncontrollable frenzy, stampeding and trampling everything in its path. Leperson and Abadie were convinced that if the Japanese dropped everything and left, Saigon would be awash in blood—starting with our own. And we wouldn't have a weapon to defend ourselves with, or even to fire a warning shot into the air.

At night on my mat, I remembered the red-ant nests that Xai and I used to stick into termite mounds we had broken open. The Vietnamese would take their machetes and hack the French to death, then madness would sweep the termite mound, and the termites would turn on each other in an endless settling of scores, with Vietnamese massacring Vietnamese. Assam had already seen several bodies floating in the river. And I wondered about what my traveling companion on the boat from Rach Gia to Ha Tien had said about the local leaders who sided with the strong—when France was the strongest.

When we were first imprisoned by the Kenpeitai, the Japanese had held all the key positions. Now those had been handed over to the Vietnamese, who controlled the Sûreté, all the police stations, the city hall, and even the arsenal. They wore brand-new pistols on their belts, and some were probably itching to try out their new toys on running Frenchmen instead of cardboard targets pinned to a wall. We had best keep a low profile and make our eyes as expressionless as possible.

My father and his fellow soldiers were still being held prisoner in their barracks. The Japanese continued to maintain order in Saigon while waiting for the arrival of the armistice commission, to which they would hand over their weapons. But this morning, while listening to the talk in the market, Minh had heard that trucks loaded with rifles and crates of ammunition were heading for Cholon; this had apparently started with the surrender. So the Japanese were arming the Viet Minh. They hated communists, but they hated the colonial system even more, or at least ours, since they themselves had tried to colonize China and the rest of Asia.

Leperson became terribly anxious. During his years with the Sûreté, he had headed off several revolts fomented by the communists. Then, they had been armed only with machetes and a few rifles fashioned from water pipes, which were extremely dangerous for their users. Now the communists would have modern firearms and enjoy tremendous prestige in the eyes of the population. If French troops didn't arrive from France to restore order soon, all would be lost. The patient pacification work that had transformed Indochina into a prosperous country where the living was good would have to begin again from square one.

_____ September 2

When the armistice commission, consisting of a few American, British, and French officers, arrived at the airport, the Viet Minh decided to celebrate Vietnam's independence. It turned into an enormous anti-French demonstration that started on the packed Norodom Boulevard and ended in a frenzy that evening on the Place de la Cathédrale. The armed Japanese soldiers responsible for keeping order didn't have time to intervene before Father Tricoire was pulled from his rectory, dragged in front of the cathedral, and murdered. Six or seven Frenchmen were killed in their homes. Others were chased through the streets, beaten, and either left for dead or brutally hauled to the Sûreté, where they were spit upon before being locked up. Today, the snake had raised its head and struck in a terrifying way. On its skin, shiny with hate, you could see hundreds of Bai Mas turned communists, who were multiplying like the germs of some deadly disease. We knew our lives were in real danger now.

_____ September 12

Crouched on the sidewalks in silent little groups, the Vietnamese watched from afar. New rumors swept through the market; voices there were lower than usual.

The Japanese troops stood at attention, their eyes lost in the distance. Soon they would sail away to rebuild their own country.

Among the French in Saigon, we had tears in our eyes; we didn't dare hope anymore. General Gracey had just arrived with his British troops in their green uniforms. They were almost all Gurkhas, an elite unit from the Army of India. And among the Gurkhas, one contingent of soldiers made our hearts beat faster.

They wore British army uniforms, but had little patches sewn at the top of their sleeves with the word "France." And they spoke French like us, with accents from Paris or the south of France.

No further parades or banners called the people to revolt; the bloodthirsty Viet Minh brandished no more red flags with yellow stars. Saigon became relatively calm practically overnight, its downtown streets alive with allied uniforms.

We hardly recognized our father when he came home that day. Aside from his shining eyes, he looked like a skeleton. Though he was only forty-five, six months of imprisonment under the Japanese had aged him terribly. The 11th Colonial Infantry Regiment barracks had been jammed with more than four thousand prisoners. There were swarms of bedbugs, a bare plank to sleep on, a daily bowl of rice with watery soup. Almost all of the soldiers had suffered from dysentery without getting medicine and had shivered with malaria without quinine or blankets.

But the last straw came in the form of a little speech by an "emissary from France" who had visited the troops on August 22, a week after the Japanese surrender. As Abadie and Leperson listened in astonishment, my father gave us the essence of that historic talk: "You, whose mission was to defend Indochina, are nothing but a bunch of traitors and Vichyite collaborators. You have been appeasing the enemy since 1940. Since you like the Japanese so much, you can just stay under their guard until real French troops arrive." As far as liberation by real French troops was concerned, General Gracey of the British Army had actually been the one to order the Japanese to open the gates of the "traitors'" barracks on the very morning he entered Saigon.

A few days passed in an uncertain equilibrium. Fresh troops, mainly Gurkhas and Indians of the British Army brought in by cargo plane, disembarked at regular intervals. But then the banners started waving again, and the Viet Minh started killing lone Frenchmen and pro-French Vietnamese. You could hear shooting all over town. Françou, who liked to slip into hot spots on his bicycle, was nearly shot. Jean Conrad, an old family friend, was kidnapped on the way home from his office.*

---

*He was never seen again. More than three hundred French and Eurasians were assassinated during the months of September and October 1945, as were a large number of Vietnamese who were hostile to the Viet Minh.

Now it wasn't just one or two bodies you saw floating down the river, but dozens. And we started to feel real hate for the Viet Minh, which wanted to destroy our beautiful Indochina.

_____ September 22

In the course of the past three days, the Sûreté building and almost all the police stations were retaken by the French with General Gracey's support. He declared martial law and had the Vietnamese newspapers that called on the people to revolt seized. In the streets, for the last several days, groups of young Frenchmen mistreated the Vietnamese, insulting and beating them. The assassination of Father Tricoire and the blind killings of September 2 still burned in our minds. Our hearts had hardened, no longer clearly distinguishing between good and evil, between what was necessary and what was harmful. Many houses belonging to Vietnamese who were suspected—rightly or wrongly—of complicity with the Viet Minh were searched by civilians who came to help the military. I was often part of those groups. We ransacked everything, tipping over dressers to see what was behind them, throwing the contents of trunks and boxes on the floor, kicking down doors which we could have easily opened by turning the handle. In short, we acted like thugs.

During those savage days, a little voice tried to tell me that I was flirting with one of the most insidious and dangerous forms of human folly. But I found it easier to chase away the voice buzzing like a mosquito in my ear. When my mother learned what we were doing, she was furious: "You and your friends are behaving not only like cowards, but like fools. You're rendering evil for evil instead of trying the other path, which would produce a little light for all, French and Vietnamese."

There she went again, telling us about the Good Lord! But if her God really existed, there was no shortage of opportunities for him to manifest himself! People had been talking about the Good Lord for two thousand years, but what did you see when you looked around you? So the hell with it!

_____ September 23

Jacky didn't come home last night. All night long, we heard shots and machine-gun fire on the other side of Khanh Hoi Bridge, which crossed the Chinese river area a few hundred yards from our house. This morning, Françou, Abadie, and I snuck over there and found Jacky firing a carbine he had taken from one of the wounded. He had spent the night in a trench defended against the Viets by marines under Ensign Romé, my old sea-scoutmaster. He and his men had been in the Japanese jails at the same time as my father.

Rifle shots were crackling all round. In Jacky's eyes, I saw a look I had never seen before. He had just shot a Viet creeping up between sand bags two hundred yards away. I begged him to lend me his rifle, so I could shoot a little too. "You've got to be kidding," he said. "You should have been here last night instead of sleeping." I almost wanted him to take a bullet in the arm, so I could hold his warm carbine in my hands at last. As Abadie and I passed ammunition, he talked a little about Verdun: "There's something fantastic about the smell of gunpowder, but you have to beware of it; it changes you into a carnivorous god."

At home that evening, I watched as Jacky ate his dinner. Just yesterday, he had been my little brother. In the space of a night, he had become my superior, by far. Because he had killed. I watched as he stood up, put down his napkin, and walked across to his room. I could hardly believe he was only eighteen. He was a man now. No, more than a man. An aura seemed to surround him, like in the holy images of my mother's prayer book.

_____ September 26

Saigon awoke to horror. During the course of the night, a hurricane of killing madness had hit Hérault, an outlying neighborhood. A massacre of terrifying cruelty, with a hundred and fifty horribly mutilated corpses of men, women, children and babies, all French, Eurasian, or Vietnamese women with French husbands. Saigon was awash in blood. Saigon was stupefied.

When Jacky and I went to see, I thought about Bai Ma and what Xai had told me the night before I left the village. If an accident of birth had made Bai Ma a Saigonese, would he have taken part in such a massacre, with women eviscerated with machetes, babies grabbed by the feet and smashed against walls in front of their screaming mothers, a young Vietnamese woman with her French husband's penis sewn into her mouth, an ignominious slaughter of innocents who had had to pay for a blind racial and ideological hatred fanned by assassins who had gone beyond any imaginable monstrosity? Had I spent last night in Hérault as an invisible phantom next to Bai Ma, would I have seen him doing that? My heart said no, but my head said yes. And I no longer knew which one to trust, which one I could still believe.

Listening to the tales of half-crazed survivors, sobbing with rage and terror, looking into their eyes filled with horror, stepping in pools of blood everywhere I walked, I became one huge fury— and my heart could go fuck itself!

The Viet Minh absolutely had to be crushed. It was an infection, a plague whose aim was clearly to destroy our beautiful country. And we had to do it very fast, very hard, and without pity. Or else there would be no Indochina left for anyone.

CHAPTER 12

Every soldier of the 11th Colonial Infantry Regiment who was able to stand was now rearmed. My father returned to his barracks just three days after being freed. French troops were arriving from France, reinforced by Gurkha and English units from Singapore and India: six British warships on September 30, five troop transports on October 6. We greeted the French cruiser TRIOMPHANT with cheers. I dreamed of doing my military service in the Navy, but berths were hard to get unless you enlisted for five years. And I couldn't imagine spending five years of my life standing at attention under a piece of tricolored cloth just to be able to go to sea from time to time if I kept my nose clean.

Other, smaller ships were tied up at the docks, and they seemed to beckon to me. But even if I could enlist for three years, it would be too long for me. So I was content to admire their big guns in Abadie's company, and especially their extremely maneuverable, powerful antiaircraft machine guns; they were fierce little beasts, capable of spraying bursts of 20-millimeter shells in every direction.

Two days earlier, General Leclerc had announced the arrival of his 40,000 men. Today he was talking about a truce with the Viet Minh, in order to begin negotiations. Leperson and Abadie were completely disgusted by that astonishing news. Why negotiate with the Viet Minh? How could anyone imagine that such a gang of thugs had the slightest intention of keeping its word? Those people from France were really naive! The French emissary, sent in August to prepare the way for the new governor of Indochina, had already been beautifully duped by the Viet Minh representatives. First he had kept behind Japanese bars our four thousand soldiers, who might have been able to defuse the Viet Minh bomb in time, or at least prevent the September 2 killings and the horrible massacre in Hérault. Then, instead of allowing himself to be briefed by the former French and Vietnamese administrators (all "collaborators" and "Vichyites," of course), he'd had the bright idea of going straight to see the Viet Minh representatives. They must have licked their chops at the sight of this pale French plenipotentiary disembarking in their midst, a white official untouched by the Indochinese sun, who was coming to ask their advice! After promising this brilliant personage whatever he wanted and escorting him back to his quarters, the Viet Minh representatives must have laughed their heads off.

And now, a truce! For God's sake, they must think we're real fools! It was high time that the new officials sent from France stopped letting themselves be taken in by the Viet Minh's honeyed words. The only language the Viet Minh understood was that of cannons and machine guns. That's what you talked to them with, not with signatures on pieces of paper they wiped their asses with before the ink was even dry.

The truce was broken a week later. The Viet Minh claimed we had fired first, the French naturally claimed the contrary. Nobody gave a damn either way; the charade couldn't have lasted.

Leperson returned to his position with the Sûreté. He told us that Saigon was surrounded by 20,000 Viets, not counting the ones in hideouts in the outlying districts. They called for a general strike and blocked attempts to resupply the city.

Diving from the sky, General Gracey's Spitfires machine-gunned the hut village of Thu Duc, which was crawling with Viets. The Gurkhas occupied Gia Dinh. Another Viet stronghold burned down, the entire neighborhood along outer Verdun Street (a mile long and three quarters of a mile wide), and the wind carried embers all the way to Catinat Street in downtown Saigon. The Phu My district and the oil storage tanks were retaken by marines of the 11th Colonial Infantry Regiment supported by the fierce commando leader Ponchardier.

Soon all of the main intersections were occupied by French machine guns. As our gunboats patrolled the rivers, dozens of

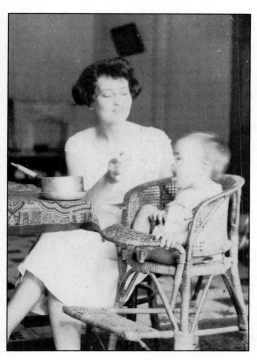

Bernard with his mother (1926).

Bernard (1927).

Assam, Bernard, and François (1927).

The three boys in a rickshaw, Saigon.

François, Bernard, and Jacky (1932).

Jacky, François, and Bernard (1933).

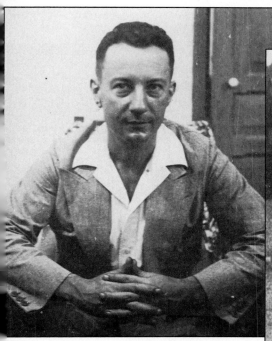

My father, Robert Moitessier
(1934).

François and Bernard (1934).

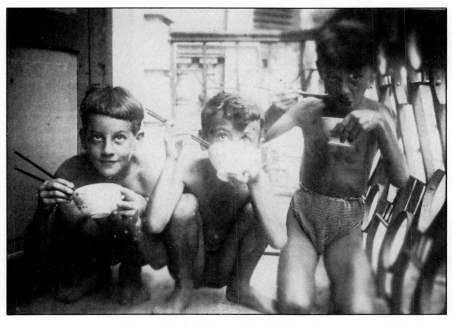

Bernard, François, and Jacky (1935).

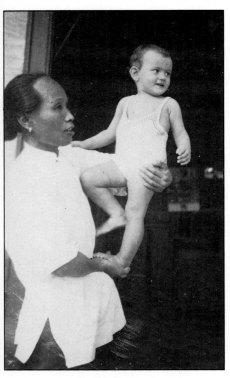

Assam and Babette (1935).

Babette with her mother (1936).

Robert Moitessier (1936).

François and Jacky (1937).

Trips to the neighboring islands aboard
CERF VOLANT, circa 1943.

Near the village, circa 1936.

(Above) "Cabriette" (1939)

(Left) Under construction in 1938.

The family at the village in 1939.

The head of the family climbing a coconut tree.

On vacation in the village aboard one of our canoes, with two friends from Saigon. Babette is in front, Jacky is paddling in the rear. Monkey Point is in the background (1943).

The three Moitessier boys on an elephant in a Cambodian village, on the way back from vacation (1939).

In the village at the same period.

(From right to left) My father, Gilbert, Bernard, Babette.

(Above) Françou is in the middle (he was second in Indochina in the 100-meter freestyle).

(Left, from right to left) My mother, Babette, Bernard, Jacky.

Weekend on the beach at Long Hai. My mother (left) with Gilbert and some Saigon friends.

Babette in Saigon (1940).

Babette and her father
at Da Lat (1939).

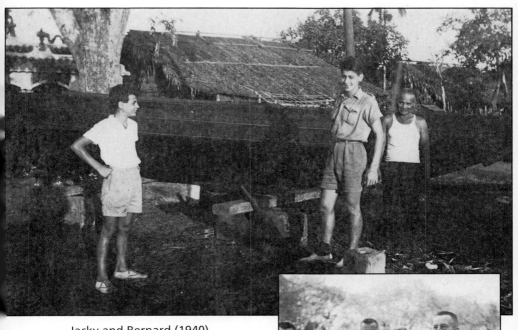

Jacky and Bernard (1940).

The Moitessier family
(1940–43)

Papa in uniform
(1941).

Maman (1941)

Bernard (1941)

Jacky (1941)

Françou (1941)

Bernard Moitessier's commercial junk in the Gulf of Siam, right after his military service (above).

Cerf Volant at anchor at an island near the village (right).

Marie Thérèse, with her aroma of pitch (1952).

MARIE THÉRÈSE II hauled out at Durban.

A little outing at Mauritius aboard MARIE THÉRÈSE II, shortly before her departure for South Africa.

Bernard Moitessier on SNARK's
deck during the preparations
in Saigon (above).

With Pierre Deshumeurs (right)
during a shakedown cruise
off Cape Saint-Jacques (left).

Picnic aboard SNARK with our
Singapore friends (below).

SNARK ready to leave Saigon (1950).

Jean-Claude Mounier (foreground) and Bernard Moitessier during the first week of preparations at Saigon (1950).

...on the dock in front of SNARK (1950).

landing craft escorted convoys of rice-laden junks. The jaws of the vise were loosened. We prayed that another stupid truce wouldn't be declared that would let the Viets regroup.

Many Vietnamese had volunteered to fight alongside the French army. The week before, Abadie had helped draft a leaflet which the air force dropped on all the villages, calling on the people to support French-Vietnamese unity.

Like several hundred young French and Eurasian men from Saigon, my two brothers and I joined the Volunteer Liberation Group (VLG). We were given an assortment of weapons, almost all Japanese: rifles, small mortars, a few hand grenades.

The Viets didn't shoot very well yet, but Japanese deserters apparently sometimes accompanied them. Kurtz, who lived in the house next to ours, had both thighs pierced by the same bullet, but it didn't hit a femur. Gashe was brought back by his buddies with a severed artery in his groin; he survived. Vidal, Claussen, Juvencelli, and Bonnier weren't so lucky; they were shot dead. The VLG unit commanded by Captain Leblanc fell into an ambush; almost no one got out alive. During a patrol in Cholon, a machine-gun burst just missed Françou and Jacky.

For us, the war had really begun. It was a war of liberation for Indochina, a war in which all of us, French and Vietnamese, had to rid our shared country of the Viet Minh cancer.

My mother, however, claimed that no war was morally justified.

"Do you mean," asked Abadie, "we should have let Hitler rule the world? That we should let the Viet Minh bring Indochina to its knees?" She answered that sooner or later the history books would be forced to tell the truth about the real reasons behind all those killings, instead of cramming our heads with a pack of lies. There she went again with her Good Lord business!

I left the table and let her argue with Abadie; he was more patient than I was . . .

During my first week with the VLG, Françou, Jacky and I belonged to a patrol led by Abadie. He didn't need to teach us how to shoot; almost all the young men in Indochina were good shots.

So he spent an hour a day teaching us all sorts of tricks in throwing hand grenades, his weapon of choice for getting out of ambushes.

Unfortunately for us, Abadie was soon assigned to General Leclerc's staff as an advisor. I was amazed to learn that he had long been a member of the French secret service in Cochin-China. He was a specialist in the Cao Dai* sect, which he had been able to infiltrate, and whose anti-French evolution over the years he had studied.

So the Japanese commander at Rach Gia hadn't known everything about Abadie—and I had known even less.

When I came back from patrol early one afternoon, the VLG section chief called me into his office.

"From what Abadie tells me, it seems you speak Vietnamese fluently."

"Not as well as a native, but pretty well, yes."

"Go over to the GAZELLE, she's tied up at the dock. Tell the officer on duty that I sent you. They may have an interesting job for you. Here, let me write him a note."

I could hardly believe my ears. I hoped it would really turn out to be true! Over my protests, he took away my grenades and my Japanese rifle. Five minutes later, I climbed the gangplank, saluted the duty officer, and handed him my precious paper. He led me to the captain's cabin.

"I need an interpreter. Can you translate this for me?"

The leaflet was a Viet Minh call to insurrection; I knew it by heart. The captain then had me translate a paragraph from a Vietnamese newspaper, checking my translation against a sheet of paper in front of him. And so I was taken on as a sailor-interpreter in the GAZELLE's marine landing company. She was a 600-ton gunboat with a 90-millimeter cannon on her rear turret, a repeating 40-millimeter cannon on the foredeck, 20-millimeter machine guns along the rails, and a crew of 125, all real Frenchmen from France! I was delirious with joy!

The petty officer led me to the forecastle, assigned me a free locker, and gave me a blanket, a hammock, and a mess-tin. Stepping out into the gangway, he spotted three guys sitting in a corner.

*Cao Dai: a sect founded in 1926, a combination of various Asian religions, Christianity and animism.

"Garguy! Escotte! Linares! What the hell are you doing here instead of being at your work stations? You're starting to piss me off, always goofing off together. I'll throw all three of you in the brig! Here, show the new guy how to rig a pipe berth."

My new comrades helped me with good grace. Garguy was a husky, nonstop joker who laughed a lot. Linares had muscles that stood out like ropes; he looked a bit like Françou. Escotte had a laborer's shoulders and a hell of a pair of biceps. To my surprise, I learned that though the ship had more than a hundred guys our age, she didn't have any real sports teams.

"You know," Linares said, "sports are pretty much for the bourgeois, who don't have much else to do except riding other people's asses. Back in France, we start working from the time we're kids, so you understand, when we get home exhausted from our jobs . . ."

He said it in a friendly way, but I realized I would have to watch my step while I was aboard this boat. I admired the fine splices at the rope-ends of my pipe berth. It was a classic French Navy hammock, made of heavy canvas stretched between two pipes that you hooked onto pegs on metal columns in the forecastle. The many columns looked like welcome places to hang on to, because at sea the deck must really heave here, right behind the chain locker. Besides their main function of holding up the ceiling, I could tell at a glance that the columns also served to support the benches and long tables scattered around the room. It was all well thought out, serving many purposes at once; really clever.

"To climb into your pipe berth," Escotte told me, "you put one foot on the bench, the other on the table, and up you go right to heaven! Give it a try. You don't seem too dumb for a rookie."

It didn't take a genius to figure out how to do it, I thought. I'd like to see him try and climb a coconut tree! But I didn't realize a pipe berth would be so comfortable. Indochinese hammocks were too rounded and yielding to sleep in through the night without waking up all stiff in the morning; they were just for taking a nap or rocking a baby. Whereas in a Navy hammock you could sleep almost flat on your back or curled up on your side, just like in a bed. It was a neat invention, and took up hardly any room.

Escotte and Linares were getting ready to go back on deck. They dragged their feet toward the gangway ladder, in no hurry to get to work. Garguy pointed out that it was dumb to go, since the chow bell would ring soon; they immediately came back. Garguy helped me stow the berth in my locker.

"Don't worry about the petty officer; he's always yelling at us. Anyway, they only use the brig back in France. Here, they put red marks on your service booklet. They aren't so dumb as to lock us up. They'd rather we went and caught a bullet for some fat colonial. What does your old man do for a living, anyway?"

Looking him in the eye, I could tell he had asked the question without aggressiveness. The four of us were simply getting acquainted, the way dogs sniff each others' bottoms to see who's who and where the new one comes from. I thought things were going just fine; we would probably wind up friends, like in *The Three Musketeers*.

A few seconds after the dinner bell rang, about thirty of us were sitting down to eat. I hadn't eaten potatoes in years, there was plenty of meat, and the bread smelled so good it was like cake, only better. The ship's baker made it fresh with real wheat flour. But the guy next to me was taking up all the room; he put his elbows on the table, shoved me, acted as if I wasn't there. So I shoved back; I like eating in peace. I had right away picked up that he didn't like me. He was a big strong guy, who looked like one of those butcher boys you saw in pictures.

"Hey, gook, why don't you tell us how you licked the Japs' asses while we were fighting the Germans?"

That piece of shit had said this good and loud so everyone would hear. All conversation stopped dead; there wasn't a single clink of cutlery on the aluminum mess-tins. Everyone was waiting to see what would happen next. Oh brother! I knew I had to set things straight right away, or they'd make my life on the boat unbearable. With the back of my hand, I slammed his plate of spuds to the deck. He stood up, but I was already on my feet. I feinted with my right, landed a left hook on his jaw, smashed my right fist in his face, then whipped out with my left to catch him again. He didn't see a single punch coming.

The fat pig was down for the count, folded up like an accordion. As Abadie used to say, "It's a hundred times better to spend thirty seconds fighting an asshole than having to do it bit by bit over six months." This had taken less than two seconds. Okay, it was all over; he would leave me alone. But I wanted the others to understand too.

"Listen guys, I don't know what people told you about the French in Indochina, but I can tell you that nobody licked the

Japanese's asses. They were here because they were stronger. If we'd made the slightest move to get rid of them, we'd all be dead. That's all there is to it, and it's easy to understand."

Soon after chow, we left the dock to sail down the Saigon River toward Cape Saint-Jacques [Vung Tau]. Around two in the morning, a klaxon started hooting all through the boat, tearing us out of our pipe berths. "Battle stations!" On the shore, near a Viet-held village, a French patrol was signaling to us in Morse code that they were in trouble. Bursts of 20- and 40-millimeter cannon rang out. I had never heard such a racket, but we were the ones doing the shooting. At dawn, we took on one dead and three wounded from among the marines we had come to relieve. The Viets knew how to shoot, too.

Jacky had been telling the truth: the Navy carbine was a little marvel. With its short barrel and wide sights, it was easy to handle and you could bring it to bear in a fraction of a second. I discovered another marvel too, the pivot-mounted binoculars on either side of the bridge. Their magnification and luminosity were so terrific that at night you could see as if you were up really close.

The war was on in earnest, and we did a lot of patrolling. I really admired our skipper, Captain Quémard, who maneuvered his boat as easily and precisely as if she were a sampan. Once when the GAZELLE ran aground on a Mekong mud-bar, the skipper got us off by having the entire crew, including the officers, run from one side to the other, one hundred twenty pairs of legs, all together when he blew the whistle. After about twenty round trips, the GAZELLE started to roll as if she were at sea, and very gradually, her six hundred tons of steel pulled free of the mud.

It felt good to be among these new friends who had come from so far away. It was as if I were breathing completely new air, filled with the cool of a dawn coming alive. In Saigon, I had moved in a closed circle of sons of good, middle-class families. We had all known each other for a long time and our ways of thinking were cast in the same mold, that of the colonial bourgeoisie, a little narrow-minded from having discussed the same subjects forever. Lucky I had my sports buddies; that was precious. But I understood that overall, I suffered a kind of anemia on the human level, just as you can get anemia from a diet that doesn't have enough variety. Now, thrown in with all these guys who had come from places very different from the one I had always known, I could feel myself expanding in a new spurt of mental activity. Garguy was a pastry cook, Linares an apprentice carpenter, Escotte a mechanic, Boiteux worked in a body shop, and the others also worked with their hands or by the sweat of their brows. Whereas I had only sweated on athletic fields and couldn't do much with my ten fingers. I used to watch people work, sometimes took an interest in how things were done, but didn't really do any of it myself. Here, thanks to the diversity I was encountering on the ship, I would be able to learn all sorts of things that would be useful later on, and make real strides on the practical level. I also decided to use my free time to make up for the huge gaps in my schooling that I had accumulated since childhood. From now on, I would spend my watches, with their long hours of mental void, in the company of my school books. Since I had to spend a year in the service, maybe two, I didn't plan to waste my time complaining about the discipline.

For the first six months, the GAZELLE crisscrossed the delta's rivers and streams between Saigon and Phnom Penh. Teaming up with the army, we retook all the provincial towns that had come under Viet control, one after another. I knew the areas we crossed, having driven through them many times. But I had no idea that Cochin-China would look so new and varied when seen from the gunboat's bridge or slipping along low in the water aboard the landing craft our company usually operated from.

Yet the rice paddies were the same, waving under the monsoon wind. The villages along the little *rachs* were the way they always were, shaded by palm trees, coconut trees, and betel palms where flying lizards lived. What had changed was the way I saw them. In the old days, Indochina had been a land at peace, and that's what I had seen. Now, Indochina was at war. We were there to save it from Communism. My eyes were no longer the same.

"Battle stations!" I had heard the klaxon screaming often enough since my first night aboard the GAZELLE. Every time, my stomach tightened, I turned pale, my heart started to race. And then I would again feel at peace as soon as my carbine was in my hands. "Move it! Move it!" the petty officer yelled. With my comrades, I climbed down among the soldiers piled in the motor barge tied alongside. According to a sampan skipper, Chau Doc was well defended by the Viets. Our gunboat was anchored in the middle of an arm of the Mekong in front of a town I had driven through dozens of times since my childhood.

The barge's motor abruptly revved up, the mooring lines were let go, we were off. The GAZELLE remained at anchor in the middle of the current, her guns trained on the shore.

"This time, I think it's gonna be hot," muttered Garguy.

I felt that way too. Escotte and Linares nodded. We were squeezed together in a corner of the bilge, as inseparable as on our first day together. The soldiers' faces were tense. They had fought hard the week before to retake Long Xuyen, thirty-five miles downstream. We had meanwhile been making little lightning raids in the area, hunting the elusive Viets.

The bank was very close now. I thought of the Chinese cafe to the right of the wharf where we used to stop for a bite to eat during our drives to the village; a cafe that smelled deliciously of beignets fried in coconut oil. No point in looking to see if it had any customers today.

A few hours later, the ship's doctor was gently pushing a gauze drain into the wound on my arm . . . Jesus, it hurt! When the bullet hit, I'd hardly felt a thing; just a slap, that's all. And really nothing compared to the pain I was feeling now. It was as if he were pulling off a piece of my flesh. Finally, it was over; what a relief. He wrapped a bandage around my arm and said, "The bone wasn't hit. You're lucky!"

No kidding! I was incredibly lucky to be alive at all; in fact, it was a miracle. And the images started to rise before my eyes . . . The dead soldier on the bank, near the wharf . . . He had been shot in the first volley and lay there, curled up in the mud on top of his rifle. I had seen other dead bodies, but they hadn't reached down and twisted my guts. They had died somewhere else, far from my eyes, far from my mind. Whereas this was my first real dead man. And I stood there paralyzed with fear before the monstrous reality . . . It's too stupid to die like that . . . And it could have been me if I had come ashore at the same time he had . . . Yesterday, he'd been fooling around with his buddies, laughing with the girls, watching the sunshine, feeling life singing before him . . . Then blam! And now he wasn't here, he'd never be here again, snatched away in the mud of the Mekong . . . Linares slammed me down to the ground, yelling, "You're going to get shot!" . . . Garguy's machine gun was firing long bursts right next to my ear . . . I couldn't hear the bullets hitting around us anymore, Escotte was feeding the clips, the blood began to pump warm and strong through my body again, I was shooting with the others . . . Death no longer existed . . . Aboard the GAZELLE, Boiteux had spotted where the shooting was coming from and let loose with the 40-millimeter cannon . . . The Viets fell quiet . . . The soldiers fanned out toward the town, you hardly heard any more shots, the Viets were on the run . . . Our group of twenty-five marines took up positions along the river, about a hundred yards to the left of where we landed, in a ditch surrounded by bushes, easy to defend in the very unlikely event of a counter-attack. Before us, along the Mekong, ran a road lined on either side by tall trees . . . Curiously, they weren't tamarinds but *cai dau*, the majestic trees which yielded the wood oil used on junks . . . At the very end of those beautiful, peaceful trees, stood a suspicious-looking pile of sand bags two hundred yards away.

Our officer called for a volunteer to go toss a grenade into it . . . If anyone had to go, I thought it should be me, because Indochina was more my country than theirs . . . Linares wanted to come with me, but I'd rather be alone, two of us would get spotted . . . I pulled off my boots, because when you're wearing shoes you can't feel the terrain; your feet can't see, and branches snap underfoot; you're much more stealthy when you're barefoot . . . There I was, halfway there, my carbine in my hand, two grenades on my belt . . . The long row of *cai dau* would let me get within twenty-five yards of the pillbox without being seen, perfect for a grenade . . . Garguy would cover my retreat with his machine gun . . . Suddenly, a shot rang out, almost in my ear. That asshole Linares! He must have followed me; it was stupid of him to be shooting like that! A second shot followed immediately. Furious, I turned around to chew him out . . . Shit, there was nobody there; I was the one being shot at, and from close range . . . And bang! a third shot rang out an instant later and my arm jerked to the side as if somebody had punched it . . . I had to think fast . . . I fell to the ground where I was . . . He thought he had shot me dead, but I had figured out where he was . . . No need to see him, he was hidden in the little ditch five yards to my left . . . I pulled the pin on the grenade, flipped off the lever, waited three full seconds to make sure he wouldn't have time to toss it back at me before it exploded, and—take this, asshole! . . . Boom! I stood up, crossed the road in two leaps, ran along the trees back to my buddies . . . They would have to deal with the pillbox without my help . . . Anyway, the GAZELLE could take care of that problem with her 90-millimeter cannon.

Garguy walked into sick bay with Escotte and Linares, bringing me the rifle of the dead Viet they had found, like a relic. They said it was what the guy had been shooting at me with. It made them so happy, I pretended to believe them. But you can't miss a man three times in a row with a rifle, even if you've never fired one in your life. The Viet who winged me had obviously been using a revolver; he had also obviously been shaking with fear. With a rifle at that distance he would have brought me down with his first shot, even if he were quaking in his boots. Whereas with a pistol, you can miss a cow at point-blank range if you don't hold it right.

I asked them if they had seen the dead Viet where I had thrown my grenade, about half-way to the pillbox.

"No, he wasn't there. Your grenade must have nearly finished him off, and then he probably dragged himself to the pillbox before dying, holding his guts with one hand and his rifle with the other."

"About how old was he?"

"I don't know; thirty, maybe forty. What difference does it make? Why are you asking?"

My buddies thought I was smiling with joy and pride at having killed the Viet in single-handed combat, like some sort of hero. They wouldn't believe me if I told them the real reason I felt so good. They had just given me the double proof that I hadn't killed that guy. He had missed me three times because he was very young and his hand was shaking as he held the revolver. And he was still alive, since they had found only one dead man in the pillbox, a much older guy who wasn't packing a revolver. So we were even, in exchange for a little blood on my shirt-sleeve.

On those rivers of the interior, barely ruffled by the northeast wind, I encountered fear on several occasions, and once a huge terror as blind death rained down around us everywhere, a hail of bullets crackling in our ears, plowing the ground I was trying to burrow into to escape my fate.

I also learned to recognize the enormous rush that you get in the Great Game of War, a kind of total alertness throughout your whole being, a heightened state where the fear of never again seeing the sun or feeling your buddies' warmth is swept away by the burning fraternity of your comrades in arms, who can change into a single, almost divine man.

That Man, when I saw him, was pure heroism, which I had never experienced before. Four weeping soldiers were carrying their comrade on a blanket stretched between two poles. He had thrown himself on a grenade that some Viet had tossed into the barracks where they were spending the night. Instead of ten dead, he was the only one, so that the others could live. His face was calm as he passed in front of me, and I recognized the god within that shattered body carried by the living.

My Tho, Ben Tre, Vinh Long, Can Tho, Chau Doc . . . even Rach Gia on the Gulf of Siam, by way of the dikes and canals. Along the way, we occupied lots of little villages, sometimes no more than a handful of huts hidden behind the palm trees lining the narrow *rachs* that snaked through the delta lowlands. The Viet Minh were swarming all over the country. We rarely saw them, but they were present everywhere in the people's minds and in the corpses of their opponents that you saw floating in the dark waters of the ponds.

It was a war of ambush against an enemy who had been poorly armed up to then, but who seemed to be learning fast. And I found myself being drawn against my will into a game that was more beautiful, larger, and more powerful than I had ever known, a terrific game in which I was both hunter and hunted, a game in which my gaze became more alive than it ever had before.

What Abadie had told me in the trench at Khanh Hoi often came to mind. "Beware the smell of gunpowder; it can transform man into a carnivorous god." Another image came to mind too, that of the little sea-snakes I used to watch with Phuoc's father when we were fishing in the Gulf of Siam, during the great calms where the sea seemed to show us all the mysteries it contained. A little snake with black and yellow rings that can swim just as fast backward as forward, as if it had a head at each end. Its venom is so powerful it can kill you in an instant. But the thing is, this snake *never* bites. It *doesn't want* to bite, it just can't. Something stops it, forbids it. You could pick one up, hurt it, do anything you like to get it angry, and it still wouldn't bite.

With my carbine, I resembled the little snake that swims in both directions and doesn't want to bite. But the snake doesn't have any choice, that's the way it's made; it thinks only about eating, living, and reproducing; it doesn't see further. Whereas I was a dead man who had been reprieved; I couldn't help seeing the Japanese officer in the jail, his hand on his holster, our eyes locked. I could also see the Viet who hadn't killed me at Cau Doc. He hadn't intended to, of course, but here I was, unable to stop thinking about him, unable to forget the miracle that had granted me life. A life I had to deeply respect . . . and not only when *my* life was involved.

I should have hated the Viets with all my soul after what they had done during the night at Hérault. And yet, since Chau Doc, whenever I had a man in my sights, I *couldn't* pull the trigger. Naturally, I fired as often as my combat companions. In fact, I was a much better shot; in ten seconds, standing up, I could put all five of my carbine's bullets in the bull's eye of a target a hundred yards away. But when I had the chance to shoot a Viet, I would shift my aim at the last instant so the bullet would brush by him, hammering in his ear, so he would only be frightened, the way I often was. And this was a secret between me and myself; none of my comrades could know this mystery, which I kept hidden like a kind of shame. If I told them about it—even Escotte, Linares, and Garguy—they would think I was a coward, maybe even a traitor. So I buried deep within me a kind of defect they wouldn't understand, and which at times I myself had trouble accepting.

I saw Abadie again at the Saigon hospital. A machine-gun bullet had hit him full in the chest; it was amazing it hadn't killed him. And he said something that I now thought about constantly: "We won't bridge the gap between Indochina and France by filling it with corpses."

We had been patrolling the delta for nearly seven months, and I believed in our military action less and less. During our brief rest stops in Saigon, I would hear the radio talking about great victories, entire areas swept clear of Viets, new provinces pacified. I would have liked it to be true, but instead thought of an ostrich hiding its head in the sand so as not to face facts or try to understand.

I could see Chu telling me, as I cut inner tubes for my slingshot: "Look with your own eyes, not those of others."

I saw my old Assam saying roughly the same thing, when I would parrot something I had heard: "Always speak with your own mouth, and don't pay attention to the thousands of mouths telling lies."

But speaking with my own mouth would surely be dangerous for an ordinary marine who didn't want to shoot Viets. I didn't think it would sit too well even if I were a general whose *képi* wore a constellation of stars and whose chest was covered with ribbons. So I chose to keep quiet instead, thinking of the mandarin's son on the Rach Gia boat: "It's simple to shut people up, much simpler than answering their questions."

Looking with my own eyes, however, that at least I could try to do. And when I really made the effort to look at things with my eyes open, what did I see? I'll tell you, but very quietly, because I'm afraid:

I saw lots of cities and villages from which we had driven the Viets. In general, we didn't do much shooting because they would turn into shadows and disappear before we attacked. We would then move on to "pacify" another city, another village, always welcomed by chiefs with smiles frozen on slightly trembling lips.

Viets? No, none here. Everything is quiet in this sector. In the others, too. So the army detailed a well-armed group of soldiers to each township. Those guys would be able to keep things under control, in case the Viets returned to harass these good peasants who asked only that they be allowed to work their land in peace.

Just the same, the Viets were there when they wanted to be.

They were everywhere.

Even if you didn't see them anywhere.

Sniff the wind a little. Look deep into people's eyes. They were there, among those obsequious village chiefs. They were there too, among those apparently peaceful peasants who prepared their ambushes before vanishing into the mystery of the rice paddies where bare feet walk noiselessly. And those who weren't quite Viets would become Viets in time; it was a lot better than finding yourself crucified on a pole in the middle of a stream swarming with corpse-eating catfish. Sniff the wind again; go ahead, sniff it, instead of hiding your head in the sand. A new wind was blowing across the paddies and shaking the leaves in the forest. It was blowing across the whole country, calling an entire people, beginning to stir their souls: the wind of freedom. And it was telling the Vietnamese that it was up to them—and to them alone—to take care of their problems without us.

I shook myself, closed my eyes again, drove all those bad visions from my mind, and went to join my buddies in the forecastle. The wind could blow where it wanted, they didn't give a damn. They got drunk as lords and went to whorehouses every chance they got. With them, I found peace . . .

But when I opened my eyes again to look into the future, I found that deep in my heart, I was afraid of someday being driven from a country which was mine, profoundly mine.

CHAPTER 13

I gathered my Indochinese past in my hands, bundled it up, and set it on fire. From the warm ashes, I took what hadn't burned away, what was real, solid, and essential: a little handful of intangibles, light as a cloud yet hard as the hardest stone. I blew on the ashes to sweep away the last specks clinging to me, and kept deep in my heart only the precious diamond, now freed from its ore.

At Chau Doc I had been twenty years old. Now I was twenty-seven, and MARIE-THÉRÈSE was spinning her first wake in the Gulf of Siam, the wake of my big departure. The day before, I had hesitated; I was afraid, very afraid. I hadn't taken the time to really learn to use the roller-furling boom during my hasty shakedown cruises. So when a terrible squall hit off Phu Quoc Island, I didn't know what to do; I had forgotten everything I knew. I was like a cat that has fallen into the water, and is trying to cling to anything it can. I felt like vomiting with shame and despair. The wind was blowing like crazy. If I could have erased everything with a single stroke, I would have just given up, in spite of my shame. Still, I was able to drop the sails before they ripped and quickly drop anchor in fifteen feet of water. In my mind's eye, I could see the page in Monfreid's book where he talks about a spiritual heaving-to, something you turn to when everything is going wrong. You hunker down, make no decisions, and let your mind wander while you wait for the wind to change. Luckily, my two anchors held; otherwise I would have wound up on the rocks the very evening I set sail. In any case, Monfreid was a great help. The squall let up at nightfall; I cooked my rice with a can of corned beef and peas, drank a good cup of coffee, and felt much better. In the heavens, the gods were already calming down. The sky was full of stars, and they were hardly twinkling. Phuoc's father had taught me long ago that that's a sure sign of good weather ahead, even when the sky still looks a bit nasty.

I watched the stars all night long. I thought of the monkey clinging to its branch, the one that had come to mind when I was swimming with Françou that evening when I made my capital decision, a trembling monkey afraid to swing into space toward a tree that was more beautiful, larger, farther away.

Next day, I was joyfully listening to the wind singing in the sails. It was the first time I had set out alone; the first time I was going to cross the sea alone; the first time I wouldn't see land for days and days, the first time I would watch the sun rise and set on the great blue disk of the sea, with me alone in the middle with MARIE-THÉRÈSE, where any land visible on the horizon could only be a distant cloud. It was something I had never experienced before. With Phuoc's father, we always stayed within sight of land and rarely sailed at night. Aboard the big cargo junk during my six months of coasting between Rach Gia and Cambodia, there had always been islands on the horizon. From now on everything would be brand-new, so new that when I made land again, a language other than Vietnamese would be spoken there. The people would wear sarongs and carry loads on their heads while worshiping Allah, instead of wearing *cai ao*, carrying bundles slung from bamboo slats on their shoulders, and thinking of Buddha while wielding machine guns to drive out white-skinned men who claimed to be following the path of Christ as they blazed away with 40-millimeter cannons.

It had taken me years to realize my dream of setting out for the peace of the open ocean, a dream that had first gripped me that night as I sailed TITETTE toward Tamassou Island while Abadie slept under the thatched cabin-roof after entrusting his boat to me.

I watched the land shrinking behind me . . . This time, the monkey had finally let go of its branch and swung out into space. I listened to the wind singing in my ears and I felt flooded with happiness. And yet I felt like crying when I thought of the beautiful tree I was leaving forever. Seven years had passed since that dawn when I put up my hands next to Abadie at the river's edge, with the Japanese soldier pointing his bayonet at my belly. Seven years already!

My military service only lasted a year instead of two. Such had been the decision of the War Ministry, in order to send all the young recruits back to civilian life without delay. We were judged to be more useful helping with Indochina's economic revival. "Pacification" became the domain of regular soldiers, professionals of the trigger and the flag.

Françou had signed up for the duration of the war. I would never see him again. Not because he had chosen the paratroop corps, but because of the drama with Bai Ma. When Françou told me about it, without apparent regret, hatred still in his eyes, I knew that we had truly lost our country. It was as if he had killed his own brother. And we had committed that murder together, one through the other, even if I hadn't been with him that day. I wanted to be able to forget . . . maybe with the sea . . . with the passage of time that wipes out all traces . . .

Jacky had left the country the year before. He suddenly got fed up, pulled his things together, bade farewell to Indochina, and left for Guyana. In a letter, he spoke about the forests of his new country, as beautiful in his eyes as those of the Central Highlands. I knew he was trying to convince himself because he didn't have any choice . . . No forest in the world would ever match the greatness of the forests of Indochina, full of tigers and deer, elephants, wild buffaloes, and the birds and little animals that crowded the jungle of our childhood, our forest with its thousand eyes.

In Saigon, my father's business was booming. The piasters poured in, his staff had increased five-fold, the profits were huge. Investing in things that lasted, he bought a ten-thousand-square-foot warehouse to accommodate his imports, which kept growing, thanks to the Indochinese war. And he seemed to believe that this blood-soaked land would remain Franco-Vietnamese for another thousand years . . .

Discharged at twenty-one and a half, I had gone right back to work in my father's company. Yet a few weeks later, I ran off to the Gulf of Siam to set up a business sailing cargo between Rach Gia and Kampot, Cambodia. Things went well at first, but six months later, I had to sell the beautiful junk I had become attached to. The French Sûreté suspected me of trafficking arms for the Viets, which put me at risk of getting killed. In those troubled times, it was all too easy to "accidentally" get a bullet in the neck. Farewell Monfreid, farewell Gerbault, it was back to the stable at the age of twenty-two. Yes Papa, you'll see, I'll work hard, no more foolishness, I promise. I gave my father enough time to forget about my sailing escapades, then persuaded him to give me six months leave in Europe at half pay . . .

Youth hostels, the Côte d'Azur, Italy, England, all by bicycle or hitchhiking, when trucks could take my bike . . . I went from marvel to marvel: new landscapes, atmosphere, the discovery of a completely new world, the intoxication of meeting young people of my generation; everything amazed me . . . And then came the big shock—Paris. An ignoramus, I let myself be swallowed up by French culture: theater, movies, museums, concerts, the Latin Quarter . . . I listened open-mouthed to students' conversations in the cafes . . . At last, I was going to learn, to understand . . . I gorged myself on culture, abundance, excess, vertigo . . . I began to feel nauseated . . . Careful, now . . . Suddenly, I started suspecting the artifice of Parisian wit, which was forever cheerfully splitting hairs amid a flood of talk . . . lots of words; many words . . . Careful, old man, don't let yourself be carried away by those wonderful flashes; they probably mask a cold and inhospitable world . . .

I went back to the countryside with my bike and knapsack, perhaps to find my distant roots in a France that was close to the earth . . . But why those fences around the gardens, which I hadn't noticed when I arrived six months before? Were people afraid of their neighbors? And why only plane trees along the roads and on the public squares of those little villages which I was now crossing and seeing with fresh eyes? They could easily have mixed in a few chestnut, walnut, and plum trees; after all, people in Indochina managed to plant tamarind and mango trees . . . Hey there, you filthy bum, go back to the hole you crawled out of, go back to your land of savages. You'll never understand the land of your ancestors . . .

Marie-Thérèse aboard the steamship carrying me back to Saigon . . . Marie-Thérèse with her golden hair . . . Marie-Thérèse looking at the stars with me . . . Marie-Thérèse gently laying her soft hands on my troubled chest . . . Marie-Thérèse, first love . . . Marie-Thérèse and our engagement in Saigon; I would soon turn twenty-three . . . A survivor told me about the massacre of the Da Lat convoy at kilometer 113, two hundred dead, sixty trucks burned . . . Assassination attempts with hand grenades in the restaurants and movie theaters . . . Marie-Thérèse dismayed by the fear that gnawed at me at the prospect of finding myself trapped with a wife and children in an Indochina full of violence that I no longer recognized after my stay in Europe . . . Tortured by remorse, I behaved like a bastard, and broke off the engagement, but Marie-Thérèse would always be in my heart . . .

Then Abadie was assassinated by the Viet Minh underground, while I got a third miraculous reprieve. I should have been lying next to him in the morgue with two bullets in my head, but the Great Book had once again decreed that my life be spared, the way it had that time with the Japanese officer in jail, then with the Viet at Chau Doc . . . At the office, I buried myself in work; my father thought I had finally developed a passion for business . . . Actually, my only passion was languages; I got up at three in the morning to study English, Spanish, Russian, and Chinese characters . . . I knew I would have to leave this land of money, this land of the blind and the insane. I knew the world would have to crack wide open if it wasn't to die of stupidity, and studying languages seemed like a trump card that might allow minds to meet across borders . . . Yet I knew that good intentions alone would lead nowhere unless they were crystallized by determination, that master trump without which nothing happens. So each night before I went to sleep I used to whisper a hundred times to myself: "I have a will of iron, I can overcome all obstacles and achieve everything I desire." It replaced the "Our Fathers" and the "Hail Marys" from the days when I still believed in them . . . I hadn't studied Latin, but I knew the phrase *mens sana in corpore sano*— a sound mind in a sound body . . . I sought a perfect balance between my work, sports, and language study, a balance between thought, sweat, and faith . . . And during the two years I maintained that discipline, starting my days at three in the morning and ending them at nine at night, my life became like a circle whose shape was more and more distinct, with Will at its center. Will held me up and nourished me with ease, power, and clarity. Will gradually transformed me by pressing outward from within.

Then, all at once, before my dazzled eyes, I saw SNARK—the escape. It was take it or leave it. Fuck my books, I thought, fuck the swimming pool, fuck the office. I would soon be twenty-six years old.

So Deshumeurs and I took off, riding our miraculous charger toward the wide world that was opening our eyes to the immensity of life . . . And SNARK gave us breath, gave us everything with the joy of discovery, until the day when she announced she had nothing left to give. Then we were forced to return to Saigon, whipping our old boat as she labored over the waves, reaching the coast on the point of sinking.

On seeing Saigon after experiencing the wind of the open ocean, that wind which blows free from one edge of the horizon to the other, there was no question of again getting enmeshed in the spider web of my father's affairs. I sold the last shares I owned in his company. Deshumeurs gave me the gear we were able to salvage from SNARK: sails, anchors, chain, line, blocks, sextant, compass, charts, the remaining stores. He gave them all to me so I could re-create the miracle. And I raced off to Kampot, to look for my next boat.

In Kampot, I was taken in by Xian's father, who had left the village to emigrate across the border to Cambodia. There you could live without too much risk of being shot by one side or hacked to bits with machetes by the other. He helped me find my little junk, thirty feet long by ten feet wide, which I baptized MARIE-THÉRÈSE. I lived in his hut at the edge of the river not far from the sea, a short walk from town. It was such a joy for me, as if I had returned to our village.

Xian's father worked with me to get MARIE-THÉRÈSE in shape. From time to time, he would give me scraps of news from the village, but very casually and delicately, to spare me pain.

And during those four weeks of intense preparation and great-hearted hospitality, neither he nor Xian's mother once mentioned Bai Ma and Françou.

Not even in a whisper.

Not even in a parable.

We knew that Françou and Bai Ma . . . no, the subject was too serious. The slightest allusion would have attracted the *ma qui,* which may even have been lurking in the squall that had so terrified and paralyzed me off Phu Quoc Point the night I set sail.

I raised my two anchors this morning before dawn. The weather was fine, and this time I really was leaving my native land . . . the Great Departure at last! I was carrying the village deep in my heart in MARIE-THÉRÈSE's bilge with its stone ballast, in her sails bellied by the wind, in her hull that smelled of the forest. And I knew that the Alliance was with me as well.

I was free for the first time in my life, really free. Before, all my freedoms had only been little ones yoked to conditions; transient freedoms, often intense but always dependent on time or other people.

Now I didn't have to account for myself; I didn't need anyone else. I could go to Malaysia or Borneo; all I had to do was choose. To make it simpler, I could even flip a coin. From Malaysia, I could continue on to Madagascar if Singapore didn't appeal to me, even try to catch up with Jacky in Guyana. I was the master of my life on new wings that carried me so high it sometimes gave me vertigo.

In my wake, which could still be seen on the horizon, the pale blue line of big Phu Quoc Island was gradually sinking into the sea. Farther, behind Phu Quoc, lay Indochina, which I was leaving forever—perhaps. A "perhaps" that held neither a real promise nor a real refusal. A "perhaps" full of questions and peopled with wandering souls who wanted to be remembered, who demanded that the past not be completely erased, so that it could one day help nurture more friendship, tolerance, and generosity between peoples.

What peace, to be alone at sea with my boat sailing on calm water toward Malaysia, running before the northeast monsoon wind. I had finally figured out how to set the tiller, and our course was perfectly straight. It was terrific to be able to rest, cook, laze on deck while watching the sea, to dream with MARIE-THÉRÈSE as she bore me toward the mysteries of the unknown.

I was alive, fully alive, and I thought about Abadie's death, which should have been mine as well. For six months, I had spent all my weekends with him and Alyette. Then just once, one Sunday, I had gone to the pool for evening water-polo practice before an important match. That was the night which fate chose to send the Viet Minh underground to shoot Abadie, Alyette, and a visiting friend (they only wounded Alyette). The next day, seeing Abadie at the morgue, I understood that the time had come for me to seriously consider leaving the country.

The sun was shining high in the sky, the northeast wind was caressing MARIE-THÉRÈSE and making her mainsheet sing as if it were alive. And I really believed it was alive, just as my boat was alive . . . But how many dead I could see still rising from the foam of the wake . . .

Linares was dead . . .
Phuoc's father was dead . . .
Hao's father was dead . . .
Xai was dead . . .
Derk was dead . . .

Xian was dead . . .

Abadie was dead . . .

Bai Ma and Françou were dead . . .

They had all died in a war that had begun with the dawn of humanity, a stupid war that had broken out before we even came out of our caves. Aboard SNARK, Deshumeurs and I had finally concluded that war was one of those calamities nobody could do anything about, like typhoons, drought, or flood. Now that I was nearly twenty-seven and was alone with myself to debate the matter, I could no longer accept the idea that war was an inevitability without appeal. My mother claimed that it was primarily France and England that had created Hitler, and not only the German people, as we were supposed to think. She brought up the Sermon on the Mount, in which Christ spoke words that would have prevented the birth of that monstrous war, if we only had had ears to hear. Abadie had shaken his head, but I was beginning to sense that my mother was less blind than I thought.

Forty million "officially" dead in the Second World War alone, almost the population of France or Indochina. I tried to imagine forty million graves being dug one after another . . . and saw a cemetery a thousand times vaster than the disk of the horizon in which MARIE-THÉRÈSE played with the wind and the white waves of the Gulf of Siam. They had all died in the name of big flags and stirring national anthems, which I would never again see or hear without wanting to vomit on them as symbols of lies, blood, pride, and stupidity.

The ghosts watched a living MARIE-THÉRÈSE running happy and free toward the Malacca Peninsula.

The ghosts departed in her wake.

And they came back to tell me never to forget.

CHAPTER 14

Only six days! The gods had blessed MARIE-THÉRÈSE for her maiden voyage in the Gulf of Siam. Steady monsoon winds, not a single day of flat calm, few squalls and none of them nasty. Just what I needed to really take my boat in hand. The six days alone at sea passed as if I were swimming in eternity, an eternity of joy and harmony. And this morning, lit up by the first rays of dawn, right in front of the bow—Malaysia!

Overcome with emotion at my first solo landfall, I gazed at the long chain of mountains gleaming in the rising sun. I couldn't tear my eyes away, hypnotized by the sight of this new land rising from the horizon just where I expected it. I had hit the bull's eye on my first try this time, and would have given anything to share the magic of the moment with my old SNARK buddy Pierre Deshumeurs. I could still remember our first landfall together, nine or ten months earlier, a week after SNARK left Indochina for the Strait of Malacca and Singapore. It had also been at dawn, like today.

On deck, Deshumeurs was squirming as if he had ants in his pants. "It's land, I swear!" he shouted. "Come here and look, for God's sake, instead of laughing. It's land, I tell you!"

I didn't budge. I wasn't on watch and I felt like quietly sipping my café au lait. I wasn't about to jump up each time some cloud appeared on the horizon . . .

But as it turned out, he was right. It certainly was land, very far off to starboard. So far away that I was completely baffled. When I climbed the mast I understood even less, because I could see more land, this time on our left. It was barely visible, but just as real. A total mystery. Land should have been dead ahead—and we weren't due to raise it for another four or five days. Even if SNARK had been making much better speed than we thought, we couldn't have seen land so far on either side of us, since the Strait of Malacca is just a few miles across. In short, we were completely lost somewhere in the Gulf of Siam between Indochina and God knows where. And for all the good our sextant did us, you might as well have given a compass to a couple of monkeys. They would have stared at it wide-eyed for a moment, turned it every which way, then gotten the bright idea of smashing the glass with a stone to taste the liquid inside, before quickly dropping the strange object in the bushes.

"Hey, Pierre," I said. "I think this time our instincts have given us a hell of a problem."

"So what do you think Christopher Columbus did when he first sighted land? He broke out a ration of grog for the crew; let's start with that. Then we'll do what he did: we'll sail closer, look for a quiet little bay to anchor in, and find some savage who can tell us where we are." The great thing about Deshumeurs is that he never worried about anything; when things went wrong, he took them in his stride and turned them around. We decided to head for the land to the right, which we had spotted first, sparing us a jibe in the stiff monsoon breeze.

SNARK tore along on a beam reach under reefed mainsail, spitting foam. The coast grew, lengthened, changed color, began to look like an almost hostile dark blue wall barring our way. Then, before our eyes, it very quickly metamorphosed into every sailor's dream. By early afternoon we were sailing on water as flat as your hand, tacking through a maze of little islands from which no smoke rose, a real flock of desert islands, all green and filled with bird song. Paradise.

A paradise where we did find ourselves scratching our heads a bit, just the same. There were two possibilities: these mysterious islands were either part of the Anambas, or they were the Natunas. On our large-scale chart of the Gulf of Siam, the two archipelagos were about fifty miles apart at roughly the same latitude. But how the hell had we managed to find land at all, with such a screwed-up heading? Even without taking into account the compass's magnetic variation—which was very slight—SNARK should have left the Anambas very far to port, invisible below the horizon. The explanation of the enigma was probably fairly simple, given that our good old SNARK was skippered by a pair of baboons sailing by a very lucky star. Also, I suspected that SNARK sometimes turned skipper herself, doing whatever she pleased when one of us was daydreaming or snoring on watch.

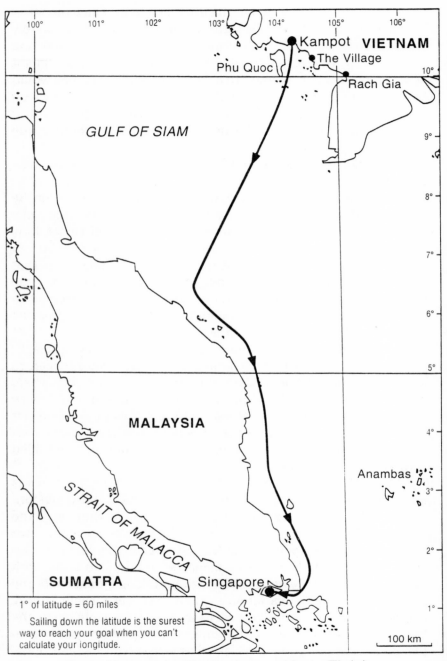

100°   101°   102°   103°   104°   105°   106°

● Kampot **VIETNAM**
● The Village
Phu Quoc   10°
Rach Gia

GULF OF SIAM   9°

                                           8°

                                           7°

                                           6°

                                           5°

MALAYSIA   4°

Anambas   3°
STRAIT OF MALACCA

                                           2°
SUMATRA   Singapore

1° of latitude = 60 miles   1°

Sailing down the latitude is the surest
way to reach your goal when you can't   100 km
calculate your longitude.

From Kampot to Singapore on *Marie-Thérèse*

Whatever the case, I never felt such joy, and I knew we would never experience it again with such intensity. We would have other joys, of course, but not like that one, overflowing with such incredible sweetness. The moment was pure Christopher Columbus. The only difference was that he thought he had reached India or China, whereas we were pretty sure that SNARK was still in the Gulf of Siam, three hundred miles north of the Strait of Malacca, with Singapore waiting for the two daring navigators with open arms. But aside from that minor detail, it was Columbus all over again, the same sense of pure discovery, that wave of warmth swelling our chests to the point of lifting us above ourselves, ready to soar up to kiss our lucky stars. And to think, we almost missed getting this incredible gift! Success and failure sometimes hang by a thread, a choice between a flash of reason or stupidity.

It had happened the day before we left Indochina, in Cape Saint-Jacques Bay, when we were wrapping up our final preparations. Deshumeurs and I were two bundles of nerves, physically exhausted. He was up the mast with a heavy pair of pliers, tightening a shackle. They slipped, and blam! the pliers fell to the deck, right past my nose. I yelled, "You asshole!"

Pale with rage, Deshumeurs tore down the mast in a flash.

"Okay, that does it! If you've got any guts, put up your fists!"

Deshumeurs had a lot of admirable qualities. He wasn't afraid of anything, he had total faith in our adventure, and I've never met anyone so willing to stick his neck out for a pal. But he was also extremely thin-skinned and it was easy to rub him the wrong way. I sometimes felt I had to put on kid gloves before asking him to pass me a saw or a hammer. To Pierre, courtesy wasn't just an asset, it was a necessity. Whereas I'm exactly the opposite, all rough edges, with a hide like a rhino. You could call me an asshole ten times in the same sentence and it wouldn't bother me. We're all assholes, more or less, otherwise the world would be in much better shape. Still, looking like a coward in Deshumeurs's eyes was something I didn't like one bit.

Luckily, I realized how serious the situation was, and that everything else depended on it.

"Listen, Pierre, we can't start punching each other out the day before we set sail, after slaving together the way we have. We've put everything into this boat—our guts, our minds, our dreams, right to the last drop. If we start fighting now, then shit, we really are assholes. Here's the way it is: If you really want to fight, then

I'm not interested in SNARK anymore. I'm dropping everything and going back to Saigon to work. Those are the breaks. It's up to you."

And so instead of fighting, here we were, blown away by the sight of all these islands. I was standing with my foot on the tiller, watching for reefs, while Deshumeurs sat in a corner of the cockpit studying the chart of the Anambas and the Natunas.

"They must be the Anambas!" he said. "Look here: we've been screwing around in this maze for two hours. If these were the Natunas, we would have seen at least one very large island with a few small ones around it, whereas here, there's just a slew of little islands. We're a pair of old salts!"

We stayed there for nearly a week, with no desire to leave. SNARK slept like a bird with its head under its wing, in a blue-green nest surrounded by flower-like coral reefs at the bottom of a tiny bay whose pebble beach was lined with palm trees. Deshumeurs went snorkeling, and erupted from the water after his very first dive with so much splashing I thought he had been attacked by a shark. But it was no shark. "It's so beautiful," he shouted. "It's gorgeous! Come see how beautiful it is. The coral! The fish! They came right up and looked at me!" And I think he began to cry, hiding his face underwater, embarrassed because of my rhino hide. Don't worry, old pal, I wouldn't have made fun of you. When I was fourteen and put on a pair of plastic Japanese diving goggles, I cried too, the first time I saw the undersea world.

A few days later, a fisherman showed up out of nowhere and anchored near SNARK. We shouted "Anambas?" with a broad wave and a great question in our eyes. And the man, with his brown skin and colorful sarong and laughing eyes, answered, "*Ya! Anambas!*" Deshumeurs threw him a line. The man understood right away; he tied it to the foot of his mast and eased off on his anchor line as I pulled him over. Soon the boats were rafted up. His was a little 15-foot lateen-rigged jewel, with staysail and mainsail halyards that doubled as shrouds, and artfully carved hardwood blocks on rope strops with the halyards rove through smooth holes in their centers.

We said, "Coffee?" and he followed us below into the cabin. He sniffed his coffee, took a mouthful, closed his eyes and said, *Bagus*. We gave him a can of Ovaltine and he said, *Terima kasih.* So we already knew how to say "good" and "thank you" in Malay.

Then we spread out the chart of the Anambas in the cockpit so the man could tell us what island we were anchored at. He looked at the chart without understanding. We put our finger on each island that had a name, pronounced it as best we could, and looked questioningly at him. Each time, he shook his head and said, *Tidak.* We could see that he was making an enormous effort to understand what we wanted. But it was always *tidak.*

Finally my finger came to rest on a small island hidden in a corner of the chart and Deshumeurs said, "Pulau Soley?" The man leaped in the air, his face transfigured, and shouted, "*Ya! Ya!* Pulau Soley! *Ini* Pulau Soley!" pointing to the pebble beach beneath the slanting palm trees.

Ini Pulau Soley! Those words were worth all the gold of the Incas!

Yes, we were old salts, and SNARK was an old salt too. True, she drove us crazy from time to time, but we still had to thank her on bended knee for getting us out of plenty of tight spots. And now, aboard MARIE-THÉRÈSE, I was becoming a real Old Salt because I had learned to use a sextant to get my noon latitude and I knew the name of that mountain I had left to starboard without having to go anchor in some cove to ask a fisherman what it was called. All I had to do was to sail along the coast at a safe distance and I would hit the Strait of Malacca in a few days! The Strait of Malacca, then the Indian Ocean . . . and then the ends of the earth. I would stop at Singapore to write Deshumeurs; I could imagine his pleasure when he got my letter telling him how I had pulled off this major crossing practically without a screw-up.

I had made a lot of progress since SNARK! Yet without that blessed boat there would be no MARIE-THÉRÈSE today.

SNARK . . . I could still see myself at my father's business in Saigon less than a year before, wrestling with an intractable problem: The inventory showed 35 boxes of Ovaltine, but we had 37 on hand. I had carefully checked the figures and counted the boxes in the storeroom three times and always got the same result. There was no accounting for it. Anyway, what difference did it make? Two boxes more or less, my father would be neither richer nor poorer, and in any case I would be at the pool in an hour for water-polo practice. Then I would hit the sack at nine o'clock sharp, after going over my Chinese homework.

"I found us a boat. Want to come see?"

Mounier was standing in front of my desk. Jean-Claude had come to Indochina with the French expeditionary force and been discharged here. We were the same age. Since Abadie's death, we had been getting together on weekends pretty regularly to talk about boats, the sea, traveling, *leaving*. But as time passed, it had become a bit like a conversation between two drunks that never went anywhere.

"She's a real Western-style boat, built in Borneo if I understand right. An amazing stroke of luck: only a thousand piasters. So I jumped on it. I have the certificate of ownership in my pocket. And I named her SNARK, like Jack London's boat."

In spite of his long legs, Mounier had to hustle not to be left behind over the four hundred yards that separated us from SNARK. And then a huge wave burst over me, carrying me along in a dazzling cascade of sparkling light. The world was right there, before my eyes, the whole world contained in that boat tied up at the dock on the Saigon River near Blagueurs Point. A 40-foot boat that would take me I didn't know where, but in any case, very far.

In a few minutes, it was all settled. Mounier would be the captain and responsible for our common funds and all decisions concerning preparations. He would invest the 1,500 piasters he had left, I the 5,400 piasters in my bank account. And soon—the open sea!

Meanwhile, there was a lot to do on SNARK. When Mounier acquired her, she had been stripped to her hull and masts. The boat had been seized by customs for smuggling and the five crewmen repatriated, but they had sold everything to the Chinese shopkeepers before leaving: anchors, sails, lines, blocks, booms, gaffs, turnbuckles, the lot. There wasn't anything left aboard! But that was no problem for two determined young guys with some money to spend.

I listened to the pounding of my caulking hammer, which rang as clearly as that of Nguyen, the worker assigned by the shipyard for the duration of the SNARK job. On the foredeck, powdered caulking pitch was simmering in *cai dau* oil that smelled of the sea. Three more days, and the cabin roof would be done; the rain wouldn't leak in anymore. Then we would start on the deck, which would take at least a week. Then the caulking of the hull. For that, we'd have to haul out and hire a crew of professionals. I had already asked around; the bill would be steep, but we had enough to pay it. And in four weeks at the most, SNARK would slip her mooring lines with new sails and two years worth of food.

Aft, Mounier was humming as he worked. He had been trained in France by a master shipwright whom he often spoke of with deep respect, and I admired his skill as he built SNARK a cockpit. Just the same, I couldn't help but feel vaguely worried at the sight of his beautiful *cai sao* planks and the boxes of expensive, hard-to-find bronze screws. A little voice told me that the captain should be giving top priority to the rigging and sails while I handled the caulking. For me, a boat comes down to three main components: a watertight hull and deck, well-rigged masts, and a solidly mounted rudder. Then you add sails, fill the water tanks, ship a good supply of rice, *nuoc mam*, and fishhooks, add a few boxes of cheap canned food, cast off the mooring lines, and you're gone. If we really wanted a cockpit, we could always build one in the next port. After all, SNARK had sailed for half a century without a cockpit; she could certainly wait another few months. We were wasting our time on non-essentials.

Nearly two weeks passed. Mounier had gone to buy sailcloth and I hadn't seen him yesterday, nor the day before.

"You really don't expect us to go cruising with sails made of woven palm-fronds, like a junk, do you?"

Now there, I agreed with him. I much preferred good solid canvas, the kind you use for deck chairs, which would last us for years. And I suggested to Mounier that Assam sew them on her sewing machine.

"I talked to her about it; she's asking a very reasonable price and can do it quickly. We'll watch out for squalls during our first passage, and then later, at Singapore or somewhere, we'll re-stitch the whole set by hand with good strong waxed thread. What do you say?"

Mounier asked for some time to think about it. But when he showed up, it wasn't with sailcloth, but a brand-new sextant and detailed charts covering half the world: the China Sea, the Sunda Islands, the Pacific, the Indian Ocean, Australia, all complete, right down to the smallest cove and tiniest atoll dotting the blue expanse of the globe. Between the sextant and the hundred pounds of charts, the bill was appalling. I had naively thought we would just wander off with the bare minimum, figuring we could always trace the charts we needed aboard freighters we met in ports along the way. And we would certainly have come across a second-hand sextant; maybe someone would even give us one, you never know!

By the start of the third week, panic was gnawing at my guts.

Nguyen and I had finished caulking the cabin roof, but apart from buying the canvas, nothing had been done about the sails. Mounier had disappeared again over the weekend and come back, proud as Punch, carrying a Winchester rifle that was all chrome, including the breech and the action—eight hundred piasters up in smoke. "That way it won't rust in the sea air, you know? There are lots of pirates where we'll be sailing, so we need a weapon we can really count on." All I could count were the few lousy piasters we had left. We weren't going to be breathing sea air any time soon.

Yet Mounier was infinitely more competent and experienced than I was when it came to craftsmanship and knowing how to rig this kind of boat. Using elegant splices, he had finally installed the shrouds, then replaced the missing turnbuckles with deadeyes; he did the job beautifully, without the slightest hesitation, in just two days. And I had to admit that his cockpit was professional-quality work. But then he started building a teak chest with metal clasps to store the charts, while the sailcloth he had been talking about cutting for the past week sat piled next to him. Mounier seemed to have forgotten that to cut a gaff-rigged mainsail, you first have to measure it, and to do that, you have to build and rig the gaff and the boom.

I had suggested an obvious solution, quick and practically free: use *cai tram* timbers. You could find them in any shipyard and the wood was strong as anything. We could cut them to length and have a gaff and the two booms in an hour. And if we worked like maniacs for another day, we could finish the rigging. Then Mounier could take the measurements so we would *finally* cut the sails and have Assam sew them while he took the boat to dry dock and got us the hell out of this country that stank of corpses. It would be so simple.

It would be so *simple* . . . Each time I blurted that out, Mounier would stiffen. As for the gaff and booms, he planned to shape them from some huge posts that were so heavy they had to be brought to the boat on a cart.

"Do you have any idea why a boom has to be heavy?" he asked. "So it doesn't fly up during a jibe. That *cai tram* of yours is a joke; it's much too light. It may be all right for your Gulf of Siam riff-raff, but I don't want that shit aboard my boat!"

Now there, he was talking complete nonsense. The greenest sailor knows how to trim a mainsheet while jibing to keep the boom from flying up. And if the boom is heavier than necessary, sooner or later it will do damage during an accidental jibe. But what took the cake was Mounier's notion that we should stow our ballast in little crates and carry them on deck when we were running or on a broad reach, to minimize rolling.

Mounier had read a lot of books, and he told me about Joshua Slocum, J.C. Voss, Harry Pidgeon, names I was hearing for the first time. He claimed that Alain Gerbault and Eric de Bisschop (whom I *had* read) weren't a patch on these three great masters' pants. That may have been true, for all I knew. But I was beginning to understand that having never actually sailed, Mounier had gotten all his book-learning jumbled up in his head. And I was feeling my way along as well. Meanwhile, SNARK's hull was making water at an alarming rate and the boat absolutely had to be hauled out. We had just enough money left to cover that unavoidable expense. I thought I knew how to caulk, from having watched Hao's father and his magic hands, but a few days before, in a heavy rainstorm, the deck and cabin roof had leaked at the places where I had pounded my oakum. At that, Nguyen quit. He was tired of my acting like the boss and throwing my weight around when I was actually no better than a monkey.

Well, all right, maybe I was a monkey! After all, inexperience is no crime. De Bisschop and Gerbault didn't know much either before they set out. *But they set out anyway, and they learned as they went along.*

If we had just cast off, everything would have worked out between Mounier and me. I was ready to learn, and he could have taught me lots of things. And he would have grasped things that become obvious after just a few days at sea. The ballast would have stayed nice and snug down in the bilge, the way it does on every other boat in the world. As for his huge booms—which he hadn't even started on—he would have decided on his own to cut them down to a reasonable size, in Singapore or some quiet Indonesian anchorage. But the real problem lay elsewhere: *the captain would never put to sea . . . because he didn't really want to.* Mounier was living SNARK's voyage in his head, in front of his charts, dreaming of horizons and atolls he would never see.

SNARK was far in my past now, thank God. And I had become a free man. For the past five days and nights, the Malaysian coast had slowly streamed by to starboard. The big Chinese junk that was in MARIE-THÉRÈSE's wake this morning passed us as I was bringing the noon sun down to the horizon for a final latitude check before Singapore.

The favorable northeast monsoon was nearly over; best not hang around Singapore too long if I wanted it to carry me south to the trades in the Indian Ocean. The southwest monsoon would start blowing in four or five weeks. A three-day layover would be long enough to see a few friends, fill my water tanks, write Deshumeurs a long letter, and then take off. Set sail again, cruise along the coast of Sumatra at a safe distance, leave the Strait of Malacca, and enter the Indian Ocean. And then head due south with what was left of the northeast monsoon to find the trades, which would take me all the way to Madagascar. The trades, those magical winds blowing through my adolescence as I read about FIRECREST, PHU-PO, and KAIMILOA,* fabulous boats that fed my teenage dreams. And no more stops after Singapore, nothing but sea, sea, and more sea!

This was only my thirteenth day nonstop at sea since leaving Indochina, but I was slowly beginning to realize what a huge treasure solitude had brought me. At last, I had time to be alone with myself, time to contemplate what was around me. Before, everything had been a blur: military service, working at my father's, my whirlwind trip to Europe, back to Indochina, studying like mad without wasting a minute, fixing up SNARK, which shot toward the horizon like a rocket but limped back on the verge of sinking, and finally, the terrific flash of the four weeks before sailing from Kampot. During all those years, I had never stopped running, looking both ahead and behind, as if time was dogging my tracks. Even while I was sailing my cargo junk between Rach Gia and Cambodia, when I had really planned to take it easy, I managed to live as if I were sitting on a hot stove. But for the last thirteen days, a great calm had been spreading within me, a calm I could savor, where bits and pieces of my past rose to the surface to come together into what looked like patterns on the sea. The sun would be setting soon; it was already behind those hills off to the right. I could see Mounier's face among the little northeast mon-

---

*FIRECREST: Alain Gerbault's boat. PHU-PO: A Chinese junk that Eric de Bisschop and his shipmate Tatibouet sailed from Asia to Hawaii, where they ran aground. They then built KAIMILOA, a catamaran with flexible joints, and sailed her from Honolulu to France practically nonstop, by way of the Cape of Good Hope.

soon clouds floating in the pink sky. Whatever became of Mounier, I wonder? I wasn't always very fair to him. True, he was sleepwalking, looking at his charts. Yet without him and his dream, SNARK would have never sailed, for the simple reason that there never would have been a SNARK. And without SNARK, no MARIE-THÉRÈSE. And without Deshumeurs, no SNARK either, nor MARIE-THÉRÈSE today, sailing toward the Strait of Malacca. Strange, how the two boats blended into each other.

It sent my mind back to Xai, shortly after he got sick from eating bad turtle meat. Kieu's father, the village healer, barely managed to save him, thanks to his black stone, which he used to crush the seven tiny sand crabs. They had been very hard to gather, since their claws all had to be exactly the same size.

Once cured, Xai had hung his slingshot around his neck, I did the same, and we walked straight to Hon Chong with a gift for the old monk in the Cave of Coins. There, Xai asked him to explain the *yin* and *yang* symbols one saw everywhere, in the temples, on the bows of fishing junks, on the little bowls filled with sand in which you stuck incense sticks to honor your ancestors, those *yin* and *yang* symbols that were said to represent balance.

The old monk put his hands, as light as feathers, on our young shoulders:

"Take a black bird and a white bird. One is called *yin* and the other *yang*. And you think you have *yin* and *yang* in your hands. But actually, neither *yin* nor *yang* could exist without a third thing: air. Without air beneath their wings, neither of the two birds could exist; they would be just be an illusion of birds. Later on, as you grow up, you'll learn to replace 'air' by 'spirit,' but the story will be the same."

Mounier was no bird, but he had been the spirit that allowed SNARK to soar and to change a little later into MARIE-THÉRÈSE. The old monk had long since gone to join his ancestors, and it was here, close to Singapore and very far from Indochina, fifteen years after the Cave of Coins, that this fragment of memory came floating up from the depths of the past. And it perfectly matched the shapes of other, more recent, images. Together, in a corner of the great puzzle, they formed a little scene where I could see SNARK, three 25-year-olds looking at MARIE-THÉRÈSE, and, far in the background, an old monk telling a couple of children the story of two birds buoyed up by a spirit.

The big Chinese junk that had passed us at noon was nothing but a dot on the horizon now. In the distance, one finger to the right of the bow, I could already make out the entrance to the Strait of Malacca. After nightfall, when it was really dark, the huge halo of Singapore's lights would appear. The glow had astonished Deshumeurs and me when we saw it from SNARK, two days after leaving the Anambas. You would have thought ten thousand spotlights hidden below the horizon were lighting up the sky to say, "Good work, you clowns, here it is. This time you hit the bull's eye." But SNARK was still very far away when dawn came, and poof! . . . there were nothing but strange coasts all around us, to the left, to the right, ahead, astern. For one whole endless day we zigzagged from one edge of the mystery to another, looking for a city that had sunk beneath the waves. All day we were carried by incredible tidal currents and puffs of wind that barely filled our sails. And then the night returned with the huge spotlight, and we sailed into the harbor at dawn, like a pair of aces!

Deshumeurs . . . I had first met Pierre by chance while paying a courtesy call on a distant relative of mine. A dandy who spoke like a book, Deshumeurs was impeccably turned out in rayon pants with knife-edge creases, a monogrammed silk shirt, a large pinky ring, and very narrow patent-leather shoes. Nothing about him appealed to me and I quickly cut my visit short to hurry back to my sports buddies at the pool.

At our second meeting, a few months later, I saw him on the dock gazing at SNARK, and nearly burst out laughing. If anyone had told me that he was exactly the person I was looking for and that one day we would perfectly complement each other, I would have laughed it off as a joke. Not only had Deshumeurs never gone to sea, he had never looked at a boat in his life. And yet, when he got word of our project through the Saigon rumor mill—"You know, the two nuts who want to sail round the world in that wreck. What a laugh!"—he came to see for himself. Of ten thousand Frenchmen in Saigon, he was the only one who bothered to come look . . . and not just with his eyes.

The great wave broke over Deshumeurs, just as it had over me. He pulled 20,000 piasters—a huge sum—out of his pocket, and laid down three basic conditions. First, he would manage our finances. Next, if a fourth person wanted to join us on the adventure, any one of us who didn't like him would have absolute veto power. And finally, we would give our word of honor that if any of us wanted to back out—before or after we sailed, for whatever reason—SNARK would automatically belong to whoever was going on, with no further discussion. There was no need to formalize

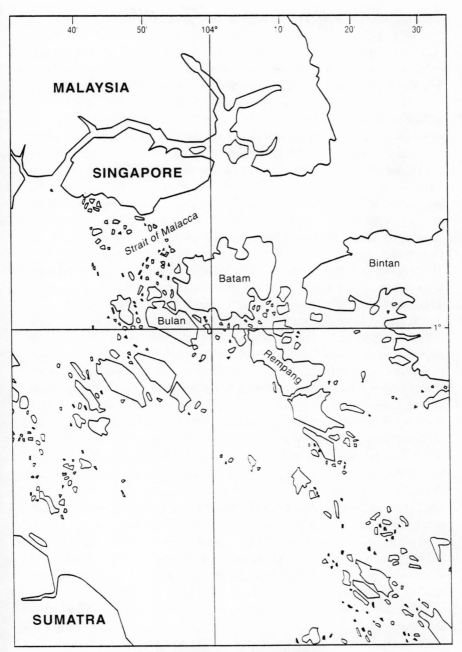

The Approach to Singapore

the agreement with a stack of signatures; our word would be enough.

Everything was becoming real again. The charts would breathe sea air after all. Mounier wouldn't back out; he would see his atolls up close. Deshumeurs was the fire we had needed.

He and I were born the same April, four days apart. Like Mounier, he had come to Indochina with the French expeditionary force and soon figured out which way the wind was blowing. Discharged in France, he returned to Saigon to start a small business. And he was no dreamer, at least not like Mounier or me. It had taken me three weeks to figure out what our problem was. By the time he pulled out his 20,000 piasters, Deshumeurs had already spotted it, and in less than two days, saw through it as clearly as an eagle. From then on, the problem began to solve itself, and a series of small miracles brought about a big one. I don't know what went on in Mounier's head, so I'll never know exactly how it happened, but a week after Deshumeurs joined us, Mounier dropped the whole thing and Pierre and I inherited SNARK.

Stupefaction. Amazement. A breath of total freedom. But now I felt an insidious fear, the fear of the unknown. As long as Mounier was part of the project I felt somewhat protected by his obvious competence. True, he had huge gaps when it came to actually sailing, but that was less important and I could have made up for them. We would have worked it out like the blind man and the cripple, one carrying the other, with Deshumeurs at our side clearing the path with wads of piasters. But here, from one day to the next, as the great adventure took shape, I could hear an intimidating question from the gods: "Will you be able to turn your dream into reality?"

I had to face facts. Deshumeurs took me for an old sea dog, but I was a captain only aboard my outrigger canoe. The sum total of my "maritime experience" amounted to a couple of fishing trips with Phuoc's father around the islands near the village, then a few months of coastal sailing aboard my cargo junk, five years before. And in all that, my role was that of ordinary seaman.

Yet now Deshumeurs and I were going to play the blind man and the cripple. He didn't know it yet, thank God, and had complete faith in me. But I had better hurry and start earning my stripes.

"You'll never be able to fix this motor unless you're a mechanic," Chu the chauffeur used to tell me when I was a boy. "But unless you start by fixing the motor, you'll never become a mechanic."

Ah, SNARK . . . I could see us getting ready to take off, Deshumeurs and I working together like a couple of live wires. We had never moved so fast; it was like watching a cartoon of two ancient Hindu gods with ten arms apiece building a three-story temple. The day after Mounier quit, the boat was hauled out to be quickly caulked. Nguyen came back to work with us. Amazing, how fast a situation can turn around. The crazy light in our eyes brought a gleam to others'. An old Newfoundlander turned bureaucrat in a dusty Maritime Affairs office saw his own youth in us, and dispatched three of his best tarpaulin sewers to stitch and seam our sails. Our dream spread like wildfire in other people's hearts and as it captivated them, they joined forces with us. Admiral Graziani sent his chief of staff to say that everything was all set to give us a tow, provided we were ready to go in exactly a week, at five a.m. on the dot. We raced around in a state of near-panic, a blazing panic, powerful as a bulldozer. In one sleepless night, we cut the *cai tram* booms and gaffs and mounted the fittings and mast hoops. Looking twenty years younger, the old Newfie gave the two baboons careful directions: mount the blocks at the masthead, reeve the halyards while you're at it, cut them to length, leaving an extra yard, whip the ends as best you can, lace the sails to the gaffs, prepare the sheets, don't waste precious time hesitating, you do this while I do that. Deshumeurs and I were in a race that was both a sprint and a cross-country . . . Three hundred kilos of rice mixed with ash to prevent weevils* stowed in nice watertight five-gallon tins; twenty twelve-gallon drums of kerosene to use with the rice for bartering along the way; two barrels of *nuoc mam;* tons of canned goods; coils of line; caulking oakum for repairs; anchors, chain, coconut-fiber mooring lines . . . we tossed it all in by the cartload, we would stow it properly later when we had the time, riding at anchor off Cape Saint-Jacques with the horizon in front of us. By moving heaven and earth, our friends located three 50-gallon metal water tanks, which we sanded, rinsed, lined with cement, and wedged tightly in the hold before filling them with drinking water. . .

*This Vietnamese old wives' tale turned out to be completely ineffective. Later on, I learned a safer and better method: you fill the container with rice, put in a wad of cotton soaked in grain alcohol, then seal it. The alcohol fumes kill the weevils and their eggs.

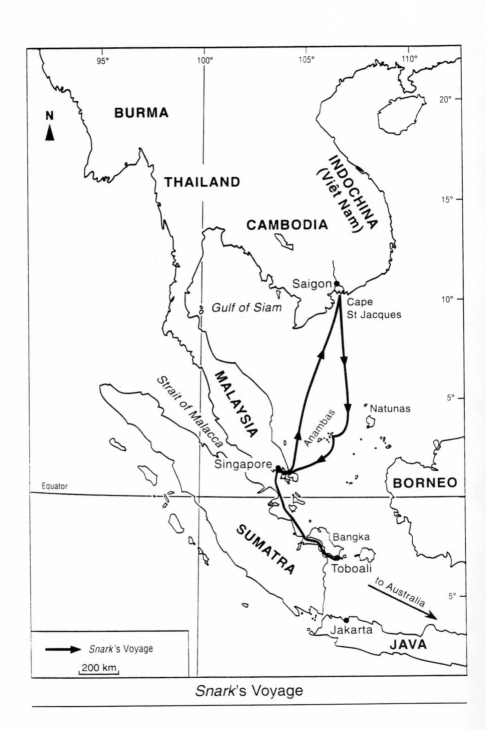

Snark's Voyage

The end is almost in sight, just a few more things to pick up at the Chinese stores and cross off the list, keep up the pace, don't pause for breath whatever you do, otherwise we'll collapse with fatigue, charging side by side, one helping the other over the rough spots, hold on, don't ease up . . . This is no time to get into a fight, this is the home stretch, we're going to burn it up . . . Seventy-two hours straight without sleep, gulping Maxiton caffeine pills . . . Check the entire rigging one last time, clear the deck, set out an anchor with a neatly coiled hawser ready to go, halyards on their pins at the foot of the mast . . . Look how beautiful SNARK is; who would have believed it? Straighten up the cabin a bit, some hot coffee to warm the heart, we won, old pal, it's almost dawn, we managed not to get into a fight once, and that's a victory too, everything's ready for departure, Admiral Graziani confirmed that the tow will be here in an hour.

And three weeks after the great wave broke over Deshumeurs, six weeks after it caught me, that evening when I first saw the hulk that would become SNARK, she was roaring down the Saigon River at ten knots, towed by a minesweeper that would drop us off sixty miles downstream at Cape Saint-Jacques Bay, the two of us staggering with exhaustion, barely able to tell stem from stern, dead tired, almost unconscious.

SNARK was but a distant memory now, and so was Singapore, as MARIE-THÉRÈSE spun her wake across the Indian Ocean more than a thousand miles from the coast of Sumatra. I looked aft, hardly able to believe it. The sun was blazing in the sky, reflected in the foam of the wake, sparkling on the back of the long, peaceful swell, stately and powerful. The swell was from the southeast, at last! And I filled my lungs with this new wind, light as a dream, which would let my pretty boat make a few more degrees of latitude south of the Equator. If this miraculous breeze would only last another day or two, it would give us time to find a safe haven in the heart of the trade wind, where the monsoon could never track us down.

The monsoon . . . MARIE-THÉRÈSE lost a few feathers there, though not too many. She was spinning out her wake toward the south under jib and staysail now because the mainsail blew out three days ago. That would be a problem, but I wasn't going to worry about it today. It was wonderful to live in the present, far from the long nightmare I had just endured.

I went below again, lit the Primus stove, and filled the kettle for a third cup of coffee. The flame sputtered a bit. I hadn't had to shield the stove from drafts in a long time, and it was the first time the forward hatch had been open in an eternity. The acrid smell of mold I had been stewing in for weeks had almost disappeared. On deck, the thin Cambodian mat and my cotton blanket were soaking up the sun between the staysail shrouds.

The Old Salt was crouched on the wide bench athwart the cabin, a steaming mug of coffee in his hand and three joss sticks stuck in front of him to thank the gods. He was contemplating the chart of the Indian Ocean. It was as sticky with salt as an old rag and covered with a spider web of nearly invisible zigzags, an end-less wake written on the sea and the waves, day after day, for a month and a half.

The southwest monsoon had hit just as I left the Strait of Malacca, soon after my over-long stop in Singapore. Fed, housed, and entertained by my friends, I hadn't noticed the time passing. So I left a bit late and the monsoon reversed direction with an army of evil *ma qui* spirits lurking in its fierce squalls. For six weeks, MARIE-THÉRÈSE and I had struggled together, a single being of wood, lines, sails, and flesh, sailing nearly flat tacks, fighting to gain latitude to the south, toward the trade winds of the Indian Ocean. It was like digging through a brick wall with your bare hands. You couldn't think of anything except dig, dig, dig. Luckily the wind was as mindless as it was furious: it changed direction five or ten degrees each night, and we took advantage of the shifts to go on the more favorable tack, slipping through the darkness.

For forty-nine days and forty-nine nights we played cat and mouse with the monsoon dragons in a chaos of angry waves, huge gaping jaws full of sharp teeth drooling for our hide. Together, we dug through a wall of wind, horizontal rain, and vi-cious seas, mile after slow mile south. We were seeking justice and protection in the trade wind, which breathes life into long ocean rambles with the sheets loosened all the way.

Fourth cup of coffee of the morning. The strong scent of the incense sticks took my mind back to the monsoon's final terrible rage, three days before. It had been in the evening, under a sky heavy with menace, as usual. In a kind of trance, one hand on the mainsheet, I was thinking of reefing the mainsail some more. Without any warning, a white squall roared in with unbelievable suddenness and violence, setting the boat on her beam ends in a matter of seconds. Thrown too far from the mainsheet to cast it loose, I could hear the big ballast stones starting to shift in the bilge. This was it, the end of the great voyage . . . Then all at once the masts rose back into the screaming wind. The mainsail had exploded into a tatter of canvas, flapping like the feathers of a hummingbird blasted by a slingshot. At the cost of a major sail, MARIE-THÉRÈSE had escaped capsizing. The mainsail was ripped to its boltrope, but I was twice as alive as before, filled with a new certainty. Reborn, standing at the mast before the sea, I looked at my beautiful boat with newfound love as she continued on her course through the night at the same speed under staysail and jib.

During the night the wind gradually slackened and shifted to the west. For the first time since entering the Indian Ocean, MARIE-THÉRÈSE was running due south, sheets slackened. Dawn brought a flat calm with a little sunshine piercing the lazy clouds. After the monsoon's grim trials, it was like watching the gates of heaven open up.

The southeast wind, gentle as a fairy's hand, had been holding for two days now. Two days in which a gentle roll replaced the crazy pitching of the past weeks. Two days without any spray on deck. I finally dared call this new wind by its proper name, the trade wind, as it drove the long easterly swell and played with the sun and the little round clouds, soft as feathers. I watched them slip across the blue sky, unhurried birds migrating on iridescent white wings. Gone were the heavy thunderclouds of just a few days ago, huge carnivorous bats with black wings filled with storms, blanketing the world with hellfire. Everything around me felt renewed.

Even MARIE-THÉRÈSE seemed transformed, full of the same sense of freedom that enveloped me like a luminous cloud. A boat is so wonderful. Leaving Indochina, I had thought I was sailing to Madagascar to settle and that MARIE-THÉRÈSE was only a tool to get me to a new country. I figured that once there I would sell my boat—so as not to be tied down! Then in Singapore I made friends with Uncle James, a rich old Englishman who had settled in the Seychelles. When he learned that I was heading to Madagascar to find work, he said it would be much easier in the Seychelles; he could soon find me a well-paying job there. Why not? I thought. And he entrusted me with a little round, richly carved ebony table and asked me to deliver it to him in the Seychelles. It just fit through the cabin's forward hatch and I was able to find a safe nook for it, out of the way near the bow. So we were off to the Seychelles instead of Madagascar, and then we would see!

A boat is freedom, and not just a means to an end, as I had believed not all that long ago. A small, Spartan house that I carry with me and which takes me wherever in the world I please. MARIE-THÉRÈSE now represented the rich solitude of wide-open spaces where the past and the future blended to become the present in the singing of the sea.

My entire being was flooded with happiness. Around noon, I finished the long task I had started in the cabin yesterday: recutting the spare mainsail I had salvaged from SNARK. I laced it onto the gaff a few minutes ago, replacing the one lost to the monsoon. Full of joy, the Old Salt watched as a completely restored MARIE-THÉRÈSE rushed down the waves. The hummingbird's feathers were all back in place and the monsoon was already far astern, almost erased from my memory.

Warmed by the sun, the deck was filling the air with the scent of Asian pitch. I listened as the sea singing along the hull told wonderful stories. Where would we be, Deshumeurs and I, if we had pushed on with our dream of reaching Australia by way of the Indian Ocean in spite of everything? SNARK was old and completely rotten. Even if we had waited another six months at Singapore for the favorable northeast winds, our adventure would have ended in some shark's belly. It was enough of a triumph to have brought our boat back to Indochina without sinking in the Gulf of Siam. Toward the end of the trip, she was taking on at least two tons of water in twenty-four hours. Maybe three. Maybe four. During the final two days, only our bailing buckets kept us afloat!

Now MARIE-THÉRÈSE was running before the trades under SNARK's mainsail, her cabin roof waterproofed with a large rectangle cut from SNARK's mizzen, tacked down and soaked with pitch. SNARK's jib and staysail were in reserve in the hold. Ever since Singapore, SNARK's two anchors lay at the ready near the bow. SNARK's compass, sextant, and charts were snugly stowed in the cabin. MARIE-THÉRÈSE was carrying all of SNARK in her wake. And next to me, I could feel Deshumeurs's warm presence.

"Want me to make you some coffee, old man?"

I had spoken aloud. I closed my eyes and the trade wind an-

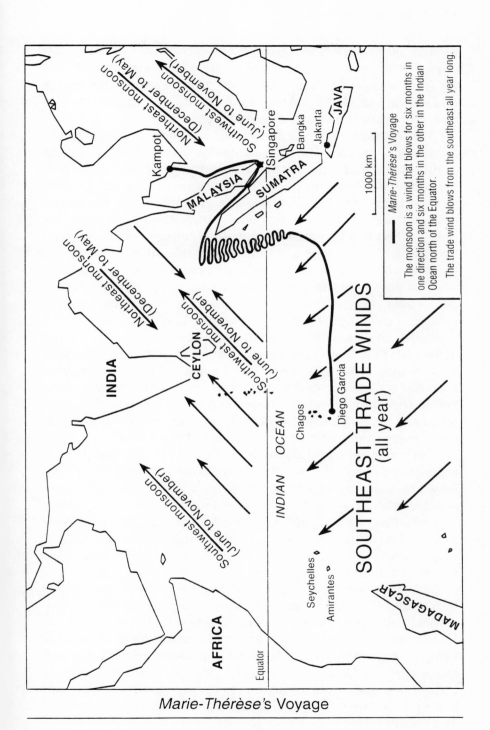

Marie-Thérèse's Voyage

swered, humming in the rigging. It had picked up a lot these last days. When it came to the sea and boats, Phuoc's father had been my teacher; but where cities and people were concerned, Deshumeurs had left his mark on me. I could still recall SNARK's arrival in Singapore and our long stay there . . .

The anchor was barely down when a reporter came aboard to ask us for an interview. A few minutes later, one of his colleagues did the same; those people must be clairvoyant! Front-page photos, long articles full of astonishing adventures about SNARK's journey and the life stories of the two intrepid sailors. And journalists don't just have antennas, they have wings. Their flights of fancy practically made Deshumeurs out to be a business tycoon who had turned his back on a dozen ringing telephones to realize a boyhood dream in the company of a former Gulf of Siam pirate.

Two guys full of fire who set off to sail around the world in a cockleshell carry in them seeds of the miraculous which people need in their hunger for magic. Give their tale a little journalistic push and it takes off for the stars. We were practically living the story of Puss-in-Boots, where a terrific bit of bluff turns two ragamuffins into princes of the realm. People on the street turned round to smile at us, doors opened wide, the whirl of invitations and parties grew faster and faster, snowballed, we didn't have a minute to ourselves, people vied to entertain the two celebrities. Our flying carpet had made us the toast of Singapore.

Deshumeurs soared above this fairy tale with the sharp eye of a great predator on the prowl. I, the timid one, quiet by nature, followed his lead, astonished by his aplomb, dumb with admiration at his confident ways. If Pierre were dropped in the middle of a foreign square wearing nothing but a bathing suit, he'd be driving a Mercedes within a month. Stumbling behind this master, I began to glimpse the terrific power of suggestion that our presence exercised on others.

Saints are surrounded by a powerful force field, but so are fakirs and other purveyors of illusion. It commands the crowds' respect and attracts the gifts of heaven as if by magic. A sailboat with a whiff of adventure and faraway horizons floats in a similar halo, which, when polished by someone with a sharp eye and quick reflexes, leads straight to Ali Baba's cave. I had already sensed this during our preparations in Saigon, but now that we had crossed the vast sea, our halo was ten times more potent. The French community, the English at the yacht club, French consular secretaries, the harbor officials, it was amazing how much they all loved us . . . A fifty-pound anchor here, a length of chain there, three boxes of supplies and a compass that magically appeared in the cockpit . . . It made me think of those dancing priestesses of ancient Greece to whom people gave little gifts in order to win the favor of Olympus. Actually, they were practicing the oldest profession in the world, the one that gives joy and consolation. I hadn't mastered it yet, but I was proving to be a talented beginner.

The little gifts continued to flow aboard in exchange for the pleasure and the dreams we gave to others. At this rate, SNARK could have sailed round the world without ever opening her cashbox.

Our time at anchor passed as if in a dream.

When we first sailed from Indochina aboard SNARK, vast Australia pulled at our hearts and minds like a magnet. Palm trees with fronds whispering in the trades, sugar-cane fields and white sand beaches stretching for miles, a barrier reef covering twenty degrees of latitude and filled with fish the color of hummingbirds, snow and ice in Tasmania, limitless space in the great central desert . . . It was this island continent, protected by thousands and thousands of miles of ocean, we wanted to migrate to. Far from Asia's madness and violence and very far from gossipy Europe's humdrum pettiness. In our eyes, SNARK represented not only a goal in itself, but also a way to reach this El Dorado in the fullness of our lives. Later, with all the time in the world, we could choose the part of Australia that best suited us, among a young, energetic people which kept its eye on basic values.

From Singapore, SNARK could take one of two routes to our goal 2,000 miles below the horizon: either the great sweep of the Indian Ocean, with the boat's bow splendidly plowing the sea for weeks beneath sun and stars, or a coastal route enlivened by human contact all the way down the Sunda Island chain.

Between the songs of these two very different but equally enchanting sirens, our hearts vacillated. My companion leaned toward Indonesia, I to the Indian Ocean. But common sense also had its say. Despite the complete caulk job in Saigon (which had revealed a hull eaten by shipworms, not to mention several rotten ribs at keel and deck level), SNARK had been making twenty-five gallons of water a day by the time we reached Singapore. That was a bit much and it wasn't getting any better. An old boat is an old boat, you can't ask too much of it. Besides, our total ignorance of celestial navigation made the vast expanse of the Indian Ocean a little intimidating.

"You know, we have all the charts. I'll bet that heading down the Java Sea, stopping wherever we please, would be pretty damned nice . . ."

To do that, however, we needed official permission from Jakarta to sail in Indonesian waters. We sent a letter to the authorities in the capital. No reply. Another letter. The French consulate backed our request. Still nothing in the mail. Time passed. A telegram. No effect. Jakarta was deaf and dumb. Not a sign. Neither yes nor no.

Two months had passed since our arrival. We had waited far too long, strutting like peacocks in the Singapore social whirl. The favorable northeast monsoon was whispering to an end and would soon start blowing the other way. We had to make up our minds.

"After all, what's the risk? If the Indonesian police ask for our visas, we'll say we're on our way to Jakarta to get them."

"In any case, we don't have any other choice. Either we raise anchor now or we'll rot here until Judgment Day."

So that's how, two weeks later, having tacked south for 250 miles against a strengthening southwest monsoon interrupted by calms, and gone ashore several times on the big island of Bangka to visit villages lost in the jungle, we found ourselves being boarded by an Indonesian launch armed with 20-millimeter guns. SNARK was swarming with uniforms and hobnail boots. *Banyak susah! Banyak susah!* (Very bad).

"Why are you sailing in our waters without permission? You say you're bound for Australia, but your passports don't show any Australian visas. And you have no proof of legal ownership of this boat. What can you show to prove it belongs to you? Why did you go ashore several times with a rifle? You say you were afraid of panthers; was it because of panthers that Mounier left you? Where is he hiding? You claim that Mounier never came with you, yet this document says the contrary. Where is he?"

Mounier . . . what a cock and bull story that was! In Saigon, the day after Deshumeurs showed up to join the SNARK crew, I had paid a visit to Admiral Graziani to ask him for a letter of safe conduct. I left his office clutching the precious signed document requesting that all civilian and military authorities give aid and assistance to Jean-Claude Mounier, Pierre Deshumeurs, and Bernard Moitessier during SNARK's journey. After Mounier dropped out, I hadn't wanted to bother our mentor a second time to have him change his letter. The Indonesian captain had confiscated the letter along with our passports and was now brandishing it as proof of our guilt.

Banyak susah, banyak susah. For the two Prince Charmings of Singapore, the tables had certainly turned. We were a pair of vagrants again, with police handcuffs in the offing. SNARK was taken in tow with two armed men on deck and three others below, searching her from stem to stern. Soon we were tied up at the dock in the little village of Toboali near the southern tip of Bangka Island, not far from the Karimata Strait that leads to the Java Sea. Thanks to the somewhat brutal tow, SNARK had made twenty miles in a straight line toward Australia against a southerly wind—nothing to sneeze at. But things turned ugly again late in the afternoon when we found ourselves in the police chief's office, surrounded by his henchmen. A bemedaled big shot had even come running from Pangkalpinang, the provincial capital, to get to the bottom of the affair.

"Where is Mounier? Where is he hiding?"

It was an obsession; they were convinced they had captured a bunch of agitators sent by France to destabilize the Indonesian government, which had recently been freed from colonial rule. Mounier—who was obviously the head of the expedition—must have gone ashore somewhere on Bangka Island to link up with a group of rebels. That was all there was to it. It was such an enormous fantasy, our jaws dropped.

Since Deshumeurs's name was the second one in the admiral's letter, the police considered him my superior in this spy mission against Indonesia's national security. It made sense, in a way. With his lordly ways, slim feet, manicured hands, and his command of English, Deshumeurs had something of the intellectual about him; probably a colonel. As for me, I was more the roughhewn roustabout type, reticent and naturally sloppy, with big hands and splayed, all-terrain feet. Besides, I didn't speak English nearly as well as Pierre; it was nearly gibberish by comparison. I could understand almost everything and follow a conversation, but had trouble expressing myself. Me, a sergeant in the secret service? That would be the day!

"Where is Mounier?"

Deshumeurs was about to patiently reply for the nth time, but the police chief cut him off with a gesture. The officer from Pangkalpinang was speaking to me. He repeated his question:

"Where is Mounier?"

"*Makan angin.*"

Makan: to eat. *Angin:* air, breeze. *Makan angin:* to eat the air, taste the breeze, take it easy. *Makan angin*, the loveliest phrase in the Indonesian language, which I had fallen in love with and been studying passionately since the Anambas. With my *makan angin*, I was handing the officer a bouquet of fresh flowers, their petals sparkling with cool, early morning dew. In its four syllables, *makan angin* held all the explanations this paranoid uniformed assembly could desire. If just one of them had the slightest gift for telepathy, he would clearly hear, deep in his heart, the very simple things I couldn't express with my clumsy tongue. "My friend and I are just wandering about, sniffing the breeze on land and sea. We're visiting this great garden of the planet for our pleasure and those of others. And we want to continue doing this for as long as possible, far from 20-millimeter guns, machine guns, hand grenades, revolvers, and uniforms in general. Because we're sick to death of all those things, see. That's why we got the hell out of Indochina and don't plan to turn around and go back. Or stay here and rot."

All that, I had expressed in a single burst of thought with my *makan angin*. But they didn't seem very receptive to the simplicity of my message. Deshumeurs immediately stepped in to pick up the thread:

"Gentlemen, let's be serious. If we really were on a secret mission, do you think it would be with a leaky boat with no motor or radio, armed only with an old single-shot rifle? Do you think we would have written your government, backed by the French consulate, and sent copies to our embassy in Jakarta? And the Mounier business is a joke. We spent nearly two months in Singapore, everybody knows us there, and nobody saw Mounier. Check it out for yourselves. I've told you all this a hundred times, but I feel I'm talking to a group of deaf people who aren't even willing to use their heads."

I could see astonishment on all the faces. I was beginning to know my friend Pierre; I'd had plenty of opportunities to see him in action. But this time I was floored. "I've told you all this a hundred times, but you don't seem to want to listen, or even think." It was so brazen I couldn't believe my ears. He dared calmly repeat it, staring right at them. Not one batted an eyelash. Pierre,

old pal, you've demonstrated your power in the most extraordinary way today. You remind me of Kaa, Kipling's great python,
Kaa with his shining scales, whom no one in the jungle could face
without becoming hypnotized.

Without giving them time to react, Deshumeurs went on. It
was then that I learned, to my astonishment, that we were writers!
The good fairies leaning over his cradle had given Deshumeurs incredible gall and a gift for oratory that might have made him a
brilliant lawyer. Nothing in our hands, nothing in our pockets, we
were—illusion! Neither Pierre nor I had ever written anything in
our lives, or even considered it. And yet, to hear him, anyone in
the room—including me—would have been ready to swear that
we spent the best part of our life with pen in hand, hunched over
our desks, mulling noble thoughts. It sounded right, and it flowed
from Deshumeurs's mouth like a clear stream running through the
woods. He spoke of our book as if it already existed. He brought
it to life with all the skill of a dazzling magician telling a story
about Mowgli to a group of children crowded around him. His
words became images, he worked the vague shapes as if they
were clay, and the clay became truth. He said that writing was a
sacred art, a present the gods gave only to the elect. It was a royal
gift with shimmering wings, he said, but also a dangerous one,
and whether it was used for good or evil depended on whom it
was given to. Where the hell did he come up with this stuff? If a
bluebird straight from heaven had flown in through the window,
perched on his shoulder, and started singing with him, I wouldn't
have been surprised. Part of me was rooted to the spot in the grip
of this music, whose terrific power I could glimpse through my
friend's dazzling flight of fancy. The other part, completely alert,
was watching a gate swing open in the fortress called "the Law"
before a man playing his magic flute, completely alone.

A scraping of boots pulled me out of my trance. The meeting
was over, everything was fine. We were sailing because that was
what we enjoyed doing. We were traveling to open our eyes and
someday tell others what we had seen on the byways of this great
earth.

Dragged there like bums this morning, we left the police station with our heads high, bathed in mystery. People smiled with
respect—a respect in which you could detect a healthy caution.
Deshumeurs had convinced them that we held the threat of a
flame that was always free: the majestic, dangerous flame of liter-
ature. In other words, what shall it be, gentlemen? A lightning bolt

that might strike you some day, or a cozy little fire we can sit around and make friends? True, it's close to blackmail cloaked in noble sentiments, but what choice do we have, gentlemen? We have to play our cards close to the vest because we're just two jokers passing through, determined to take our own sweet time graduating from our chosen school of "making the best of life." So we have to defend ourselves against the masses of right-thinking folk draped in someone else's laws. You understand.

The Bangka authorities sent our passports to the central government in Jakarta, and the Toboali police chief enthusiastically backed our request. He was sure we would soon receive permission to continue our voyage through the Java Sea to Australia.

Life is so great! You take off, not knowing where you're going, and bingo! you find yourself in heaven. Anambas, Singapore, Toboali didn't seem to have anything in common, and yet they were all heaven. Even the police chief was heaven. He liked us, and twice a day sent his little boy to bring us a pot of *makan*: rice, vegetables in a spicy sauce, chopped fish or chicken in lemongrass. The only times that hadn't felt like heaven were when SNARK was at sea, because she had two captains who rarely agreed on which course to take. The Chinese say that the best way for a shipowner to wreck his junk is to entrust it to two *tai congs*. SNARK had managed to pull through so far, though she sometimes gave us glimpses of hell close up. But whenever the anchor was down, it was heaven again. Maybe even more so in Toboali than in Singapore.

Toboali . . . A peaceful village where everyone wore sarongs and walked barefoot, where *makan angin* filled the air like a soft cocoon after the day's toil. What hospitable people they were, always ready to invite a newcomer across the threshold of their pretty huts on stilts.

Selamat hari! (Hello!) People gestured for us to enter. We wiped our feet before climbing the narrow betel-palm ladders. Inside, the spotlessly clean huts were almost bare, the floors made of lashed split bamboo. Instead of furniture, woven mats with brightly colored geometric patterns were strewn about. Crumbs and food scraps fell through the cracks in the floor to be dispatched by chickens and ducks under the house. The kitchens were outside, right on the bare earth. This being a Muslim country, there were no pigs.

Minum kopi? They served the coffee in bowls, generously laced with sweetened condensed milk. And, as in Singapore, they wanted to know all about the two travelers from afar. "How do the people live in the country you sailed from? There are only two of you on your boat. Aren't you afraid?" And their eyes asked questions, hungry for amazing stories that would stretch the bounds of their imagination. The world is so full of prejudice. If we had stayed in Saigon to stew in our juices, we would have gone on thinking that Muslims despised unbelievers and would have nothing to do with them. In days of old, troubadours wandered around without a care for the morrow, sure of being welcomed, fed, and spoiled all along their way in exchange for a little bit of the miraculous. So I played the harmonica for the villagers, made slingshots for the kids, and we understood each other with our eyes. And Deshumeurs told stories in short sentences, gestures, smiles, and eloquent silences.

Indonesian and Malay are practically the same language, and the two months we spent in Singapore had helped us pick up a good number of common words. *Ya*: yes. *Tidak*: no. *Orang*: man. *Perempuan*: woman. *Anak*: child. *Saya*: me. *Kamu*: you. *Hari*: day. *Mata hari*: sun (eye of the day). *Malam*: night. *Awan*: clouds. *Hujan*: rain. *Bicara*: to talk. *Mengerti*: to understand. *Besar*: big. *Kecil*: small. *Bagus*: good, nice, kind. *Susah*: bad, difficult. *Apa*?: what? *Ini*: this, that. *Di mana*?: where? *Jauh*: far. *Dekat*: near. *Jalan*: to walk. *Besok*: tomorrow. *Kemarin*: yesterday. *Makan*: to eat. *Minum*: to drink. *Panas*: hot. *Dingin*: cold. *Cepat*: fast. *Pelan*: slowly, gently. *Api*: fire. *Masak*: to cook. *Nasi*: rice. *Ayam*: chicken. *Itik*: duck. *Telur*: egg. *Ikan*: fish. *Susu*: milk. *Gula:* sugar. *Susu gula*: sweetened condensed milk. *Rokok*: cigarette. *Minum rokok*: to smoke. *Rumah*: house. *Desa*: village. *Pulau*: island. *Kapal*: freighter, ship. *Perahu:* sailboat. *Rusak*: broken, damaged. *Memperbaiki*: to repair. *Kayu*: wood. *Batu*: reef, rocks, stones . . . To this I added the words for mango, papaya, grapefruit, lemon, finished, more, enough, sail, mast, rudder, oakum, to caulk, waves, current, and shark. The notebook I kept handy since leaving Singapore filled up with words we learned from people along the way.

In the longhouse where the men gathered after work, we all listened to a big radio, and Deshumeurs and I gradually began to understand snatches of the news. "Hey, there's been a fire at such-

and-such a place . . . a flood over there . . . They say the rice harvest has been good elsewhere . . ." The villagers were delighted by
our progress; several wanted to help us build a hut on a piece of
land near the beach so we would stay with them for a long time.
Though still very recent, Dutch colonial rule hadn't seemed to
have left any trace of bitterness in its wake. Had freedom been
won without too much bloodshed on either side? Here, whites
were treated like brothers.

Three weeks had already passed. Our passports still hadn't
come back with our visas. Jakarta was in no hurry, but neither
were we. Bureaucracy, with its mania for papers and complications, is one thing; people are something else again. And we
thanked heaven for having arranged things so that we wound up
here. Not only were we warmly welcomed by the villagers, but the
forced layover at Toboali gave us the unhoped-for chance to completely recaulk SNARK, which had been making water at an alarming rate since Singapore. We took advantage of the tides to careen
and spruce her up . . . and not just the tides.

Ali Baba's cave stood a hundred yards from the dock. We had
spotted it on the very first day: the storehouse of a government
tin-mining operation in the area. The watchman was an old guy
who liked to play the harmonica at siesta time, so I taught him "La
Paloma," "Le petit vin blanc," and "Marinella." When I had lulled
him with my harmonica, a big smile of Deshumeurs's accompanied by a hearty *Selamat hari!* would open the cave door a crack.
Once inside, larceny awoke in our hearts: oakum and caulking
compound, 3/16" sheet metal which we made into extra chainplates to spread the mast's tension on the hull, heavy galvanized
wire we could twist into shrouds, a box of screws and lag bolts, a
few round-head bolts that would surely come in handy some day,
thirty feet of new half-inch manila rope to replace the port jib
sheet. All right, that's enough for today; well, just a minute, another box of oakum, it's amazing how much SNARK uses, and next
time we'll have to make off with that can of tar to swab on the
hull. But don't worry, good Toboali officials! We take such pleasure in these little gifts for our boat, you can see that we don't
have sticky fingers, and you know how small presents can feed a
friendship, don't you?

We had been in Toboali for two months and were making the most of it. We took advantage of every favorable tide to completely recaulk SNARK from keel to gunwales. Six weeks of almost daily caulking, not counting other jobs to get the whole boat in shape. Like two migratory birds busily smoothing their feathers and pecking at a few more goodies before taking wing again, we were ready to go. We were just waiting for our visas.

The police chief gazed at our pretty SNARK, her hull gleaming with fresh tar, sporting new fittings and twisted-wire shrouds. As a policeman, he must have known where all those marvels came from, including the lag bolts on the eight chainplates which had come from Ali Baba's cave, and all the rest. When I felt he was frowning a little and might have been about to say something about it, I would give him a smile as bright as the sun. Wonderful, how a well-timed smile can melt someone's heart, even a policeman's. So he started liking us all over again and his son was never late in bringing us the *makan*.

But each time the chief strolled along the dock at high tide, he would see us pumping. It made no sense; SNARK was leaking like a sieve, much more than the day we first tied up here. Were we twisting the oakum too tightly? Or pounding it in so hard and deep that we were splintering the half-rotten planks? And it seemed that the chief always showed up at high tide to watch us pumping.

We sensed that it was starting to bother him. That was hardly surprising. Watching Laurel and Hardy getting ready to set sail for Australia while pumping a leaky scow four or five times a day would weigh on the conscience of anyone who planned to stay on nice dry land.

The police chief called us into his office one morning to talk about what was troubling him. Deshumeurs quickly cut him off, saying it was no problem for us, since we didn't mind pumping. While Deshumeurs was setting him straight, I nodded my head up and down to make sure the chief understood that I agreed with my pal.

The chief tried to speak again, but this time I cut him off. I told him that the long way the two of us had come since Indochina had forged us into an alloy, the way copper and tin make bronze. The chief was taken aback to hear me say so many words at one sitting. Maybe he thought I was practically mute, able only to say *makan angin*, make slingshots for the kids, and play the harmonica.

With that, we left the chief with his problem and quickly went back on board, because the *makan* would be ready soon, and also because we had to pump before the tide got too high.

In the end though, the chief decided he didn't want us continuing toward Australia after all. He pointed out that Australia was 1,600 miles from Toboali, on the other side of the shark-infested Java Sea. He would just as soon the much-beloved Laurel and Hardy crew went and sank somewhere else. The chief returned our passports, but with the following written in red ink on the visa page: "Not authorized to land in Indonesia." And he ordered a military launch to tow us, practically nonstop, the 300 miles back to Singapore. There at least, SNARK could peacefully sink in a good harbor, near our consulate.

We stayed in Singapore for a while, to plan and very carefully prepare for our next passage, which would be almost 600 miles of open ocean. And though we almost sank, we managed to bring SNARK back to Saigon six months after leaving there.

Once back in Indochina, we took stock of the situation. What I had told the Toboali police chief had been true. The long trail of joys and pains Deshumeurs and I had traveled together really had brought out the best in each of us; we had practically become each other's double. But we would be taking separate paths toward the future.

Pierre decided to go back into business to earn enough to build a real boat, and to have a ship's cash-box that could keep the lean cows at bay for a while.

I hung around Saigon for four long weeks, looking for someone to buy my remaining shares of stock in my father's business. Once that was done, I set out from Kampot two months later aboard MARIE-THÉRÈSE without a penny in my pocket. Too bad for the lean cows, they would have to make do with rice and *nuoc mam*. As for the rest, I would trust in the Good Lord, who always looks after the birds singing in the sky.

MARIE-THÉRÈSE was now running before the trade wind toward

the Seychelles. The Old Salt looked at them on his chart, at the other end of the Indian Ocean. MARIE-THÉRÈSE wasn't making a drop of water. Well, eight or ten gallons a day, but to anyone who had known SNARK, that was hardly a drop. Still, she had come through some rough spots.

So had I. During my stop at Singapore, MARIE-THÉRÈSE had nearly sunk at anchor, just like that, smack in the middle of the yacht club. The leak opened up one night when I was sleeping at some friends' house. When I saw MARIE-THÉRÈSE the next morning, her deck almost awash and tins of rice bobbing around inside, I thought I'd die. I bailed for hours, then towed her aground with my dinghy. I really did feel dead then, but dead of despair, not fatigue. There wasn't anything I could do. It was too much all at once. I was screwed; I didn't have any money, and I didn't know which way to turn. Crouched in the mud in front of that wreck, my head in my hands, I didn't even feel like crying, just going to sleep and never waking up again.

I felt a hand on my shoulder. It was Orner, a Singapore ship chandler I knew slightly. "Pump all night while the tide rises," he said. "I'll be here tomorrow morning when it starts to ebb. Don't think about anything else, just pump. I'll take care of the rest."

So I pumped all night long. At about four in the morning, when the tide turned, Orner showed up with ten Chinese caulkers and three apprentices to twist the oakum, prepare the putty, and tend the lamps. As the tide began to drop, the caulkers went to work. Waist-deep in water, they started on the upper planking, working by the light of arc lamps hung on poles rigged around the boat. When the tide was completely out and the sun was high, the caulking was finished. And before the tide came up, everything was taken care of, including spreading the putty mixed with cement so it would stick to the wet planks and harden underwater. At high tide, Orner helped me return MARIE-THÉRÈSE to her mooring. And there, he told me something surprising.

He said that what he had done for me was exactly what someone had once done for him, at a time when he couldn't see a glimmer of hope, the way I'd felt the night before. So I didn't owe him anything, he said, but I shouldn't forget to pass this gift on someday when the right time came along, without a second's hesitation. And he left me alone with a miracle.

Since then, every time I thought about it, I could see that it really had been a miracle.

A miracle very different from the one that made the Viet's three bullets miss me at Chau Doc.

Very different from the one that kept me late at the pool the night Abadie was shot.

Different from the one that caused the mainsail to rip during the monsoon's final squall, saving my life.

Those miracles didn't have any real meaning; you could just as easily call them "luck" or "chance." Whereas what Orner had done was a true miracle, born of a blend of action and conscience. To be a miracle, something must have a meaning that can be neither chance nor luck.

It had been nearly two and a half months since MARIE-THÉRÈSE sailed from Singapore. On the chart, my last reliable fix was forty days old, at five degrees of north latitude. I had taken it in mid-monsoon, when a break in the clouds revealed a glimpse of the mountains of Sumatra. I was stunned. My close-hauled zig-zagging against the monsoon had thrown my dead reckoning completely off. I thought I was two hundred miles farther west, when in fact, I was only twenty or thirty miles offshore. I quickly headed out to sea to get clear of that dangerous neighborhood.

But that was all far behind me now, maybe more than a thousand miles astern. For two weeks, MARIE-THÉRÈSE had been running due west in the trade wind along the eighth parallel south. But I couldn't even estimate her speed by timing the foam as it passed the length of the boat anymore; my sweep-second alarm clock had conked out long ago. So my dead reckoning was becoming more uncertain as the wake lengthened. Aside from knowing my exact latitude, thanks to a daily sextant fix at noon, I didn't know where I was in that vastness.

What I did know was that ahead, some thirty miles north of this eighth parallel I had been blindly following, the Chagos Archipelago was hiding. It forms a huge shallow bank spread spider-like over nearly 180 miles of latitude and 90 miles of longitude; shallows cut by unpredictable currents where the sea probably breaks very hard in some places, with reefs lurking a few feet beneath the surface, and small, low islands hidden here and there, level with the waves. On the large-scale chart, the Chagos reminded me of a clutch of crocodiles in a swamp. Only Diego

Garcia, a large atoll at the extreme southern tip, is visible from ten or twelve miles away, by day and in good weather. At night, forget it. And I had no way of telling whether MARIE-THÉRÈSE was a hundred miles away from the Chagos, or three hundred. Or five hundred. Or fifty.

The Old Salt had given the matter a lot of thought.

I didn't have a chronometer, a radio, or anything else to help me calculate my longitude, but I still had a way to locate MARIE-THÉRÈSE on the Indian Ocean chart to within twenty or thirty miles: by sailing due west at exactly latitude 7° 45'. That would safely put me eighteen miles south of Diego Garcia, and the sea birds living on the island would let me know when I passed it, since I was sure to see plenty of them fishing around the boat.

Then I would continue due west for at least forty-eight hours to be sure I was clear of the entire bank, head north until the latitude of the Seychelles (4° 30' S.), and stick to that latitude for the next seven or eight hundred miles until I reached them. The Seychelles are high islands and visible a long way off, so sailing down their latitude would be a piece of cake.

Three days passed. The Old Salt was full of doubts now. I had been seeing birds constantly since hitting the trades, even a thousand miles from Sumatra. Every single day, almost without exception. Sometimes just a few, other days a lot.

I had no idea where they slept; maybe on the wing or on the water, but certainly not in their nests. Yesterday I spotted at least thirty; today not more than ten or twelve. How many tomorrow? Or the day after? Or next week?

I was now almost sure that the sea birds wouldn't warn me when I passed Diego Garcia.

"Forget about the Seychelles," a small voice insisted. "Head for Madagascar where the sea is free of dangers. Madagascar has high mountains you can see a long ways off; they'll help you make a perfect landfall by sailing down the latitude."

The problem was, I no longer had a choice—because of that little round ebony table carefully stowed in the forward compartment. I had to deliver it to Uncle James, who was expecting it at

Mahe in the Seychelles. When I saw it come aboard the evening before I sailed, the little voice shouted, "Beware, beware, you're giving up your freedom!" But Uncle James was so nice, I didn't want to disappoint him, and he was so attached to the table, a work of art too heavy to take on the plane with him. Besides, I could feel how much he liked me. One day he said that I reminded him of the son he would have wanted to have, something my own father had never told me. If I could bring his precious table to the Seychelles, he would protect me, become my patron. When you're broke, when you don't have anything, and you're neither blessed with a head for business, like Deshumeurs, nor crazy about working yourself to death, you need a patron. A Vietnamese proverb says that a minute of protection is worth more than a lifetime of labor. The little voice continued to shout, "Beware, beware!" while I was securing the pretty ebony table forward, the night before sailing. But if we had to pay attention to all the little voices that babble in our ears, life would be pretty dreary.

Just the same, I would have given a lot not to be dragging that particular ball and chain right now.

I had figured out the problem. Uncle James would get his pretty table and I would get my patron. But just then the Child appeared, standing between me and the chart. He said my heart was no longer what it was, that I was in danger of losing the Alliance. But I had better things to do than listen to his nonsense, so I told him to go play somewhere else.

I carefully studied the chart and adjusted my course a little to the north. I was borrowing a tactic the great navigators of old must have used to learn their longitude in the days before chronometers. Uncle James would be proud of me. Deshumeurs too, when he got my letter from the Seychelles. I was going to head north one degree of latitude, to the seventh parallel. There, I would resume my course due west, hugging my new latitude. And MARIE-THÉRÈSE would sail through a 30-mile-wide channel between Diego Garcia to the south and a group of six small islands which are awash but clearly marked on the chart. That way, the relative calm of the sea in the lee of Diego Garcia would give me my position, even at night. And if I passed Diego Garcia in daylight, I would have a chance of spotting the tops of the coconut trees that cover the atoll.

After that master stroke, all the Old Salt had to do would be to set a course for the Seychelles, as initially planned.

Once upon a time, a Crow watched a Royal Eagle carry off a newborn lamb in its talons. And the Crow said, "I will do the same." He chose the biggest sheep in the flock and swooped down on it, but his claws got so tangled in the thick fleece that he couldn't fly away when the shepherd came. He wound up in a cage, with all the time in the world to meditate on the fable of the Crow who wanted to play at being an Eagle.

There was no Old Salt anymore. There never had been an Old Salt. Just a poor jerk sobbing as he watched his beautiful MARIE-THÉRÈSE being torn apart in the middle of the night on the Diego Garcia reef.

Come on, don't cry like that. That's life, it has its ups and downs, you should know that. Open your eyes and look around. You see that very rich gentleman over there? Dry your tears, give him a nice smile, and pull up your rags to show him your pretty legs. He's the one who will give you the keel of your next boat, as a present.

What's that you're saying? The little ragged whore doesn't want to smile at the very rich gentleman? She says she doesn't want to be tamed, even a little? She's afraid of losing her freedom? But what freedom are you talking about? You need a boat, that's the only thing that spells freedom for people like you!

And it will be freedom for others, too. Deep in their hearts, all they want is to fulfill their dreams through you. But there are rules to this game. So give a nice smile to the very rich man, and to the others, too. It's how the game is played. Come on, don't be shy, show them your pretty legs, give them a smile as warm as the sun, you know very well how it opens hearts and wallets. Anyway, it makes everybody happy. You understood that perfectly at Singapore and Toboali, so why not here?

There we go . . . The sweet little whore isn't a complete fool, she lets herself be tamed a bit while staying a little wild, it makes her even more charming. She's really gifted, she understands it all, the little whore is even wearing her dazzling smile of Singapore and Toboali . . . Now that wasn't hard, was it?

After Diego Garcia, three years slipped by like a dream. And in that dream, I invested a lot of sweat, thought, and sacrifice to get back to sea. And now I could shout with joy aboard MARIE-THÉRÈSE II, headed for South Africa and the ends of the earth, alone on my beautiful boat.

In my heart I carried all the tenderness of Mauritius, where I spent the three years it took to get back on my feet. I was given so many gifts: a nine-hundred-pound keel, bolts, nails, fittings, ribs cut from a handsome piece of black wood, two masts, sails, most of the planking, a sextant and chronometer. I don't think there is a more generous people on earth than the Mauritians. A noble people, open-handed with their friendship, a great deal of friendship. And they taught me to take a sun sight properly, so I could get both my latitude and my longitude.

MARIE-THÉRÈSE II was racing toward Durban on the long Indian Ocean swell. She wasn't quite finished. I wasn't quite finished either; I still had a lot to learn; getting a fix by the stars, for example. But that would come later, when the opportunity arose.

The same was true of my boat. If I had waited for MARIE-THÉRÈSE II to be a hundred percent ready, I might well never have set out. Because I would have stayed forever at anchor, fiddling with unnecessary things I thought I couldn't sail without.

I was thirty years old, and I was checking my position. Not with sextant and chronometer, but by looking to the heavens. They told me that I had been able to preserve the Alliance, and that all would be well so long as I remained true to it.

The Child came to crouch next to me in the cockpit. Durban was far ahead. Farther on, much farther, lay the awesome Cape of Good Hope. We listened to the sea singing along the hull. Born of sun and spindrift, a rainbow played in the lee of the bow. And the trade wind hummed in the rigging, singing its song of wind and sail.

I now understood what all those songs meant. They were saying that I was a citizen of the most beautiful nation on earth. A nation whose laws are harsh but simple, a nation that never cheats, which is immense and without borders, where life is lived in the present.

And they were reminding me never to forget that in this limitless nation, this land of wind, light, and peace there is only one Old Salt, and that is the sea.

CHAPTER 15

Twenty years had passed since
I left Mauritius. The vast Pacific with its thousands of islands lay
all around me; Tahiti was eight days in my wake. Whichever way
you headed, all the other islands were from two days to several
weeks' sailing away. All except one. And I gazed as the soft reflection of its pearly lagoon colored the underside of a fair-weather
cumulus. The atoll was still a ways ahead, and the wind was light
today. If it were good enough to rise, I would make the pass by
early afternoon.

This morning, the Fairy Tern* came out to say hello, flying
around JOSHUA's masts to tell me I was within twenty miles of the
atoll.

I already knew that; the stars and my sextant had told me before dawn. But to make her feel appreciated, I pretended to be a
bit lost and thanked her for her welcome, which she had carried
so far on her light wings.

It wasn't at sea that I was lost, though. The real navigation
problem was deep inside me, and I had come to Suvorov to get a
fix on things. This atoll is magical; no other place on earth gives
me so much peace in which to quietly think things through, bring
out of my heart the images accumulated during the last twenty
years, sort out the essential ones and arrange them in the great
picture album that still has so many empty pages to fill . . .

In my mind's eye, I could see MARIE-THÉRÈSE II, my proud little
sailboat, arriving at Durban from Mauritius. We'd had a bad capsize in the Mozambique Channel; everything inside got soaked,
but nothing broke in the rigging or on deck.

---

*The fairy tern (*Gygis alba rothschildi*) is the *only* sea bird that never flies out
more than fifteen or twenty miles from land.

Coming to that great South African port without a penny, I'd had to work like a slave. I got myself hired as a shipwright, though I was no more a shipwright than a nuclear physicist! As a full-time apprentice building my boat, I knew how to plane, drill holes, saw a straight line, and drive a nail without bending it, but that was the extent of my skill. Luckily, real shipwrights were hard to find in those days, and the boatyards had to settle for whoever came along.

I sweated for a year in that yard, saving my pennies. On weekends, the sweat and pennies went into MARIE-THÉRÈSE II. My boat, which had limped in from the horizon, metamorphosed like a chrysalis: a bowsprit; a new jib; a Marconi mainsail instead of the old gaff-rigged one; all the chainplates removed and hot-dip galvanized; a slab of poured cement with iron filings finally replacing my old ballast of rusty anchor chains; a decent bunk and cupboards to make the cabin comfortable; a sheet of Plexiglas heated and shaped into a dome which I screwed to the hatch cover; and little portholes that let me see out in all directions and might someday allow me to steer from inside the cabin.

Another boat was getting ready to see the world at the same time: Henry Wakelam's WANDA. When you're lucky enough to meet a guy of Henry's caliber, you try not to split up too soon. So we spent two years roaming around together. Henry had a brain that worked as fast as an abacus; it gave you answers as quickly as you clicked the numbers in. Unbelievable. Plus he had incredible energy, could jury-rig anything, and was the best scrounger I ever knew. The Durban garbage cans were our main source of supplies—and sometimes even of food. One day, as we were pulling a nice stew bone with some greenish mutton still on it from a pile of garbage, a German shepherd happily trotted over. We promptly drove him off with a couple of kicks. That bone would make us some good soup! I'll never forget the look of crushing contempt the dog gave us as he turned tail. You could read it in his eyes: two scummy wharf-rats, stealing a bone from him!

One day after I arrived in Durban, Henry and I were moored side by side. Each weekend we worked as a team, making our boats shipshape. We also worked at getting each other's courage up for the next great hurdle: leaving the Indian Ocean. We were both afraid. For Henry, it would be his first real sailing passage. And it would be all new for me, too. Every time you go to sea, it's for the first time.

Two weeks after we left Durban, when I saw the Atlantic

sparkling before my bowsprit as I rounded Good Hope with its playful albatrosses, my chest was filled with a joy that had no name. If Henry and I had been able to, we would have kept straight on to Saint Helena, so as not to have to put into port, and then sail clear to the Caribbean, at the other end of the Atlantic.

We had dreamed of the Caribbean during our preparations. But we had sunk what money we earned in Durban into our boats; our few remaining supplies wouldn't get us far. So we were forced to stop in Cape Town, find a new boss, and again work like a pair of yoked buffaloes so we could leave South Africa like princes, with our pockets jingling with coins and our holds crammed with rice. That would really do the trick; we'd really be able to live the good life for a good long time, with WANDA and MARIE-THÉRÈSE II winging across the Atlantic to go and laze side by side among those enchanted islands . . .

But MARIE-THÉRÈSE II died in the Caribbean, and it hit me like a bullet in the gut. It was also a resurrection, though I didn't realize it at the time.

That night, I thought I would die along with my boat. I thought I had lost the Alliance and might as well let myself be broken on the rocks by the breakers that were smashing her hull. I would pay my debt once and for all. Two shipwrecks, one after another—it was just too much. The first one, okay, but not this! But the Child screamed that I shouldn't do it, that I shouldn't heed that evil voice! He said that I hadn't lost the Alliance, nor the old monk's jar from the Cave of Coins. True, this shipwreck was a big test, harder than the last one. But I had to take it like a man.

I shipped out of Trinidad as an ordinary seaman on a tanker and reached France a few months later. I was almost thirty-four, with half my life already behind me, and I was starting from scratch with no money, no degree, and no skills—not to mention a résumé that was so checkered it would turn off any potential employer.

For two months I wore out my shoe leather on the hard pavements of Paris. I could have found a construction job, but that would have been a fatal blunder, a kind of quicksand I'd never be able to break free of. I had known the old routine of sore muscles and empty head all too well at Durban and Cape Town, where I used to come home each evening so exhausted that I only managed to read three books in two years.

Paris was a great desert: garrets, sandwiches, the *France-Soir* classified ads. The money I had saved from the tanker job was melting away, with no relief in sight. I was like a sewer rat skittering along the sidewalks, tracked by danger in a heartless, completely alien world. I would have given anything to find some nice warm hole where I could curl up and forget about it all.

Life was harshly reminding me there are only two kinds of people in this world: those who make money easily, and the group I had belonged to for so many years, the sweat-hogs and shit-eaters. For them, each penny saved represents a huge effort spent scraping by, doing without, and rummaging in rich people's garbage cans. The Good Lord may watch over the little birds singing in the sky; I was proof of that, still alive and all in one piece. But going hungry at times and grubbing around a lot doesn't exactly yield pheasant under glass. Like a coolie sweating in the sun digging some rich landowner's field for a skimpy ration of rice and *nuoc mam*, all I had to offer was my sweat and my shovel. Nobody wanted the rest of me.

Then a patch of blue sky suddenly appeared among the dark clouds: a dream job, a real coat-and-tie affair. Choosing to over-look my somewhat unusual résumé, the Midy drug company hired me as a detail man. So the grasshopper would have something to eat and might get through the winter without freezing to death after all. Then, two weeks later, as I was pitching an article to *Le Yacht* magazine, I came across a journalist named Jean-Michel Barrault.

A series of teachers and guides have appeared at key turning points in my life, and I've learned a lot from them: Phuoc's father, Hao's father, my old *amah* Assam, Chu the chauffeur, Abadie, Deshumeurs, Henry Wakelam—all living signposts along my path. And now I could thank the skies of Paris for sending me Jean-Michel. "Write a book," he said.

"Are you kidding? I'm no writer. And besides, having had two shipwrecks doesn't exactly qualify me to write a book; people would die laughing!"

"First, you've got a lot more in you than your two shipwrecks. Second, I had never written anything either, before I decided to give it a try. Just write down the stuff you've been telling Dany and me, it'll be terrific. In any case, you don't have any choice. Do you really think you'll be able to buy yourself a boat in less than ten or fifteen years of dragging your sample-case from one doctor to another? And in that time, you'll have lost your faith; you'll become like one of those great cats locked up in a zoo far from the jungle. Just write about the wide-open spaces you've known; that's the way to get them back. And if I think you're really working at it, maybe I'll be able to lend you a hand."

Until I met Jean-Michel I had been wandering in a kind of fog, trying to forget the caress of tropical sun and breezes on my bare skin. Then "luck" put him on my path. He took me by the hand, shook me up, opened my eyes. And I saw that life was beautiful and gave it a smile—which was all it asked of me.

My job as a drug salesman left me a lot of free time. Snug in some warm bistro after a day's work, I would watch the snow falling, and write and write. Pencil in hand, Jean-Michel read the chapters as I brought them to him.

"In four nicely linked paragraphs, you can say everything that's in these three pages. Look, get rid of this part, and this, too. It just slows the story down without adding anything. Pick it up again here. Okay, that's better. Here, boil this down to a few punchy lines. And this technical section is interesting as hell but it's much too long, it breaks up the rhythm. Wait, don't start bitching, we aren't going to spoil anything. Give me a minute to think . . . Okay, look here. We split it into two parts, leave the first one as it is, then change the second a bit and put it right after the story of you and Henry with the cormorants and your slingshots. See, now it really flows, it's got a nice rhythm, and it's all there. What do you think of it now?"

What I thought was that I was the luckiest guy in the world. I had a no-pressure job that gave me all the time I needed to work on my book, a more than generous salary, and a friend who was helping me discover a taste for writing. I gradually began to spread my wings, and Jean-Michel and Dany's warm friendship sustained me when I hesitated. One look from them was enough to pick me up when I might have started spiralling downward.

I drew on distant, long-buried memories, brought them to life, cut out an unnecessary detail here, added a little atmosphere there to recreate the mood, shared my old feelings, followed through, composed, constructed, stepped back a little, checked to see that I'd gotten it right . . . The underwater caulk job in Durban, the tin tub we rigged as a diving helmet, penguins and tortoises with Henry . . . And suddenly the sails were sliding up the mast and the breakwater slipping away astern . . . I had no idea writing could be so transcendent. I felt I was flying, I could hear the sea singing, the wind, the sun, the rainbow in the spray, the flowing phosphorescent tresses of a star-strewn wake in which a wharf rat becomes a lord of the wide horizon, enjoying a kind of freedom no amount of money could ever buy.

My book, *Vagabond des mers du sud* [*Sailing to the Reefs*], was touched by grace. Seeing it in bookstore windows, I would run my eyes lovingly over its beautiful color cover, which showed MARIE-THÉRÈSE in the Gulf of Siam, sailing from Kampot.

Marie-Thérèse, my first love . . . I gave you my entire soul.

Jean Knocker, the boat designer, liked the book and drew up the plans for my next boat for free. I named her JOSHUA, in honor of the great sailor Joshua Slocum.

Fricaud liked the book too, and built JOSHUA for the cost of the steel plates and welding rods.

Oh yes, it happens . . .

From then on, the first pieces of the great puzzle of my future began to fit together as if by magic, forming a luminous image that would remain forever unchanged in the great album of my life. In the foreground stood Françoise and the three beautiful children she brought me from her first marriage. In the background, my two seasons of cruising school in the Mediterranean.

Teaching people about the sea, after losing two boats through blunders not even a beginner would make, may have seemed a bit arrogant. But in fact, I enjoyed enormous prestige in the eyes of my crews. They saw me as some sort of phenomenon. They all knew the broad outline of my story, a guy who started sailing almost empty-handed and pulled it off anyway. How was that possible?

And through JOSHUA, they could get in touch with the basics: a solid hull that was proof against anything, two telephone poles I had shaped into masts in a week, a set of sails with many bands of reef points, a good water supply, and room under the floorboards for food. Ready to go! To prove it, we're heading for Corsica. No storm-jib? We'll reef the jib. No genoa? We'll do without for now; a storm jib and genoa will come along some day. So the shrouds are made of phone-company galvanized wire; what's wrong with that? First chance we get, we'll replace them with good stainless steel; that's not the sort of detail to keep us from setting sail. This is our fifth round trip to Corsica, we've already covered more than a thousand miles and it's still early in the season. Whether I replace the stays next week or two years from now doesn't make any difference, except that in the meantime more than ten thousand miles will have passed under JOSHUA's keel without our fretting over details that aren't worth the trouble. And if reefing the jib and staysail isn't enough to get us through a real blow, there's always a simple trick: you heave-to and wait for it to pass. Heave-to with plenty of sea-room, of course, not too close to the rocks.

No winches? We really couldn't care less! The main thing is that we're covering miles instead of wasting time installing gadgets that cost a fortune and aren't needed for the time being. Check out "Attila," the little block and tackle rig I threw together in five minutes. Work with it and learn; its two blocks symbolize our whole story! "Attila," the little darling, light as a feather and strong as an ox, does the work of ten winches, hardening sheets, seating the halyards as tight as steel bars. Sure, maybe JOSHUA will get real winches one day; they'll be faster and more convenient. But meanwhile, thank "Attila" for everything it has already shown you.

I can also thank my crews, because a "master's" teaching benefits not only his "disciples," but also the "master" himself. Each person brings some scrap of knowledge that feeds the entire group. Knead some enthusiasm into that rising dough and it becomes fantastic, pure creation.

After two seasons of cruising school and a hundred and fifty "student-teachers" passing aboard JOSHUA, life was one joyous song. Gone were my lousy days as a sweat-hog and a shit-eater. The broken coolie sweating over his shovel in other people's fields had become the master of a tractor with a three-bladed plow who would someday reap rich harvests from his own land.

Three plowshares under one hand.

The main plowshare was JOSHUA, my beautiful, indestructible boat. She would furrow the sea wherever we went together, powered by wind and salt water, which are free for the asking in every ocean, in exchange for the most basic maintenance, just a coat of paint from time to time.

The second plowshare was my cruising-school certificate. A

gift from the gods, that certificate let me do this wonderful work I loved, work I could give my heart and soul to—and earn a handsome living while I was at it.

The third plowshare was writing, which requires pen and paper, but can soar skyward on the wings of inspiration.

Unbelievable, to have come so far in so little time! And now that I had my tractor in hand, I was well on my way to finally achieving an old, once-impossible dream: what Deshumeurs used to call "reaching escape velocity."

Escape velocity . . . the speed that puts a rocket into orbit. And this time, old man, you're going to cruise so high that life can never again shoot you down like some wild duck . . . It's going to happen before too long, I can feel it . . . sail on and on until I've had my fill of it . . . drop the hook awhile, once I'm drunk on salt spray . . . write a second book, then do a few more seasons of cruising school to crack the whip again, keep the top spinning long enough for another orbit around the world . . . way high in the sky . . . very far away at sea . . . escape velocity . . . and then, a very long time in the future, a very, very long time, when I'm all wrinkled and preserved by salt, quietly spend my old age with a spade in my hand in a nice garden, close to a simple little cabin with Françoise inside still looking gorgeous, a cabin made of solid round logs, and me still in love with my wife in this dream shelter that smells of the pitch of my childhood, solidly planted in our own land . . . close to the sea where JOSHUA waits, ready to set sail at the first call from the far horizon, the way MARIE-THÉRÈSE waited in the Gulf of Siam.

And wham! Barely five years after the shipwreck that left me naked as a worm on that Caribbean beach, Françoise and I were raising the sails on my miracle boat, bound for the unknown.

When I convinced Françoise to come on our far-ranging adventure, it was with the promise that we wouldn't stay away too long from our three children, who were in boarding school. How would I keep my word? I didn't have the slightest idea, but I've learned that life is full of crossroads. You come to one, you take the best path, and that always leads to another crossroad, another choice. And when you're beloved of the gods, a little soul rocked in a warm heavenly hand, you always manage to take the right path.

Deep in my gut, I knew I had to leave, and fast. Every fiber of my body longed for wide-open spaces. Raise the anchor before it gets stuck in the mud of Marseille's Vieux Port. Don't ask too many "how" questions; don't try to solve impossible problems the first time out. Music has its own rhythm, and so does immensity. Everything becomes clear when you're at sea, that's when you have the time to see what's true and what isn't. Make sail, and the rest will follow. Return to your beloved tropics, get yourself under a real sun, far from noise, money grubbing, and complications. Get the hell out; once you're in the heart of the trades with your wife and your boat, everything will become crystal clear.

We started by making little hops as far as Gibraltar. It was our first key passage, and we scuttled into Spanish ports every time the ugly winter sky turned threatening.

Then came Morocco, the Canaries, the Atlantic trades, Martinique, finally the Panama Canal and the mind-blowing flash that hit me when I first saw the vast Pacific.

Then things really took off, with JOSHUA's bow purring with happiness . . . days, nights, days, nights, the sun rising astern and setting ahead . . . the sea, the sea, the sea . . . Go for it, JOSHUA, rush down the waves! Show us what you can do, catch up with the flying fish! And JOSHUA sprinted before the Pacific trade winds that reach all the way to Asia, and were blowing fair that year . . . JOSHUA kissing the rainbow at her bow, turning into light, singing deep in my heart: *Give me wind and I'll give you miles . . . I'm a good boat . . . thousands of miles . . . thousands of miles . . .* The Galapagos, the Marquesas, Takaroa Atoll in the Tuamotus . . . and there was Tahiti, born of the horizon after this half-circumnavigation with the Alliance dancing before my magic boat's bow.

What next? asked the Tahitian gardener with his eyes as he watched me puttering on the quay, in the shade of a century-old mahogany tree. But I wasn't puttering; I was working on something extremely important. Henry Wakelam himself couldn't have come up with a better idea. Tapping with the shaft of my hammer, I was rounding out the bottom of a tin basin I had bought that morning in the Papeete market. The Chinese shopkeepers must have wondered what I was up to, trying out every model they had, putting the basins upside down on my head one after another, like hats. I made the rounds of all the stores before finding the right one, neither too big nor too small, with a rim at least a quarter of an inch wide so I could bolt the basin down solidly. I was turning a dime-store tub into a miracle: a dome over the inside steering seat.

We had made up our minds, you see: we were going to try to return nonstop to the Mediterranean . . . And as I made JOSHUA shipshape for Cape Horn, an image buried in my memory rose before my eyes.

It had been just after *Sailing to the Reefs* was published, before Knocker and Fricaud came along. I had caught up with Deshumeurs, who was growing roses in Vence, in the south of France. I stayed with him from time to time while I was on the road. One day, to my surprise, he told me about a woman in Antibes he said was a psychic.

I'm not one to get taken in by tarot readers or the like, because I don't believe any of that stuff. Maybe astrology, but that's as far as I go. Just as our genetic inheritance affects us physically and mentally, I'm willing to accept that the moon and planets, depending on their respective positions in the sky at the moment of our birth, can leave a permanent mark on our life here on earth. Of course it's up to us to then make the best of this "destiny" by making whatever choices our free will encounters. So I'll grant you astrology. But you'd have to get up early to make me swallow a story about some crystal ball that can tell the future . . .

But Deshumeurs, who could have made his living as a professional poker player, wasn't the kind of guy to let some fortune-teller put one over on him. So I took down the address he gave me, partly to make him happy, partly so I could see for myself.

I was passing through Antibes a few months later and had a free afternoon, so I stopped by to see the psychic—the first time I'd ever visited one. I was dressed like any traveling salesman, my hands hadn't coiled a line in ages and the smell of tarred oakum lay far in my past. So unless she was a goddess from Olympus in disguise, nothing in my appearance would tell her where I'd come from or who I was, much less where I was going.

The woman was fiftyish and a bit plump. She spread out her cards without even asking me why I'd come. If she had, I couldn't have told her, for the simple reason that I didn't know myself. I just came, that's all—and had almost turned around on the stairs, I was so embarrassed. The psychic stared at her cards for a long time. I hadn't opened my mouth except to say, "Good afternoon, madame." If she was looking for hints, I wasn't about to give her any. I waited. She was in no hurry, and neither was I. I had the whole afternoon free, and it was chilly outside.

She gathered up her cards for the third time, shuffled the deck, and spread them out again. She sat still for a long time, as if fascinated. And then she started to speak, in a steady stream, about water: "Water . . . a lot of water . . . lots and lots and lots of water . . ." No sentences, just the word "water," but so much of it that her eyes widened, unable to believe that such a mass of liquid could exist on the planet . . . It was all she could say: "I see water . . . I see water . . . I see water . . ." And suddenly she went into a trance . . . she was beneath Niagara Falls . . . completely out of her body . . . carried into some other world where a huge torrent was crashing down on her . . .

After five long minutes that felt like a century, she came to, panting, her forehead damp with sweat, her gaze still far away. With a kind of surprise in her eyes, she noticed me sitting there. That did it, it was finished, the crisis was over, she was back on earth. She mopped her brow. By then, I was intrigued. I wanted to ask her a few questions, even if I wasn't about to believe in any crystal ball—or her deck of cards. "This water, madame, is it fresh or salt?" She didn't know. "Ahead of me or behind?" She said she saw water ahead, in the future. If there was any behind me, she hadn't seen it; she only saw water ahead. And that liquid churning held neither death nor misfortune, just water, water, water as far as she could see. She couldn't tell me more, that was all she had seen.

Our Tahiti pals were bringing us their farewell presents. Françoise was stowing the last things in the cabin. We hadn't stinted: six months of stores and two hundred gallons of water. I had written to Jean-Michel Barrault, by then the editor of *Neptune* magazine, to let him in on my crazy scheme. But I asked him not to publish anything before we reached port, whether somewhere in Chile under jury rig or in Europe, if the gods were with us. "You understand, old pal, we don't want to attract the Evil Eye by blowing our horn too soon."

Life is so fantastic. If you had told me when we left France that JOSHUA would attempt to return by way of Cape Horn instead of the Torres Strait and the Indian Ocean, I would have bust a gut laughing. Me, go to Cape Horn? You've got to be kidding. And yet, it would soon be time to head there.

Crouched on the quay, I ran my eyes over my boat. Everything on board was ready. God, JOSHUA was beautiful; a real bird of the capes. Bolted to the cabin roof hatch, the tin basin had become a bombproof cupola; with its five tiny Plexiglas windows, it looked like a tank turret. I had also finished rigging a seat on gimbals near the inside wheel. In case of a hard blow, we would be able to steer from inside the cabin, out of the cold and spray, safe from breaking waves. JOSHUA, my bird of the capes! She was the one who had given me the answer to the problem of being away from the children too long. She gave it to me as she rushed before the trades, asking for wind, more wind, and still more wind . . . real high-latitude wind, the wind of albatrosses, the wind that has howled since the beginning of time, and, before JOSHUA's bow, thousands and thousands of miles, all the water you could ever dream of . . .

. . . And JOSHUA succeeded in returning from Tahiti to Alicante, Spain in one shot. For six days and six nights, Françoise and I had taken turns at the inside wheel in a gale that felt like the end of the world, in squalls that sometimes blew like a hurricane. The sea was surreal, huge in its beauty, bursting with life, a sea you could never describe, with waves five hundred to seven hundred feet long that broke over hundreds of feet without tumbling down the swells that bore them. Six days and six nights of taking one wave after another, drunk with exhaustion and amazement . . . one after another . . . one after another . . . a million times, with water everywhere . . . water to infinity . . . water all the way up to the steering dome at times . . . water that roared and sang with the same voice for six days and six nights, binding us to JOSHUA forever.

Then Cape Horn in fair weather, seven weeks after our departure, with the white glow off the pack ice very far to starboard in the night . . . and the great calm in the lee of the Horn, the unreal calm, sheltered by the Horn, in which we made love for the first time since Tahiti, like little woodland animals, honey I love you, I love you too, under a high-latitude sky that melted into that of the tropics . . . Then bidding farewell to the albatrosses, heading north toward Gibraltar with all sails set, dorados and flying fish, the Southern Cross sinking in the sky while Cassiopeia rose a little higher each night.

Time flowed like a peaceful river through four months of limitless horizons and space, with the high latitudes imprinted on our souls forever, the near-perfection of an immense journey pulled off without a hitch along a blazing wake in which the passage of time had ceased to exist.

It was the story of the little boy who left his village with the little girl he loved, to seek the Enchanted Bird which had always called to him. And she followed him deep into the jungle to the place where it became magical, to the foot of the Tree That Stands Alone where the Great Bluebird sings. There they stood together and looked, in front of the Sacred Temple. And the gods entrusted the boy with the Stone of Power to help him remember the long, beautiful journey the two had made into the unknown to come see them. But when the boy returned to his village, he was greeted by the scent of incense sticks and lots of noise. It was such an uproar that it made his head ache, after the songs of the fairies that spoke silently in the deep woods. The noise was all about the marvelous stone, a nugget so big and beautiful that no one on earth had ever seen the like.

A world record!*

I hadn't thought about it before or during the great journey. I had pulled off the biggest triumph of my life just like that, without planning to, almost by chance, a huge triumph that smashed through a barrier no one had ever dared attack before.

Halfway around the world by way of Cape Horn!

Fourteen thousand miles with the anchors stowed away in the forepeak!

Four months at sea, fully half of it in the most ferocious seas in the world, arriving with crew and boat intact!

I didn't get puffed up over it, nothing to worry about from that point of view. But you really won the lottery this time, old man, a stroke of luck for the ages . . . You aren't about to let this slip through your fingers, are you? Open your eyes and look: You've got luck, *baraka*, it's right in front of you, reaching out for you . . . Are you listening, or daydreaming? If you're too dumb to get it, I'll lay it out for you. Look here, this is the *baraka*. And inside, what do you see, shining through as clearly as the sun in a blue summer sky? Look closely: it's your escape velocity!

All right, I can tell you're getting interested, you're finally

---

*In early 1966, JOSHUA's four-month journey by way of Cape Horn was the world's longest nonstop yacht trip.

starting to wake up! So get busy and light the fuse of the shooting star that will carry you into orbit, hurry up and write a terrific book about the great voyage to the ends of the sea, that's what will put a concrete launching pad under your rocket.

But wait, there's just one more thing you have to get through your skull: your book absolutely must come out before the Salon Nautique, that is, in ten months at the latest. At the boat show you'll really hit the jackpot. Listen to what I'm saying: the media are still in a frenzy, they'll use the Salon to spread the word that you have the magic stone, and they'll make a hell of a noise about it. It'll be like that day the monks at the temple beat their drum to call people from the other villages to come to the big *badamier* tree when Phuoc's father caught a sawfish that was longer than his boat. So don't give the monks time to slow down, hurry up and write the book while the media drums are still pounding, and your escape velocity is a done deal.

And that's exactly how I lost the Alliance. I worked too quickly . . . No, not too quickly; not long enough. It isn't the same thing; in fact, it's very different. For *Sailing to the Reefs*, I had done my best, and I could feel proud of that book. For *Cap Horn à la voile* [*Cape Horn: The Logical Route*], I did my best too, I really did. But I didn't go all the way, not in the last three chapters, which were just copies of my log entries. I had scribbled those entries on the run, between putting in reefs, handling sail, recovering from days of fatigue and tension—in a word, everything involved in a sailing passage, whether long or short. When you're writing in a log, you don't have the leisure or the perspective to do more than set down the high points, the landmarks that might help you write a real book later on. Provided you then take the time that is essential if you want the third dimension to emerge in the final writing.

The third dimension—the only thing in writing that puts anything real across to a reader—was exactly what I had failed to convey in my three final chapters. Yet they covered a key section of the book, the whole second part of the passage home, from rounding Cape Horn until our arrival: two and a half months out of the four at sea . . . the passage of time becoming more and more magical . . . time stretching out to infinity, with a song vibrating within me like a guitar chord linking me to the sky.

In those vital pages of the book, I had failed to transmit that sacred song from afar, that message from the skies. I had produced a fake. And by the time I realized what a crime my unforgivable blindness had led me to commit, it was too late. The presses were rolling furiously to make the opening of the Salon Nautique.

The book was a smash hit. People fought to get their hands on it, praised it, even gave it a so-called "literary" award. But I had lost the Alliance. I couldn't look myself in the mirror without wanting to spit in my face. On bookstore shelves, the book was like a finger pointing at my soul and saying: "Traitor . . . you're a traitor . . . you've betrayed everything!"

And it couldn't be fixed. When a book has been published, you can't just rewrite the last three chapters for the next printing. Everything is already set. A publisher's production department couldn't care less about the regrets and metaphysical anguish of its authors. Especially with sales booming and orders pouring in from distributors.

The few months of summer that followed gave me a kind of respite. I didn't have too much time to think. The wheel was spinning at top speed. Things were busy aboard JOSHUA, with cruising-school students vying to sign up for my classes. On the outside, everything looked normal; the captain was doing his job. But when I looked within during my few quiet moments, it all rang hollow, like those beautiful shells people stick in their windows. I praised "Attila," the little block and tackle rig as strong as a pair of buffaloes, which had now seen the Horn; I immersed myself in taking reefs and trimming sail between Toulon and Corsica; I taught and taught and taught . . . but it was all a façade masking the deep wound inflicted by my conscience.

Then came September, the end of the season. The last crew went ashore and I was left face to face with myself. A great emptiness lay before me. I alone knew the crime I had committed. I couldn't confess it to anyone; even Françoise wouldn't have understood what I was talking about. And besides, what was the point of talking? What could I say? What would I explain? When a thing is done, it's done; you can't go back, take a big sponge, wipe it out, and start fresh. I was trying to solve a problem that had no possible solution. And I knew the finger would keep pointing at me until the end of my days, without my ever being able to escape it.

October was devastating. Wrapped in total silence, sucked down by a huge inner emptiness, I sank into the abyss. Wandering the same labyrinth that Françou had known years before, I met the Monster that had killed my brother. That's where he had died, to pay for shedding Bai Ma's blood. I felt madness burrowing into my guts like some hideous beast. I found myself wondering what last thoughts come to someone who has swallowed a lethal dose of poison and is watching his being becoming lighter and dissolving, just before tipping into the void. I saw my brother's ghost with hallucinatory clarity. Standing between me and the Monster as if to protect me, Françou was screaming words I wasn't able to hear, frantically waving, seeming to show me the way to save myself. But all I could see were the slimy walls of the labyrinth, with no way out except that of paying my debt the same way my brother had.

I must have been on the point of suicide when the Child hurled the lightning bolt that paralyzed the Monster. In one blinding flash, an entire part of my future appeared before my eyes, and I saw how I could redeem myself. Since I had been a traitor by knocking off my book, what I had to do was to write another one to erase the first and lift the curse weighing on my soul.

A fresh, brand-new book about a new journey . . . a gigantic passage, on the scale of the Alliance itself.

Drunk with joy, full of life, I was flying among the stars now. Together, my heart and hands held the only solution, and it was so luminous, so obvious, so enormous, too, that it became transcendent: a nonstop sail around the world by the three capes!

The Antibes psychic . . . water, water, water . . . so it wasn't Tahiti-Alicante that had broken like a wave across her deck of cards spread out on the table . . . it was something else, something absolutely colossal, further, much further, infinitely further. I could already feel that "something else" rumbling and singing within me in a surge of emotion. Tell me, old man, do you have any idea what you're going to be attempting? I mean, do you have the slightest idea?

Incredible, how energy can expand and accelerate to smash all obstacles, once the goal can be clearly seen. Without wasting a minute, I started readying my weapons, down to the smallest detail. The four months nonstop of Tahiti-Alicante had shown me exactly what JOSHUA still lacked to become the superb traveling companion with whom I would soon confront the Dragon that had robbed me of the Alliance. And this time I was setting out for the battle of my life alone.

At Toulon, I worked through the winter and early spring of 1968, sustained by my vision and helped by friends anchored nearby. A second bobstay; a sturdy bow pulpit made of galvanized pipe; ladder rungs of quarter-inch galvanized rebar screwed at regular intervals all the way up the masts so I could climb them to check halyards and oil blocks whatever the state of the sea; four solid sheet winches—a gift from the Goïot firm—and two little boom winches to make reefing easier (though my faithful "Attila" would be ready just in case); stainless steel wire to replace the old galvanized shrouds. The Ferrari company gave me all the material I needed for brand-new sails, and Loiseau sewed it into several sets, in all sizes, with bands of reef-points and reinforcements that would stand up to the nastiest blows.

By early April, I considered JOSHUA ready. I would wait for the first days of summer to take her to Gibraltar. Once there, on the threshold of the ocean, I would wait a while longer, listening to the song of the wind. And the sky and stars would tell me when the moment had come to set out.

While making the technical preparations for the trip, I spent many evenings rewriting the three last chapters of *Cap Horn à la voile*, and produced thirty tightly written pages to replace the fifty loose, uneven ones of the first edition. Deeply moved, I took the train to Paris to hand-deliver the new copy to Jacques Arthaud, my publisher.

"Listen, Jacques. You don't know it, but I'm ashamed of that book. If ever a second edition comes out, even in the distant future, and it could be published in this new form, you can't imagine what a relief it would be for me. And in case things go badly on this trip, I mean, if I end up as shark bait, it would be really nice if you remembered what I'm asking of you today.* Seriously— well, not too seriously—let's say this is my will, and you're my executor."

Aboard the night train back to Toulon, I had to smile as I recalled my little scene in Jacques Arthaud's office about becoming shark bait. The sea isn't like aerobatics or mountain climbing, you

---

* Since 1987, all editions of *Cap Horn à la Voile* have included the text Moitessier gave his publisher that day.

don't go over the edge just like that. Still, the contract for my next book was signed, and Jacques hadn't flinched at the generous advance I asked for. He promised to pay Françoise a stipend for ten months, so my family would be taken care of until I got back. I would spend the rest of the advance on stores—enough for a year, to be on the safe side—and two hundred reels of 16 mm color movie film. Maurice Choquet of the Beaulieu company loaned me a little marvel, a new Angénieux camera with three lenses on a rotating turret. I planned to bring back some beautiful images this time; not like Tahiti-Alicante, where we took off with two pitiful rolls of 35 mm black and white film!

It's crazy what you can accomplish in Paris in a week if you hustle and knock on the right doors. At Jacques's suggestion, I asked the Ministry of Youth and Sport for help—I couldn't believe my nerve—and got it on the spot! My boat would be hauled out for free at the Toulon navy yard, which would also give me all the charts I needed, plus stores, gear, and French navy cold-weather clothing!

Dawn . . . I felt I hadn't slept during the trip. Lyon, Valence, Marseille, I saw all the stations go by. We reached Toulon. In a few minutes, I would be on board. In my mind's eye I could see JOSHUA, more beautiful than ever, eager to spread her wings for this enormous marathon. A feeling of total completeness filled my chest. It was one of those rare moments when life is racing full steam ahead while speaking very simply. All clear astern. All clear ahead.

At that early hour, the quay was still deserted. Heavy dew; a *mistral* sky. The wind hadn't risen yet, but I could feel it coming. It was chilly. France isn't really my country; I had spent only five years of my life there, perched like a bird on a branch. The gods of my native Asia are different from those in France. Still, I love the atmosphere of French bistros, with their human warmth. It was in those sometimes noisy places that I wrote all of my first book and much of the second. The hubbub didn't bother me; quite the contrary, the mood helped my inner wanderings.

Sitting in front of a café-crème in my favorite harbor bistro, I contemplated JOSHUA's beautiful red hull extended by the powerful bowsprit with its double bobstays, the little steering seat dome, which had seen Cape Horn, the two rugged masts with their ladder rungs . . . my boat, pure and simple. She lay twenty yards away, between Henri Cordovéro's CHALLENGE and Michel and François Feuga's magnificent BLUE TROUT. I owed those three pals a lot; they had really pitched in to help make JOSHUA what she had become.

When I came in earlier, I had noticed a guy chatting with the bistro owner. Now he came over to my table.

"Are you Bernard?"

I invited him to sit down. He said he worked at the London *Sunday Times* and that his paper had sent him to talk to me about a very interesting project. Another sailor, Bill King, was getting ready to attempt the same journey I was. The *Sunday Times* wanted to organize a race between the two of us, hoping to attract other competitors. The more boats that entered the race, the greater the media impact.

The rules had been carefully thought out, and could be stated in just a few lines. Each competitor would sail from the English port of his choice on any date he chose between June 1 and October 31. He would bring his boat back to the starting point after sailing around the world solo by way of the three capes, without putting in and without outside help or resupply during the journey. Each was free to leave when he wanted to; the only condition was that he set sail from England. Two big prizes were at stake: a check for five thousand pounds sterling for the fastest passage and a splendid trophy (the *Golden Globe*) for the first boat to return. The rules specified that the same boat could win both prizes if she was both the fastest and the first one home.

"We would be happy to welcome you in England for your departure."

Sitting there, I'm pretty sure I turned pale. The journalist looked at me, probably surprised by my silence. Maybe he expected me to leap up with excitement at the prospect of winning such big prizes. He was waiting for my answer . . . I would have to tell him how I saw things without beating around the bush. He would get it the first time, even if he didn't understand a thing . . .

I told him that the *Sunday Times*'s proposal made me want to vomit. Such a journey, beyond time and right to our very limits, a voyage so fantastic, with so little chance of success, given what we were attempting, belonged to a sacred domain where the spirit of the sea had to be respected above all. We didn't have the right to muck about in such a beautiful story with our grimy fingers, to turn it into a circus where a bunch of clowns would set out to beat each other for money and a gold globe while the media pounded the drums. I left boiling with rage. Thunderstruck, the journalist remained rooted to the spot.

A week later, he went back on the attack.

"My paper is really counting on your participation. We aren't asking anything of you, so why refuse? Four new boats have signed up since the announcement in the *Times*; we expect at least another two, maybe more. Your Tahiti-Alicante trip was a catalyst. The following year, Francis Chichester did his round-the-world sail with just one stop. So did Alec Rose, soon afterward. Now some exceptional sailors are readying their boats, hoping to raise the ante. And you know, except for the sailing magazines, no French newspaper is paying any attention to your project. Whereas in England, from London to the smallest town, people are talking about nothing but this race, where a dozen boats are going to risk their all.

"It's an incredible adventure, and we want tell the whole world about it. Because it's *big*; because it's *beautiful*. That's the main reason we want to cover this terrific story, and we will. It would be really stupid of you to stay out of it. The *Sunday Times* asks only one thing, that you sail from an English port. For everything else, you're free to do as you please. I beg of you, think it over."

As a journalist, he was sincere and conscientious; he obviously believed in what he was doing. But he needn't have bothered to ask me to give the matter further thought. I had already made up my mind. In fact, I had thought of nothing else, day and night, since our first meeting the week before. So I told him I was leaving Toulon as soon as possible to sail to Plymouth. When he saw how completely I had changed my mind, his eyes bugged out of his head. "Just a week ago you were furious at the *Sunday Times* and rejected the whole idea of a race out of hand. Yet now it seems completely natural to you, since you've decided to participate. Can you explain why, for my readers?"

It's true that some things seem hard to understand for someone on the outside looking in. But I couldn't tell him about the Monster that had tried to kill me in the labyrinth after killing my brother . . . nor about the Child's look as he threw the lightning bolt . . . nor about the Dragon I was preparing to fight on the long way to the three capes, alone . . .

And yet everything within me could be summed up in a simple formula that unfortunately doesn't translate into journalistic prose: *I have made a pact with the gods to recover the Alliance, and must remain pure as the driven snow if I ever hope to succeed.* That was the absolute rock-bottom truth. But unless they could gaze directly into a person's soul, people hearing that would think I'd gone completely bonkers. There's a fine line, a hair's breadth, between the sublime and the grotesque. So I figured I better take the direct path, even if it was a bit steep and stony.

"I've decided to leave from England because it suits me from every point of view. Each of us will run the race he wants to. I'll run *my race*, on my terms. Obviously, given what we're undertaking, not many of us will make it to the finish line. Perhaps none. Maybe our boats will be scattered to the four corners of the world, limping along under jury rigs. But suppose the gods grant that I return safely and that I'm also both the first one home and the fastest. In that case I'll snatch the check without saying thank you, coolly auction off the *Golden Globe*, and leave without a word for the *Sunday Times*. That way, I'll be making a public statement of the contempt I feel for your paper's project. It will be my way of protesting, loud and clear. And don't think I'd have any scruples about cashing the check, because the five thousand pounds will have been purified in the public square. Try to understand this as best you can."

A feeling of friendship had sprung up between us. He looked me straight in the eyes, and my eyes answered him. He was "him" and I was "me," but together we could see that it didn't make any real difference.

We went off to have dinner in some harbor joint and ended the evening over a mug of coffee aboard JOSHUA. And there I told him another side of the story, which related only to sailing. Without all my inner turmoil caused by the *Sunday Times*'s getting involved, I would have blundered past something essential: my decision to sail from Plymouth was a blessing from a technical point of view. As in target shooting, it would give me one last chance to adjust my sights.

At first glance, JOSHUA seemed absolutely ready. But a boat is never a hundred percent ready after spending six months in port and nearly two years without feeling the spray of the open ocean. I had realized this during my days spent mulling things over, with the image of the Atlantic in the back of my mind. The little Toulon-Gibraltar trip—in boring calms, within sight of land—which I thought would be enough to get me going, wouldn't really challenge me or my boat. Whereas Toulon-Plymouth would be a true test: east winds and west winds with my eyes wide open, the Bay of Biscay, ocean swells with no land on the horizon, the approaches to the Channel, time spent observing and feeling tiny details that would take on enormous importance in the future. And then I would adjust my sights one last time during the few weeks at Plymouth before leaving, and the team of boat and man would be perfectly in tune for the great leap into the unknown. "Destiny deals the cards, but we play them." I might as well stack the deck which destiny would be dealing from with as many lucky cards as I could.

My companion returned late to his hotel that night. Next day, he would take the train to London and announce to the *Sunday Times* the good news that I'd been "recruited" to join the race that meant so much to them. In the final analysis, everything was falling into place, the way the last pieces of a puzzle fit into a picture to create a larger, unified whole. This crazy race would take place whether I liked it or not. So if I could take the *Sunday Times*'s money without compromising myself, it would be a nice tankful of fuel to help me reach my beloved escape velocity. Because with the small fortune I'd sunk into preparations, I was just about flat broke.

Stretched out on my berth, eyes wide open, I listened as the gods of Asia came to hold a meeting in JOSHUA's cabin. They said that everything had now fallen into its proper place. If I succeeded in my nonstop sail around the world, that would be good. If circumstances forced me to stop en route, that would also be good, because there, too, I would have done my best. They knew that I would accept no compromise . . .

. . . and JOSHUA pulled off the biggest triumph of her career. She took me far beyond my dreams, to where time ceases to exist. Together we had rounded Good Hope . . . Cape Leeuwin in south Australia . . . Tasmania . . . New Zealand . . . and finally Cape Horn! All without breaking stride across three limitless oceans, in under six months—though I had long since lost any sense of time. It was just a question of holding out, which was in the present.

On the little globe my friends on DAMIEN* gave me, I spent hours hypnotically contemplating the huge loop drawn around the world with JOSHUA. And the loop stretched on toward infinity in my thoughts, with the highest points of future and past embossed like markers along the long way. I would dream, holding

---

*DAMIEN: Gérard Janichon and Jérôme Poncet's boat, aboard which they undertook a splendid voyage from the far north to the far south, by way of the Amazon.

that globe of pale blue cardboard, far purer than gold, which told of the colossal journey that had become frozen in time . . . the touching loyalty of the albatrosses carrying JOSHUA on their wings all the way across the great emptiness of the Southern Ocean . . . the tame sea birds who recognized my rallying cry and came to eat out of my hand in the great supernatural calm off the Kerguelen Islands . . . and the friendship of the porpoises whose shrill whistling warned me of a deadly reef hidden at wave-top in the fog off New Zealand . . . I also saw the spirits of the forest where I used to walk barefoot with Xai and my slingshot . . . and the islands of my past in the Gulf of Siam with Phuoc's father, who taught me to read within the waves, he who had never been to school and wanted me to know how to do without a compass so I could absorb the sea's messages through my bare skin . . . Phuoc's father, my teacher, who taught me the language of the stars that would announce whether the next day would be calm or windy. In my solitary days full of life and light, I could feel among the familiar objects the presence of the little jar given to me by the old monk of the Cave of Coins. I still hadn't found the key to it, but it had been through two shipwrecks, plus all the labyrinth's darkness of the previous winter, and it was still there, as intact as when I left Indochina aboard MARIE-THÉRÈSE.

The Child would often come sit next to me on the inside steering seat. Together we looked at the sea through the portholes of the dome, that tin basin I had hammered out with so much hope in my heart on the Tahiti quay three years earlier. Unbent under the weight of the breaking waves, it said that we should go on, that JOSHUA could reach the other side . . . where beings and things and time meet in one and the same substance.

When I left Plymouth, I had just wanted to sail around the world without stopping. An immense project, yet based on some very simple elements. A meticulous technical preparation, in which I drew my past experience into the present. I wasn't worried about the physical demands of such a journey and being able to face the long solitude. It would all be new, but as if I had already lived it. I knew the story by heart already; it just sounded a deeper, broader note, on an octave that wasn't unfamiliar. But so as to not lose its meaning, I had to follow the Great Law which the sea had written in my very fiber: "Always keep your boat in perfect shape, sail her as fast as possible, but be careful never to go beyond your or your marvelous companion's limits."

At another level, my voyage to the end of time could be compared to a marathon swim, where body and mind join in a kind of sacred union. JOSHUA was the flesh, I her consciousness, and each became the extension of the other. But for the miracle to occur, everything had to rest on that balance point where every gesture, every effort, even the tiniest detail, all tended toward the same goal: the search for an absolute through the highest possible level in the art of sailing. From that moment on, it became possible to *enter the crack*, as Hao's father used to do, working with his caulking tools on the junks of my village. Hao's father, who saw everything as a whole, with the eyes of the water and those of the caulk.

I don't know exactly when I entered the crack. Imperceptibly, the old rules of a game I once believed in began to blur in the distance as the prodigious shape of brand-new rules, rich with incredible promise, appeared in the bow rainbow. In them I saw the story of the old alchemist seeking the secret of the magic stone . . . But with the passage of time, time frozen in the plain-song of the universe, the seeker after illusion changed shape himself and lost interest in a worthless stone that merely transformed lead into gold.

Then the giant wave returned to carry me further, still further, to the highest parts of myself. With my boat, I glimpsed heights where my heart was on the point of bursting, like some balloon that had flown too high. And in the vastness where wind and sea scatter sparks to the sky and merge beneath the great breath of the stars, I recovered the Alliance.

When I reached the Atlantic after rounding Cape Horn, all my senses picked up the fetid smell of the Dragon. The stink came from the north, in gusts. Tahiti-Alicante had shaken up only the world of cruising. The nonstop sail round the world would be a far more devastating bomb. An eventual victory would bring me only future disillusionment. I would find myself caught in a web of contradictions spun by the Dragon, who was waiting at the finish line to fight me on his own ground, ready to use every dirty trick he knew.

JOSHUA would soon begin her sixth month at sea, as beautiful and powerful as she was the day we left. The long line of foam on the DAMIEN globe would soon intersect the old one marking my descent from Plymouth to Good Hope. When I left, I had expected it would take seven or eight months to turn that dream into reality, barring a major accident. That original goal was now practically at the end of my bowsprit, but everything would be wiped out if I settled for it. The truth I was unconsciously seeking would reveal itself by and by. And I now knew that it was calling me much, much farther.

To return now would amount to never having left at all, to tacitly accepting the old rules of a game imposed by others. It would be to betray myself. The sun, the sea, the wind, the Southern Cross so high in the sky, and the albatrosses that see all things alike, gliding at wave-top, brushing the troughs and the crests to show me the way . . . all were telling me this in the song of the great luminous silence where I had been sailing my soul for so long.

To have recovered the Alliance wasn't enough anymore. It had to be fed on space and light, vastness and beauty, to strengthen it further in my heart . . . follow the magnet of the vast emptiness that reaches to the stars . . . beyond the stars . . . follow my long way in the heart of that peace where spirit fires up the blood and helps it overcome its fears . . . the vertigo can't be helped . . . leap into space at the furthest limit of my thoughts . . . continue at whatever cost and cross through the dream, go beyond it to reach the other shore at the true limits of myself . . . farther than the ends of the earth!

After the Falklands, when the Dragon saw that I had set a course for Good Hope instead of obediently sailing north as I had once planned, he came winging at top speed. Disguised as a Bird of Wise Counsel, he tried to convince me that I was passing up the chance of a lifetime. "Don't you see? There'll be crowds waiting for you up there, with microphones and television cameras. It'll be a frenzy, with glory and money by the shovelful! Can't you see what you'll be missing if you continue on this idiotic course? Especially since you won't get out of it alive?"

Sure I did, I realized it perfectly! I had listened to that song and dance after Tahiti-Alicante, and it cost me dearly. With a single stone from my slingshot I sent the Dragon's feathers flying and left him wallowing in the water, naked as a jaybird. Off Cape Town, I catapulted this brief message to the *Sunday Times* onto a tanker's deck: *I am continuing nonstop toward the Pacific islands because I am happy at sea, and perhaps also to save my soul.*

Right afterward, I saw that the "perhaps" was superfluous. I had been afraid of looking ridiculous when I wrote those few lines addressed to the press, and I yielded to a bit of cowardice and wrote "perhaps." But there was no "perhaps" about it. I was continuing because I was happy at sea, and *also* to save my soul—period.

"The higher the monkey climbs, the more he shows his behind." That's what Assam, my old *amah*, said one day as I climbed a coconut tree with a hole in my shorts. It's true: the fear of looking ridiculous is deeply rooted in every culture; it's been handed down from generation to generation since the dawn of time . . .

Because of that "perhaps," I hadn't quite sent the Dragon down for the count, but I'd given him a hell of a black eye. The Child thumbed his nose at him, which I backed up with my middle finger, and JOSHUA rolled him in her bow-wave before sending him astern like a gob of spit.

We then rounded Good Hope for the second time, roared across the Indian Ocean under shortened sail, left Australia and New Zealand to port, and raced into the Pacific without being able to shake out the reefs. Winter's jaws were already gaping wide, and the glittering stars spoke only of gales that sometimes put the keel in the air among the breaking waves. But the breath of the gods had made me invulnerable, like those knights of old who set out to seek the Holy Grail. And my magic boat with its fabulous wings had eaten up thousands of miles of ocean, had given me the entire ocean sea so I could someday offer it to the lady of my thoughts.

Gazing at my salt-stained chart, mesmerized by a track that seemed destined to go on forever, I nearly went too far in the Pacific. Only brief moments of lucidity let me see that a second rounding of Cape Horn would take me past some outer limit beyond which eternity lies . . . a world totally new, free from ever having to turn back, where one could sail until the end of time among blue dolphins and airy sea gulls. In my extreme fatigue, I tried to say no, but could feel myself being penetrated by the siren song of a white country where a ghost ship from another age sails on and on, never to return.

JOSHUA pulled me from that fatal dream by plunging her masts into the trough of a breaking wave one last time. She was clearly telling me that the time had come for us to find a peaceful anchorage in the calm of the tropics, some lagoon protected from the wind where my boat could rest a while, go to sleep without worrying about anything. A Polynesian lagoon where I could write of the long and beautiful way we had come together.

So we set a course for the trade wind. Two weeks later, the Fairy Tern came to play around the masts to announce the sweetness of her luminous island. We followed her, and the next day sailed through the pass at Tahiti, all lined with white and gold.

And on the DAMIEN globe, the incredible track wrapped one and a half times around the world in ten months of horizons where time and the sea had become united in one immensity.

As soon as I had seen to JOSHUA (hauling out and an overall coat of paint), I set to writing my book, at anchor in Papeete.

When I had signed the contract with my publisher, I honestly believed I would be able to give him the manuscript six months after I arrived, at the latest. To be on the safe side, I had said, "One year, maximum." What wild optimism! I soon realized that this book was beyond my capabilities.

Ten months alone on a boat making her way between sky and sea is something that can hardly be expressed in all its fullness. The blank pages made incredible demands on me; I was face to face with something enormous. This voyage, both physical and spiritual, that I was trying to convey in writing, was made up of gestures that were too simple and feelings that were too intense to be expressed in our poor, everyday words.

The beginnings were harder than I could ever have imagined. What followed was just as hard. It was all hard, from start to finish. From one end of the book to the other, I lived what Steinbeck called "the terrible majesty of writing." I felt like a primitive hunter who had undertaken to turn a half-dozen acres of dense forest into tilled fields with only his poor muscles and his tiny hatchet, praying to the gods for the faith not to give up, not to pick up his bow and run off into the woods before finishing his impossible task. I spent two years slaving away before I saw the end of that Herculean task. I don't know if I managed to enter the crack. If I did, I don't know how deep I went. As the months passed, I very slowly began to feel the text taking on its true dimensions, the way, during a great voyage in uncharted seas, islands appear one by one as you sail on. I knew those islands already, but was discovering them a second time, under a new light, seeking the link that bound them together in the weft of time.

In JOSHUA's cabin, the patient rumble of the trade-wind swell breaking on the distant barrier reef kept me company. The book was coming to life, paragraph by paragraph, page by page, through a mountain of drafts ripped up as the chapters came together. I was feeling my way through my memories, carried along—and sometimes constrained—by my log-book.

It took two years of misery, but also indescribable joys, to recreate in *La longue route* [*The Long Way*] what I felt was a faithful reflection of the incredible journey. In any event, I could do no more. I had put everything I had in me into that book, feeling at times that I had smashed through my own limits, as I had during the most trying periods of the real-life journey.

One final chapter to write . . . and the book would be finished!

I had sailed the long way to make up for my previous book. The old debt no longer existed; it was more than paid off, in every sense. Beyond the deep satisfaction at having produced a work that was far better than I had hoped for at the outset, substantial royalties would soon be coming my way. The jackpot! And with that, no more worries for the rest of my days! That little plot of land, for when I would be old . . . and my magic boat JOSHUA forever nearby, ready to take off at the drop of a hat.

My escape velocity! The thought hadn't even occurred to me, during those two killing years. But I'd be getting the money too, and so much the better; I damn well deserved it!

And then, halfway through what I expected to be my final chapter, the sky and sea lit up very far ahead of my bow to show me the ultimate Cape rising from the horizon—a colossal Cape, completely unexpected, whose existence I could never have suspected at the start. And the message it delivered to me like a thunder-clap couldn't possibly be misunderstood:

"What you expressed by continuing on your way instead of returning to Europe, *you can* now express in your book by an identical act. But to do that, you have no choice but to refuse to accept your royalties from *The Long Way*."

I staggered under the storm's power. The world was crashing in on me. I was lost, I no longer knew what I was about, I was completely at sea. I hoped I had misunderstood, that this was a nightmare I would wake up from. Two years spent working like a galley slave on my book . . . all to give up a reward I amply deserved? You've got to be kidding . . . !

But I had understood perfectly. It was crystal clear. I could see the last piece of the great puzzle of this beautiful story, which had borne me so long on its wings, falling into its rightful place within a quandary I had to resolve with myself once and for all. And from then on, it all became *obvious*.

The day I set my course for the east after the Horn was the day I made the capital choice. *The Long Way* had to carry the same weight as the voyage; exactly the same weight. Accepting my royalties would amount to denying myself, to implicitly erasing the entire passage all the way from Plymouth. For the book to deserve to exist, it had to go as far as the dream that spawned it. Otherwise, it would simply be a nice sea book where fine words told of an exceptional adventure, nothing more. It would lack the deep truth I had glimpsed during my quest for the absolute, during which my thinking had transmuted into a fundamental act joining my flesh and my faith. Just as I had gone to the very end at sea, I also had to go to the very end in my book.

The message I had sent with my slingshot onto the tanker off Cape Town had shaken the public up; it was front-page news for quite some time. The shock wave caused by the news of my "quitting" the *Sunday Times* race was still reverberating on the shores of the Western world two years after my arrival in Tahiti. The ashes of the May 1968 revolution in Paris hadn't yet cooled. I could use that conjunction of events to once again raise questions people had been asking themselves about the meaning of life and its ultimate purpose.

I believe our purpose in life is to participate in creating the world. Each of us according to our sail surface, our draft, our tonnage, our ability to point up, to heave-to, to bear the weight of breaking waves while running before the wind. And I believe in the depths of my being that no one can break that law without cutting himself off from the human race. I became aware of that during those ten months spent in the company of the waves, decoding the faint messages carried by the wind, which had received them from the skies. Those voices-turned-intuition had cleared my path, causing me to turn my back on the stable where mounds of delicious hay were waiting, set out by the Dragon.

To participate in creating the world . . . Yet I couldn't just hand over the royalties I was abandoning to some charity or other. Such a childish attitude would have been a shot in the dark. What was involved wasn't the money, but what money represented: the *material security* I had been chasing ever since my youth.

Giving up my royalties had to be an act both public *and political*, a question I was asking of everyone in my book, the one I had asked myself during the great journey of which *The Long Way* was the fruit. I was aiming high, very high, as far as I could see, right at the edge of my instinct, to where things change their shape. And the Dragon, who had picked up my track, sneered to see the little monkey with a hole in his pants meditating before a gigantic tree whose top reached nearly to the gates of heaven. Far astern were my old days aboard SNARK, when we had simply wandered off to invent the future and accomplish miracles. "To change the world by transforming men"* required not only a strong dose of faith and naiveté, but also a stroke of tactical genius. How could the writing and substance of my last chapter fan the ashes of the great revolt of May 1968?

The Western world reminds me of a truck crammed with millions of human beings roaring full speed toward the abyss. It's nearly there, and is picking up speed every second. It's too late to veer aside; the truck would tip over and go tumbling over the edge. It's also too late to hit the brakes, the wheels would skid and the truck would certainly wind up in the chasm. Nothing can be done to avoid catastrophe, and yet the solution is obvious: *take off*. We've invented the airplane, so why not create its analog in another domain, that of conscious thought?

Back in Paris, the printing presses were getting impatient. I was already a year past the deadline extension my friend and publisher Jacques Arthaud had given me. The book absolutely had to

* The French phrase, *Changer le monde en transformant les hommes* was a key slogan of the May 1968 revolution in France. *(Tr.)*

be wrapped up. Yet as I faced the blank pages of the decisive chapter, I was adrift, hove-to in a dense fog.

Which way should I aim the missile of my royalties to give it some chance of hitting its target? I had run into a brick wall. In despair, I even considered giving my royalties to the Glénans sailing school.

I know of an old legend in which a hunter sets out to feed his village armed with a sling and a magic stone that can as easily kill a hummingbird as a mammoth. But the stone's power lasts only a day, and for one shot. And the hunter can't see the huge animal right next to him, hidden in the shadows of the jungle, while thousands of birds all around call to him. In vain, I listened closely and opened my eyes; I still couldn't see the mammoth. Les Glénans is a wonderful sailing school, a great place for those who hope someday to slip their moorings to learn about life at sea. But choosing it as a target would be laughable compared to the real target I wanted to hit, that was lurking invisible, deep in the fog of my brain. At times, I seemed to catch a glimpse of something, only to have it immediately vanish. I was going in circles, lost in the jungle, searching for the unreachable. And the sun would be setting soon, carrying away with it the power of the stone I held in my hand.

That was when the Child hurled the lightning bolt that raised the book's end to the level of the final passage between Good Hope and the Pacific. And I was dazzled at the enormity of the act revealed by that flash, which would finally make *The Long Way* the perfect reflection and physical extension of the long, beautiful voyage. I finished my book the way a jeweler cuts a precious stone that is unique in all the world. In it, the disposition of my royalties appears in the form of an allegory with three symbols: the *Pope*, the *Friends of the Earth*, and the *abandonment of my future security*. A letter sent to my publisher with the manuscript spelled everything out.

My domestic and foreign royalties were to be paid to the Pope "to help rebuild the world." In case the Holy Father didn't accept them, the new organization called the Friends of the Earth was to use the money as it saw fit.

That all seems pretty vague, I'll admit. So I'm going to describe the pieces on the chess board very plainly. It will help people to better understand how I tried to spark an explosion.

On one side of the board stands the Pope. In my heart, he symbolizes the almost dying flame of spirituality that still flickers in the West—a "Christian" West that furiously builds weapons to feed wars in the Third World so as to perpetuate a system from which any sense of the sacred has disappeared. A "Christian" West which deliberately bankrupts poor countries solely to guarantee its material "welfare." And this "Christianity" is born of the wonderful Sermon on the Mount which was given to people two thousand years ago, a message of immense hope that reached right up to heaven . . . and which we turned into a huge swindle backed by our businessmen and our machine guns.

On the other side of the chess board stand the Friends of the Earth. To my mind, they symbolize a *summons* addressed by simple common sense to the Rule of Shame—that blind, crazed West guided by the principle of "anything goes so long as it's legal." A West whose mental and spiritual level is no higher that the tops of daisies. A civilization capable of transforming the world, but which absolutely must find a higher path if it isn't to disappear in the dark pit of a moral, existential, and ecological catastrophe.

By placing the third symbol, the abandonment of my material security, between the Pope and the Friends of the Earth, I was shooting for the moon: a checkmate to our entire political, economic, and moral system. A checkmate that could stir the West's conscience, make the masks fall, and perhaps lead to a kind of cultural revolution. Nothing less!

As you can see, I was playing for the highest possible stakes—no holding back! Best of all, the whole thing held together. I mean it; it could have worked.

If the Pope accepted my royalties, the Friends of the Earth could challenge him in the press to ask *how* he planned to use them to "rebuild the world." And if he refused the money, the Friends of the Earth could then demand to know *why.**

In either case, there would be no escape; the Vatican (representing Christianity) would be summoned to explain itself, not in arcane language before some little committee, but in broad daylight, before the whole world, before the media—whose fundamental mission is to seek out the truth *and tell it*, as a matter of

---

*The Friends of the Earth had a number of media outlets it could use: *Whale Mail*, the magazine *Le Sauvage*, plus a number of other press outlets.

professional conscience. As a matter of conscience, period. Without worrying whom the truth will please.

In my eyes, Christ's message is the greatest, most beautiful message we have received since the world began. So I wasn't attacking religion (or religions), but the false values of the West. I wanted a straightforward answer to the following question: "Are we a bunch of pigs and slobs, yes or no? Is our only goal a full plate and comfort at any price?"

Since the answer to that is obvious to anyone honest enough to face things, a second essential question follows from the first: "Are we condemned to continue being pigs and slobs, or do we intend to assume a human shape?"

In exchange for the material security I was giving up, all I wanted was an answer to those two questions about the meaning of life. And I wanted the debate to take place in full public view.

"The higher the monkey climbs, the more he shows his behind." All right, no argument there. But the monkey didn't feel embarrassed at people seeing his behind; I had forgotten my fear of appearing ridiculous once and for all.

I had also licked the Dragon. He could hang around to his heart's content, he would never be able to make a fool of me again.

Françoise and I had long since broken up. "Being in love doesn't mean looking at each other, but looking together in the same direction." We had chosen different paths. They would not cross again.

I had met Iléana seven or eight months before finishing *The Long Way*. I considered myself unattached; she was too. Coming from God knows where, she stepped off a tramp steamer with nothing but a suitcase in her hand. Just a little suitcase and Rimbaud, Verlaine, Musset, and Baudelaire, treasures she had carried around since her teens, their pages yellowed with age.

A kind of evolved hippie with a very open mind in a head solidly planted on her shoulders, Iléana got a job in a travel agency two days after arriving in Tahiti. The day after that, she found a tiny run-down *faré* facing the lagoon, three minutes by bike from the harbor. The rent was next to nothing; a real miracle. We put a mattress in a corner of the floor, and Iléana swept the place out while I snipped patches out of tin cans and carefully nailed them over the holes in the roof.

It was the prettiest *faré* in the world, right out of a fairy tale, with mice so tame they used to eat with us. I would leave early every morning to go work on my book aboard JOSHUA, then meet Iléana in our dream *faré* at the end of the day. She was a good typist, and did clean drafts of my chapters whenever she wasn't too tired from work.

Then Iléana's belly started to swell. At first, I was afraid. The pregnancy was both too unexpected and too serious. Then, as the weeks went by, I began to feel the baby living and kicking in her body. My fear disappeared, and I started to long to hold this precious little thing in my arms.

But we also had one very serious conversation. I told her that I would always need my freedom, that I couldn't live as a prisoner of anything, or anyone.

I told her that my nonstop trip around the world wasn't my last battle. Nor was *The Long Way*. I would face other trials, and while I didn't know what shape they would take, I knew that they would come, and I refused to fight while locked in a cage.

Iléana said she had understood all that from the very first day, and that she would never blackmail me into staying.

Her belly continued to grow. How could such a slim woman carry such weight? She often had to get up before dawn to meet her travel agency's clients at the airport and deliver them to their hotels; or else the flights would come in at eleven o'clock at night. She spent her days at the wheel of a minibus, driving tourists around the island, with practically no weekends off. I had to make a stink to get her to quit the job, which was much too hard for a woman already six months pregnant. In the past week, she had finally gotten some rest.

Once in a great while, magical moments come along that leave their mark on us forever. One evening, we were going over the final chapter by candlelight, pencil in hand. I was going to send it off by certified mail the next day with the letter about my royalties. I tried to imagine Jacques Arthaud's face when he read it. On the table, our two mice were nibbling scraps from our plates, which I had pushed aside to give us room to work without disturbing them. They were tame, but wouldn't yet let us pet them.

It was nearly midnight when I saw the Dragon between me and the candle. He looked a bit twisted. I knew why, and so did he. In my mind, I gave him the finger and told him to shove off. He answered by saying that he wasn't going to leave before telling me two things. I said, "Okay, but just two things, and then you're out of here."

So he said:

"First of all, you're completely nuts. You've wasted your time writing this final chapter and you're going to waste your time with this royalties nonsense which the media won't possibly understand. The media! They're a pile of shit dressed up in cynicism; you don't really think you're going to give them wings, do you?"

I told him to go fuck himself. He said that I could yell all I liked, I still had to listen to the second thing he had to say. He nodded toward Iléana, who was rereading the chapter, and said:

"Look at your girlfriend with her big belly. She doesn't have a penny. She isn't even sure you'll stick around after the birth of this baby you've given her. She's wondering how she'll get by without any money after you take off for 'new adventures.' It's staring her right in the face, and she's afraid of the future, afraid of being poor. As long as she was alone, it was okay, she could get by. But the kid will be coming along soon, and that's something she can't stop thinking about. She knows she'd have a hell of a time raising him properly with what she can make at her little dead-end jobs. So go ahead, ask her the Big Question, and I'll get a good laugh, watching you come tumbling down from the clouds."

I looked at Iléana for a long time. I will never forget that moment. Lounging in her chair, her head bent back, she was looking up at the rafters where a pair of mice were building a nest. She had sustained me with all her tenderness and all her strength during the hard trial of the ultimate cape I had to round in my final chapter so as not to lose what was essential.

But what was essential for her? I looked at her face in the candlelight, looked at her huge belly, and I could see a future ahead that wouldn't exactly be a bowl of cherries. *She couldn't not be afraid*, just as I had been afraid as I rounded the great cape, tossing all the baggage overboard to save the one thing that really counted. And I was still a little afraid, even though the stormiest waters were already astern. But there was still one final reef, more or less hidden in the fog, to get past.

I absolutely had to know what she considered essential: the security which money represented to raise this child without too many problems, or letting go of the comfortable branch and flying through space toward the great unknown that awakens the spirit? I needed her answer, *beyond the shadow of a doubt.* Then I would know whether the depth of her soul was rock or mud. And I proved myself as vicious as the Dragon when I put the Big Question to her, well wrapped in cowardice so it would really hit home.

"Iléana, listen to me. Everything will be played out tonight; it will be white or black. I'm due to mail the chapter tomorrow, but we still have time to think it over. And I'm beginning to think it would be stupid to give my royalties to the Pope or to anyone else. I thought I'd been touched with grace when I wrote that last chapter, and maybe that's why it's as good as it is. But cutting the two pages about the Pope won't make any difference to people who read the book, since those pages will never have existed. If you think it best to burn them, without anyone being the wiser, then I'll go along."

As the probe sank home, I had the impression Iléana was dying. But I had to be absolutely sure she would answer me truthfully. And when the probe reached bottom, what it hit was rock. The pain in her eyes was no lie. "To think that I was so proud to be carrying your baby!" she said. "And here you are, bravely talking about future battles, yet you're turning tail at the first *real* fight! Your nonstop sail around the world wasn't a real fight to the finish: you went on *mainly* out of love of the sea and your boat, not just to save your soul. This book brought me all the way to tonight because it's pure—and you want to kill it?"

I entered into her eyes then, and as she felt my great joy, her heart instantly understood everything. I put my hands on her shoulders in the dancing candlelight and said: "There have been other women in my life, and there may yet be others. But you will always be my Queen; because now and forever, you are the Lady of my Thoughts."

And the Dragon skulked off, crawling. The business of giving my royalties to the Pope had nearly broken him; now he had lost a leg after what we had achieved together, Iléana and I.

CHAPTER 16

The wind picked up soon after the Fairy Tern's visit at dawn to tell me about the atoll. The bow rumbled with pleasure as it plunged through the sea. Suvorov was very close.

Four years before, I had been in Tahiti when I received the first copy of *The Long Way*. That very evening, Iléana went into labor and was rushed to the hospital, where she delivered premature twins. Erwan, who weighed two pounds, twelve ounces, died two days later. Stephan, at three pounds, one ounce, developed jaundice and turned as yellow as a lemon. I didn't think he would live either, but he hung on. It was both terrible and wonderful to see that tiny bit of our flesh clinging to life in his incubator in the hospital, without our even being able to warm him a little with our hands. Slowly, he began to make his way toward the light; it had been a near thing. After forty days in a Plexiglas box, the miracle baby would finally get his mother's breast and the tenderness he needed so much.

Stephan grew into a little boy whose eyes sparkled with curiosity, and who delighted to hear his mother read from Kipling's *Jungle Book* or *Just So Stories* each evening in his bed in the *faré*.

Before leaving for Suvorov, I had made Stephan his first slingshot. We went into the guava groves together to look for a forked stick that was just the right size for his hand. I showed him how you hang a real magic slingshot around your neck so as to never lose it. And Stephan learned how to choose the right stones, neither too big nor too small, as round as possible. I promised him I would return to Tahiti in six weeks at the latest, for his fourth birthday. By the time his papa returned, he would surely have made great progress in handling that fabulous weapon which makes streetlights tremble and scares away dragons.

High in the sky already, the sun was glittering on the crests of the swell, turning it into billions of tiny pearls as it crashed on Suvorov's barrier reef.

The deep emerald-green pass was before the bowsprit, wide and straightforward; you could run it under sail alone, whatever the vagaries of the trade wind. Dozens of terns and noddies wheeled above JOSHUA's masts, welcoming my pretty red and white boat with their piercing cries.

Once in the lagoon, the magic of the island took over, with only the rustling of water at the bow, the murmur of the wind caressing the sails, coral heads clearly visible here and there, with plenty of open water around them. Tom Neale's island was less than a hundred yards on the right. Bird Island was two miles to the left.

First I would anchor in front of Tom's place, like all the visiting yachts that called here on their way west. I was bringing him supplies, as well as a new machete; his old one had been pretty worn the last time JOSHUA called, already two years before. Then I would make my pilgrimage to Bird Island.

The old hermit was happy to see me again. Into Tom's *faré* we carried a hundred pounds of rice, a sack of flour, three jerrycans of kerosene and four sleeves for his Aladdin lamp with the circular wick—it burned a lot of kerosene, but gave him light to read by—two boxes of condensed milk, sugar, coffee, oatmeal, and cans of vegetables and fruits. (The hurricane season was coming and Tom wouldn't have any visitors for six months.) He was especially pleased that I had remembered his machete. Then we dined on one of his big, plump chickens.

The next day, I waited for the sun to climb into the sky a bit, so as not to have it shining in my eyes, and took JOSHUA to anchor off the place Iléana and I had baptized Bird Island. The terns were so numerous they made a deafening cloud, their thousands of cries drowning out the rumble of the barrier reef. Stephan had been two years old when we first visited, and we had to watch him. We also had to walk carefully, lest we step on the chicks; little brown balls of down that ran every which way, they were forever throwing themselves under our feet.

When we first "discovered" the island, only twelve coconut trees were growing on it. I planted a hundred and thirty more, using my machete to clear space around each one so the relentless underbrush wouldn't shade it or crowd it out. A coconut tree needs light to spread its fronds. It took a lot of sweat to cut the dense *tahinu** shrubs back. But on the third day, I came across a miracle.

It was late in the afternoon. Staggering with fatigue after ten hours of planting under the blazing sun, I was digging in the sand with my bare hands to plant a beautiful sprouted coconut. It was the last one of the day and I wanted to make a particularly nice nest for it.

As I dug, the sand started getting damp. When I reached water, about two feet down, I knew it would be salty. Without thinking, I tasted it . . . and got the shock of my life. It was as sweet as the water in the frog pond at my childhood village!** Iléana was weaving palm fronds to make a hut for Stephan. I called her over and we widened the hole into a funnel shape and lined it with flat pieces of coral to keep the sand from sliding in. Then we planted three sprouted nuts around the well, which would be the heart of Bird Island.

Iléana had made a stink when I raised anchor the week before, leaving her and Stephan in Tahiti. She'd had her heart set on coming to Suvorov as well. But I had a compelling reason for setting out on this pilgrimage alone: *inside, I was completely wiped out.* I felt an enormous need to come back here, to think about these last years, to have an intimate talk with this mystical island, which might answer my question.

Ever since *The Long Way* came out, the Dragon had been tracking me. He was still limping, but was accompanied by a little slimy animal whose name I now knew; it was *Doubt.*

In the beginning, I hadn't paid him any heed. But the two intense years spent finishing the book had brought me to my knees. Then came the anxiety about our son's birth and our worry about

---

**Tahinu:* The Tahitian name for *Tournefortia argentia*, also called *Messerschmidia.* A shrub normally ten to twenty feet tall, though it can grow to thirty-five.

****At the time, I didn't know that in all atolls, a layer of rainwater lies on top of the seawater beneath. No mixing occurs in the sand, so the fresh water, which is less dense, "floats" on the salt water the way wine will float if you gently pour it into a glass of water.

his delicate health. A year passed before we were really sure he would make it.

Besides the two coats of paint I had given JOSHUA when we reached Tahiti after the great journey, I had completely neglected my boat. Until I was finished with my writing project, I had carefully resisted the temptation of the marijuana that was being passed around on the quay. But once the proofs were corrected, I felt drawn to this herb, with its flavor of the East. I already knew what it smelled like, and I really wanted to try it.

Those were the great days of the Papeete quay, with visiting sailors of every nationality debating philosophical questions, holding discussions that went on late into the night by our boats, near the banana trees we had planted along the waterfront to try to slow the steamrollers that were killing the greenery.

The magic joints went round and round among my group of pals on the quay, like a game of "Button, button, who's got the button?" We wanted to remake the world, based on new principles. The marijuana went round and round, and I was rarely the last one of the bunch to grab a joint as it went by. The more I smoked, the more I saw the world through rose-colored glasses, while missing the realities under my nose. Insidiously, total laziness took hold of me. I became a chatterbox who had forgotten the point he wanted to make. I quit taking care of my boat. I let my guard down.

When I realized the danger, it was already late. Not too late, but late just the same. And I learned a lesson about myself I won't soon forget. Grass can easily turn into something that saps your willpower; you start to think, "Everything's cool, man." That much was clear . . .

From that moment on, I launched a feverish effort to save JOSHUA from disaster. She hadn't been touched by so much as a paintbrush in three years, and much more than a paintbrush was needed now. I had to go at her with scraper, metal brush, and a hammer to chip at the rust—and all the rest. A steel boat will forgive your hitting a lagoon coral head at six knots, a chunk of flotsam, or even a very angry sperm whale. But it won't stand being denied the most basic maintenance for three years. It may seem hard to believe, but it took me nearly a year to dig my boat out of the hole we were sliding into together. And the cost in sweat and guilt was high.

I had to get out of Tahiti right away. Stephan would soon be two; we were finally ready to set sail for new horizons: New

Zealand. Miguel, a twenty-two-year-old American who had crewed to Tahiti on a big yacht, had fallen head over heels in love with JOSHUA the first time he saw her. He was an excellent sailor and had been a real help when I hauled out. So when I asked him, "Do you feel like coming with us?" I thought he would faint with joy. His sea bag was on board within five minutes.

I had often heard about Suvorov and Tom Neale. The atoll was on the way to New Zealand, a perfect stopover where you could take care of final technical details before heading for the less friendly seas where the westerlies blew.

Iléana had done some sailing before, and was eager to make the New Zealand passage, which would be her first real taste of blue-water cruising. And she wanted to get away from Tahiti for a while as much as I did. We needed a change of scene, to shake things up, to try something new.

Crouched on the Papeete quay, my chin in my hands, I looked at my beautiful boat, as good as new again. Miguel was at his girl-friend's this evening, saying goodbye. Iléana was taking care of a few last things at the *faré*. I watched as the sun set behind Moorea, etched in mauve against the sky. God, that island was beautiful! I closed my eyes, the better to keep the image deep in my heart, the better to say goodbye.

When I opened my eyes, the Dragon was in front of me with his slimy little sidekick. "See how happy the monkey is to have saved his boat," he said. And the little animal fell on the ground in a fit of laughter. I knew why they were mocking me: my big play of giving my royalties to the Pope hadn't generated the slightest re-sponse. Two years after the book came out, the money was still quietly waiting at my publisher's.

In spite of my natural naiveté, I had known at the outset how huge the bet was. But I still hadn't expected such a complete de-feat, such a dead calm after my attempt to shake up people's con-sciences. Since *The Long Way* had come out, neither the Friends of the Earth nor the Vatican had reacted. Nor had any of the media. It was as if I had passed the ball to a center-forward who was completely in the clear ten feet in front of the goal; all he had to do was shoot . . . and he had been looking the other way.

Instead of puffing on joints with my buddies on the quay, maybe I should have started making noise the moment the book was published, roared off to Paris like a rocket, moved heaven and earth. But we all have our limits, and I know mine. I'm a modest monkey who is happiest on the lower branches, naturally lazy and shy. I'm not a gorilla with nerves and muscles of steel who can shake the jungle with a roar. And even if I had been, what difference would it have made? I didn't dare ask myself that troubling question; I was almost sure I knew the answer.

You can't act for other people. If overnight someone with a magic wand had planted millions of fruit trees along all the roads of France, along all the streets of our cities, and in all the public parks, they would be ripped out . . . so our children wouldn't be stung by wasps hiding among the ripe fruits, so they wouldn't get diarrhea from eating the green ones . . . so our dear babes wouldn't get scratched climbing in the branches . . . so our darling children wouldn't risk falling and splattering the sidewalk like so many cow pies. You can't play other people's games; you can't see for them if they don't want to look.

JOSHUA had forgiven me my long neglect, thank God. At least she was safe, and hadn't suffered too much with the business of the Pope's royalties. Gleaming with fresh paint, with new shrouds all around, she was saying that the time had come to raise anchor, to go back to feeling spray and reefing sails, to thinking only about those simple things you do with your hands. In time, maybe the insidious wound inflicted by doubt would heal.

Iléana and Stephan came aboard, Miguel and I raised the anchor, and we were off for New Zealand by way of Suvorov. Our three-month stopover came as a revelation. Nothing I had heard about Tom Neale and his atoll was more than a pale reflection of what I actually saw there.

Tom was the soul of Suvorov. At seventy-two, he had been living on the atoll so long he had lost track. One day, he had fetched up there, perhaps guided by fortune. And stayed.

They say that fortune is God's logic. Even if I sometimes pretend not to believe that, deep down I know it's true.

Fortune had created that blue-green lagoon protected from the great ocean swell by its crown of coral. Over the millennia, a few rocky islands had risen, shaped by innumerable hurricanes whose gigantic waves slowly ground the chalky rock into sand. Then seeds carried in the feathers of sea birds nesting on other distant islands had sprouted in the desert. And a coconut drifting on the great ocean current had washed up there, carried by a wave higher than the rest.

Thus, thanks to fortune, are born all the world's atolls. But without Tom and his love, his conscience, and his sweat, without his magic shovel and machete, this speck of dust lost in the middle of the Pacific would never have become Suvorov. And if there is one place in the world I am sure to return to, it is this enchanted atoll protected by Tom's aura, which the Dragon would never dare approach.

With his slimy little cohort, the Dragon was waiting for me when we reached New Zealand. I had barely set foot ashore when he said, "The monkey should read the newspapers and find out what's been happening, he'll find it fascinating." And the slimy little animal laughed so hard, he nearly choked.

I knew the broad outline of the story he was referring to; it had been all over Tahiti before we left. But I didn't know the details, because of our long stopover in Suvorov, where I quit listening to the radio except for weather reports. So I picked up the newspapers, had all the press clippings on the subject sent from France—and something in me snapped. After this, I would never have faith in humanity again. Because the story could be summed up this way: *Once again, mediocrity had triumphed by dragging a great and miraculous event down to ridicule and oblivion.*

Here is the story of that thwarted miracle. I am telling it after a lot of reading and having spent many evenings in New Zealand with the people who had sailed on FRI.

FRI, a barge-like 65-foot sailboat, had left Auckland seven or eight months before, bound for Mururoa, the French nuclear test site about eight hundred miles east-southeast of Tahiti. There were thirteen people aboard, including three women. Their purpose was to sail into Mururoa's territorial waters and stay there, hove-to, to prevent the detonation of the next bomb. They were simply saying, "The Bomb is bad for everyone; we have to try something else."

When they saw the old tub coming, the French authorities in their wisdom decided: "Better not bother them, it will just make for bad press. We'll ignore those jokers, they'll soon get tired of bobbing around and will leave on their own after a face-saving last stand. And we'll set off the bomb as planned. There's no hurry, it isn't even ready yet."

An old wooden boat, FRI was making water at an alarming rate and the crew had to take turns at the pumps day and night. Pachouli, one of the women, had been pregnant when they left Auckland. The Bomb knew about it because FRI was in radio contact with the New Zealand press. It was one more point in favor of the Bomb's policy of cautious waiting. The FRI people would have to knuckle under eventually, if only because of Pachouli. They would leave soon; human endurance has its limits. But the Bomb had no way of knowing something unimaginable: that thirteen gods were living in FRI's heart, thirteen gods who held in their hands the power to create a miracle. They would never knuckle under. And they spent four months standing up to the Bomb. In spite of a woman so pregnant she was about to burst. In spite of short rations. In spite of the exhausting work of pumping day and night to keep afloat an old rotten boat that would neither sink nor leave.

Finally, the Bomb got angry. It couldn't stand FRI's taunting any more. The carefully planned nuclear program couldn't be delayed any longer. So it came out to hail the damned boat, planning to tow her away somewhere, far from Mururoa. But when it stepped aboard with its helmets and truncheons, it was knocked for a loop. Because in addition to the thirteen nuts, they found a general aboard. And not just any general, but General Jacques de Bollardière, who had arrived a couple of days earlier after tacking two thousand miles from the Cook Islands aboard a little sailboat with Brice Lalonde and the priest Jean Toulat. It was a bolt from the blue, and with all the world media in the know, there would be no way to hush up the "scandal." A French general . . .

As I re-read the Paris newspapers for the nth time, I felt like throwing up. When a guy with hippie tendencies tries a stunt like giving his royalties to the Pope, I can understand that well-meaning, docile people with their noses in their plates might shrug their shoulders, scratch their heads, and say, "He's just crazy, he'll outgrow it."

But here a general, respected by his fellows and by the entire nation, had proclaimed loud and clear at Mururoa, that "Not only is the Bomb dangerous, it's unnecessary. We can stand up to a military invasion and triumph with nonviolence." And his country's media had quietly covered it up—and the bigger the audience, the bigger the cover-up. I felt like shooting myself, like never believing in anything anymore, and never wanting to hear anyone talk about humanity again—and especially not about France.

"Go see Philip in Jerusalem," said Iléana. "It'll give you something new to think about. And maybe you'll find an answer there."

By then, we had been in New Zealand for six months. I was turning in circles. I didn't know what to do with my life, and couldn't see so much as a glimmer on the horizon. "Go to Jerusalem," Iléana insisted. I could leave JOSHUA in complete safety in Peter and Pachouli's care at Opua Bay. Iléana and Stephan would wait for me with some of our other FRI friends who lived in Auckland.

But what could Philip teach me? Since finishing *The Long Way*, I hadn't spent my time just getting stoned with my Tahiti pals. I had read and meditated about almost everything written about life's great questions: *The Tibetan Book of the Dead*, René Guénon, Sri Aurobindo, Satprem, Carlos Castaneda, Lanza del Vasto, *The Center of the Cyclone* by John Lilly, the works of Lao-tsu and Confucius, *Be Here Now* by Ram Dass, the Bhagavad-gita, Yogananda, Gurdjieff and Ouspensky. In the course of two years, I had met all those masters through their writings. But they apparently hadn't been able to teach me much, beyond a few fragments that quickly dissipated. So what could Philip show me that would help get me back on track—or at least see my existential problem a little more clearly?

Still, I was at a complete dead end in my life, and I knew Iléana was right. I had to go to Jerusalem. It was my last hope.

I had met Philip shortly before leaving Tahiti. He spent three days aboard JOSHUA and when he left, gave me his address at Ein Kerem, a small village on the outskirts of Jerusalem that was the birthplace of John the Baptist. Philip said he would be glad to have me spend a few months in his little community if I ever felt the need to come. "You never know," he said as he hugged me before leaving. And if I hadn't known from the first instant that Philip was a true master—in the flesh, not just one of those masters in books—I would have sensed it at that moment, his embrace radiated so much power and peace.

So I took the plane to go see Philip. Before continuing on to Jerusalem, I stopped in Paris and told my publisher to deposit the royalties from *The Long Way* in my bank account. Sales had surpassed 100,000 copies in less than three years. Money doesn't bring happiness, as I well knew, but it didn't bother me a bit to suddenly find myself rich. Having resolved the conflict between my dreams and reality once and for all, I then caught a flight for

Tel Aviv to spend two and a half months in Philip's community at
Ein Kerem.

There were three of us besides Philip: two old-timers, Jim and
Maurice, who were very far along in the "work," and me, the newcomer. From time to time, others would come to spend a few days
or a week in the tent set up for them thirty yards from the house,
between the orchard and the garden.

Philip's teaching can be summed up in one deceptively simple
sentence: "The spirit is a tool that can be sharpened like any
other tool, not only to give it an edge, but to prepare it for a work
of creation which each one of us on earth can choose to accomplish."

As for the actual sharpening . . . whew! It wasn't a matter of
just pushing a button and watching it happen. I found myself pro-
pelled into the discovery of a world whose existence I would
never have suspected without having had a glimpse of it thanks
to Philip.

The "work" began with a group meditation from 4:30 until
dawn, followed by a variety of mental exercises largely based on
the teachings of Gurdjieff and Oscar Ichazo (a Bolivian master
who had been the teacher of John Lilly, among others). Not a
minute was wasted between rising and going to bed, and the least
of our actions had to be *conscious*, even the few minutes of rest
we took during the day. Philip also wanted me to keep a diary, in
addition to my group activities. I resisted at first, but he insisted.
So I had to get out of bed several times a week at three in the
morning to keep up the rhythm of my writing.

In addition to theoretical study and the difficult *mentations*
(which I won't try to explain here), tai chi chuan played an important role in our program of *self-awakening*. Philip and Maurice,
who were both tai chi masters, made us practice the discipline for
a solid hour, morning and evening. In the beginning, the extreme
slowness with which you accomplish this martial art drove me
completely nuts. As a former competitive 100-meter swimmer, my
entire life up to then had been a series of bursts of speed followed
by peaceful moments of complete rest in which I recuperated. In
fact, I had always been lazy, hurrying to finish my job as fast as I
could in order to take it easy for as long as possible. Ten weeks of
tai chi under Philip and Maurice's guidance helped me to glimpse

the benefits of slow movement, when its major purpose is the repatterning of the brain.

During my entire stay with the group, Philip made me work intensely on the mental level; you had to sharpen the tool. I worked hard on the physical plane as well, spending as much time as I could with a spade or a pick in hand among the fruits and vegetables. I took on the project of enlarging the garden and planting more fruit trees. I've always believed in giving sweat to the earth. And if I were to forget everything I learned during my stay at Ein Kerem, one thing would remain: a good cucumber hole will feed you for a few weeks, whereas a cherry, plum, or walnut tree will yield for fifty or a hundred years. Planting a walnut tree takes no more sweat than digging a cucumber bed, and the tree has a chance of lasting longer than our good intentions.

As I said, whatever the work, whether mental or physical, it had to be done *consciously*. Knowing who was working, who was thinking. Was it a machine, or *me*? The aim was to move to another plane, to see from above, to try to see more clearly inside yourself, to separate from the function, to strip away the "mechanicality," to try to act on the working of the machine instead of letting it just carry you along. Well, enough about that. It's too complicated to explain in words, and I'm already starting to feel like a monkey who accidentally puts his hairy hand on an electric switch and then thinks he can tell others how you make light in the darkness.

The last I heard, Iléana was about to board the plane to fly back to French Polynesia with Stephan; she hadn't been able to renew her visa to stay in New Zealand. So I would be sailing JOSHUA alone back to Tahiti after my stay at Ein Kerem.

Philip thought it useful for me to take advantage of my visit to Israel to get to know the country a little in the short time I had left. So I spent eight days traveling in the desert with a group of about twenty pilgrims. What I saw blew me away.

I dipped my hands in the aqueduct that carries water from Jerusalem to Jericho, winding for twenty-five miles along the hillsides. Less than three feet across and lined with unmortared stones, it had been built before the birth of Christ.

I swam in the Dead Sea, a thousand feet below sea level, in

water so saturated with salt I could hardly dive in it. I bathed with my companions in the Spring of David in Ein Gedi, a crystal-clear oasis in the middle of the desert.

I meditated before the ruins of Masada perched high on a seemingly impregnable plateau which the Romans had besieged. They had spent three years building a huge ramp leading to the little encampment, and when they reached the top, found only corpses. The warriors and their families had all killed themselves, preferring to die rather than accept Roman slavery.

I climbed the majestic stairway of heavy stones, cut by monks more than a thousand years ago, that rises from the plain and climbs hour after hour to the top of Mount Sinai, where Moses received the Tables of the Law. Overcome by emotion, I looked out over an immense expanse of desert where no sound reaches your ear, not even that of an insect. A desert of sand and stone where a people had wandered for forty years, listening to the voice within. And among my companions hungry for God and miracles, I noticed a beautiful woman of twenty-two (I was nearly fifty) gazing at the grandeur around us. She had done some sailing and read a few sea books, including *The Long Way*, which she thought wonderful. When I told her I had written it, her eyes widened, and she made it clear that nothing would make her happier than coming to spend a few weeks aboard JOSHUA, visiting the bays of New Zealand before I sailed for Tahiti.

So it was at the very top of Mount Sinai, with my head in the sky and my feet solidly planted on the rock, that I felt the Old Monkey beginning to get back on his feet, after all the wonders I had witnessed in the Holy Land.

During my last three weeks at Ein Kerem after that pilgrimage, Philip worked me with such intensity, I would never have believed I could stand the effort. We focused on three kinds of nourishment for the human machine: food for the body, breath for the soul, and impressions for the spirit. And when Philip accompanied me to the airport the day I left, he told me the story of all those who are seekers like him, like me, like many others here on earth:

"Sooner or later, the truth-seeker finds a 'master' on his path. He receives his teachings and after a while leaves to go dig in solitude, sure he will find Truth. Then come doubt and fatigue, and he goes to look for a new 'master' who will enlighten him further.

And this continues until the day he finally understands that the master's teaching is no more than the shovel you use to dig with.

"Because the master can only teach his own technique for making the tool. The Truth-Seeker has to make his own, shaped to his hand and unique in the world. Some need a narrow, pointed shovel. Others a wide, rounded one, either somewhat flat or very scooped. The handle will be every shape imaginable, short or long, thin or thick, flexible or stiff, and either straight or slightly angled at the top or bottom. It depends on each person, and no shovel will be quite like any other. But don't mistake the shovel for the Truth.

"In any case, you always dig alone. And the shape of the shovel is much less important than the thought, sweat, and faith with which each of us digs his well in search of Truth."

When we parted, Philip hugged me very tight and said, "When you see the light, you'll want to cry. But don't forget to laugh in the darkness."

Back in New Zealand, I took stock of things. I had been away for six months. To keep in close touch with Iléana, I had regularly mailed her my diary about Israel and the rest of my travels: two and a half months with Philip, three months visiting in France, and a two-week stay in Hong Kong, where I rediscovered some of my old Asian roots. JOSHUA had been waiting patiently under the vigilant eye of my friends from FRI. I hauled her out, then spent another four months waiting for the end of the hurricane season. I spent the time helping Peter and Pachouli create a beautiful kitchen garden surrounded with kiwis on their land at the end of Opua Bay. The corn grew thick, the beans climbed up their stakes day after day, and the tomatoes flourished. Then I said goodbye to everybody and headed for Tahiti, happy to be back on the great ocean which is so simple, with its west winds to keep you on your toes.

Philip was right to think that the "work" and the sea had a lot in common. I talked to my boat, asking her how long my soul would retain a little of Ein Kerem in the coming years. In her wake, I could see the naked Indian of the Amazon forest who set out to discover the ends of the earth. After walking for ten days, following the sun, he saw a giant dragon-fly land in a clearing with a terrifying noise. The gods that came out of the enormous insect's belly gestured for him to draw near. So he came close; he even touched the gods. But none of his people would ever believe the story, so he didn't speak of it, except to his wife, who awaited him back in their hut of woven branches. He already knew that he would someday forget the great dragon-fly which had taken him far into the sky with the white-skinned gods, and had set him down in the same clearing at moonrise. He also knew that his village would never look the same to him again.

I had an exceptional passage from Auckland to Tahiti; eighteen days without once dropping the genoa. I anchored at Papeete on April 10, my fiftieth birthday. Iléana had found a *faré* ten minutes by bus from the harbor and was making beautiful *pareu* wraps which she dyed on the lawn and sold in the local stores.

My boat was in need of attention. The sails were old and worn; they dated from the time of the long way, already seven years before, and had to be completely re-stitched. I wanted to do it by hand, pushing on a sailor's palm like in the good old days, when things lasted. I brought the sails to the *faré* so I could be close to Stephan, who hadn't seen his father for more than ten months. Sewing helps you think; your fingers pull on the needle and stroke the fabric, and your mind wanders. What was I going to do with my life? I wondered. What could I devote it to? I listened to Stephan's babbling. Together, we planted papaya seeds along the embankment by the road.

"You see, you just dig with your pick, drop three papaya seeds in the bottom, cover them up, and someday there will be papayas for people who pass by here; it's easy. And on the other side of the road we can plant mango pits if you like, just for a change."

What will this handsome little boy with his eyes full of curiosity be like, when he is my age? I wondered. Since the beginning of the world, parents everywhere have wanted their children to be better than the previous generation. Yet the world has remained pretty much the same. Egotism and stupidity are very firmly rooted.

More than six months passed.

I was watching Moorea in the setting sun, but with new eyes. That island, which I had thought so beautiful when I said goodbye to it two years before, I now found stupid and useless. Its neglected slopes, covered with worthless vegetation, didn't make any sense. The place was only good for postcards. A large part of Moorea could have been covered with pines, mahogany, and trees for lumber. Looking across the road, to Tahiti's highlands, the panorama was just as depressing. Hundreds of thousands of acres should have been planted with trees years ago. In our own *faré*, which was like every other *faré* in Tahiti, *none of the building materials were local*: corrugated iron, imported lumber rafters and lintels, plywood walls and partitions, cement floor and stoop—everything had been shipped in from somewhere else. Freighters came here loaded with food and supplies, and left empty. People ate things they didn't produce.

Except for a tiny minority—held in check by a bunch of vultures and a wall of general passivity—an entire people had simply given up. "In his hands, man has everything he needs to create a wonderful world, but he prefers inertia."

There I was again, overtaken by a huge depression. I hadn't seen the Dragon since my stay at Ein Kerem. I thought I had gotten rid of him, yet here he was, circling around me once again. Ein Kerem hadn't solved the problem. I hadn't been the one to create the light I had seen; it was fortune, a stroke of luck. And the light had gone out without my being able to rekindle it.

It was then that I heard Suvorov, the magic atoll protected by Tom's aura, calling to me. I had to go back there, to think. But it wouldn't be to practice meditation in the lotus position, tai chi, *mentations*, and other stuff that was too complicated for me. It would be with sweat, pure and simple, the sweat that would help my coconut trees flourish on Bird Island. Maybe they would help me answer the question that had been tormenting me for so long: "What should I do with my life; what should I devote it to?" Ein Kerem hadn't answered it; maybe Bird Island would.

So I hugged Iléana and our little boy tight and promised I would be back in seven weeks at the latest, in time for Stephan's birthday. And I set sail with old Tom's supplies, not forgetting his new machete.

And thus, a quarter of a century after leaving on SNARK and MARIE-THÉRÈSE, twenty years after MARIE-THÉRÈSE II, a monkey in search of the truth was anchoring his beautiful JOSHUA off Bird Island, where the Dragon could *never* come bother him.

I hadn't stirred from the boat since my arrival the day before yesterday. Like a lover who rejoins his beloved after a long absence, I was gently becoming reacquainted with Bird Island. Stretched out on deck, I filled my eyes with the lagoon's emerald-green reflection on the bellies of the terns flying by the thousands above my anchorage. I had been careful to anchor fore and aft, in case the wind changed. But I knew it wouldn't change. It was blowing fair from the east-southeast and JOSHUA was floating on a lake, sheltered by the magic island.

I daydreamed as I looked at the carpet of ten- to twelve-foot *tahinu* covering the island. My coconut trees were still much too young to have risen above them. A few more years, and they would win out.

Of the hundred and thirty coconut trees we had planted two years before, how many would have raised their fronds toward the light? Surely a good hundred, maybe more. Before leaving Tom, I had collected fifty sprouted nuts; they would be the second generation. Tom showed me how to select the best ones: big, heavy nuts, with only three leaves, young enough not to have become accustomed to their native soil, so they would adapt easily to a new habitat.

The sun was beginning to sink. I piled my fifty coconuts in the dinghy along with my shovel, pick, and machete. Then I swam to shore, towing the overloaded boat onto the little submerged sand bar in front of the beach. The coconut tree I had planted at the very tip of the northwest point was no longer there, which I sort of expected. It hadn't had any chance of making it; the spot was too dry, too windy, blasted by the sun from dawn to dusk. I had tried, telling myself, "You never know." But I couldn't help but feel a little twinge in my guts just the same. I had lavished care on that tree, almost certain I was averting the unlucky fate that attended its birth. I had even built it a windbreak against the trade wind that blew across the point.

I unloaded my nuts, shovel, and pick under the big *tahinu* at the edge of the lagoon. Ever since Ein Kerem and the garden at Peter and Pachouli's place at Opua, a shovel and pick had become part of JOSHUA's tool kit. I wasn't planning to do any work that day. I took only the machete with me as I went to say hello to my island.

The trail leading to the well had almost vanished, but my bare feet picked up its trace. Incredible, how bare feet can find a path that your eyes can't see. I was walking on a cloud, my entire being filled with the pleasure of rediscovering my island. In no rush, I moved without hurrying, chopping here and there with my machete, clearing the dark green tunnel of *tahinu* branches as I went. I heard a little voice whispering, "The brush sure has grown quickly." But another voice answered, "Brush can't win out against a good machete, and I plan to use it."

I reached the well . . . and doubled over with a sudden stab of pain in my gut. The little voice had been preparing me, but I couldn't believe what I saw. Of the three coconut trees planted in a triangle around the well, two were dead and the third nearly choked by the *tahinu*. As for the seven coconut trees we had planted in a large circle forty feet across, like a crown to protect this sacred spot that symbolized the heart of the island, none had survived. The *tahinu* had smothered them all.

Two hours later, I was back at the edge of the well, my gaze in the distance. I had checked everywhere; not the smallest corner had escaped me. Of the hundred and thirty coconut trees we had planted with gallons of sweat and tons of faith, only five remained.

I thought of Ein Kerem. Gather energy by meditation. Create emptiness within. Like heaving-to, with the staysail aback and the tiller down. A little tai chi near the well to see if it worked while hove-to as well; it did. I watched as my body slowly split into two; one part of my being was here, while the other part, keen as a well-sharpened machete, floated lightly over the magic island to prepare the next movement, which was already taking shape. Within me, the sea began to calm, the sky began to clear.

Now I was watching as Suvorov blurred in the wake. My body was numb with fatigue, my hands full of blisters, but the job was done. It had taken me fifteen days to put the fifty sprouted nuts in the ground. It hadn't been lightning work, but this time the trees were well planted, each one set in the middle of a large area cleared of all noxious roots and watered with sweat. Philip and old Tom had labored at my side, Philip in *self-awareness*, Tom in *tenacity*. And the Child had played with the clam shells, perhaps a thousand years old, that my shovel turned up here and there in the sand.

Before leaving, I stopped off to see Tom and talked with him about Doubt. Perhaps a few scraps of it were still clinging to some dark part of his being. Tom burst out laughing, and said, "Sure, I often used to feel doubt in the beginning. But very rarely now. And when it happens, I piss in the crack of his ass, and he gets the hell out!"

Coming to Suvorov, I hadn't known what to think. I'm not sure that Bird Island completely answered my question. But one thing is certain: I would never give up on the great love affair between Man and Creation. I would pass this way again after the hurricane season, bring Tom fresh supplies, and plant more coconuts on Bird Island. And keep on doing that for another few years, until the day when Stephan would need fresh mental stimulation. Maybe head for China or America then. There was plenty of time to think about it.

But always, now and then, I would make my little pilgrimages to Suvorov.

Two weeks of tacking against the trades. Tahiti glimpsed at dawn before the bowsprit. The Fairy Tern coming very far out to greet me and confirm that I was on the right heading. Tahiti growing as I approached. I would reach it in a few hours if this easterly wind didn't back around to the southeast too soon, as it usually did early in the afternoon. But no, here it was veering ten degrees—perfect! Everything was going right. I eased the sheets slightly and JOSHUA took off.

I was arriving five days before my little boy's birthday. I hoped he hadn't lost his beautiful magic slingshot. Anyway, he would be getting a big cake with four pink candles stuck in it. I would get my own cake a few months later, with five big candles and one little one.

I was amazed to see Iléana standing on the quay, ready to catch the mooring line I threw her. How could she have guessed the day and hour of my arrival, when they had still been mysteries to me this morning? With eyes like two glowing flowers, Iléana gave me some wonderful news. She had been busy during my Suvorov escapade, and had taken Stephan to visit the Tuamotu Archipelago on the copra schooner that resupplies the islands. And she had found a wonderful atoll, neither too big nor too small, where Stephan could go to school until he was seven.

The atoll had a safe anchorage for JOSHUA, she said, with a tiny dream island nearby. We could build a *faré* together there, an easy two-minute walk from the village across tide flats that were covered with seashells.

She said everybody there was expecting us, that Stephan had made friends with the villagers and they hadn't wanted him to leave.

And I said that life was just fantastic!

CHAPTER 17

AS we pounded into the waves, the miles added up with agonizing slowness. Sailing is a long lesson in patience. I checked to see that the halyards were good and taut, the sheets not too tight, the heading about right. Okay, that would do. Everything was clear ahead, with no squalls on the horizon, so I took off on a little trip into the great beyond. My boat and I had been sailing together for so many years, no formality was called for when I drifted away on one of my frequent mental escapades, disappearing into a parallel world where time no longer existed. In a deep reverie, I was contemplating a long line of covered wagons from the last century. They had left the east coast of the United States, drawn by the lure of California, where people and things would be different. I could see those families, hungry for open spaces, covering thousands of miles and shaking the past from their shoes as they went. With hearts full of hope and wagons loaded with everything they would need, they had set out in search of something new.

JOSHUA alerted me that the wind had shifted against us and I quickly leaped back into the cockpit. We had to come about; the other tack would take us past the north side of Rangiroa Atoll during the night, which was much less dangerous than the unpredictable currents off Rangiroa's southern point. Iléana and I exchanged a glance. Even though the sea wasn't her element, she was in seventh heaven. We had kicked the dust of old dreams from our bare feet and were forging a brand-new path toward the future, following JOSHUA's bow. The future was called Ahe, an atoll in the Tuamotu Archipelago, two hundred fifty miles east-north-east of Tahiti.

Barely heeling in a force five wind that occasionally gusted to nearly six, an overloaded JOSHUA was grudgingly beating into the trade wind. She had never been so low in the water, her deck awash at the slightest wave. Loaded to the gunwales, she looked like a half-submerged submarine. In the cabin, we had to slither like eels among crates and sacks to reach the galley and the sink pump. Stephan crawled behind the mountains of supplies, teased the cat, got scratched, cried a little, then went to sleep with the cat in his arms. Thank God, he didn't yet know that his pretty white mouse with the pink eyes had chewed through her cardboard box and escaped . . . I thought of the damage she could do . . . How would I ever catch her? . . . Lord, I hoped she wasn't going to have babies . . . What a mess!

We were stewing in a damp cabin that was crammed to the ceiling, the hatch sealed tight so waves wouldn't wash in and soak everything. Crouched on a sack of flour wedged in front of the stove, Iléana was thinking about what we would have for dinner. In a quiet voice, she wondered aloud if we could make do with a pot of rice and a can of mackerel. The only thing that mattered to me just then was making miles toward our goal with my overloaded boat, whatever the cost.

My eyes half closed, I mentally ran through our incredible load: a ton of topsoil in hundred-pound sacks, plus four sacks of chicken manure to get our garden plants off to the best possible start; three rolls of wire fencing to keep the village chickens from wrecking our tomatoes and pumpkins; five lemon trees in pots; four 5'x3' sheets of glass I could use to make a still to condense seawater into fresh if the rainy season was late; ten sacks of cement for a cistern; four sheets of aluminum, two glass panes, and styrofoam, which I was thinking of using to build a solar oven for cooking (to see if it really worked, as I had read in a book); three almost new mattresses, a gift from the Navy, which had been about to auction off a batch of them; ten five-gallon drums of kerosene, with handles that would make them first-class outhouse and garden buckets; seventy pounds of nails to build the main *faré* and Iléana's studio (she planned to send her *pareus* to Tahiti); four gallons of Xylene; three lengths of wide-diameter plastic piping for gutters to collect rainwater from the thatched roofs; a large clay filter which could produce five or six quarts of drinking water a day in case the water from the roofs turned out to be questionable; four bundles of empty sacks which were sure to come in handy. To this mass of supplies, we had added a year's worth of food, not to mention the many gadgets and tools that would be invaluable on an atoll that didn't have anything remotely like a hardware store, where you had to make whatever you needed with what was on hand. And that was just what was in the cabin.

As for the load outside, it took me back to the days of my Gulf of Siam junk, whose deck had been piled so high with logs that you had to make the slightest maneuver very carefully, so as not to capsize. It included all the planking for our future *farés*, which would be built on stilts, all the beams for the floor joists, and sheets and sheets of old plywood we had salvaged from the navy shipyard. Four empty fifty-gallon drums were lashed to the railing, which would hold our precious water supply while the cistern was being built.

At sunrise, Rangiroa was still visible astern. I watched as JOSHUA struggled against the wind and the sea. Six months earlier, I would have spluttered with indignation if someone had predicted that one day my beautiful bird of the capes would look like a fat water buffalo staggering through the mud, pulling its plow.

But the past was already far behind us. Like characters in a Mickey Mouse comic book, we were off on new adventures.

If I hadn't had an engine, the Ahe pass would have given me real problems. It is relatively narrow and parallel to the direction of the trade wind, so you have to tack into it. Doing that under sail alone would be unthinkable in JOSHUA, a heavy, long-keel boat that didn't maneuver very well in tight spaces. But the little ten-horsepower diesel roaring along at full revs helped the sails a lot and eliminated the risk of a failed tack, which would have put us on the reef. Just the same, I breathed easier once the foam-laced coral was all behind us.

The lagoon welcomed us into its open arms and dressed for the occasion, with luminous colors and silvery pearls thrown up by the bow. We were charging along on a broad reach under a cloudless southeast trade-wind sky. Dangerous coral heads stood out against the surrounding blue and could be spotted well in advance. My belly was filled with terrific joy. I wanted to play with the wind and the coral, skim past the great scattered polyp-covered shelves, their carpets of sea urchins close enough to touch, the bottom dropping from zero to a hundred feet and more. Here, sailing took on a whole new meaning. After the open ocean swell, it was wonderful to crisscross this beautiful calm, blue water in every direction, to make love to this lagoon which had seduced me from the very first moment, to breathe in the scent of the nearby islets that protected us from the great waves beyond. A long time ago, when he was ending his trip around the world aboard CHIMÈRE, Jean Bluche came up with the most beautiful image of what an atoll is: "Not quite land and not quite sea, but a union of the two, a gift to the sailor in an azure jewel-box surrounded by immensity."

The time had flown by so fast, we were already at Tenukupara, the village a few miles beyond the pass. What awaited us was an anchorage you see only in dreams. It was protected by a horseshoe-shaped coral outcropping awash at low tide. A concrete quay about a hundred feet long extended almost to that natural breakwater, leaving just enough room for one last tack before you entered the nest.

With her anchor well set in three fathoms of water, fifty yards from a beautiful white sand beach in front of the village, JOSHUA was resting as if on a lake. Total protection. I couldn't believe it; only a real hurricane could threaten my boat in that exceptional harbor. In the Tuamotus, the least sign of bad weather usually sounds the alarm for the crew, which has to be ready to cross the lagoon in search of some other more or less questionable anchorage while waiting for good weather to return. And you can get in serious trouble if you're slow to make up your mind. But this place, whichever way the wind blew, held the promise of total peace.

Soaked with spray, dazed by the sun, we felt elated; best turn it to our advantage. We finished the unloading that very evening, temporarily storing our tons of supplies behind the *faré* on Poro Poro *motu** where Patrick and Diana lived with their two children Josh and Loïc, aged five and seven. Stephan was overjoyed to be with his pals again.

---

*The coral islands or islets which surround an atoll lagoon are called *motu*. Some *motus* can be six or seven miles long, others are tiny. In Polynesian, *u* is pronounced like the *ou* in "you."

After the briefest of showers (not a drop of rain had fallen for months), our friends showed us around. Twice as long as it was wide and running east-west, Poro Poro was about an acre in area. Half of it belonged to Raumati and Tepuku, a couple who lived in Tenukupara a few minutes' walk away on the main *motu*. The other half belonged to five or six families who also lived in the village. After Iléana's visit the month before, Patrick and Diana had spoken with all of them. We were free to occupy the part of Poro Poro located near the outer tide flats, on the ocean side.

Some thirty coconut trees, planted here and there as if by the hand of fortune, dotted the western half of Poro Poro, along the lagoon. Halfway between the two ends of the island, a white sand beach stretched as far as its western tip. To the left of where the beach began, facing the anchorage, was a deep-water cove hemmed in on either side by coral rock as hard as a lava flow. Facing this swimming pool-aquarium stood Patrick and Diana's *faré*. Built completely of Polynesian materials, right down to the smallest detail, it rested right on the ground at the edge of the beach, practically in the water. Search my memories as I might, I had rarely seen a more beautiful place, or a corner of the world that more clearly made you feel the sweetness of life.

I did wonder about the rest of Poro Poro, though. The eastern part of the *motu*, facing the barrier reef on which the ocean rumbled, was nothing but sand, which gradually became solid coral as you walked out on the tide flats. Except for a big century-old *kaaia* tree (*Guettarda speciosa*) with branches twisted by the wind and one stunted coconut palm, there wasn't a scrap of shade anywhere. A rotten tree trunk had somehow washed up here; when I kicked it a bit, it crumbled into dust. The soil was arid on this part of the island, with parched bushes that held on any way they could when the trade wind blew hard. But it was the only place we could settle without disturbing our neighbors.

A tough day. From the moment the anchor hit bottom this morning, and except for a snack eaten on the fly, the sweat had flowed nonstop. Now the sun was setting. The entire sky facing the lagoon was pink. The wind dropped. A little cumulus cloud edged with mauve floated above Poro Poro as the *motu* prepared for a quiet night. Seated at Patrick and Diana's dinner table in front of a generous helping of rice and fried fish, we were getting better acquainted with our hosts.

Patrick Humber was French; Diana was American. After building a 50-foot ferrocement boat near Los Angeles, they had left bustling California behind and set sail for Polynesia. A stopover at Ahe had blown their minds, leaving them speechless with awe. When they first sailed into the lagoon, they had expected to stay only a week or so, since they were anxious to go find work in Tahiti. Two months later, they still hadn't raised anchor. Time no longer existed. They learned to speak Paumotu, the Tuamotu dialect. Ahe had become their home port, with the village of Tenukupara symbolizing real Polynesia, where life unfolds as in a mystical dance centered on the present.

Living at the atoll's rhythm, Patrick developed a quasi-religious veneration for Raumati, an outstanding fisherman and *patia* (Polynesian spear) champion, who operated a fish pen. His wife Tepuku became like a second mother for Diana and the children. And Raumati and Tepuku told them:

"It would be nice if you built a *faré* on Poro Poro. Nobody has ever wanted to settle there; people prefer to be together in the village. That way, Diana and the children could live nearby, but in their own place. And then Patrick could start his business shipping fish to Tahiti."

With the help of Raumati and his brother Metu, the *faré*'s framing had gone up in four days. Working at top speed, Tepuku and her women friends wove coconut fronds into the sheets of niau that would cover the roof, walls, and canopies. Patrick and Diana had their *faré* a week later. They also had absolute peace and quiet, because a *tupapau* haunted the island. A *tupapau* is the ghost of someone with a guilty conscience who died long ago. They are much less dangerous than the *ma qui* of Indochina, and Polynesians don't usually worry about them. Just the same, they avoid their immediate vicinity, especially at night. But the *tupapau* never bother *popaa* (Westerners).

As soon as his family was comfortably settled, Patrick sailed for Tahiti with Tepuku's son Siki to equip the boat with a refrigerated hold. He then started hauling fresh fish from the Tuamotus to Papeete. Even though he paid the fish-pen producers almost twice the price set by the commercial schooners, his business was surviving and paying its way.

A few months later, however, fate dealt Patrick a heavy blow: he lost his boat on an atoll near Rangiroa. She was a total loss, and he didn't have any insurance. He had returned to Poro Poro six months ago to sort things out, let some time pass, heal the wound, and help Raumati with the fish pen. Now everything was clear in Patrick's mind. He would soon leave for Tahiti with Diana and the children on the schooner that brought Ahe supplies every five or six weeks in exchange for its copra (dried coconut meat). He wanted to build a new boat and then return.

Two days after our arrival, I was raising JOSHUA's anchor with Patrick and Luciano Ladavas. Luciano and his wife Léo had arrived the day before from Tahiti aboard their sloop GUIA*, en route for the Marquesas before heading for Italy by way of Cape Horn.

In his outboard, Raumati joined us as we sailed for the northern end of the lagoon, where we would gather the wood we needed to build our *faré*. That part of the atoll was covered with *kaaia* trees, crowded so tightly that they grew perfectly straight. "The more we take, the better the next ones will be," said Raumati, "since each sapling you cut puts out four or five shoots. In a year they'll be good for *patias*; in three years, rafters and poles; and in five or six years, good-sized posts for the fish pens."

After three days of machete and hatchet work, JOSHUA looked like one of those inland junks that used to ply the canals of Indochina, loaded so high with bamboo you wondered how they stayed upright. We sailed back to Poro Poro under jib and mizzen because the main boom couldn't swing over the stack of wood.

In our absence, the women had organized the pile of supplies unloaded the week before. Iléana had transformed JOSHUA's boat cover into an awning that covered everything. The women had leveled and raked the site where the *faré* and *pareu* studio would stand. As we unloaded the wood, they peeled the bark the way Diana showed them. By pounding the trunks with a mallet, it came off in big sheets, without any effort. They worked fast, because *kaaia* dries out very quickly. Once it's dry, you can't use the mallet technique; you have to peel the bark with a machete, which is much slower and more laborious. Caught up in the general enthusiasm, the children had joined the peeling work too, banging on the trees with their little mallets of *miki-miki* wood.

With Poro Poro echoing with their rapping like a forest full of

---

*Skippered by Luciano, GUIA had taken part the previous year in the first race with crew around the world by the three capes.

woodpeckers, Luciano, Patrick, and I used a crowbar to dig the holes for the posts. To keep them from rotting, we charred the ends that would go in the ground, a trick known to peasants the world over. We had decided to build the 18'x13' *faré* and the 13'x8' *pareu* studio at the same time.

In the old days I had been like Kipling's "cat that walked by himself," the one who walked alone through the wet wild woods, "and all places were alike to him." But Poro Poro had made me see things in a new light. Something ineffable was stirring within me. For the first time, I felt the need to pitch my tent somewhere for a good long while, to stop chasing after mirages, to look nearer than the horizon, to ally myself with the earth.

Three days after unloading the wood, all the posts were up and the bark peeling was proceeding faster than ever. A week later, the framing for the two buildings was nearly done and we were setting the *faré's* ridge beam. Too bad if all the rafters weren't peeled, we were nailing them on as we needed them. Léo had sewn us canvas belts with a large pouch for nails and a hammer loop.

Laying the floors presented a few technical problems, which slowed the work down a bit. Getting the measurements right and the joist beams nice and level wasn't easy, since no piece of wood was quite straight. We had to constantly come up with new tricks, improvising a level by using a watering hose, resisting the temptation to nail too fast. Patrick was our crew boss; he was calm, quick, and competent, and it was a pleasure to work with him.

In the village, Tepuku, Mama Fana, and Mama Tehua wove palm fronds into sheets of *niau* with their agile fingers. Each evening, they brought us a batch, which Iléana spread out near the tide flats with the leaves facing up. She soaked the *niau* with seawater three times a day, and the salt dried in a thin layer on the inner side. I figured that this treatment would keep our roofs in good shape for four years instead of three, before they would have to be replaced. We would see . . .

It was terrific to be building with your own hands this way, using wood you cut yourself, a machete, hand saw, hammer and nails, and palm fronds picked up from the ground—and surrounded by everybody's warm friendship. Unlike the Polynesian *farés*, ours were being built on stilts, four feet off the ground. It's a bit of a luxury and takes longer to build, but gives you very useful extra space where you can store supplies out of the weather. It also helps keep the sand out, so the inside of the *faré* stays much cleaner. I now know that it's possible to build a traditional *faré* on a deserted atoll, using only a machete and a sharpening stone. Instead of nails, you would use coconut-fiber lashings, as was done all across the Pacific before the great European voyages of exploration.

With the copra schooner that would take our friends to Tahiti due in two weeks, Patrick suggested that we build a family fish pen before they left. He had noticed a *hao* near the tiny *motu* to the left of ours, less than a minute's walk away. A *hao* is a natural channel that the fish on the flats use to return to the lagoon when the tide ebbs.

"If we all work together like crazy, we can get it done in a day. If you agree, we can start tomorrow."

Of course I agreed; having a fish pen would change my life. I had been wasting precious energy spearfishing in exchange for a few mediocre catches. The last time I went looking for something to eat, I'd had to settle for a moray eel after swimming around for almost an hour in water that was none too warm. People think that fish are plentiful on an atoll, but that's only true around the pass and the coral outcroppings far from the village. Off Poro Poro, the pickings were slim.

I asked Patrick why nobody had built a fish pen on that *hao*. The answer was simple: by hopping into an outboard that could do twenty knots, the locals could reach good fishing grounds in five minutes. Or else they would spear fish on their way back from gathering copra on the other *motus*. Besides, Polynesians have hearty appetites; a ten-pound jack or grouper is barely enough for one family meal, and you still had to feed the dogs. Only the little tide-flat fish used this *hao*. Our pen's yield would be modest, but sufficient . . . and far more delicious and pleasant than opening a can of sardines.

Patrick took Luciano and me over to the *hao* to show us what we would be doing. Using the crowbar to dig with, we would set eight posts in the coral at the *hao*'s mouth in a circle a dozen feet across. We would connect the posts with poles nailed to their tops and tack chicken wire around the circle, to a depth of six feet. We would then snip an opening a foot across, and stick a short cylinder of chicken wire through it, close to the water's surface and open to the current, with its end curving downward into the pen. That was how the fish would get in. Once inside, they would swim in circles in the trap, never thinking of leaving through the hole above them.

The next day at dawn, we were on the site. Patrick, Luciano, and I set the posts and hung the chicken wire while Diana, Léo, Iléana, and the three children built two low walls with chunks of coral collected on the tide flats. To work properly, the walls had to extend about a hundred feet on either side of the pen entrance at a ninety-degree angle, like a pair of arms, so the fish would be herded toward the trap. There was only a foot and a half of water over the flats at high tide, so the walls were easy to build, but they required a lot of coral to make their bases strong enough to resist the powerful current of the ebbing tide.

Three hours after noon, we men had finished the post-and-wire trap and we could finally get out of the water to go help the wall-building team. At sunset, we were carrying the last chunks of coral, which had to be brought from farther and farther away on the tide flats. Our shoulders were sore and our hands laced with cuts, yet nobody thought of quitting, not even the children.

Shortly before nightfall, the job was done.

Since our arrival, we had been sleeping aboard JOSHUA while waiting for the *faré* to be finished. The first light of dawn would find us rowing to Poro Poro in the dinghy. We usually all ate lunch and dinner together at our hosts' place.

But that routine changed abruptly, and for the past few days we had been alone. Patrick and Diana had gone to help Raumati and Tepuku at their fish pen near the pass. We let them take Stephan along, who hadn't wanted to leave Loïc and Josh. He also had a third pal, Tutaina, who was Tepuku's son. As the result of an accident in infancy which had damaged his spinal column, both his legs were paralyzed, and he got around with the use of his arms. A very precocious mind made up for his physical handicap. Eleven years old at the time, Tutaina could speak pretty good English, thanks to Diana's lessons. He looked after Stephan like a little brother and would take him fishing for the jacks that were plentiful along the pass.

Léo and Luciano had also left, for good. They had been a great help during their three-week stay. But the best part was what we discovered the morning of their departure, as GUIA's sails were disappearing on the other side of the lagoon en route for the Marquesas. With a pickaxe, they had dug the plot where we had been talking about planting bok choy someday, and spread a thin layer of the black topsoil we had brought from Tahiti in JOSHUA's hold. They built a fence around it, which they covered with dried palm fronds to protect our first plants from the wind. All this, they had done the night before leaving. Working by the light of a kerosene lamp, they must have sweated buckets to give us this wonderful farewell present. They left a little note on a twig stuck in the center of the plot: "We sowed the seeds; don't forget to water them."

At that, I heard a kind of click in my head. All at once, I was back at Ein Kerem and Philip was saying: "When a *shock* from outside comes to wake us up for an instant, that's the time to immediately respond with a *conscious act* and *do* something, instead of simply looking on like a dreamer." Iléana and I started by carefully taking stock of the situation. And we understood that the planting had to start right away, without waiting for the *faré* to be finished.

When they returned from the pass a week later, Diana and Patrick could hardly believe their eyes.

The embryonic garden created by GUIA now had three additional beds and its fence had expanded accordingly. Strands of wire stretched over the beds were draped with coconut fronds to shade the young shoots that already covered Léo and Luciano's initial plot like a soft green carpet.

Scattered among the bushes like hidden Easter eggs and sheltered from the wind, were seven watermelon holes, seven cucumber holes, and seven pumpkin holes. The pile of topsoil from Tahiti was considerably smaller.

Tomato seedlings were beginning to sprout in flats under the *faré*; with luck, we would be able to plant them near the watermelons in a week or two. That trick would save space and work. And ten little bags which Iléana had cut and stitched from a sheet of plastic were filled with soil and planted with three papaya seeds apiece.

Under the big *kaaia* near the tide flats, our compost pile was getting underway. We had started it with the rotten tree trunk we found lying there and palm fronds chopped up with a machete and mixed with some good soil and a half-sack of chicken manure; we watered it with our urine to activate the fermentation. And we had inaugurated our "honey bucket." It was set up right at the water's edge behind a *miki-miki* thicket. I was anxious to see the level in the bucket rise, because the combination of human manure and compost is dynamite for plants.

Best of all, though, was the well! Getting drinking water had been a real problem. The rainy season was late, and we had to haul water in jerrycans from the village cistern. Poro Poro was so small, I was afraid I would only find brackish water under it, which we couldn't use to water our plants. But after ten hours with the crowbar breaking through a cement-hard layer of coral, I reached the water pocket—and found it was as sweet as the water at Suvorov!

Crouched side by side next to the well, our backs aching and our hands covered with blisters, Iléana and I together saw that the game could be won. The water would turn dryness into greenery, and the greenery, as it grew, would give both welcome shade and fruit. We no longer had to worry about the rainy season being late.

One month to the day after first anchoring here, we moved into our *faré*. We had finished the roofing two days before, with Raumati, Patrick, and me nailing the *niau* to the rafters, and Tepuku, Diana, and Iléana tossing it to us in big sheets as we went along. In six hours of work, it was all done. The next day, Iléana's studio was finished as well.

It was fantastic! I felt I was dreaming. All this in four weeks, and there we were, listening to the wind singing in the *niau* of our roof!

Then Patrick and his family sailed for Tahiti and we were alone. One night, by the light of our gas lantern, Iléana was reading Stephan a few pages of *The Call of the Wild*, a book that had enchanted my childhood. By a stroke of luck, I had recaptured the white mouse hiding in the boat. We would set her free tomorrow on another *motu*, far from Génie, our cat.

When Stephan fell asleep, Iléana joined me outside. Hand in hand, we slowly walked around the island. The moonlight splashed the white sand of our kingdom. The old *kaaia* near the tide flats sent us the sweet scent of its tiny flowers. An infinite, otherworldly tenderness enveloped Poro Poro. The night was soft, soft, soft.

By day, though, everything was different. Except for the small, somewhat shady spot where the Humberts' *faré* nestled, and not counting the thirty coconut trees, the *motu* was a blinding desert of sand and coral, hammered by the sun and scoured by the wind. Since our arrival, we had drunk only a dozen coconuts, because of the rats that destroyed everything. And mosquitoes rose in swarms as soon as the wind fell.

But the mosquitoes, rats, fierce wind, and burning sun were vicissitudes of fate, and we would deal with them, and master them.

When a great adventure is launched with a powerful thrust, fatigue in the muscles and doubts in the mind are swept away by a fullness that moves life along like a breath from the depths of the soul.

I had encountered that breath several times in my life, and had learned to recognize it. So had Iléana. It was related to love in the broadest sense, we knew. Love of the sea and love of the earth are the same thing. We had felt that love wash over us when we sailed into the Ahe lagoon. And Poro Poro had picked it up, with all its power.

We didn't know what the earthly paradise that man had lost was like, but we were aware that its seed lived on in our heads and in our hearts. And we could re-create it here, right beneath our feet, by bringing out the god within all of us from the depths of our being, giving this desert the sweat of our bodies and the breath of our souls.

CHAPTER 18

YOU either love an atoll from deep in your guts, or you don't love it at all. If you just love it a little, the feeling soon changes to not at all. There are mosquitoes, *nonos**, flies drawn by the smell of fish, rats that scavenge everywhere, dangerous sharks that cruise the tide flats in a foot of water, terrible stonefishes hidden like chunks of coral among all the rest of the coral, animals that sting and animals that bite. Coconuts fall without warning, seemingly aimed at your head. The sun blazes straight down, then is reflected back up in flames from the calm water to hit you again from below.

But when you look more closely, you notice the lagoon's colors, the light of the pass, the living coral, the breathing of the atoll.

And you see further.

You begin to learn.

And the rest comes very quickly . . .

The first thing we had to learn, and right away, was how to avoid being stung by a *nohu* (stonefish), which can be fatal for a child. Chameleon-like, the stonefish changes color to blend with its environment; you can hardly see one, even on a sandy bottom. It remains motionless and the deadly spine on its back can pierce a plastic sandal. Its venom is similar to a cobra's. No predator would dare attack one; it could probably kill a shark. Like Raumati and the other villagers, we learned to shuffle our feet through the water, especially when blinded by the sun reflecting off the rip-

---

*The *nono* is a tiny sand fly whose bite can itch terribly. It is also found in the Hawaiian islands and the Caribbean (where it is called *yeng-yeng*).

ples. That way, there is no danger; a stonefish's lateral fins are soft as silk, and if you bump into one, it will swim away.

The rainy season had finally arrived, or at least we hoped so. It seemed a bit tentative, and we were anxious for it to begin in earnest; the land was thirsty. I may have learned that "man's sweat is the best irrigation for the earth," as a reformed dunce at my agriculture school, but a little water from heaven would make everybody happy.

After the period of intense activity that had gotten us settled on Poro Poro in record time, we were trying to find a suitable pace at which to cruise along, a tempo somewhere between "too much" and "not enough." We had been here nearly three months, and things had certainly moved ahead. Doing a little every day meant a lot of ground covered by the end of the week.

Cruising along . . . a little every day . . . I looked at Iléana, who was drenched with sweat, and we burst out laughing. Up to then, we had worked like animals from dawn to dusk, pausing only when I made my daily trip to the fish pen while Iléana fixed the rice. We hadn't taken a siesta in ages. But we had beaten the sweltering heat that was killing this part of Poro Poro, by covering the ground with dry coconut fronds in a wide area around the *faré*. It took many, many bundles of fronds, which we brought from the neighboring *motu*. The bulk of the job had taken us nearly a month. We would pack a picnic and set out in the morning, towing the dinghy across the shallows; Stephan would cling to my neck as I swam across the *haos*. Early in the afternoon we would carry a load of palm fronds back, along with a raft of poles for windbreaks. We would then spread out the fronds, not too tightly at first, covering as much ground as we could.

You can rarely tell in advance where a project with a specific objective will lead you. When the first goal is achieved, you see the next one, which was barely visible at the start, like an island rising from the horizon. And in a slow metamorphosis, the story gradually changes.

In the late afternoon, when Iléana went to fetch Stephan, who was playing with his schoolmates, she would come back dragging a few palm fronds. With the heavy labor behind us, I also went to the village after work to practice throwing the *patia* with the team practicing for the Pacific Games. Before returning home, I would tie a big bundle of fronds and carry it on my shoulder across the flats. If we didn't take the fronds, they would be burned, "to make everything nice and neat."

Our layer of fronds was getting thicker. A little each day . . . a little each day . . . Insect colonies were beginning to inhabit this kingdom of the sun where nothing had been able to live a few months before. They fed on the rotting palm fronds, which retained moisture as they decomposed. They were transforming them into waste matter, digging their tiny tunnels, laying millions of eggs, working all together to enrich what had once been a desert. Under the layer of fronds, the sand had turned gray. I didn't need a microscope to detect the tiny organisms coming to life at ground level. The face of our shared habitat was already changing; once severe, it was now almost smiling.

We had also beaten the mosquitoes. They needed fresh water in which to lay their eggs. When they hatched, each egg produced a larva. They didn't seem to have gills, since they rose to the surface every minute or so to breathe. In ten to twelve days the cycle was complete, and a mosquito emerged from the water and flew away.

In Indochina, we used to fight malaria and dengue fever, which are mosquito-borne, by putting a few spoonfuls of kerosene in our cisterns. The kerosene covered the surface without affecting the water's taste, and the thin film was enough to prevent the larvae from breathing.

But here, and probably throughout the Tuamotus, the mosquitoes found water deep underground, thanks to their ally, the *tupa*. The *tupa* is a large sand crab which burrows down to the water table. Mosquitoes lay eggs in its holes in complete safety. We counted more than a hundred and twenty *tupa* holes on Poro Poro alone; some were even under the *faré*. There was no point in plugging them, they would be back again the next day. And as for pouring kerosene down the holes, it would soak into the sand without a single drop reaching the water table.

The problem seemed insoluble. Then one night, after thinking long and hard . . . What if I ran a flexible plastic hose into the hole, with a funnel stuck in the other end? . . . I could pour a quarter-glass of kerosene and a jug of water down the hose all at once, and only the devil could keep the kerosene from reaching the bottom . . .

We treated the hundred and twenty *tupa* holes that way. It was a big job and it took us three days of squatting by the holes with the sun scorching our necks. But we hadn't seen a single mosquito in the past two weeks. And the crabs didn't seem to mind; they were doing just fine. Stephan, who was getting better and better at it, shot at them with his slingshot.

Raumati and Tepuku, who often came to visit us on Poro Poro, were amazed. "There were always mosquitoes here before, almost as many as in the village."

I explained the mystery to them, and gave a demonstration using the hose, kerosene, and water jug.

"Digging the Panama Canal was the same thing," I said. "Where they started, the ground was dry; no problem. But then they reached the swamps, and malaria broke out. A lot of people died, nobody wanted to work, there were too many dead. So then a guy got an idea, and glug-glug-glug, drums of kerosene were poured into the swamps. No more malaria, everybody went back to work, and the canal was finished."

"You ought to tell that to everyone during the Sunday meeting at the village hall, after the *boules* game," said Raumati.

I intended to. But first I wanted to be sure I had guessed right in treating the *tupa* holes the way we had. Iléana and I hoped so, because a severe epidemic of dengue fever had hit Tahiti. The radio gave advice to avoid contagion: "Turn over any coconut shells around your *faré*, and don't leave any containers out in the rain. Otherwise mosquitoes will lay their eggs in them. That's what spreads dengue fever." Nor were the atolls spared; the epidemic had already reached Rangiroa and Apataki. A single person carrying the virus could come in on the schooner and infect a village that was infested with mosquitoes.

Raumati had alerted Papa Toa, the mayor, and they called an urgent meeting; everybody came. I filled a glass of water from the cistern at the village hall. Three mosquito larvae were zigzagging up and down in it. I added two drops of kerosene, and by the time I counted slowly to sixty, they lay motionless on the bottom. Then I described the method which had worked on our *motu*, and ended with the story of the Panama Canal.

"The village is exactly the same," I said. "It's up to you to decide if you want to do anything about it."

But except for Neti and Raumati, who treated their *tupa* holes and covered their water tanks with cloth, the others let fate decide for them. And fate hit hard: of the sixty villagers, more than half came down with dengue fever. The epidemic was checked by a team of health workers quickly sent from Tahiti, but they came too late to save little Hina, a three-year-old girl.

Hina lay dead in the cemetery and life went on. I made a chicken-wire trap to catch the rats that were raising Cain with our supplies. The Ahe rats were very small, lively as squirrels, almost tame; when we caught them they looked at us without obvious fear. If they hadn't been so numerous, we would have gladly gotten along with them. So we offered them a truce: "We won't drown you just because you come to steal a few grains of rice, or knock the lids off our pots and pans and fight in them at night." Each capture was the occasion for an impromptu picnic on the palm-tree *motu*. First we bundled up some fronds and loaded them into the dinghy; may as well stay ahead of the game, no point in walking around empty-handed. Then we released our rats, after clipping their ears with scissors. That part wasn't so easy; you had to half-drown the rats to be able to hold them without getting bitten; but once we set them down in the sunshine, they quickly revived. We clipped their ears to see if any returned, hopping from rock to rock across the mile of shark-patrolled tide flats. None ever showed up in our trap.

Tuamotu rats are known for their ravages in the coconut groves. They are excellent climbers, and gnaw into the young nuts for food and drink. In the whole of the archipelago, they damage thousands of tons of copra. Whatever the situation elsewhere, the rats on Poro Poro had been more or less neutralized once we ringed our thirty coconut trees with plastic sleeves. Normally, thin sheets of tin are used; a rat can't climb the slippery two-foot metal barriers. The plastic wouldn't last as long, but it was a lot better than nothing. I planned to replace it when I could get the proper materials during our trip to Tahiti over the school break, in six or seven months.

So within a few months, we had beaten the sun, which had once turned our place into an oven; the mosquitoes that sometimes made our nights unbearable; and to some extent the rats that kept us from drinking our coconuts. That left the wind, a formidable adversary.

The periods of *maramu*—when the trade wind blew from the south or south-southeast—were terrible. The wind would howl across the barrier reef, carrying spray right to our *faré* at the highest tides. After a strong *maramu*, salt crystals glittered on the carpet of fronds and the watermelon leaves. I couldn't see how I could stop that colossus with what I had on hand. We would have needed a couple of staggered rows of ironwood trees all along the ocean side of the *motu*. Ironwood is a hardy tree that grows quickly, even on almost pure coral. In Tahiti, I saw ironwood hedges in the sand along the sea that had grown to more than twelve feet in two years. They look like bushy pine trees, with needles so fine and dense that they catch the salt spray.

Okay, enough dreaming; we didn't have any ironwood plants on hand. And even if we did, they wouldn't solve the problem for a year or two. But the battle was joined, and we were already winning it a little at a time.

From the right side of the *faré*, starting at the corner post, ran a tall fence covered with palm fronds that protected what we called our "patio" from the *maramu*. Iléana had planted flowers all along the fence. In the patio stood a breadfruit-tree sapling, a gift from the village, and five young papaya trees we had grown from seeds. They seemed to be doing well; the biggest was already nearly two feet tall. At that rate, they would be bearing fruit in a year.

Another fence to the left of the *pareu* studio sheltered three more papayas and two of the lemon trees we had brought from Tahiti aboard JOSHUA. We had planted the other two near Patrick and Diana's place as a surprise for when they came back. Near the *pareu faré* fence grew an aloe vera, a kind of dwarf agave that Iléana had brought from Tahiti, and which she tended like a baby. Aloe vera has amazing medicinal properties; if you cut a leaf and rub the juice on a burn, it heals almost before your eyes.

Behind the *faré*, the watermelons were prospering, protected by individual windbreaks, which I had carefully angled to minimize turbulence. The biggest melon weighed forty pounds, and we had given it to the village the previous Sunday, after church services. Everybody got a slice, and their "oohs" and "aahs" came straight from the heart. The villagers could hardly believe that Ahe had produced a watermelon so beautiful or so sweet. I gather that Pastor Toto spoke of a miracle on that occasion. I just nodded and smiled broadly, while thinking about the way I made my compost; that was the real miracle! But I thought it wise not to give the villagers the exact recipe just yet. They would suspect me of practicing black magic and might not dare accept any more of Poro Poro's good vegetables, which were grown in the best Asian manner.

Of our seven watermelon plants, however, four died. That was before we got the idea of protecting the soil by covering it with palm fronds. The cucumbers, hidden in the bushes, came through like champs, and Iléana often brought some to the village. She would almost always come back with a papaya, a fish, or a few eggs or lemons. Life wasn't complicated here. Nothing was sold, traded, or calculated; it was simply given.

Land can't be divided between heirs in Polynesia, thank God. Twenty or thirty people might own even a small piece of property. To sell off so much as a corner of it, they all had to agree in writing, in a lawyer's presence. The law protects the Polynesians, who are generous to a fault and quick to bend an elbow whenever a bottle of rum comes out. They could lose everything else, but not their land.

Like the seventy or eighty other atolls that make up the immense Tuamotu Archipelago, Ahe lived on copra, dried coconut meat which is refined into oil.

The men left in the morning in their outboards to work on the *motus*, and returned to the village at the end of the day, after a round trip of sometimes as much as fifteen miles. *Ohipa copra*—copra work—consisted of collecting the dry, fallen nuts, piling them up, then splitting them open with a hatchet. The men scooped the coconut meat out with a sharp tool shaped like a big, shallow spoon. They then put the copra in 130-pound bags and took it back to the village, where it was dried in the sun. The schooner that came every five or six weeks picked it up and took it to the refinery in Papeete.

Ohipa copra also involved tending the coconut groves. The dried fronds were piled in windrows between the trees; *kaaia* shoots and other weeds were cut down with machetes and piled neatly on the stacks of fronds. That part was first-class work, but then everything was burned.

Some sixty people lived in the village, which covered a dozen acres. There were twelve widely spaced *farés* with plywood walls and corrugated iron roofs, and three concrete buildings: the Protestant church, the village hall, and the school. The houses and public buildings were surrounded with flowers, the yards raked twice a day. Not a leaf lay on the ground. Polynesians seem to have a kind of phobia about finding a single blade of grass, and immediately pull it up. There was no greenery except for the coconut palms, banana trees, a single mango tree, many flowers, and a few lemon and breadfruit trees that must have suffered from the heat when they were young. The coconut palms didn't have sleeves, but the many dogs, who were always hungry, kept the rats away from the village.

Each *faré* had at least two or three dogs, often more. They were very good at fishing, and would gather in packs to chase mullets and little surgeonfish in the barrier-reef shallows. It seemed to me that their paws were slightly webbed, perhaps from having lived in an aquatic environment for generations. But the dogs on the atolls were mainly a valuable form of livestock; the Paumotu all ate dog meat from time to time, as a change from the usual fish and corned beef. There were also a few chickens, which laid their eggs wherever they pleased. You saw few chicks, probably because of the *tupa* crabs that infested the village, as they did on all the other of the atoll's *motus*.

Nobody did any gardening. People ate plenty of coconuts, bananas, breadfruits, and fresh-speared fish, plus canned beef, sweetened condensed milk, flour, oil, white rice, sugar, and instant coffee brought by schooner. It was a diet based on protein, starch, and refined sugar that would give a dietician fits. In the old days, the people of the atolls grew taro to satisfy their need for starchy food, but the practice had died out long ago. According to one account, only eight coconut trees were growing on Ahe in Captain Cook's day. The 2,500 acres of coconuts growing here now had been planted at the beginning of this century. The groves were almost an accident, a byproduct of the Industrial Revolution, but they had changed the face of Polynesia.

The Paumotu people look to the sea. Water is their element, they feel comfortable with the *patia* they always carry on the reef and a *pupui* (speargun) in the bottom of their outriggers. And when the Paumotu eat fish, they don't eat only the best parts, as Westerners often do. Except for the gills, intestines, and the biggest bones, they eat the whole fish—including the fins, skin, eyes, brains, and small bones. When I learned that, it reminded me of what Professor Jean Rivolier once told me when I visited him for dietary advice while preparing for the long way. Rivolier said that an entire Swedish polar expedition had once died of malnutrition because they used only the "best" parts of the seals they killed. A group of Eskimos got through the same winter without any trouble because they ate every part of the seal, including the fat and organs.

Stephan was going to school. He would cross the tide flats every morning, eager to see his fifteen schoolmates, boys and girls aged four to eleven. The teacher, a sturdy Tahitian woman, made them start the day in front of the cistern faucet, where they all brushed their teeth. She didn't want them to grow up with mouths like their parents', full of rotten stumps. She also made sure the children spoke French in class. The older ones helped the younger ones, whispering words to them. That was allowed, but the little ones then had to repeat the word three times, to show they remembered. She snapped at the children occasionally, but never hit them.

Class ran from 8:00 in the morning until 12:30, with a couple of recesses during which Stephan learned Paumotu from his classmates. He would join them on the fringing reef after lunch to search for "pencil urchins," whose large, harmless spines are used for necklaces, to hunt the little moray eels that slithered between the coral rocks, and to collect seaweed and shells. On the tide flats, they watched for sharks, which can be extremely dangerous when you're walking in water up to your calves; seeing only that small part of your body, they can attack "by mistake." During their outings, the children always carried a *patia* or a stick; the slightest splash was enough to scare off a shark, even a fairly large one. There too, the older kids looked after the smaller ones, and no parent ever dreamed of worrying about them.

We weren't sure that school was doing Stephan much good, but he was developing his "body intelligence" out on the tide flats among his friends, learning to open his eyes and see what was right in front of him. Very independent for his age, he split the rest of his time between Poro Poro and the village, where each *faré* welcomed him as a member of the great Polynesian family. Children grew freely here, within a community consciousness that let them learn about life on their own.

On Sundays, not a sound could be heard in the village. The men played *boules*, the women braided wreaths of flowers, the children didn't yell. After the *boules* match, the men came to crouch in a half-circle under the big *maioré* (breadfruit) tree near the village hall, where Papa Toa, the seventy-two-year-old mayor, awaited them. This was the time to discuss municipal projects: building a new cistern to catch water running off the copra warehouse roof; asking the Agriculture Service in Papeete for ironwood seedlings to plant upwind of the village, in case a hurricane ever hit the atoll; finding a crew of volunteers to cut the weeds in the cemetery, etc. Papa Toa would nod and talk about the budget. And shortly before dusk, everyone went to church to hear Pastor Toto's sermon. Along with Neti and Tuarue, Toto was considered one of the best skindivers around.

I'm sure Pastor Toto talked about the Good Lord, but I think those Sunday get-togethers mainly served to settle little disputes and smooth any waves that may have been kicked up in Ahe's calm. That way, the next week got off to a good start. It was clear that religion here had found its most obvious, useful daily expression: it united the village.

After the sermon and the singing in the church, Papa Toa would play the harmonica; mine wasn't tuned to the same key, so I couldn't accompany him. Then the guitars took over from the harmonica and the party continued. Each person brought a small gift which Toto auctioned off for the upkeep of the church. But Iléana and I could never quite understand what happened next: those who had bought the presents then gave those same presents back to the minister, who shared them with everyone. Our contribution to the party usually took the form of a watermelon or a little basket into which Iléana had put a few tomatoes and cucumbers decorated with flowers.

Nobody got to taste our pumpkins, alas. They were a total loss. Scorched by the sun, not a single plant survived. Again, that had happened before our coconut-frond idea. So I dug seven new holes for the next generation.

This time, I dug deep. As usual, I was using a pickaxe and shovel, the way I had at Ein Kerem. I had barely begun when I saw Philip next to me, who said, "Make each swing of your body and every thought in your mind a tai chi movement. That's the way to do things when you want them done well." So I took a heavy crowbar and in five hours broke through the slab to the water table. It was a stroke of genius, and well worth my five hours of sweat. Rising to the surface by capillary action like oil in a wick, the water would moisten the roots, which would then need less watering. Later, we would see whether theory and practice came together and triumphed. The next day, as I was starting on the next hole, Stephan came over and said, "Why don't you dig at the *tupa* holes? They know where the ground isn't so hard." And by digging where my four-and-a-half-year-old son told me to, I finished the hole in under forty-five minutes, right down to the water table. And I didn't encounter any slabs, only blocks of coral I could pry loose fairly easily with the bar.

Stephan had a new pal, a white-fronted noddy. It was a sea bird, slightly larger than a tern, and he fed it every day. During one of our expeditions to the palm-frond *motu* to release a rat, Iléana had found it as a chick, lying on the ground. It had wandered away from its nest and was trembling, almost dead. A month later, it was able to fly, and roosted on one of the *faré*'s rafters. Génie the cat caught the licking of his life just for looking in that direction. Whenever the noddy saw Stephan and me leaving for the fish pen, it would accompany us, wheeling overhead.

We also had a blue-footed booby, who was Iléana's special sweetheart. We found it the same way; the chick had broken a wing falling from its nest. Iléana splinted its wing and nursed it back to health; the booby tried its first flight a month later. It would disappear in the morning, come back to greet me when I returned from spearfishing or tending the fish pen, and sleep on the *faré* roof each night. I liked both birds, but dreamed of having a fairy tern. We hadn't been able to find any, though there were plenty of them around. They laid a single egg, perfectly balanced on a branch. It was a miracle it didn't fall, because it wasn't even stuck there; I had checked several times. In hatching, the chick breaks through the shell, pushes the pieces aside, and stays there until it flies away.

The rainy season was spotty: just a shower from time to time, enough to wet the leaves but not enough to fill the gutters. So we continued to use the village cistern for drinking and cooking water. The plants tolerated our well water, but it wasn't really potable; the coral made it too alkaline. And we used it sparingly, because the lens of underground water was probably very shallow on such a small *motu*. After Patrick and Diana had used their well water for a year, it became almost as salty as the lagoon; it was a serious warning.

So as not to waste a drop of water, we washed while standing in a big basin, and used the waste water in the garden. The plants didn't seem to mind the brown soap we used. In fact it provided them with potassium, fats, and probably other useful substances. We recycled our dishwater the same way. And our daily urine (three to five quarts, depending on the weather) enriched the compost pile. I would carefully check the pile's humidity by sticking my hand into it: too dry, and the compost would take too much time to ripen; too wet, and it would turn acid—without ripening—because of the anaerobic bacteria growing in it. When our production of urine exceeded the needs of the compost pile, we diluted and used the surplus on the plants, in a ratio of one part urine to three or four parts water.

If Léo and Luciano could see the garden they had helped start, they'd know they hadn't wasted their time. Our tiny tomatoes wouldn't win any ribbons at a county fair, but they were delicious, and more were growing. The radishes produced only leaves, which tasted good in soups. The bok choy astounded us, spreading at an incredible rate; we ate some almost every evening. In the West, we speak of the "quality/price" ratio; on Poro Poro, we used a "sweat/yield" calculation. Compared to the tomatoes, watermelons, and cucumbers, our bok choy had by far the best "sweat/yield" ratio. We always planted its seeds very close together, a technique I had learned from Peter and Pachouli in New Zealand. Systematically crowding vegetables whose leaves are eaten, such as lettuce and bok choy, saves on work, space, and watering. As the plants grow, you pick off a leaf here and there, enough for a small salad. At night, the remaining leaves spread out and cover the ground, which keeps the compost and soil from drying out.

Producing maximum yields in a minimum of space is what is technically known as "intensive cultivation." We had to practice it to the highest possible degree because of Poro Poro's very poor, sandy soil, which was always in need of water and organic matter.

Time had passed quickly; we'd been here six months already. Beneath the blanket of palm fronds, which grew thicker by the week, a thin layer of sand had turned black. Insects were teeming in the dampness of that first humus; they didn't bother our plants, except for a few attacks on the tomato leaves, a minor aggression which Iléana deterred with soapy water.

When we first arrived, the villagers said that nothing would grow on Poro Poro except coconut palms; there wasn't any point in trying. I remembered sitting next to Philip as he drove his Volkswagen from Tel Aviv to Jerusalem. I was looking at a pine forest that covered thousands of acres. Then, without any warning, the road continued across empty desert. There wasn't a single tree, just bare earth and stones. I couldn't understand it; I would have expected the forest to thin out gradually before disappearing. Philip explained the mystery:

"This expanse of forest was once nothing but desert," he said. "We created one of Israel's first miracles by planting millions of young pine trees, all drip-irrigated. Hundreds of miles of plastic pipe were laid, with a little hole at the foot of each tree. The trees were irrigated for two or three years, long enough for the roots to grow down to the underlying natural moisture. And the desert turned into a forest."

The problem was a little different on our sand and coral *motu*, but the basic situation was the same. And life on Poro Poro was now in full swing, without costing us too much sweat.

Dividing her time between the garden and her studio, Iléana had gone back to painting *pareus* again. She had a keen appreciation of her surroundings and magic fingers, and when she filled her paintbrushes with the seven colors of the rainbow, the atoll's light, nuances, and joy all came together in her art. But I had counted off enough one-piaster bills in my father's office to realize that my companion—who could spend an entire day on a single detail—had no head for business. So I suggested she use a stencil to increase her output a little; that way, she could flood the Papeete market.

"Any idiot can use a stencil," I said. "You choose the patterns and colors, I'll be your robot, and bang-bang-bang, it will zip along, you'll see."

Iléana responded with shrieks of horror.

As for me, I had completely repainted JOSHUA, from waterline to masthead. I would spend a couple of mornings a week on board, to putter, restitch the mizzen, which was showing signs of weakness, and enjoy my boat's company, writing a few letters on the chart table. I felt moved each time I saw that table. I had spent so many hours sitting there, listening to the bow singing during the long way. And I could hear it singing again as I wrote my friends—Philip in Israel, pals in France—telling them about our existence in the midst of all this coral. But words are pale things when speaking of Ahe. You *live* an atoll, not only with your mind, but with your whole being. "Go ahead and love Ahe," JOSHUA told me, "I'm not jealous. I know I will always remain your great, beautiful love, the symbol and proof of your real freedom."

Now that Poro Poro required much less work of us, I went swimming every day in the calm water of the anchorage, admiring the coral and taking an interest in the intense life it attracted, as little blue and red fish darted among the multicolored polyp flowers to avoid being eaten by bigger ones. But I had become much more vigilant since almost being attacked by a four-foot shark. Absorbed by the familiar scene unfolding before my eyes, I only spotted him at the last minute, a few lengths away. The shark had already started his war-dance, with arched back and pectoral fins lowered. I slowly backed away, and he immediately calmed down.

Normally, a black-tipped lagoon shark will never attack unless there is blood in the water or a fish struggling at the end of a spear. When I told Raumati about my encounter, he explained that the shark's dance was caused by my invading a space which for some mysterious reason he considered belonged to him *at that particular moment*. As for why it was that particular moment, nobody could say.

"Ten minutes earlier, or a quarter hour later," he said, "nothing would have happened. You just showed up at exactly the wrong moment, and were lucky to see the shark in time. Otherwise, he would have mauled you."

The episode didn't keep me from swimming every day, but after that, it was with heightened awareness. On Saturdays, if the ocean swell wasn't breaking too hard on the barrier reef, I would go spearfishing behind the village with Toto, Neti, and Tuarue. You really had to watch your step there, because the gray sharks of the outer reef could be dangerous. We never went alone and always stayed in a group, ready to make a stand after one of us had fired. Jacks were plentiful, and the parrotfish and groupers were much bigger and less wary than in the lagoon; it didn't take much time to get a meal for the family. Because of the sharks, I tried to aim for a fish's lateral line, so as to kill it outright, without its flapping. I did my best, and while my best was well below Paumotu standards, it didn't keep me from joining the group.

Spearfishing with Polynesians is a real treat. They become gods underwater, masters at holding their breath and stalking, and unbelievably good shots. I was a good swimmer, I had plenty of wind, and had been the best carbine shot on the GAZELLE. But mastering the *pupui* isn't only a matter of swimming, wind, and aim. To even begin to approach the skill level of a Polynesian, you have to be on totally intimate terms with the fish and the water, to *become* them. The Tahitian Jean Tapu was the spearfishing champion of the world, though Polynesia has only 120,000 inhabitants, compared to billions for the rest of the planet. When you think of the ratio, that's fantastic. Nowhere else could I have found better teachers.

One image remains fixed in my mind . . . Four large jacks were swimming our way, but I knew nobody was going to shoot because Neti had just speared a big grouper and the sharks were already restless . . . One of the jacks passed slowly in front of a shark, six feet from Tuarue . . . and click! Tuarue's *pupui* nailed it *right under the shark's nose*. The shark didn't notice a thing, because the fish was killed instantly.

Raumati rarely joined those *pupui* hunts. He seemed to feel a certain contempt for spearguns; they were so accurate and easy to use, they lacked nobility. For him, only the *patia* counted. The undisputed master of Ahe, Raumati used his *patia* the way Paganini used a violin bow. From afar, on the edge of the reef where the waves broke, he looked like a ballet dancer, in total symbiosis with the coral. Raumati had insisted on making me my *patia* himself. It was almost identical to his, eight feet long and straight, but a little lighter, to suit my more modest musculature. After using it for weeks without result, spearing my first parrotfish gave me a rush of joy, the same blinding flash I had felt as a boy when I hit my first bird with my slingshot.

Compared to the Paumotu, I was still a baby at the *patia*. But I was getting better at spearing reef parrotfish to feed my little family when we took JOSHUA to go anchor on the other side of the lagoon. To be honest, the fish there were less cautious than the ones near the village.

Every afternoon, I joined the village team practicing for the
patia javelin competition. That *patia* is very thin and extremely
light. Just five and a half feet long, it flies like an arrow—provided
you know how to throw one. The target was a coconut on top of
a twenty-five-foot pole thirty-five or forty paces away.

I had been practicing for months without success. Raumati
and the others urged me to keep at it and applauded when my
shots didn't miss the target by too much. "You'll make it, you'll
see. It takes time, that's all." Sure, I would make it—but it would
be in some future life, when I came back as a Polynesian, with
Polynesian chromosomes.

In the meantime, I struggled to transform the *popaa* flesh I
was born with . . . which might yet happen, this time around . . .

Though the rainy season was over, a terrific storm hit the atoll
one night. The sky lit up with a thousand lightning bolts, and the
subtle smell of ozone entered our lungs, sending its magic down
to our deepest nerve endings. It brought out our animal instincts,
and we stared, fascinated, into the distance. Then the wind
dropped and a deluge replaced the calm. After that, the sky went
on emptying itself very gently in a fine rain that lasted until dawn.
The four fifty-gallon drums were full, and the level in our cistern
rose two and a half feet—almost two tons of water collected from
our roofs in a single night! Next morning, the cucumbers and watermelons radiated happiness under a sky that was blue from one
edge of the horizon to the other.

Crouched near the cucumber hole I had dug the day before, I
was drinking a cup of tea with Iléana. She was about to transplant
some tomatoes, taking advantage of the wet earth. Stephan was
practicing throwing his little *patia* at the mullets close to the
beach. Quick and skittish, they were in no great danger. Still,
Stephan was making a lot of progress; he understood refraction,
and how it varies with the angle of the shot and the depth of the
fish.

Together, Iléana and I had decided to take him out of school
after he came home one day mindlessly reciting: "The shepherdess tends her white sheep on the green grass of the
meadow." When I was a boy, we five little French children and our

thirty-five Vietnamese friends used to sing-song, "Our ancestors the Gauls, who had blue eyes, etc." the same way.

When she took Stephan back under her wing, Iléana told the teacher that he was still a bit young for school, and that she would teach him to read herself. The teacher agreed, and praised Stephan as a very affectionate little boy who often brought her flowers, but who was perhaps a bit dreamy in class, and very undisciplined at recess with his slingshot, which she'd had to confiscate several times.

Once I finished my tea, I would plant a few cucumber seeds. Then Stephan and I would go gather sea slugs. That way, he could practice throwing his *patia*, which was much more fun than going to school. Sea slugs were ideal targets to help him master the refraction problem; and when we had collected a bucket-full, we would add them to the compost pile.

Iléana was gazing at our garden. It had started from scratch, and Lord, how beautiful it was now! But without compost, it certainly wouldn't have looked so wonderful—in spite of our sweat, our careful water rationing, all our good ideas put together. Even in spite of the good topsoil from Tahiti, which we had mixed with the sand in the beds. The topsoil was all gone; we finished the last sack a long time ago. But new watermelon and cucumber plants were starting to grow in their sand-and-compost mix.

I created that miraculous compost in the shade of the *kaaia* tree by mincing the banana-tree trunks I brought from the village. Raumati or someone would alert me when anyone harvested a bunch, since the tree was then chopped down to make room for new shoots. And they were glad to give it to "Tamata," which was the nickname they had given me. (In Paumotu, *tamata* means "to try" or "why not?") Sheltered from the prevailing southeast-northeast winds, the village had many banana trees, and I usually got three or four trunks a week.

Once I had chopped up that raw material with my machete and crumbled the pieces with my hands, I mixed them with a sack of topsoil gathered under the *miki-miki* (*Hedyotis*) thickets from the palm-tree *motu*. The layer of good soil there was so thin, I had to scrape it up with a spoon. It usually took me half a day to gather four or five seventy-pound sacks of soil, which I brought back in the dinghy with a few bundles of fronds. I then added a couple of buckets of sliced sea slugs to my banana tree and soil

Catinat Street, shaded by tamarind trees, like almost all
the streets of Saigon and the provincial towns.

Bernard at Bandol in 1962
(left), and with his mother
in 1964 (above).

A crowd of sampans on the Chinese estuary in Cholon (Saigon's sister city; together, Saigon and Cholon form a huge urban area).

Joshua reaches Alicante, coming from Tahiti (1966).

Joshua at Bandol for her last cruising-school season in the Mediterranean (1967).

At a friend's house in Tahiti, in 1975 (Photo by Dominique Charnay)

Tahiti, July 1977: first meeting with Antoine, whom we would soon see again at Suvorov atoll. (Photos by Dominique Charnay)

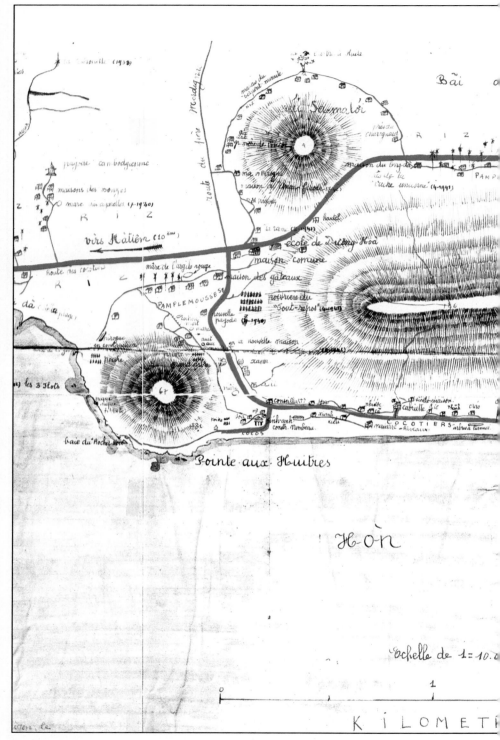

Map of the village drawn by Françou.

Talking with Arii, the mayor of the village of Tenukupara on Ahe, a little Tuamotu atoll 250 miles from Tahiti. (Photo by Dominique Charnay)

Setting out to go spearfishing (Photo by Dominique Charnay)

With Iléana, Stephan, and Génie the
cat at Poro Poro, in our faré on
stilts, with its roof and walls
of woven coconut fronds.

Iléana weaving coconut fronds.

Stephan (front row, second from left)
with his classmates of all ages in the
single class at Ahe.

(Photos by Dominique Charnay)

Views of the faré on
Poro Poro motu,
at Ahe atoll.
(Photos by Dominique Charnay)

Salvaging old banana-tree
trunks for compost to
fertilize the coral soil
of the motu, using some
good topsoil and a lot of care.
(Photos by Dominique Charnay)

Planting a sprouted avocado seed in the village at Ahe,
and chopping banana trunks and leaves. (Photos by Dominique Charnay)

Heading across the lagoon to the village. (Photo by Dominique Charnay)

Meeting Gaston Flosse, president of the Territory of French
Polynesia, campaigning through the Tuamotus. (Photo by Dominique Charnay)

ith the children and the
mayor of Lachelle (Oise),
ges Lambert, the first to
r my open letter calling
rance's elected officials
plant fruit trees in their
communities. (1986)
(Photo by Dominique Charnay)

At Croisic, at the
house of an old
friend, the former
solo sailor of
KURUN:
Jacques-Yves
Le Toumelin.
(Photo by Dominique
Charnay)

JOSHUA in the Ahe lagoon
(above, 1977),
(Photo by Dominique Charnay)

TAMATA at anchor at Raiatea
(left), and off Bora Bora
(below). (Photo by Véronique Lerebours
Pigeonnière)

mix. Sea slugs (also called "sea cucumbers") were everywhere on the shallow sandbar between Poro Poro and the village, and provided organic matter rich in nitrogen and organic compounds. Naturally, our kitchen scraps also went into the compost: vegetable peelings chopped very fine, fish guts, and sometimes a diced shark. Each time Raumati came back from the pass, he would leave jack heads and a bucket of fish guts at the foot of the *kaaia* tree, and bring us a nice parrotfish or grouper for dinner. The villagers also often stopped at Poro Poro to bring us a big fish if the spearfishing had been good after their day's copra work.

Two compost piles were always underway beneath the *kaaia*, covered with sheets of plastic to keep them moist. We used the older, ripe one, as needed in the garden. The other gradually grew as I added chopped banana-tree trunks and other ingredients, which I varied as much as possible.* Plants are like us; they crave variety, and are very good at choosing the nourishment that best suits them.

Our compost was ready for use in three weeks, or a month at the most, which is extremely fast. This was due first to the fact that it consisted of very small pieces, which accelerated its transformation into assimilable humus. The second favorable factor was the Tuamotus' warm, relatively dry climate. Its nutritional richness came from the variety of elements that composed it. But without the addition of the Big Secret, the compost would never have ripened so fast or been of such high quality.

I could see myself once again sitting in my school at Ben Cat, listening as our teacher Jean Bouillère revealed the Big Secret of market gardening. Thirty-five years after that outstanding class, I could remember it almost word for word.

"The compost produced by Indochinese peasants is the best in the world, along with China's. By comparison, the manure used by farmers in Europe and America isn't worth a thing. The *human* manure used in Asia makes all the difference; that alone is what makes Indochina's compost so unbeatable. Get it into your heads that human fertilizer is far superior to that of any livestock. As

---

*Fifteen years later, Pierre Deshumeurs told me that he had created excellent compost on Pukurua Atoll that required much less sweat. It consisted entirely of *tahinu* (*Tournefortia argentia*) leaves, with no other organic matter, and ripened in ninety days. *Tournefortia*, which is very prolific, is the pioneer plant on the atolls.

you well know, peasants sell the contents of the country's out-houses to specialized merchants who re-sell it, well mixed and ready to use, to market gardeners. France has professional wine tasters who can recognize vintages and spot imitations. Well, Indochina has the profession of *thài thu cúc*—or "shit-tasters," to put it plainly. And they really do taste it; I wouldn't have believed it if I hadn't seen it with my own eyes. And a market gardener needs a *thài thu cúc*'s experience if he doesn't want to be cheated on the quality of the merchandise. It is easy to stretch it by adding cow, horse, or pig manure, or even water. The *thài thu cúc* is there to spot the cheaters."

At Poro Poro, our production of human fertilizer averaged about fifty pounds a month, and I fed that good slurry to the com-post pile every other week. At fifty pounds a month, that came to about one and a half brimming fifty-gallon drums a year. If I were ever to spend time in a Western country again, I think I would al-ways feel a bit guilty whenever I flushed a toilet.

Stephan was screaming, and Iléana and I rushed over to him. It had finally happened, he had been stung by a stonefish! But no, it wasn't a *nohu* at all; he had finally speared his first mullet, and was beside himself with joy. His pal the noddy was beating its wings overhead, shrieking hungrily at the sight of the fish quiver-ing at the end of Stephan's *patia*. I was so happy, I felt like crying. I hugged my little boy tight, then went back to my work.

My eyes lost in the distance, I was stirring the honey-bucket near the compost pile in the shade of the *kaaia* tree. And way off in the distance, I could see a guy running around, waving his arms like a madman. That nut was myself, always chasing after some goal that retreated as he got closer to it. Except from a few calm periods, that was the way I had lived ever since leaving Indochina. But all that was behind me now. I was right in the center of my goal, and it had happened all by itself.

It certainly was the first time I felt so totally at peace with my-self. It was a long-term peace, without any crazy projects in mind, without my hatching some big plan to save the world.

I watched myself, an exhausted swimmer cast up on the beach by a wave. The sun slowly warmed me, and I opened my eyes. Everything had become simple. No more generous flights of fancy to carry me up for a moment before dropping me, bruised and battered, back where I started. The planet and its inhabitants

could go wherever they wanted, that was their business. Total retreat. I was living in the present. I had JOSHUA, my family, and Poro
Poro. The friendliness of the village was close at hand, and all
around me, the atoll sparkled with beauty.

The rest was no concern of mine.

CHAPTER 19

The parabola was perfect . . . and my *patia* hit the coconut on top of the pole thirty-five paces away. From fifteen chests burst a tremendous ovation—no, it was much more than that: it was *the shout*! I recognized it in a flash. I had encountered it for the first time when I was twenty-two, at the end of our finest water-polo match, against the Burmese team. The shout had burst from the stands as from one enormous chest, and our victory wouldn't have meant a thing without that crowd, which had been transformed and overwhelmed by its own shout. It was in a different context now, but it was the same shout.

I stood rooted to the spot, in a kind of trance. It had taken thousands of throws, over months of practice, for my *patia* to finally become magical. Raumati was hugging me in his huge arms, and I sensed he was crying; Neti's eyes shone with happiness; everybody was congratulating me. An aura surrounded us all. This victory was as much theirs as it was mine.

"Bravo, Tamata! We knew you could do it! From now on, you aren't a *popaa* anymore. You're a real Ahe *taata* [a citizen of Ahe]!"

Carrying a watermelon on my shoulder, I was walking in the clouds. At dawn, Doubt had come to buzz in my ear while I was drinking my coffee. I hadn't seen that slimy little beast in ages; I thought I was rid of him. Then I remembered old Suvorov Tom's method and followed his advice—and Doubt took off like a rocket. And now, on this Sunday morning, I was walking in the clouds as I crossed the tide flats, heading for the village with Iléana.

Patia in hand, Stephan had left long before us. He had joined his friends on the barrier reef to hunt the little red-spotted surgeonfish that darted through the foam left by the waves breaking on the coral; to spear one, you need a good eye and a quick arm. If the swell hadn't been rumbling so loudly, we could have heard their happy shouts even at this distance.

As usual, Iléana was carrying a basket of cucumbers and tomatoes; they would be no loss to her. A cucumber here, a tomato there, all were repaid with lots of smiles and words of welcome that came straight from the heart . . . And she would return to Poro Poro after visiting Tepuku, her basket heavy with an *uru* (breadfruit) and a few lemons, maybe a fish as well. Everyone knew that the current and the sharks had torn holes in the rusty chicken wire of our fish pen.

I was carrying our superb thirty-five-pound watermelon as a prize for the winners of the *boules* match that was underway. They would have fun sharing it with everybody . . . But that wasn't the only reason my feet were running in the sky and my head was full of images. In a few moments, when they were all gathered around the watermelon, I was going to talk to them about something very important.

During our picnics on the *motus*, I had already raised the subject with little groups of two or three of the men doing copra work, trying in vain to convince them.

They answered with friendly smiles: "Fire drives the rats away and the ashes help the earth. You're a *popaa*, you must know that."

I told them that burning the coconut fronds was a disaster for their *fenua*, their land. It was the scourge of the Tuamotus, whose coral soil, poor to begin with, was slowly dying because of the fire that was supposedly doing it good. The ashes contained potassium, but that was also found in the fronds, along with nitrogen, which was essential to the coconut trees' growth and health, not to mention all the known and unknown compounds contained in organic matter.

"If you would only leave the piles of fronds stacked between the coconut trees to rot, then the potassium, the nitrogen, and all the other good things would go back into the earth. By burning them, you keep the potassium, but everything else goes up in smoke. And potassium can't act alone, without being combined with the other elements."

It had been like discussing painting with the blind; I was wasting my breath. Nitrogen, potassium, phosphoric acid, organic-thingamabobs and all the rest didn't mean a thing unless you had at least some vague notions of chemistry. So how could those things exist outside of my cock-and-bull stories? Besides, all you had to do was to look up; anybody could see there were coconuts up there. Wasn't that plain enough?

I had never dared speak at a village meeting before. I knew I was still too new to Ahe, too *popaa*. It was just as well. They wouldn't have understood a thing. I would have gotten caught in a tangle of incomprehensible words.

Now I felt ready. I had finally understood that what I wanted to show them would only make sense when told in a metaphor. And I was going for broke; I wanted to attack ignorance, explode old, fossilized habits, cause a revolt. Thank God, I'd had the wisdom to wait until my *patia* was ready, nice and sharp, easy in my hand, easy in my mind . . . But there, old man, you're really going to have to surpass yourself; you'll be alone in the arena to face the Dragon of Ignorance, with your watermelon as a witness. And the villagers' eyes accompanying your soul will decide alone where the truth lies.

Deep in my reverie, I hadn't noticed how long we had been walking. The coral tide flats were already behind us. Here was Maiere's *faré* on the right side of the road leading to the mayor's office, then Mama Fana's *faré* on the left, Tehua's *faré* by the lagoon, and Old Cowboy's right next to it, with its mango tree out front. And then I was in the clearing where the *boules* match had been played in the shadow of the big breadfruit trees. The Raumati-Toto-Vetea-Siki team had won. Everyone was there: the men, the women with their babies, even enormous Sopo, who was so fat he could hardly walk, and one-legged Mama Teri who had hopped all the way there . . .

I told them about the earth. I drew on the simple images my teacher Jean Bouillère had used to illuminate our minds, clothing the microorganisms in a marvelous aura which made them magical, like in a cartoon where children's hearts sparkled. The village couldn't take its eyes off me, it was listening and watching with all its soul . . . I could see Jean Bouillère next to me, lifting me above myself . . . He was speaking through my mouth . . . as we spoke of "this world" of the villagers, which blended into "the world below" of the *taata nai-nai* (little beings), that fabulous world right under our feet.

"The *taata nai-nai* need to eat and drink and find shelter, just like we do," I said. "We sleep in our *farés*, we drink from cisterns and coconuts, we eat breadfruit and fish from the lagoon. They eat and drink things that rot, which also give them a *faré* when the sun is too hot. Leaving them the coconut fronds makes them happy, and they make love like crazy and have babies all over the place. And their children become adults in a few minutes, they get married, billions at a time, all together, and they have children of their own, who have billions and billions more children in turn. You think I'm talking nonsense? You think 'the world below' doesn't exist? If I had a microscope, I could take a little bit of Poro Poro soil, where there used to be nothing but sand, and you could see with your own eyes the *taata nai-nai* swarming under the palm fronds we put down for them.

"But to live and have babies, they need a lot to eat; they can't live on coral and ashes. They aren't picky, they just want to be left in peace and be given all the things that we don't need. They eat all the *kaaia* shoots we cut down and the fronds on the ground, once they're good and rotten. That's what lets them multiply into infinity, and work the earth and enrich it with their piss and their shit, which feeds the coconut trees the way it fed this delicious watermelon we're all eating together.

"But when you burn the coconut fronds instead of leaving them for the *taata nai-nai*, they don't get anything to eat or drink, and with nothing but stones and ashes and no way to escape the heat, they all die out. It would be as if a giant *tupapau* set fire to our *farés*, chopped down every last breadfruit and coconut tree in the village and the whole atoll, and dynamited all the fish in the lagoon. What would be left? We'd be screwed, like a bunch of *houri taata* (monkeys) in a desert surrounded by water, without even anything to use to make a raft and get away, and soon we would be eating each other.

"Yet that's what you're doing to the *taata nai-nai*, and that's what you're doing to your *fenua*, which belongs to your children, your grandchildren, and your unborn great-grandchildren. This land, which isn't just yours, is slowly dying before your eyes. By burning the coconut fronds, you're acting as if tomorrow will never come because it isn't here yet, and you can't see it. But 'today' is yesterday's 'tomorrow,' *so you can see that 'tomorrow' exists*! And in this true story that I'm telling you, the only difference between 'creation' and 'destruction' is a match. But you're the ones holding the match, and the choice is up to you."

Hand in hand, Iléana and I walked back to our *motu* after picking up Stephan on the reef. We would have jack for dinner, grilled *uru*, a bok choy salad with lemon juice, and a fresh coconut apiece. I could hear Pico della Mirandola's poem singing within me, a message that had already crossed five centuries of human history to show us the way for centuries yet to come: "I have given you neither face, nor any place of your own, nor any special gifts, oh Adam, so that you should desire, conquer, and possess face, place, and gifts yourself. Nature encompasses other species within Laws I have established, but you, who are limited by no bounds, define yourself by your own free will, into whose hands I have put you. I have placed you in the middle of the world so you can contemplate what the world contains. I have made you neither celestial nor terrestrial, neither mortal nor immortal, so you can find your own form freely, in the manner of a skilled painter or sculptor."

The sun rose and set in our trade-wind sky. The days followed one another like waves on the reef. The weeks passed. From time to time, our magic boat took us on trips in the lagoon. We had been living on Ahe for nearly eight months. Our booby and noddy had left us in search of mates on the other *motus*.

Stephan was beginning to read, not only French, but also a little Chinese, thanks to the wonderful little book by Rose Quong, which contained some thirty elementary ideograms.*

We were amazed at how easily our five-year-old son memorized them. I often thought of the *ang hai* I had met on that boat after the Japanese takeover, when I was twenty. He had let me glimpse that basic communication between East and West was possible, provided we could grasp the terrific cultural power of those ideograms; a hundred and fifty well-chosen ones would be enough to bring about the miracle. Perhaps Stephan would prove to be a better student than his father. Without asking our opinion, he had returned to school and to his classmates who brushed their teeth under their teacher's watchful eye. Anyway, what difference did it make if the shepherdess was blond or brunette, or if she tended her sheep in green meadows instead of braiding flower wreaths in the shade of a coconut tree? Our child was happy, that was the main thing. And he loved his *patia* with a passion, the way I loved my slingshot when I was his age.

Chinese Written Characters: Their Wit and Wisdom, by Rose Quong (Cobble Hill Press, 1968) (*Tr.*)

Iléana, who had been a psychiatric hospital nurse for ten years before coming to Polynesia, divided her time between occasional routine visits to the village dispensary and the dyeing of her *pareus*. She decorated the *farés* interior with them, gave one to every woman in the village—and hadn't sent anything to the Papeete shops. I couldn't blame her. Time had ceased to exist for her, the way it does during a long ocean passage, where the horizon always remains the same, even as it changes day by day.

As for myself, I couldn't quite tell what was happening. Life was good here, but I had started to see things differently. Poro Poro was running too smoothly, like a well-tuned engine: a little oil now and then, check the gas tank, put-put-put, no problems . . . Once we added a few watermelon holes to the ones we already had, they yielded continuously . . . Thanks to the plastic sleeves, the rats left our coconuts alone, and the trees gave us all the green nuts we could drink . . . The compost pile had reached its full glory . . . Fifteen ironwood saplings I had had brought in by copra schooner were planted along the tide flats . . . I had built three extra windbreaks and planted thirty nice sprouted coconuts behind the *faré*, plus ten new papaya trees . . . There wasn't much left to do . . . And the put-put-put was beginning to sound like snoring. I was getting bored by the routine. The Poro Poro paradise was already no longer enough for me.

Neti suggested I spend a week with him gathering copra on a *motu* that belonged to his family, four or five miles from the village. I accepted immediately, happy for a break in my daily routine that would let me share the life of the atoll in a purely Polynesian activity.

"I'll come pick you up tomorrow morning after coffee," he said, "and I'll take care of lunch. In my *cao*, it's about half an hour from here by outboard. Don't forget your *pupui* for the way back; I know a good coral head full of fat parrotfishes."

It's often said that Polynesians are somewhat lazy, but everything is relative. They may be experts in the art of kicking back and playing the guitar, but they don't waste any time when they're doing work they enjoy. Cutting brush with a machete, gathering the fronds at the foot of the trees, then piling them in windrows between the trees, I had a hard time keeping up with Neti. In a few hours we cleared a good-sized area, about a hundred yards by fifty, with no time out to rest.

But no matter how hard he works, no Polynesian can gather a ton of copra from an area where only a few coconuts have escaped disaster. On every *motu* I visited with Stephan and Iléana, the ground was littered with young coconuts that had been gnawed by rats. Neti's *motu* suffered from the same calamity which affected the whole of the Tuamotus, according to what I had read and heard. Neti figured we would collect barely one sack of copra from the plot we had cleared this morning. I found myself thinking that this would just about pay for the gas we used for the round trip . . .

We broke for lunch beside the water, had a cigarette after the rice and corned beef. I asked my companion if he had any idea how many young nuts a rat destroyed in a month. He said that the Agriculture Service figured it averaged about five.

In front of us, the reflected sun sparkled on the blue-green lagoon. The acrid smoke from a little fire of frond stems kept the mosquitoes away. How peaceful it was, here in the *kaaia* tree's shade. My body soaked up all that beauty while my mind did a laborious mental calculation. I was thinking aloud, and Neti listened while sipping his coffee. Five mature coconuts yielded about two pounds of copra, so each rat destroyed twenty-five pounds of it a year. On Poro Poro, which was about an acre, we had trapped thirty-two rats since our arrival. The charts showed that Ahe had some 2,500 acres of coconut groves. So if you figured thirty-two rats to an acre, then eighty thousand rats were each destroying about twenty-five pounds of potential copra a year . . . that came to a thousand tons of copra!

Neti checked my calculation by drawing the figures in the sand, carefully lining up the zeros; it came to a thousand tons all right!

"Your math is correct," he said, "but it doesn't make sense. Even without the rats, Ahe could never produce a thousand tons of copra. There aren't enough people here to maintain the groves, so brush grows everywhere between the rows of trees."

He was right, of course. But even if my estimate of eighty thousand rats was far too high, and had to be divided by two, or three, or even four, that still left more than two hundred tons lost every year, a figure Neti thought was about right, but could hardly believe. He looked baffled.

Neti and I worked side by side for a week and spent a lot of sweat to reap a meager harvest: just eight sacks of copra averaging a hundred pounds each. During our final trip back to the village, with the eight sacks in the bottom of the *cao*, we both found ourselves thinking about a mass of two hundred tons of copra that should have been sitting on the dock, ready to be shipped to the Papeete refinery. But the huge pile had died stillborn; all that remained was a ghost swarming with rats, who were very much alive.

Sunday. Rest. While helping Neti pull an anvil out of a jumble of supplies stored behind his *faré*, I nearly fainted. I'm not exaggerating when I say I was bowled over with astonishment. Because there, under a pile of junk, lay a big package of the very sheets of tin that are used for sleeves on coconuts trees to stop the rats from climbing them. I counted four hundred and fifty sheets. Stopping by Raumati's, I asked if he had any, too.

"I don't know; maybe. Let's take a look."

By rummaging in his tool shed, we found about a hundred sheets under some bags of cement. I didn't get it. Raumati and his family spent every other week at the fish-pen camp on their *motu* near the pass. I had gone there several times with Stephan and Iléana for a change of scenery and to give Raumati a hand. About thirty coconut trees surrounded the camp, but because of the rats, there wasn't a single coconut to drink. And if there is one thing a Paumotu *really* needs, it's being able to collect a few drinking nuts every day. Yet God only knew how many years those sheets of tin had been there, gathering dust.

"If you need them at Poro Poro," said Raumati in a friendly tone, "help yourself."

I took about thirty sheets, to replace the plastic ones on our coconut trees, which were beginning to shred. The next day, accompanied by Iléana and Stephan, I raised anchor to sail JOSHUA over to Raumati's fish pen. It wouldn't be the first time Stephan cut class with his parents' consent. And in a quiet day and a half of work spent deep in thought, I nailed sleeves on the thirty-two coconut palms that graced and shaded our friends' camp by the pass.

Iléana told me she had never seen eyes as luminous as Raumati's and Tepuku's. It didn't have anything to do with the sleeves I had put on their coconut trees; it had been that way ever since we arrived at Poro Poro. They loved us deeply, and we returned that love with the same intensity. To us, they represented everything that was most true and pure in the mirror of Polynesia, where the heart embraces everything.

With Neti, it was different. We had recognized each other from the very first day, like two brothers reunited after being separated for forty years, during which time they had lived completely different lives. Twin brothers, born of the same flesh, suckled at the same breast, rocked and told the same stories by their mother. When we worked together, I found myself traveling far back into my past, to when Xai and I used to run through the forest seeking the Enchanted Bird. And, as in the old days with Xai, Neti and I could communicate without needing language, by joining our thoughts directly.

So as Neti towed his *cao* across the sandbar between Poro Poro and the village this morning, he didn't have to open his mouth for me to hear his question: "You want to go do a little more copra work?" And I didn't have to move my lips for him to hear my answer: "No copra, but we can work on the coconut trees if you like; it's up to you."

And he kept on walking and towing his *cao*, wearing a smile so luminous I immediately guessed he had a surprise in store for me. When he reached the beach in front of our *faré*, the big stack of tin sheets lay in the bottom of the *cao*, along with a hammer and nails. So I took my *pupui* and my hammer and we set off together to put sleeves on the coconut trees on the same plot of land that had given us the eight sacks of copra two weeks earlier.

Blam-blam-blam-blam . . . and another one was done. I climbed down my ladder, which I had fashioned out of *kaaia* branches. Neti was working on the next row of coconut trees. For the past week, we had averaged seventy trees a day between the two of us. I moved my ladder and leaned it against the next trunk. If the sleeves were set only as high as a man, a rat could get past them by taking a running jump. You also had to anticipate that the vegetation would grow back between clearings; a rat could climb *kaaia* saplings and easily get past the sleeves. For both those reasons, they had to be nailed fifteen or twenty feet off the ground.

Blam-blam-blam-blam . . . it was simple, but terribly repetitive. You had to stand perched on the next to the last rung of the ladder, nailing with your back arched, head back and arms in the air. Over time, your neck and shoulders started to cramp. Next!

Blam-blam-blam-blam . . . I couldn't stop thinking. The coconut trees were planted fifteen feet apart; there were four hundred for every two and a half acres, which came to 400,000 trees
on Ahe's 2,500 acres. Working at a steady thirty-five sleeves a day,
that came to 12,000 man-days—forty years for a guy doing the
work by himself, perched on his ladder three hundred days a year
with his deltoids in knots. Next!

Blam-blam-blam-blam . . . With a bunch of nails between my
lips, I kept pace with Neti. We were working in parallel, each on
his own tree, and thinking the same thing. The village had fifteen
guys in it, sixteen counting me . . . So even if we could get the
400,000 sheets of tin, it would take all of us three years . . . Three
years of doing nothing but this from morning till night . . . Forget
it! Next!

Blam-blam-blam-blam . . . Right after the Second World War,
the government had wanted to deal with the rat problem in the
high islands—Tahiti, Moorea, etc. So it gave away the tin and offered a substantial premium for each coconut tree sleeved. An official I considered trustworthy told me that it had taken twenty
years just to finish the high islands. In other words, you give me
the tin, deliver it to my *faré*, pay me to put sleeves on my own coconut trees . . . and I take twenty years to do the job . . . That was
no joke . . . And Iléana would be rubbing my shoulders tonight.
Next!

Blam-blam-blam-blam . . . For the Tuamotus, the government
tried something it figured wouldn't take so long or be so hard—
and in theory, it should have worked like a charm. Each atoll was
given thousands of little boxes and a free supply of rat poison.
The villagers were to grate coconut meat, fry it so the smell would
attract the rats, mix it with the poison, and set out one box for
every couple of acres, nailed to a coconut tree trunk. Next!

Blam-blam-blam-blam . . . Grating lots of coconuts, setting out
lots of boxes, replacing the poison every month . . . The wonderful Polynesian people live in the present, and they aren't at their
best on long-term projects . . . So the little boxes were left to rot
in somebody's yard and the poison was buried at the foot of a coconut tree. Next!

Blam-blam-blam-blam . . . Rats were scurrying through my
mind . . . You can't just let them call the shots . . . They come and
go as they please, they don't have any predators . . . My eyes
widened . . . What's that I see there, in the back of my mind, come
out of nowhere? Could it be the silhouette of a cat?

Blam-blam-blam-blam . . . I had hammered so many nails in the past week I could work with my eyes closed . . . Yes, it's a cat all right, no doubt about it . . . A cautious little voice whispered in my ear: "Watch what you're getting into; don't get involved in this adventure, it's going to cost you. Stay Paumotu, it's so much simpler." Another voice rose from deep in my heart: "You have to move life upward, otherwise we'll continue being monkeys until the end of time." And the Child danced before my eyes shouting, "Yippee! We're going to have a ball with this business; it'll be terrific!"

Lunch break in the shade of the *kaaia* at the edge of the lagoon. Neti went out on the reef with his *patia* but didn't find any fish, so he brought back a few clams. I lit a fire to cook the rice. Water for coffee was heating in a can near the coals on which we grilled the clams. We smoked cigarettes while waiting for the rice to cook. Neti was silent, as usual, and my mind was wandering far afield, back to the period when my only reason for living was sailing the sea without any other goal than to get the most out of the beautiful things of existence. Then followed that long period alone with myself during the nonstop sail around the world, the start of a higher and broader view of our responsibilities to the planet. And then I had tried my big play of offering my royalties to the Pope . . . Had I aimed too high? Of course not. You never aim too high when a matter of evolution is involved. At most, you get a black eye by tackling something that's too big for you. That time, I had gone to the canvas, no two ways about it, and then the FRI affair sent me down for the count. Philip and Ein Kerem managed to get me back on my feet, but it hadn't lasted. All those adventures had left me punch-drunk. That was when Suvorov reached out to me, and then Ahe, like a miracle. I then resolved not to waste another minute looking to the past, and even less to the future. I thought I had found a safe harbor here where I could build a double watertight bulkhead between "before" and "after," with a well-protected nest where only the present would exist. I had wanted to become a Paumotu. The graft had taken, but I now realized that the other branch of my being still had sap flowing in it, fed by roots sunk deep in the distant time when I was searching for a new path toward the future.

Now everything was clear in my mind. The cat I had barely glimpsed earlier had come to life; the rats were starting to lie low. And I could see a great wave rushing in from the horizon to lift me on its crest and take me I knew not where.

"Neti, I think we can pull off something really terrific! Give me some time to think it through carefully."

A few days later, I learned that except for Neti and Raumati, all the others were still burning the fronds in their coconut groves, to keep them nice and clean, because it was the custom. That was just great! It reminded me of a Leo Ferré song about the coming of the Great Day: "Yes, in ten thousand years/When the germs of stupidity have all died out."

When I was younger, I often used to go flying on the wings of my illusions. I had lost them some time ago. Not in the negative sense of "What's the use?" But decisively in the spirit of "Okay, we'll continue on foot." And this whole business of coconuts and rats was starting to fascinate me. I could feel myself swelling with a kind of excitement. My mind was racing, trying to figure things out, looking for a chink in the armor of fatalism that seemed to hang over Polynesia . . . Little Hina had died, even though it would have taken the village only two days to wipe out the mosquitoes . . . This beautiful atoll being impoverished by fire . . . The teeming rats . . . Mango pits tossed in the garbage when it would be so simple to plant them instead, and have a mango tree near every *faré* . . . The enormous waste caused by technocrats in their Tahiti offices, cut off from reality, throwing huge amounts of money out the window on big showy projects, when that same money could be used to plant useful trees on every hillside in the high islands . . . It brought to mind that scene from Greek mythology where the guy is pushing a boulder up a mountain; just as he's about to reach the top, kerbang-crash-bang! the rock rolls down the hill, and the guy has to go down and start rolling it back up again, until the end of his days.

But I held a master trump card: *I have never believed in fate.* Destiny hasn't written our future in indelible ink. If it's written at all, it's in pencil, and we're free to erase a word here and there, replace one with another, change the meaning of a sentence we disagree with, and thereby shift the future in a direction shaped by humanity and not by some so-called fate leading us by the nose.

While spearfishing this morning, I had been lucky enough to immediately spot a very big rainbow-colored parrotfish. I speared it just behind the gills and climbed out of the water thirty seconds after diving in. Iléana was waiting for me at the edge of the barrier reef. She didn't like me hunting by myself out in the open ocean where the sharks can be troublesome. She used to say I enjoyed cheating death. That's somewhat true at times. The Child loves to feel emotions that make your heart pound and your senses come alive; it's as important for him as it is for me. Playing at cheating death feeds our friendship, adds spice to my life, gives me a sharper awareness of reality. JOSHUA certainly cheats death, and we've often enjoyed doing it together. Yet we have never taken undue risks, any more than I had taken any real risk on the reef with my *pupui* today. Besides, we needed a big fish for tonight's banquet. We were having five guests, three of whom were big eaters. Stephan and Tutaina would spend the night in the village with Neti's parents.

Across the lagoon, the sky was turning pink. The air was calm, and Génie the cat lay curled up in my lap. He loved to have me scratch his head between his ears, and would close his eyes with pleasure when I stroked his neck under his chin. The two of us weren't dreaming about the same things, but we were both completely happy. I thought of the political party I had formed the day before, the "Tamata Gang." It had six members all told: Raumati, Tepuku, Neti, Iléana, and me; Génie the cat had been enlisted willy-nilly. All our plans depended on him; he would be our torch, our symbol, our standard-bearer.

I used to think that politics was the battleground of a race of short-sighted, extremely talkative and sometimes dangerous monkeys, where each band had its own leader. They had long ago been immunized against the slightest metaphysical anxiety, and their genius lay in seizing power while carefully avoiding the essential question raised by the age-old clash between Intelligence and Idiocy.

My feelings about politics had become much more refined since living in Ahe, which was really a microcosm of our planet. I could see to what extent my atoll with its sixty souls responded to the same mental mechanisms as all humanity, just as my Rolex worked on the same principle as the first watch built two centuries before. And I was now convinced that those involved in public affairs devote a great deal of their mental and spiritual energy to trying to create a better world.* So, as the poet says, "Please do not shoot the piano player. He is doing his best."

---

*Women, more than most men, have what can be called "intelligence of the heart," and they represent 53 percent of the electorate in the West. With women in power, I think the world would take on a more human face. Fifty-three percent . . . The choice is up to you.

The Tamata Gang was also going to do its best. Iléana and Tepuku fixed a bowl of *poisson cru*—raw fish marinated in lemon juice and coconut milk. I felt proud of having speared the eighteen-pound parrotfish in so little time this morning. The rice was almost ready; we would soon be sitting down to dinner. In our case, that was literally true, since the *faré* had no furniture, and we ate squatting around a mat on the floor. Iléana started frying a piece of fish for the cat, just the way he liked it, nice and crunchy. Raumati was already there when Neti arrived. Our political party was now complete, meeting at Poro Poro to fully debate the big project I had mentioned to Neti the previous week while we were nailing sleeves on the coconut trees.

Cat, pretty cat, lazy cat who had never been curious enough to catch and eat a rat, pretty, plump cat purring on my knees as the delicious aroma of frying fish comes to tickle your delicate nostrils . . . If you could read our minds, you might cock an attentive and slightly worried ear. Because after we eat this meal together, we will be mainly talking about you. When Kipling told his marvelous stories about the Wild Wood in the Time of the Very Beginnings, he never imagined that Man, your enemy, would ever be able to put you to work. But I can't see what Law should have decreed that you should be the only animal on earth never to do any work, the only one to purr while waiting for supper time, waiting for Woman, your ally, to bring you nice crisp fried fish three times a day, forever.

Well, guess what? Things have changed since the Time of the Very Beginnings when you made your pact with Woman. It may come as a surprise, but we've finally found the perfect job for you. Now I promise to respect the ancient Pact as far as you personally are concerned. So don't worry about a thing. You can laze around our *faré* for as long as you please, playing with Stephan and rubbing against Iléana's soft legs. We're saving the heavy work for your descendants. Okay now, scat! The rice is cooked, stop clawing my knees while purring like an idiot! It's our supper time, too.

Polynesian cuisine will never be as refined as Vietnamese, but both here and there, it is eaten in the same restful, almost religious silence. Around our mat, as on the family platforms in my village in Indochina, you really savor what you eat, you fill your stomach, and nothing else matters. And when you lick your fingers at the end of the ceremony, it isn't just a figure of speech.

After coffee and a cigarette, we moved on to copra, rats, and cats. During the last few days, I had carefully prepared things.

Everything was in perfect order, with figures clearly written in felt-tip pen on the back of a condensed-milk carton. I gave a running commentary as we went along, as if I were building a strong, waterproof *faré*.

"One: A rat destroys 25 pounds of copra each year, so one hundred rats destroy 2,500 pounds. And three hundred rats represent 7,500 pounds of copra lost.

"Two: If you turn a cat loose in the wild (with a water hole so it can drink when it wants to), it will have to eat at least one rat a day. The water is there, the rats are there, it will have to figure out how to get by; that's the cat's problem, not ours. And since a cat isn't a stupid animal, this will mean at least three hundred rats wiped out every year, and about three and a half tons of extra copra for Ahe. With ten cats, that comes to thirty-five tons, at a cost of some extra sweat spent digging water holes.

"Three: A female cat normally has two litters of kittens a year. Given the difficult living conditions, we can figure that she will instinctively limit the number of births to one kitten per litter, say, or two a year. That's the bare minimum." (Tepuku and Neti agreed with that figure; Raumati and Iléana thought there would be more kittens, at least two per litter.) "To be on the safe side, let's keep the figures low and stick with the initial estimate. And we can be sure the kittens won't be attacked by rats, because Tuamotu rats are tiny, more like mice than rats.

"Four: So each female becomes three cats by the end of the year. Ten females become thirty cats. And those thirty ratcatching cats will save about a hundred tons of copra by the end of the project's first year."

"Five: Therefore, the ten initial females (with a few males thrown in) will have metamorphosed into thirty hunters after a year, seventy or eighty after two years, and more than two hundred by the end of the third year. After that, no problem. The Big Project's pump will be well primed. Ripe coconuts will rain from the trees and the schooner will have to start coming more often to load all the miraculous copra."

Our meeting went on late into the night. Nobody spoke much. When someone put forth the germ of an idea, it took shape slowly, the way a seed sprouts, or the way the pieces of a puzzle slowly come together over time.

"All the young people who go to Tahiti looking for work will finally come back," said Tepuku.

For years now, the exodus of the young from the Tuamotus had been a major problem. Babies grew up, became adolescents who stared at the horizon . . . and the young people gradually started leaving the atolls, where copra was getting harder and harder to find, leaving the old folks to get by on the *fenua* . . . They would find work in Tahiti, where the money was easy, or so rumor had it. And when they got *fiu* (fed up) with all that, they would hop a schooner back to the calm of the Tuamotus with a brand-new radio, gifts for their parents, and lots of stories to tell about the big city . . . Then they would leave for Tahiti again to make lots of easy money before coming back . . . They would keep one foot there, in the bustling hubbub of city life, and the other next to the lagoon where they were born, *patia* in hand . . . But the dream never came true; there wasn't enough work in Tahiti for native Tahitians, much less the Paumotus, and many of the young people streaming in from the atolls turned to delinquency and wound up in jail.

"When they come back to the *fenua*, there will be enough people to replace the old coconut trees," murmured Raumati after a long silence.

At that, something clicked in my head. It was no longer just a matter of Ahe, one little atoll lost in the middle of the Pacific. The Papeete technocrats drawing up grandiose plans in their air-conditioned offices dreamed of developing Polynesia with tourism and pearl farming. They didn't realize that all that was just so much hot air. If they took the trouble to open their eyes, they would realize that their plans were nothing but glitter. Polynesia was an underdeveloped area that had been wallowing in artificial wealth for decades, entirely supported by subsidies orchestrated by speeches in which self-interest and mud-wrestling idiocy dominated the debate. Meanwhile, the *fenua* was drifting away, like a boat that has lost its anchors. Nearly eighty percent of the coconut groves on the Tuamotus and the high islands had been planted before I was born, a half-century ago. And everyone knows that after sixty years, a coconut tree yields practically nothing; it has been squeezed dry. It doesn't take a prophet to understand that some day, sooner or later, the coming economic crash will smash the Golden Calf and rock the entire planet. And when it does, neither speeches, nor hotels, nor pearl necklaces will feed this ravaged land where asphalt and concrete will have replaced breadfruit trees. Copra is a coin of the realm, an edible substance that can always be traded for other foods, whether flour, sugar, condensed milk, etc., or traded for lumber to build the schooners that supply the islands. But only if the copra is there when you need it. Replanting coconut trees was an absolute priority in guarding against a future that many signs were announcing, the way you know a hurricane is coming by observing the sky and the sea.

Our friends returned to the village at two o'clock in the morning. Iléana was dozing peacefully with the cat nestled against her. I felt so excited, I couldn't sleep. "When they come back to the *fenua*, there will be enough people to replace the old coconut trees . . ." Raumati's words echoed deep within me, harking back to a distant past in which I saw the first canoes leaving Asia, setting out to put down new roots beyond the horizon. I felt gripped by a tremendous power that tore me from the ground. I was soaring over the Tuamotus, an immense archipelago. I climbed a little to try to glimpse the future. It wasn't just the Tuamotus I could see from up there, but all of Polynesia, its land and its people. Our cat would be surprised to learn that he would be taking part in saving not only Ahe, but all the atolls and the high islands as well. Seriously, I'm not crazy. Look: cat = copra = young people returning to the atolls where they find work that is financially and creatively rewarding = less delinquency and social unrest in Tahiti = Polynesian consciousness moving toward a higher path. It was more beautiful than the Golden Calf and made a lot more sense than blindly following the West, that giant with feet of clay. Perhaps the young would figure out how to stop their parents from destroying the soil with fire. But that wasn't the main thing; the earth is patient, it abides. What was really important was that the young people would come back, stop crowding into Tahiti, and start planting coconut trees for the future.

JOSHUA hadn't left the lagoon for more than eight months. Yesterday, I filled her water tank and dove down to brush the hull. The last time the copra schooner called, we bought a sack of flour, three boxes of condensed milk, sugar, cooking oil, kerosene, batteries, and a lot of other things—all of which were now carefully stowed under the bunks. The sails and sheets were ready, the deck cleared, the sextant mirrors checked. Everything was ready for our departure.

JOSHUA, my faithful boat, you bore me to the heights during the long way. You gave me faith. You carried soil and everything we needed so we could flourish on this chunk of coral. And tomorrow, your bow will sing with happiness as it drives across the sea to Suvorov, where Old Tom needs fresh supplies, where the young coconut trees on Bird Island need my and Iléana's hands. We'll plant another thirty trees and then beat against the trade wind to Tahiti, where we'll find cats for you to carry to Ahe. It will be our second visit to Poro Poro, and we'll probably stay seven or eight months. Then we'll head for Tahiti again and bring back a load of fruit trees, so that there will be mango, lemon, and avocado trees around each *faré*, against the day that the young people return to their *fenua*.

You can fall in love with a people the way you fall in love with a woman. My love for Polynesia goes back to my first visit, years ago. I knew I wouldn't live in this country forever, but I was here now and felt ready to give a lot to help this people awaken from its torpor and see things clearly. And yet I could tell how much Ahe now reminded me of a space that had become too narrow for a bird whose wings had grown and who was looking further, higher, toward the vast world.

Seated at my chart table, I wrote a letter to France's mayors and town councillors:

Here is an idea I think is a good one, even though it came to me in a dream: to plant fruit trees along our city streets, along all our roads and paths, in all our public parks, and even in our forests, using species that would yield fruits and good wood for building or cabinetwork. Because a fruit tree gives both the shade and greenery we need, as well as fruit. But beyond these practical considerations, fruit trees that belonged to everyone (including the bees and the birds) without being anyone's private property would stand as a symbol of the era of change we have to embark on if we want to re-build Europe and the planet. As they grow, those fruit trees could become real, silent participants in creating something bigger than our small selves, a work both generous and simple which would help to unite people on the path to the evolution of the intelligence of the heart. This dream, which isn't mine alone, will be opposed by all sorts of laws, warning us against wasps hiding in the ripe fruit to sting our children, diarrhea from eating green ones, and every other ill one can imagine. But if we have made laws, it is our duty to modify them in the direction of Creation, so we don't remain as we are, that is, not really much, for the time being. People have built cathe-

drals, and I think that a country whose roads, paths, and streets were lined with fruit trees would be more lovely than the most beautiful cathedral imaginable.

I had told Iléana that I was going to spend the night on board to quietly prepare JOSHUA for our trip to Suvorov. The sun was beginning to set on the other side of the lagoon. Absorbed by my writing, I hadn't noticed the hours passing. A heap of rough drafts littered the floor, as in the days when I was working on *The Long Way* while listening to voices from afar. The Child had come to crouch next to me on the berth and together, we re-read the letter to the mayors. That Child, whom I had brought with me when I left Indochina, had been my friend forever. He had been the one to teach me always to aim as high as possible, even if the goal seems out of reach, even if you can scarcely see it through the fog. I thought of the palm fronds Iléana and I had spread on Poro Poro's bare sand, not knowing how much they would change what was once a desert—as well as the way we saw things. Writing is much like the business of the palm fronds: you scribble a still-vague idea on paper so as to see it more clearly, you work at it the way a potter works the clay without noticing the time passing, and the clay takes the shape of an act that slowly grows. If all this sounds like nonsense, no matter. The idea was beginning to take shape and would go its own way, borne along by other hearts. Ahe had taken me time, like this letter to France's mayors. The Child and I worked on it by the light of the kerosene lamp that cast dancing shadows in JOSHUA's cabin. And then we were off to the countries of Africa, India, the rest of Asia and Latin America, where entire populations were struggling to survive. I could see myself on Poro Poro, shovel in hand, meditating on the obvious fact that a cucumber hole that produces for a month requires the same work as planting a breadfruit or a mango tree that could feed and shelter generations. The essence of this letter to the mayors should water the entire planet; we may as well aim right for the heights while we're at it! But you can't do everything at once . . . I would get involved in that beautiful story in a few years, after I wrapped up the job started on a small scale in the microcosm that was Ahe.

The sky was lightening already. Deep in thought, I hadn't slept a wink all night. Dawn was here, the sun would soon be rising. I found myself back at Ein Kerem next to Philip, who often used to say: "The work is teaching you the work." He must have meant that by contemplating a mental image and adding the necessary sweat and faith, the image takes on perspective and precision. Like the *patia* that winds up by becoming magical, and hits the coconut stuck on top of the pole.

CHAPTER 20

Josephine Baker used to sing that she had two loves: her own country, and Paris. For us, the two were Suvorov and Ahe, separated by the immense Pacific with its millions of pearls cast up by JOSHUA's bow wave.

The trade wind was blowing fair, and our boat happily ate up the thousand miles that separated us from our dream in a week. The bowsprit could already sense the entrance to the pass; no treacherous currents, reefs safely off to port and starboard, everything was clear ahead for the final sprint into the lagoon of light.

Time stopped there.

Suvorov!

We found old Tom splitting sprouted coconuts with his hatchet and feeding them to his chickens. Those forty or fifty hens were the linchpin which kept his whole existence in balance. To keep fallen mature coconuts from turning his island into an impenetrable jungle, Tom gathered them before they took root and fed their oily, slightly sweet meat to his chickens. In exchange, they gave him half a bucket of manure a week, which was essential to his garden. With a laugh, Tom said that the chickens had taught him the secret of perpetual motion.

Tom was a fountain of youth. Standing, as if for eternity, on his seventy-four-year-old legs, he never stopped moving. All alone, he had built a coral jetty as sturdy as he was, that extended from the beach out to deep water. Hurricanes had several times scattered the coral blocks; each time, he started over, with the patience and determination of an ant. I couldn't imagine how he had been able to pile up that enormous mass over such a distance. Men have built temples and monuments that inspire other men. Tom had built this colossal wall while creating his island.

After spending a few days with Tom, JOSHUA went to anchor off Bird Island, where we stayed for three weeks. Of the fifty coconut trees planted the year before, twelve had survived; the rest had died. Twelve out of fifty wasn't too bad, considering how poor the soil was; we couldn't complain. The face of Bird Island was gradually changing. "The buffalo is slow, but the earth is patient." We planted another thirty sprouted nuts before raising anchor.

We returned to Tahiti by a roundabout route, with a month-long stopover at Bora Bora; we were in no hurry. In Papeete, we hauled out at a slip owned by our friend Ellacott, whose father had seen Gerbault, Eric de Bisschop, Le Toumelin, and Bardiaux all come through.

Once we had hauled out, we started looking around—for cats. Lots of cats. As many cats as possible. No dawdling, but no undue haste, either. We had to prepare the big Ahe project carefully.

A few weeks later, JOSHUA raised anchor with a cargo of sixteen kittens, all weaned and in perfect health, plus two nearly grown females. The adventure reminded me of a truck loaded with young nursery fruit trees which were being taken to be planted, to beautify a landscape and make it productive as well. Iléana, who was sensitive to smells and tended to get seasick, would leave with Stephan three days later aboard the copra schooner. I had Neti along; I had sent him a telegram, and he hitched a ride on a passing yacht to come join me in Tahiti. He was an excellent sailor and a valuable presence on a sailboat.

The weather was fine and we were making good time. The two female cats explored the cabin without seeming too intimidated; I was relieved to see them sniffing the litter-box full of sawdust. The sixteen little ones were housed in a big cardboard box with about twenty holes cut in the sides; to get fresh air, all they had to do was stick their noses out. The box was carefully wedged in the forepeak, with water and food in cans tied in the corners.

However, we very quickly discovered that cats need lots of room, and can't stand being cooped up. By the next day, several had managed to enlarge the air-holes by shoving their heads through as far as their necks. They then tried to push their shoulders through, got stuck, started to panic; they were drooling, on the point of strangling. Others lay completely inert, carried by the heel of the boat into a heap in a corner of the box, where they lay in their vomit and droppings, suffocating. One more day and they would all be dead. I had to free them, to keep them from dying of asphyxiation. They revived in a few moments, eyes alert, a new spring in their step . . .

After four days of tacking, the boat had turned into a real hell-hole. Shit and piss were everywhere: on the bunks, the cushions, the floor, under the sink, in every possible corner. When I returned a pair of pliers to my tool-box, which I had foolishly left open while I was on deck loosening a shackle, I found a kitty curled up in it . . . and got a sticky mess all over my fingers. A locker swung open, and I quickly slammed it shut; it contained the precious fabric that Iléana used for her *pareus*. An hour later, when I went below to light the Primus to heat a can of food, I heard scratching. I listened carefully. It was coming from that very same locker . . . and I found a cat inside. I'll never know how it managed to get in there without Neti or me noticing.

Having scattered throughout the boat, the cats now took it over. Every personality imaginable was represented: timid, impudent, cunning, hungry, cautious, noisy, sneaky, whiny, and diplomatic. The only thing they clearly had in common was a smell that was becoming more pestilential by the hour. And nothing we did could discourage them from doing whatever they pleased, whenever they felt like it.

Aita péa-péa (it doesn't matter) is the key to Polynesian philosophy, the "Open Sesame" which lets you soar so high that the worst calamities fade away in the distance and disappear.

Aita péa-péa . . . The cats were here, but we had wings and were elsewhere, far away in our minds, daydreaming. We handled sail to keep the boat moving as fast as possible. And what a pleasure it was to be sailing with Neti!

Aita péa-péa . . . We joyfully took the pass with our eighteen lively cats.

Aita péa-péa! Hello, beautiful Ahe! Mission accomplished!

Iléana and Stephan joined me at Poro Poro. She had found six more kittens at the last minute, and brought them on the copra schooner. Then a yachtsman friend showed up at Ahe a few days later with another three kittens. So we had twenty-seven future rat-catchers, far more than the dozen we had originally planned on.

For the village, it was like a party. Three kittens went to Neti, three to Tepuku and Raumati, the two young females to us on

Poro Poro. Iléana's own lazy Génie, whom Tepuku had cared for while we were away, was already paying court to the older of the two young ladies; she would soon be a mother. Papa Toa doled out the nineteen remaining kittens at a rate of one or two per *faré*.

The following Saturday we held a general meeting of the "Tamata Gang" at Poro Poro around the traditional meal of rice and fried fish, supplemented with green papaya salad and a bottle of wine. The object of our meeting was to plan the best possible next step for our cat project, which had begun so well. On Sunday, after the *boules* match in front of the village hall, Raumati spoke up:

"Instead of putting the cats to work as soon as they're old enough to fend for themselves, let's keep them in the village, where they will have lots of kittens. It will be like choosing coconut trees and caring for them, and then planting the *motus* with the ones that produce the best nuts."

Papa Toa nodded. Everyone agreed. Within a few months, each *faré* could become a real cat factory. Some factories produce cans of peas or sardines, others produce tanks, jet planes, or guns. Ahe would produce cats. It was simple: the twenty-seven cats from this first batch would be well fed and cared for in the village, and would regularly produce lots of kittens, which would be sent to work on the *motus* once they grew up. It was more than simple, it was a real stroke of genius. It was clear that the cats kept in the village as breeding stock and fed fish and rice would be much more fertile than cats struggling to survive in the wild, eating rats when they could catch them. Moreover, if the feral cats had too much trouble raising their young, the *motus* could be regularly restocked with new cats being raised in the village. After Raumati spoke, Neti added that the villagers might even send cats to Manihi atoll, a dozen miles away, where each Ahe family also owned a coconut grove. No doubt about it: the Tamata Gang's big project was getting off to a great start.

Our absence had lasted four months, what with visiting Suvorov, tacking back to Polynesia, stopping in Bora Bora, hauling out in Tahiti, gathering the cat harvest, and then coming home to Poro Poro with our morale high and batteries fully charged.

The papaya trees planted nearly a year earlier were heavy with fruit. The thirty young coconut palms behind the *faré* were spreading their fronds in the sun, bringing some coolness to that previously desert-like area. And the wind over the *motu* seemed to have eased a bit, thanks to the ironwood trees staggered along the tide flats beyond the old *kaaia* tree. They were growing quickly, living only on coral and salt air.

The garden, on the other hand, had to be restarted from scratch. Pickaxe, shovel, crowbar, ten watermelon holes, ten cucumber holes, ten pumpkin holes, three beds for tomatoes and bok choy, seeds started in flats, new posts and fencing for the fish pen, endless bundles of fronds brought by dinghy from the neighboring *motu* to keep enriching the soil. We also had to pour fresh kerosene down the *tupa* holes; the old kerosene had evaporated during our long absence.

Completely absorbed in getting Poro Poro going again, Iléana and I hadn't been to the village since our return four weeks before. We were even busy on weekends. Our only breaks—if you could call them that—were spent doing odd jobs around the island. For the time being, I had lost all interest in *patia* throwing, for which the men continued to gather on the soccer field in the late afternoons. I also stopped going to the meetings after the *boules* games in front of the village hall. For her part, Iléana had too much to do to pay any calls, what with her *pareus*, gardening, Stephan's Chinese lessons, and cooking; if someone got sick and needed her advice or help, she would hear about it.

Up before dawn, aching with fatigue at sunset, we had gone back to the rhythm and sweat of the first days of our settling here. One of our female cats had a swollen belly; she would soon have kittens. The other was still a bit young, but it would happen soon enough. And our evening's exhaustion turned into immense satisfaction when we thought of the twenty-four kittens in the village, well fed, well cared for, which would soon go into action on the rest of the atoll. A new era was dawning for Ahe. We would see the difference in a year at the most. And that handful of cats would spread like wildfire. In just a few more years, the rats would be under control in a good part of the Tuamotus. No more wearing out your feet zigzagging between rows of coconut palms to fill the copra sacks. And the most amazing thing would be the way we had accomplished it, by sniffing the wind and carefully acting in concert with the village. So much ground covered in so little time, it was hard to believe!

And then Stephan came back from school with crushing news.

I dropped my crowbar, Iléana put down her spade, and we stumbled across the tide flats like sleepwalkers.

The parabola had been terrific all right, but the *patia* had hit an invisible barrier on the way to its target. Except for the kittens belonging to Tepuku, Papa Toa, and Neti, who were in fine shape, all the others were dead or nearly so. Two or three survivors were still hanging on, but they looked like skeletons, and wouldn't last long. Wiped out! Destroyed! It seemed incredible!

Yet it was easy to see how it had happened. The villagers just tossed food for their dogs into a corner of the yard and left the animals to work things out themselves. The kittens didn't even have time to get close before the dogs had eaten everything, and had died hungry and miserable. All the villagers had to do was feed them separately from the dogs. It wouldn't have taken much, just a little rice or fish—and a tiny bit of mental effort directed a step or two toward the future.

But the future, what was that? Very complicated, the future. Maybe the future will be full of stuff we don't want to deal with, things that are too new, or a little worrisome or unsettling, which might force us to use our brains a little. Just harvesting copra was enough of a grind; you don't expect us to think too, do you? So *aita péa-péa*, it's so much simpler, no point in worrying. If the kittens didn't feel like fighting the dogs to get something to eat, that was their business. *Aita péa-péa*, and life goes on its merry way, that of an eternal present where no surprises would ever upset our blessed routines.

I had to restrain myself not to show how outraged I felt at such callousness. It would have been a violation of a fundamental rule: in Polynesia, you don't stick your nose in other people's business. There was once an avocado tree in the village that belonged to a smiling old man. Naturally, kids stole avocadoes from it each time his back was turned, and he didn't like it. So nobody interfered when they saw the old man take a hatchet and chop down that lone avocado tree so the children could never swipe his fruits again. It was not to be believed. And yet Polynesians are infinitely generous; there isn't a speck of meanness in their soul— even if they had let the kittens die of *aita péa-péa*.

Back at the *faré*, Iléana blew up. She was so disgusted, she talked of leaving Polynesia. Plus she reproached me for not uttering a word of pity for those poor animals. We had been responsible for them, and they had died miserably. But I don't express my feelings much; I was like Françou in that way. Anyway, you can't bring the dead back to life. In a flash, I saw Françou standing in front of me, with Bai Ma—because of the word "responsible" that Iléana had said.

For two days, she didn't say a word, her eyes in the distance, sometimes wet with tears. And I looked inside myself—and remembered a story old Assam used to tell.

A craftsman was carrying on his head a bronze pot he had made; he was taking it to his new hut. His foot tripped on a stone, the pot fell to the ground, and the craftsman went on his way without turning round. He had heard the dull thud made by the pot the moment the metal hit the rocky ground. Rather than fix a cracked pot, he would make another one, stronger and more beautiful.

I continued to sort out my feelings. We really had taken a beating with our grandiose dreams, I had to admit. But it would be stupid to just drop everything now, get our things together, and set sail. Where would we go? And what would we do? If only for Stephan's sake, we had to stay here a few more years. No other place in the world that JOSHUA could sail to would give him a childhood that was so happy and rich, so fully animal . . . his bare feet, his friends, his *patia*, the endless horizon beyond the barrier reef where the primeval ocean broke, sharpening reflexes and forging the intelligence of the body. We didn't know what this boy would do later on in life, but Ahe would remain deep in his heart, as a beacon, an essential landmark.

Come on, Iléana, don't cry . . . I know we wanted this business with the cats to be a beautiful love affair between us and Polynesia, a love affair that could have gone far . . . It got shot down, there's nothing we can do about it. Don't cry . . . It's true that we're feeling pretty low, but let's forget all that, let's become Paumotu again, the way we were when we got here last year. Listen, here's an even better idea. It's a trick I perfected when I was on MARIE-THÉRÈSE during the monsoon in the Indian Ocean when everything was going to hell and I was so depressed I could cry. I just turned into a protozoan, depression couldn't touch me, and the boat went on its way as if nothing was the matter. Well, we'll do the same thing. I guarantee it: all our problems gone, not a single thought, the great inner calm, not a blip on the encephalogram. Come here, we'll start with a little snuggle, then a good night's sleep, and tomorrow we'll wake up as protozoa in an *aita péa-péa* of the highest order!

Sunsets on the mauve of the lagoon . . . toes spread to the per-
fumed breeze rustling the palm trees . . . our minds working in extreme slow motion as a healing fog blurrs the outlines of things.
From now on, nothing urgent. Back to square one. The past was
buried, the future didn't exist. We spent the greater part of our
days making Poro Poro beautiful. Poro Poro and our well-being.

The *tupa* became our guru. By observing it, we decided that it
functioned at a level barely more sophisticated than that of a protozoan, but probably much better adapted to the passage of time
on a Tuamotu atoll. Safe in its shell, lazy as the day is long, it
didn't rack its brains about existential problems. It didn't even
have any brains, much less problems. It saw only to its little com-
forts, picking up pebbles here and there to decorate its hole,
chewing a twig it happened to run into. If anything seemed a bit
far away—a couple of yards, say—it didn't go. No risk of getting
any bruises, no point in making life complicated. When the sun
was out, it basked on the sand; when the rain poured down, it
made use of it. It had everything all figured out, without thinking.
Once the *tupa* had transmitted its teachings to us, we took to living at a similar mental level, centered on the present, in the en-
joyment of the moment. It took little toll on our bodies and hardly
any on our brains.

One fine Easter weekend, we left the *tupa* daydreaming near
its hole and went out for a trip on the lagoon. I had the feeling that
JOSHUA was telling me to let her find her own way, not to interfere
until the moment came to drop anchor. Whenever a coral head
appeared in our path, a gust from the side would hit and correct
the course just enough to send the bow past the danger. Then the
wind would shift back to its previous direction, and the boat returned to its original heading. It was as if the boat, the coral, and
the breeze were playing at scaring each other a little. I watched all
this out of the corner of my eye just the same, but hardly had to
touch the tiller during the whole trip. Iléana was singing, sitting
on deck weaving a palm-frond basket, and Stephan was carving a
forked *miki-miki* stick for a new slingshot with his Opinel knife.
When I was Stephan's age, I had been crouching beside Hao's father next to one of the village junks as he showed me how to
comb the *cai tram* bark so it would fit snugly into the caulk seams.
In that way, JOSHUA quietly sailed all the way across the lagoon to

its farthest northeast point. That was where she had wanted to take us.

At first, I thought JOSHUA had chosen that spot to show us a place where the *kaaia* grew in especially dense clumps, where we could cut perfect saplings for the new windbreaks we needed at Poro Poro. But just a little farther, we discovered a small forest of gigantic trees. Stephan had spotted it, by watching a noddy's flight while Iléana and I were peeling our bundle of poles.

I couldn't believe my eyes. How could such giants be growing out of such a poor sand and coral base? Some of the trunks were twelve feet or more around, and they were as tall as the highest coconut palms. Frigatebirds, boobies, noddies, and fairy terns nested by the hundreds in their branches, so high up that their cries were muted by the time they penetrated the dense foliage, through which only pale shafts of blueish light came to dapple the ground. An aura of supernatural mystery emanated from the place, which Stephan dubbed "The Land of Birds." The coolness, the chiaroscuro, the deep majesty that reigned in the underbrush gave Iléana the feeling she was visiting a cathedral with a dome surrounded by stained glass windows, supported by huge, marble-faced columns.

As we walked in silence, I could hear the gods speaking. I recalled the endless forests of the stories of my childhood, inhabited by dragons, genies, and fairies. Some days lift me up on their wings this way, to drop me at the edge between two worlds, this one and the next, where a glimmer from the beyond rewrites familiar laws in its own image. The ground under our bare feet was spongy, covered with fine vegetable debris mixed with sea-bird droppings. It would be excellent in the Poro Poro compost. Our supply of empty sacks was back at the *faré*, but Iléana thought she could find four or five in a locker in the forepeak. She would also bring back some water, a nice snack, instant coffee, and dry wood for a fire. Stephan, who had left his slingshot in the cockpit, went with her.

I continued exploring alone. The place was about an acre in area, hidden behind the screen of *kaaia* trees lining the beach, inaccessible from the lagoon because of a large scattering of coral heads that protected it like a secret. The forest was invisible from the anchorage and nothing hinted at its presence when approaching it from any direction on land. Only Stephan, by looking at just the right spot, had made it reveal its existence. I had spent a lot of time in the forests of Indochina and elsewhere, but had never encountered one so dominated by a single tree species. There, even when one dominated, you always found creepers, ferns, and various other small trees living in symbiosis or conflict in the shadow of the giants. Here, there was no break; every single tree in the grove belonged to the same giant species (*Pisonia grandis*).

Two white fairy terns accompanied me part of the way. I walked slowly. Their translucent wings drew arabesques above my head, so close I could almost reach out and touch them. They led me to the edge of the grove, where the *motu* took on its usual appearance. There, a very long mound, about three feet high, caught my eye. It reminded me of the shell of a huge sea turtle. I sat down on it to rest a few minutes. I was thirsty. The "turtle" intrigued me. It was obviously a natural accident, created by some ancient hurricane, but nothing grew on it. The coral it was made of was almost smooth, covered only with dead leaves and a little moss. It wasn't normal. There should at least have been a few ferns growing there.

I stood up, planning to go on exploring. Suddenly I felt dizzy, seized by a kind of vertigo. I was very hungry and terribly thirsty. I sat back down on the turtle's back. I felt a presence near me, as if I were being watched, but nobody was there; I was alone with myself. And then, in a blinding hallucination, I saw Françou and Bai Ma, who looked at me and then disappeared. From the time Françou had appeared to me in the labyrinth before the long way, this was the third time I had seen him, with Bai Ma, close together. The first time was when I rounded Cape Horn, no longer in the Pacific but not yet in the Atlantic. The second time was when Iléana had said the word "responsibility." And I had just encountered them once again. So the passage of time hadn't erased their trace. That was the way it was; there was nothing I could do, and I had to live with it.

I re-entered the cathedral of tall trees. The soles of my feet could detect the smell of humus through their very pores. It had been a long time since I had felt such excitement. I was floating in a dream, yet I wasn't dreaming. I probed here and there with the tip of my machete. The layer of humus was between two and four inches thick pretty much everywhere. Around the tree trunks, between the big roots, it was much thicker, both light and dense with life, real compost . . . tons and tons of compost concentrated in this forest like a heart beating in the center of the atoll. Lacking a shovel, I scraped the humus up with a clam shell and piled it up with my arms. It was effortless. To think that we had spent eight months on this atoll during our first visit and nearly four since our return, twelve months during which Raumati had watched me busting my ass to make compost . . . and had never mentioned this inexhaustible supply!

As my pile of humus grew, I could hear the silence singing within me. I was floating in a cloud, in a kind of altered state. How much time had passed? Twenty minutes? Two hours? Iléana returned with four sacks which could each hold between sixty and seventy pounds of humus, if we packed them tight. She stared dumbfounded at my enormous pile. Poro Poro would explode with joy to see this fabulous treasure brought straight from the Land of Birds on JOSHUA's deck.

We filled the sacks. My body was busy here, my mind far away, my head filled with stars. At Ein Kerem, Philip used to tell me that thought resembled matter to the point that it *was* matter, weighing practically nothing, but matter nonetheless, just as this shiny clam shell in my hand was matter, or the invisible air I breathed, or the rustling of the wind high in the branches, or the smell of this humus that was carrying me to the heavens . . . all were matter born of a common origin, all composed of atoms clustered in a nucleus and surrounded by electrons traveling at speeds faster than thought could apprehend. Later, I found a definition of the electron written in a book by a Nobel prize-winning physicist: "A negatively charged twist of nothingness." And yet there I was, *me*, yes, *me myself*, body and soul inhabited by billions and billions of these twists of nothingness, like a Cro-Magnon man sitting in front of his cave with his chin in his hands, trying to understand the mystery of fire.

When we returned to Poro Poro two days later with our first four sacks of humus, we saw Tepuku and Raumati waiting for us under the old kaaia near the compost pile. They *knew* where we had come from. *Mana* had told them.

The Paumotu *mana* refers to something which under certain conditions can transmit thoughts. I really can't say what that "something" is; in that, I was no better than my brother the monkey, perched on the same branch before the void of space. Yet Iléana and I could affirm that the Paumotu *mana* had winked at us several times since we moved to Ahe. After all, since thought was matter, as Philip says and I believe, made up of the same elements as a stone you can throw on purpose or not, nothing prevented it from skipping on the lagoon or flying through the sky to another shore if it felt like it.

Whatever the case, Tepuku and Raumati were waiting for us under the old *kaaia* tree. We were impregnated with the Land of Birds, its scent, its beauty, its aura of mystery. The impetus we had been given there would get our *motu* off to a fresh start, thanks to the tons of humus we could gather in the magic forest. But they were worried because we had discovered it. It was haunted, they said, by a dangerous *tupapau*.

Raumati spoke in short sentences punctuated by silences in which I could almost hear a kind of primitive music where nothing was superfluous, like a throw of his *patia*. And the story he told us had its roots in the *namua roa* (the very distant past), long before the arrival of the first *popaa*, when the islands fought terrible wars with each other. He took us by the hand, Iléana and me, and led us back in time to the *namua roa*. There, he showed us the big double canoe that had hurtled over the barrier reef, carried by the breaking waves. And we could see it really rushing ahead in the thundering waves, as if it were about to crash down on us.

"Look: no women or children; only men with *patias* and rosewood clubs, very sharp and heavy and hard. The first day, many from Ahe died. But we were better with our *patias*; much better. You should have seen them fly, our *patias* with their sting-ray points.

"And before the second day ended, all the men out on the coral had been killed. All but one, who was so incredibly strong and agile, you can't imagine. That one, we didn't manage to get. When he saw the others were done for, he dove into the breakers, and didn't come up again. He preferred to let himself be eaten by the sharks and moray eels."

Deep in Raumati's eyes, this ancient epic was turning into images so vivid that I found myself back in the Saigon trench where Jacky had just shot a Viet two hundred yards away. At the same instant, I could hear Abadie telling me about those carnivorous idols that the smell of powder could cause to be born within us ... war ... war ... and then, the past when I was twenty years old began to unfold relentlessly deep in my conscience ... the past when I was twenty and betrayed Bai Ma ... It was right after the horrible Hérault massacre by the Viets, when my sandals were splashed with blood and my heart swollen with hate ... I had told Françou about the rifle that Bai Ma was hiding in his hut ...

Françou had used Abadie's influence to get himself assigned to Ha Tien . . . and from Ha Tien he showed up at the village at dawn with his Cambodian infantry patrol . . . And he shot Bai Ma in the head at point-blank range in front of the entire village . . . Later, he volunteered for the paratroop corps . . . And one day Françou committed suicide, because he saw that Bai Ma was his brother, like all the other people on earth.

Raumati paused for a long time. He rolled himself a cigarette and pushed his package of tobacco toward me without taking his eyes off the horizon. In the sand, his finger was drawing circles and squares in a way that reminded me of Xai in the shade of the big Rach Gia mango tree when the junks were resting on the river waiting for the wind to rise.

"But a few months later, we saw him again near the place where you found the humus. At first, the people thought it was his *tupapau*. But it wasn't a *tupapau*. He was alive. We watched him for a long time from a distance, because we feared his strength. Each morning at dawn, he dove into the lagoon to look for food, and would spend the whole day there. He very rarely came to the surface. He knew how to breathe like the fish. There was no question of attacking him in the water, he would have drowned us one after another.

"He really could breathe under water, but he had to return to his *motu* after sunset to sleep. We couldn't find his hiding-place; he didn't leave any tracks and avoided all of our traps. At one point, we thought he could turn into a tree; maybe he had become part man, part fish, part *tupapau*. And then one night, by the light of the full moon, someone saw him climb an old, broken-off tree trunk, and jump down inside it. That was where he slept. And the next day, we stuck four *patias* at the bottom of the trunk with their points sticking up. He was impaled when he returned from the lagoon. And that's the way we finally got him!

Mai-tai roa (very good), concluded Raumati, his eyes shining with a savage flame as he recounted this exploit from his people's past.

Aita mai-tai (not good), answered Tepuku. Her voice seemed to be coming from somewhere else, shaping images as palpable as Raumati's, but to which she brought a beauty that lit up her woman's eyes with a different flame, by whose light even a blind man could see that killing the warrior had been a terrible sin.

"You have to give the last one a chance," she said, "even if he isn't worth much. And that man had qualities that made him worth a lot. He was tall, strong, and brave, and he had powers. He could have brought new blood to Ahe and its descendants. With a little effort, we could have tamed him. We didn't even bother to try. Right away, the men thought of their *patias*, though they could very well have put a sign of peace in the bottom of his tree trunk, instead of spears. Offered him a place in the atoll's community. Let him repay the blood spilled on the reef. That's what we women asked for, and we were beaten for it. The men could only think of their *patias*. And they killed him like an animal. Worse than an animal.

"Ever since, his *tupapau* has haunted that forest. And it is *really* dangerous, because he was very strong when he was alive and hadn't been forgiven. You would do well not to go back there. But we know that no warning will stop you, so take very careful precautions: don't leave any footprints, and cover all the places where you collect humus with branches and dead leaves. And return to your boat before sunset."

Every weekend, JOSHUA dropped anchor at the Land of Birds. For the tons of humus we were bringing back to Poro Poro; for the outings on the lagoon; and for my secret rendezvous, though I avoided mentioning those to Iléana. With her experience as a psychiatric nurse, she might have worried that Ahe's isolation and apparent calm were driving me to a terrible breakdown.

According to Raumati, the turtle-shaped hillock had formed all by itself, at the site of the hollow tree where the last warrior had been killed. That was my secret rendezvous; at that tomb, risen from ancient times, I would meet Françou and Bai Ma.

At each of those encounters with my distant past amid the chiaroscuro of the cathedral of great trees, I could see the Child by my side like a sentinel, holding a lightning bolt in his hand. The gentleness of the past returned to Françou's eyes, the gentleness of the days when he wrote his poems. But Bai Ma's eyes remained hard, and would never meet mine. And I found myself alone in the enchanted forest again, alone before my own mirror, not knowing how to exorcise this very old business that linked the three of us together.

And yet someday I would have to succeed in untying the knot, in some way other than by shrugging my shoulders and thinking, "All that's too long ago, the statute of limitations has run." Françou's ghost accepted the statute of limitations, but not Bai

Ma's. I still lacked something fundamental that I needed to find forgiveness in his eyes, which refused to meet mine.

Two coats of white paint on JOSHUA's deck, two coats of red on her hull, a black stripe along the bulwark and another at the water line. Our second stay on the atoll had lasted nearly ten months; it was time to think about leaving. I also painted the mooring bitts, sheet cleats, pulpits, bowsprit, stanchions, and handrails with black enamel, the way I always had. Against all logic, black is very easy to see at night *at sea*. Because even on a stormy night, the sky and the sea are never pitch-black, but dark gray. And against that more or less dense gray backdrop, anything on the boat that is painted black can be spotted at first glance.

Some more straightening in the cabin and on the chart table and we would be nearly ready. All I had to do was dive and brush off the hull while Iléana signed Stephan up for the next term's classes. We almost certainly wouldn't be back in time, but so what? Stephan's school was everywhere: on the boat, on the reef, at Suvorov, as well as in the Papeete harbor parking lot, where he would make lots of new friends before coming back to brush his teeth at the cistern faucet under his teacher's eye. A real zigzag school . . .

The kittens who had survived the earlier disaster were nearly grown and able to hunt. There were twelve of them, including the three kittens born to our female. With Neti, Tepuku, and Raumati, we settled them in families of three on various *motus* far from the village. We dug a water hole for each colony. The water was perfectly fresh, and since it lay about three feet below the surface, we built a coral-lined ramp to it; the cats would be able to walk down to drink whenever they wanted, and sand wouldn't slide down from the edge to fill the hole. All in all, an hour's work per well.

We had regret in our eyes and a tightening in our hearts. This was a far cry from the Big Project we had once planned, with the village turned into a kitty factory, cats spreading throughout the Tuamotus, the salvation of Polynesia. True, not much was left of our dreams . . . But as Chu used to say as he fiddled with the big Hotchkiss's engine with wire and bits of inner tube, "When you don't have what you want, you make do with what you have."

Now the cats could fend for themselves; they had water, they had rats, it was up to them.* We wished them good luck and set sail for Tahiti to pick up supplies. Then we would be off to Suvorov, where old Tom and Bird Island would be glad to see us once again.

---

*When we returned six months later, we found far fewer coconuts gnawed by rats on those *motus*. We subsequently learned that the same experiment had succeeded on Tetiaroa Atoll, where a settler had released a dozen cats. They had reproduced and eliminated the rats. A simple and efficient trick which could have been extended to the whole of the Tuamotus long ago.

CHAPTER 21

The light was so bright today, it reflected the blue and green of Suvorov's lagoon onto the underside of a cumulus cloud that was visible long before the atoll itself came into view.

A few hours later, seen from atop the spreaders, the back of a single wave seemed to stay frozen on the horizon. It was the atoll, all right . . . It stayed in the same place, growing larger by the minute. Then its crown of coconut palms appeared, looking like a pincushion.

From then on, time hurried to meet us; everything accelerated, everything condensed . . . great rollers, laced with pearls, were breaking on the barrier reef . . . we took the pass in a single rush into the great blue heart of the lagoon . . . and a huge joy swept over us, the way it did each time we entered Suvorov!

JOSHUA anchored off Tom's island, about fifty yards from a big ketch flying an American flag. A Zodiac was pulling away from it, with a man in a wetsuit, a woman, and a child aboard. They waved to us and headed for the pass. This was a treat; meeting another boat with a child aboard is always a pleasure for both crews.

As soon as the anchor was down and the deck straightened, we loaded the dinghy and went to bring old Tom his supplies. He was as alert as ever, still busy with his chickens, his garden, and his perpetual motion.

While Stephan stayed behind to play with Tom's cats, Iléana and I crossed the *motu* by a trail leading to the outer reef. There, a deep crack let you get into the water without being pounded by the waves too badly. It was a good spot, and I had always managed to spear at least a fair-sized grouper there, sometimes a jack.

Iléana planned to gather dry wood and wait for me under our usual pandanus tree near the coral sand beach.

Less than a quarter of an hour later, I climbed out of the water, completely disgusted. This year, for some reason, the place was full of sharks; there were as many as six black-tips around me at once. Sharks of that species are normally fairly timid, but only if you can keep an eye on them. Six at once was at least four too many, and hunting alone under those conditions would have been foolhardy. We would have to make do with leftover rice and a can of green beans heated on the coals.

Heading back aboard in the late afternoon, we passed by the American ketch to deliver some coconuts and meet our neighbors in the anchorage. Coconuts are always welcome on a boat. Few Westerners know how to climb a coconut tree, and at Tom's, the smallest ones were fifteen or twenty feet tall. "Thanks for the coconuts, we really appreciate them. Dinner will be ready soon. Why don't you come aboard and share it with us? That is, if you like fish and spaghetti."

The invitation was in French. Aboard, we met Ugo, Isabella, and their son Maurice. He was a year older than Stephan and led him off to play in his cabin. The women went below; Ugo and I stayed on deck.

The head of a jack was hanging from the rear pulpit. On the cockpit bench, where Ugo's neoprene wetsuit was drying, a powerful compressed-air speargun caught my eye. The spear's size and weight were impressive. Compared to the light spears used with the rubber-powered Polynesian spearguns, it was strictly big-game caliber.

"How accurate is it?" I asked.

"Five feet from the end of the spear, I can hit a fish no bigger than two fingers across. Well, eight times out of ten. Tom tells us that you come to Suvorov often and that you get nice groupers with your Tahitian speargun. What did you get today?"

"Zip, zero. I've never seen so many sharks. Just black-tips, but they still managed to scare me. Did you get that jack near the pass? I went out there once, our first year here. That was enough for me. The pass is strictly gray shark territory, and those guys don't fool around."

"I use a kind of close-up stalking technique. We anchor the Zodiac at the edge of a coral head. Maurice and Isabella stay aboard and I get into the water, always staying within six feet of the boat. As long as I haven't actually started hunting, the sharks ignore me, and the jacks come to see what's happening; you know how curious they are. And you've seen my speargun, a real bazooka. It can kill even a big fish dead as a doornail if I aim carefully for its head three fingers behind the eye, or its lateral line. But I never fire unless it's a sure shot, and then I quickly toss the jack into the Zodiac. So far, I've managed never to give the sharks time to get nosy. Still, it might be more fun to go hunting together . . . and probably safer for both of us."

Ugo gave off a feeling of quiet strength, in which I didn't sense any bluff. He introduced me to PHOBOS with a quick tour of the deck. She was a sturdy 50-foot wooden boat of traditional plank construction, well maintained and without any flourishes. Plenty of freeboard, with good lines; she was probably pretty fast. Ugo confirmed my hunch: in the North Pacific trade wind PHOBOS had often covered 180 miles and several times 200 miles in twenty-four hours. The rigging fittings inspired confidence, and the bowsprit was a pleasure to look at. She felt like a true high-seas boat. Everything was clear on deck, sheets properly coiled, halyards cleated at the foot of the mast; no lines to trip over when you struck the sails in a hurry. Ugo had cut his halyards with enough additional length to avoid tangles while allowing for a little extra to accommodate wear at the blocks. No radar, no Satnav, no autopilot, not even a windvane. The lack of any kind of self-steering device on a blue-water cruising boat surprised me.

"One of us is always on watch in the cockpit," he said. "It's a matter of safety, to keep an eye out for fishing boats or freighters. But more than that, standing watches twelve hours out of every twenty-four brings us closer to the sea and the boat. Later on, we'll get a solid self-steering rig, but it isn't time yet. Meanwhile, the old system of steering by tying a sheet around the tiller forces us to fiddle with the set of the sails and stay alert to the needs of the boat. For us beginners, it's the best way to learn."

Ugo, a beginner? I wondered what he meant by that. Everything about PHOBOS spoke of a sure sense of the sea. He merely smiled and pointed to the companionway.

"It smells good down there. We'd better eat before the food gets cold."

Dinner was delicious: jack stew fines herbes with onions, a huge pot of spaghetti, and two bottles of California wine. I stuffed myself shamelessly as Iléana tried to keep Stephan from bolting his food so he could rush off to read comic books with Maurice, who had finished before him. Our hosts were hearty eaters too. Ahhh . . . that was better. Sea air, swimming, and being in the sun all day gives you a real appetite. It was all I could do to keep from stretching out my legs under the table and loosing a gigantic belch.

Ugo and Isabella were Italian-born and had taken U.S. citizenship a few years before. After finishing their studies in Rome, they had pooled their savings and left to drive through Canada in a Volkswagen bus equipped with bunks and a galley, stopping here and there. They didn't want to put down roots too quickly; the tempo was *piano, piano*. Staying mobile was the main thing.

They worked at whatever turned up, Isabella as a maid and Ugo in electronics. They reached Ontario, crossed into the United States, drove down the East coast from New York to Florida, and eventually headed out to California, looking around, getting a feel for things. They were very impressed by the United States, a huge country, fast-paced and efficient; a place where people weren't afraid of hard work, where unions and management knew how to bargain, putting their cards on the table to work out satisfactory compromises without blowing the business sky-high.

While finding well-paying jobs along the way, the two started sending their résumés to various universities. But they didn't want to settle on anything too soon; they still wanted to go a little farther, to see what Mexico was like. On the Sea of Cortez, with some friends they met along the way who were also living from this and that, they shot a documentary film, part of which dealt with spearfishing.

Meanwhile, several California universities had responded; Ugo and Isabella had only to choose and sign up. They picked the University of California at Berkeley, where Isabella started teaching psychology while working on her doctorate. Ugo earned a second doctorate, in geophysics, then got a job doing research in geophysics and engineering. He also worked on a project to detect minerals by using the radiation emitted by giant storms on the sun's surface . . . It was all a bit complicated for my little brain, especially with the wine flowing.

So I asked Ugo to explain something simple to me: "Why is it that the flames of a fire manage to create such beautiful shapes, so lively and unpredictable?" It was a question I had often asked myself, and I was sure a scientist of his caliber could finally answer it. But his answer astonished me:

"Like the eddies in a river or the ripples of waves breaking on a rock, flames are a chaotic phenomenon. People are using the most powerful computers available to understand the laws of chaos, but so far, nobody has been able to lift the veil. Chaos seems to hide behind an impenetrable enigma. But to answer your question, the only thing science has figured out in this area is that it is *theoretically* impossible to predict the shape and nuances that the flame of an ordinary wood fire will take."

Well, I was no wiser than before . . . But I better understood our fascination with that mysterious flower which dances so freely and has delighted our eyes since the cave days.

The children were asleep, snuggled together on Maurice's bunk. Around the three candles burning on the big cabin table, bottles were being drained and hearts warmed. We had the whole night before us. Total relaxation. Ugo and Isabella knew a little about me from my books and had seen the documentary about the "long way" on television. In their eyes, that fantastic trip was a kind of miracle, a symphony orchestrated by the gods, with the sea, a boat, and her skipper as the instruments. Under other circumstances, that kind of talk would have driven me right into my shell. But nothing of the sort happened here; our contact was as pure as bird song at dawn; no mask could resist Suvorov.

Until recently, Ugo and Isabella hadn't known anything about sailing except what they picked up in books and sailing magazines. They bought a boat, renamed her PHOBOS, added two backstays to better support the mast, and took her out on San Francisco Bay a dozen times. Then they headed for the horizon. They wanted to take three or four years to sail around the world, get things straight in their heads, get some perspective, discover the open ocean and overcome their fear (hence the name PHOBOS). I could see that it was the same, universal story . . . the story of us all . . . a story about the Dragon. And I reflected on the fact that one of the great privileges travelers have is the ability to communicate with each other very quickly, the way ants touch antennas to transmit messages. You either want and need to get to know each other better, or there's no mutual attraction; either way, the question is settled quickly. Sitting at the cabin table, we already felt connected by a very subtle bond.

When you're sailing around the world, your stopovers tend to be fairly short and carefully planned. PHOBOS had been preparing to raise anchor the previous afternoon when a leak in the seawater pump delayed her. By the time Ugo had taken everything apart, cleaned under the floorboards, replaced two nuts corroded by electrolysis, changed the membrane, and reassembled everything, night was coming on and it was too late to sail out through the pass. Then, when they saw JOSHUA arrive, they decided to stay another week.

Three o'clock in the morning already! Talking with Ugo and Isabella was so engrossing, we hadn't noticed the time passing. They were passionately concerned with the problems facing the planet. And they had a surprising view of the nuclear arms race that the United States and the Soviet Union had been engaged in for decades:

"For the first time in human history, a country can be less 'powerful' than a potential adversary without putting its own security at risk."

I glanced at Iléana, whose eyes had widened. Neither of us understood. Seeing how baffled we looked, they explained the paradox:

"Imagine two neighbors, John and Popov, who can't stand each other; each is afraid the other will attack. Suppose they each have a hundred incendiary grenades. When Popov makes ten more, John quickly follows suit. They continually monitor each other. It's the escalation of terror. All they can think about is their grenades. They don't have time to weed their garden, and their vegetables are shriveling from lack of care. No time to patch their rusty rain gutters or clean out their polluted wells. And they don't have time to look after their kids, who aren't doing a thing in school and are turning into delinquents. That's exactly where America and Russia are now, in 1977; they each have thirty thousand nuclear intercontinental ballistic missiles ready to launch. It's complete insanity.

"Now suppose the United States gets rid of nine tenths of its nuclear weapons. Is this *unilateral* decision risky? Absolutely not. Two thousand missiles—or even two hundred—have the same deterrent power as thirty thousand. And de-escalating the arms race would allow the United States to devote its financial, intellectual, and creative potential to ends that are a lot more useful and exciting: social progress, agriculture, teaching, scientific research. Everybody would benefit, not to mention the lessening of international tensions. Besides, such a unilateral gesture by one of the two superpowers would contain the seeds of greatness that our poor world desperately needs."

Next day, the trade wind shifted to south-southeast and strengthened, raising a steep chop. Our taut anchor chains were grating against the bobstays. The anchorage would soon be untenable. So I suggested we move together over to "our" island, which was completely sheltered from the weather. We quickly covered the two miles. With a bow anchor in six feet of water on a sandbar and another one off the stern on a coral head, our boats lay quietly in the lee of Bird Island.

Stephan took Maurice to go look at the frigatebirds and boobies that nested on the western part of the island. Iléana and Isabella began cleaning out the well and weaving palm fronds to make a hut for the kids. Later, we would help them gather firewood for lunch and finish setting up our camp. Ugo had been dazzled by my jury-rigged Zodiac, which was JOSHUA's second dinghy; he wanted to try it before buying one at his next port of call. When there are several people aboard a boat, having a second dinghy is like having a bicycle when you live in the countryside with a single car: the bike represents freedom for the person lounging by the fire when the other is out driving around. Our dinghy-bicycle was simply a huge inner tube (13.00-24/14.00-24) in a heavy canvas sleeve with a set of carefully tensioned straps to give it an oval shape and a longer waterline. It was very light, could carry two adults or be used to go set an anchor, and could be deflated and stored in a forepeak locker. After a few minutes' practice, Ugo pretty much mastered the reverse sculling movement that sent the boat through the water in a straight line—the same way the "basket boats" used by the junks of Indochina are paddled.

Then we went looking under the *tahinu* foliage for a *kaveu* to eat for lunch. A *kaveu* (*Birgus latro*) is a kind of huge hermit crab, but without a shell; it can grow to eight or nine pounds and tastes something like ordinary crab. This prehistoric-looking crustacean lives on most of the atolls, feeding on young shoots and vegetable debris. Using its huge claws, an adult can burrow into a sprouted coconut. Their number had risen sharply since our first visit, nearly five years before. Maybe that was one reason our coconut trees had had such a hard time of it. Of the two hundred we had planted, in three successive waves, only about twenty had survived the *tahinu, kaveu,* drought, and wind. But those twenty trees were out of danger, and the veteran shading our well was about to put forth a cluster of nuts.

"It would be cool to plant a few coconuts together," said Ugo. "I'd like to work with you a little, to leave something of myself on this island."

So we did, planting seven more in a nice day's work that strengthened the link between us. Seven sprouted nuts, each with three healthy fronds, which we had selected from beneath the tall coconut palms that Tom had planted fifteen or twenty years before.

"Remember the spot where I'm planting this one," said Ugo. "I'll admit I don't quite believe this is going to work, but I'm giving it all my best wishes. When we get back to San Francisco, I want you to write and tell me that it came through in good shape. And say hello to it when you come back here next year, you lucky bastard!"

The week passed as if in a dream. Nobody said the word we feared, "departure." Bird Island was enriched by twenty more young coconut trees which Ugo planted. Our two families got together each noon and evening around a fire for meals of fried grouper or surgeonfish. We hunted jacks in the pass, where we knew they were waiting for us.

Ugo was fourteen years younger than me, and had the sleek muscles of a swimmer; he was as comfortable in the water as a seal. Cautious and determined, he had quick good judgment that was shaped by reason, experience, and instinct. He never hunted for show, only for food. I couldn't have hoped for a better spearfishing partner. He turned out to be an expert with a slingshot, too. We laughed like a couple of kids as we recalled our adolescence, when he used to shoot out streetlights in Rome, and I in Saigon.

Ugo also exploded a dangerous misconception I had long held. From not having read Alain Bombard's book* carefully, I was under the impression that a shipwrecked sailor could survive by *eating* raw fish. It seemed obvious. Seabirds, porpoises, and seals don't need to drink any fresh water, so they must get enough of it

---

The Bombard Story, by Alain Bombard (Grafton Books, London; Sheridan House, Dobbs Ferry, NY, 1986). (*Tr.*)

from fish, which supplies them with both food and drink. But Ugo said that what is true for them is completely false for us. It seems marine mammals and seabirds produce certain enzymes that allow them to digest protein despite the small amount of fresh water contained in fish; but we humans don't have those enzymes.

"If you just *eat* fish without drinking any water, your stomach will draw water from your cells to digest the protein, leading to faster dehydration of your body. The only way to survive is by *drinking* the serum contained in the fish meat, the way Bombard did. And waiting for rain before eating anything, as he did. Unless you thought to bring a solar still along, of course."

There you had it: you sail for years, race through a major book on survival at sea and think you've grasped a fundamental lesson—and twenty years later, a chance encounter on a Pacific atoll forces you to revise your ideas.

Since the dazzling flash Iléana and I had experienced on seeing it for the first time five years before, we had considered Bird Island our secret garden, a retreat protected by Tom's aura, a little piece of heaven that effort, faith, and great patience were gradually transforming into a flowering of creation. But having PHOBOS nearby hadn't broken the spell. Quite the contrary, a powerful current was flowing between us.

During the eighteen months we spent in Ahe, some thirty yachts had come to drop their hooks off Poro Poro. Their visits lasted a few days, occasionally a week, rarely longer. They soon went on their way, anxious to pick up the mail awaiting them in Tahiti before it got stale. And we were left unsatisfied, because the shortness of their stopovers prevented any deep contact. Our meetings were warm but necessarily superficial, limited to whatever words we exchanged in conversation around a few meals eaten together at our *faré*. Words are certainly useful as vehicles for thought, which they transform into mental images. But if you're seeking *real* contact, those images must be transformed again by minds *and* hands. In other words, it's essential to *do* something *together*. And it's important that what is done together be new, created out of nothing, because that leads to another level where real contact is established.

PHOBOS' anchor had worked its way deep into the sand; she gave no sign of an imminent departure. Stephan and Maurice met every morning at dawn to go off together searching for treasures they later brought back to the well, with lots of wonderful stories in their eyes. The women, too, had become inseparable. From what I understood, Isabella's doctoral thesis dealt with creativity and the mental and emotional processes that promote it. And she was fascinated by the way Iléana's ten years of psychiatric work had been put to the test by her hard-won experience at Ahe.

As for Ugo and me, we were living through each other in a kind of accelerated symbiosis. We were conscious that our time together was running out, and were determined not to waste a minute of it. He practiced throwing the *patia* at the parrotfish in the lagoon. A *kaveu* can crush your finger with one of its claws, but I taught Ugo how to lure one out of its hole barehanded. I then showed him how the Paumotus, with a single machete-blow to the spine of a palm frond, obtain a strong cord with which to tie up those monsters. And after only three of my "coconut lessons," Ugo learned how to climb a coconut tree by using the Asian trick of tying a scarf around your ankles, so your feet grip the slippery trunk. He sent a coconut falling down . . . then a second . . . a third . . .

Amazed, I watched him as he climbed down. Ugo had found a style perfectly adapted to his body type, which was something I couldn't have helped him with; nobody could. Beyond a certain point, you have to figure things out for yourself—and he had! It brought to mind a meeting between an Australian aborigine and a white explorer. One makes his way barefoot among desert snakes carrying a boomerang he shaped from a bent tree branch with a stone. The other strides along in leather boots, gripping a Winchester with an infrared scope that allows him to shoot even at night. And despite the light-years that separate them culturally, they instinctively recognize each other as brothers, go off hunting together, and mutually reveal two amazing worlds which come together in magic.

People usually think of scientists as lost in the clouds, much more comfortable dealing with abstract theories than with daily life. So I was all the more impressed by the level of practical intelligence with which Ugo had turned his own Zodiac into an avant-garde masterpiece. He had added two slim leeboards shaped like airplane wings, a flexible mast solidly stepped on the floorboards, and a large Sunfish sail. The result was an inflatable that surfed in a following breeze and could sail into the wind almost as fast as a racing dinghy—with the two of us hiked out so as not to have to swim home!

But Ugo confided to me that his Zodiac was only the first draft of a much bigger dream, which he meant to pursue once PHOBOS returned to California: a 28-foot super-Zodiac capable of crossing oceans in relative comfort and safety. There, I had to draw the line; I wasn't about to swallow that one! A self-contained inflatable raft, well equipped for survival, okay; but let's not get any nutty ideas. Then one night around the campfire, Ugo sketched out his dream in my head, almost as if by hypnosis. Raumati had been able to bring the past to life; Ugo was describing the future with startling clarity. And as we returned to our boats, I realized that his dream made sense.*

And at each sunrise—like Stephan and Maurice, and like Isabella and Iléana—Ugo and I felt the urgency to imbue each other with the best parts of ourselves. We were like two sorcerers with different powers who had met briefly at an oasis to share their secrets. Aboard JOSHUA, Ugo measured the metal rungs that let me climb the mast while at sea. He tried out my "perch"—a strong plank nailed across the mainmast, three feet from the top—where you can sit in complete safety to change a halyard or check on a block, without the inconvenience of a bosun's chair. He noted the ingenious system that prevents my halyards from getting wrapped around the spreaders when sails have to be struck in an emergency. And he immediately noticed the tie-downs permanently attached to the booms, which allow me to quickly furl the sails without having to fumble in the dark along the lifelines or in a cockpit locker; each tie-down is in place and can't blow away. Naturally, all of those improvements, which had lasted for years, bore my "monkey-work" trademark, like my inner-tube dinghy. Everything was extremely simple, efficient, and easy to make without any headaches. . . . But it was still monkey-work, tricks so primitive they would be an embarrassment at a

*Four years later, alone on an inflatable boat he named EMTEESS, whose design, rig, and sail plan came straight from the future, Ugo Conti sailed from San Francisco to Honolulu, a distance of 2,500 miles. He averaged 100 miles a day, and covered 140 miles in twenty-four hours three times during that epic journey. The name *Emteess* was Ugo's acronym from the Latin phrase *morituri te salutant*—those who are about to die salute you.

boat show. At a glance, Ugo grasped how those details could make a boat safer and the sea friendlier. He then took out his tools and improved PHOBOS in his own way; and his work was really professional, worthy of a top-notch boatyard.

I would never have imagined that an engineer with so many diplomas (I figured he must have lots, to be doing research at Berkeley) could have such a broad range of manual and inventive abilities. Ugo composed music, could improvise, played the guitar, and whistled beautifully. For the past several years, in fact, he had been working on a device to modulate his whistling. Ugo figured that perfecting it would require many more attempts and a lot of thought. The current model resembled an African gourd crossed with a jungle tambourine. But as I looked into the future, it was wonderful to watch him join electronics, poetry, and mathematics in his own search for the Enchanted Bird.* I was beginning to see why Ugo Conti so often reminded me of Henry Wakelam: they both had a scientist's mind, a craftsman's skilled hands, and the vision to grasp both the big picture and the details and to extract what was essential. Henry created his miracles rummaging through garbage cans, Ugo his amid the swirling energy of ultra-sophisticated laboratories, yet the two of them walked along side by side within the same symbol.

What with *patia* throwing on the barrier reef, planting coconuts, the well, the hut that the children had lined with shells, spearfishing, and working on our boats, three weeks had passed. Our friends would soon be raising anchor. The hurricane season was about to begin and PHOBOS had a long way to go before reaching New Caledonia.

In the days when WANDA and MARIE-THÉRÈSE would spend months in port before heading out to sea together, planning to meet further on, time had stretched out before us forever. But here at Bird Island, time had shrunk to the point of an almost tactile intensity.

Our meetings in the evening around the fire were precious moments of reflection. That was when the day rested and souls listened. Ugo and Isabella would talk about their Berkeley friends who were groping through the fog surrounding the high peaks of

*Conti patented his "Whistle Synthesizer" a decade later, in 1986. (*Tr.*)

science. One was involved in a prodigious project involving ele-
mental particles sent to collide with each other at nearly the
speed of light. Another was working on genetic mutations of certain *graminae* that would produce harvests in soil so poor only
reeds could grow in it. And a third had gone so far in chemistry
that you could no longer tell at what point matter ended and
spirit began.

"Fantastic, all these things you're telling me!"

"Yeah, sure . . ." said Ugo, "but you can wind up wearing blind-
ers. I was working at physics problems that were so tough, I was
like some sweaty lumberjack who sees only his tree and has lost
sight of the forest. Luckily Isabella stepped back and saw the trap.
So we dropped everything and headed out to sea, so as to have
time to sort things out and get some perspective."

The red and yellow flower was dancing above the coals. The
children fed it twigs, played with it. By this time tomorrow, PHOBOS
would be gone. As a *kaveu* roasted near the well, Ugo and Isabella
helped us see the outlines of the great challenge that mankind's
conscience would be facing in the near future. They were pulling
us from our *tupa* hole, pushing us outside, bursting our bounds,
and waking us up to the urgent realities of the vast world being
stalked by the Dragon. Raumati had taken us into a *namua roa*
dominated by the law of the *patia.* Ugo and Isabella were guiding
us through the twists of another *namua roa* which blended at
once present and future.

Isabella stood up, chose a nice *tahinu* branch and stuck it in
the fire that was bringing us closer together each day. Then, like
a sorceress, she made an immense band of monkeys appear in the
flames . . .

They came from the very first glimmerings of our humanity,
millions and millions of monkeys who were all trying to move a gigantic tree trunk. They wanted to bring it to the other end of the
plain, where they would turn it into the Temple of Knowledge.
Putting their shoulders to the trunk, they pushed with all their
might, but the tree wouldn't budge. So they invented vine ropes,
braided hemp, fifty-two-speed multi-part block-and-tackles, steel
cable, titanium, and all the rest, including the nuclear reactor and
television. The huge trunk only sank deeper into the ground. And
yet, from the very beginning, smothered by the multitudes, some
of the monkeys had been crying out. They were trying to say that

to reach its goal, the group had to look higher, to seek inspiration from above, to find another future freed from the chains of both past and present. Without this the magic tree trunk would disappear and drown consciousness in the great swamp of mediocrity.

"Lost in the mists of time, one primate branch took a *Step of Thought*. And when it experienced that incredible flash, it opened its eyes a little, and saw that it could gain understanding. But in order for the Original Monkey to acquire a human face, it had to take the next step, which is now essential: the *Step of Intelligence*. And here we aren't talking any more about intelligence with a small i, which has closed its eyes and ears to go build the Carnivorous Temple erected to the glory of Finance and Technocracies."

Isabella's eyes were as beautiful as Tepuku's. This was our final evening around this fire, which had so enchanted our souls. Tomorrow, when the sun lit up the sheets of coral scattered like lily pads on this jewel-box lagoon, PHOBOS would raise anchor to continue on her way toward the Great Horizon.

CHAPTER 22

Two and a half years had passed since PHOBOS. Around our campfire on Bird Island, Ugo had told me something truly astonishing: that scientists had proven that the *same* electron can go into two *different* holes *at the same time*. It seemed impossible. Unless it splits in half, no object can hit two separate targets at the same instant. But when you think about it—and add the necessary pinch of magic—you can begin to see that it makes sense. And that was exactly what I was about to try, no more, no less.

Toward noon, I shook out the reef in the mainsail, replaced my working jib with the genoa, and raised the big staysail. A little rainbow danced in the spray in the lee of the bow; Tahiti's mountaintops were already beginning to blur in the distance; the sky announced a beautiful night. The way ahead was clear. I felt happy. Destination: The United States. I was going ahead on a scouting mission; Iléana and Stephan would join me after I had carefully studied the lay of the land. It's going to be fascinating, I thought. I was almost sure that Hao's father had already told me about the electron trick—but in other terms—one day when we were caulking Bai Ma's junk under the big *badamier* tree. He had been having a hell of a time plugging a leak where the water came in at two places. He paused often, chewing his betel nut; I think it helped him collect his thoughts. He stroked the *cai tram* bark between his fingers, as if he were speaking with the gods. Hao's father didn't talk much, but when he did, his words turned into moving images in my mind. And what was wondrous about the stories he told was the way they could leap across time to shape themselves to circumstances in the present.

The trade wind was blowing just right, neither too much nor too little. The genoa was pulling like a horse; the staysail too. But

I had to be careful not to blow them out; they were three years older than Stephan, and patched everywhere. I'd look real smart if I ripped them one after another. Especially since the working jib wasn't likely to reach San Francisco in one piece; it was twice as worn as the genoa and the staysail.

I listened to the water flowing along the hull. Doing seven knots on a reach without pounding, JOSHUA was in heaven. As for me, I was finding my center again after the tiring, tense weeks before my departure. Sitting at the chart table, I daydreamed as I took stock of the situation. At first glance, it seemed simple. Stephan would be nine soon. In school, he was an even bigger dunce than his father. The *tupa* had taught him how to get by . . . But enough is enough. It was high time that our lovely, lazy boy discovered another culture, which would make him bilingual at the same time. As for Iléana, ten years of wall-to-wall coconut trees were enough; she'd had her fill of it. She desperately needed to get back to a lively, stimulating environment. Besides, she had been dreaming of the California climate, where snow and desert exist side by side. As for me, I needed neither snow nor desert; I was perfectly happy in the tropics. But we had to make the move, raise the anchor before it—and we—sank too deeply into the ambiguities of Polynesia.

Begin with a change of scene.

Point the bow toward something new.

Along with those noble considerations, though, another much more down to earth problem had shoved us toward the exit. After spending so many years living like grasshoppers under the Polynesian sky, we were almost out of money, and the lean cows were getting closer. I had hung out with that herd for long enough in the days of my two MARIE-THÉRÈSEs. But I was young then and had good teeth, and could gnaw on their hides and find them tolerable. At fifty-five, with a wife and child, dodging those aggressive beasts was a lot more risky.

So the time had come for me to try a new path, in search of dollars. Sure, there would be a few detours down the ethereal byways of universal consciousness, but first I wanted my dollars! All of which left the Dragon flat on his ass, wide-eyed with astonishment. He must have figured we had finally walked into his trap. But he could keep his idiotic thoughts to himself; I wasn't going to waste a minute bothering with him. As many dollars as possible! But there, old man, you're going to need a good eye and be fast on your feet; better get your *patia* ready. Ugo and Isabella would be waiting in San Francisco; they would help me sharpen my aim. And once the cash-box was full again, my mind would be free to tackle the second part of the program.

The sun would be setting soon. Tahiti was out of sight. Behind me, everything was clean, all the crumbs swept away. My heart felt as light as those fair-weather clouds drifting across the sky, telling tales of the far horizon. I had rarely felt such peace while looking at the sea where JOSHUA was sailing, on course for our big adventure—an adventure with two targets which were actually one and the same. The Monkey was really determined to grab the high branches! Needless to say, waking up our neurons and getting our finances in shape would be only one of the electron's twin paths. If that were all that was at stake, I wouldn't be satisfied. My real motivation involved the second target: *the book*. A book I felt responsible for writing since that bright dawn when MARIE-THÉRÈSE left Phu Quoc Island in her wake and all those wandering souls had kept me company. They had become more insistent since Ahe.

Next to me in the cockpit, the Child listened to the singing of the waves while I told him the story of the "smart" electron. He didn't understand a word I said. It was too complicated for him. So I broke it down to its basic principle, the crux of the matter: "You and I, we're *two*. And yet we're *one*. Get it?" The Child burst out laughing, and I could see how happy he was that I had finally taken myself in hand and moved on to something new. Still, I knew what writing was like; I had already danced to that tune three times before. *Sailing to the Reefs* had taken me six months, *Cape Horn* a year, and *The Long Way* two full years of grinding labor. I wasn't kidding myself; this next book would be tougher than the other three put together. What would it cost me? How many years would I need to put together the pieces of the puzzle scattered in my distant past? I could expect a long ordeal, facing a blank page where ghosts from long ago demanded to be resurrected. To engage in that combat without being pressed for time or getting knocked out in the first skirmishes with the past, my family and I absolutely had to be on a solid financial footing. In other words, I had to earn enough money to keep us from want during the years of writing. And if the gods of my native Asia would be good enough to lend a hand for the sake of our old friendship, then I would reach my goal without killing myself.

Sirius, Aldebaran, and Orion adorned the sky, the trade wind hummed on the genoa's leach, the swell was regular, and JOSHUA's bow stirred up pearls as she made her way through the night. I was feeling the same excitement I had felt twelve years before, when I pointed the bow toward the great capes in answer to their call. Deep down, I knew that this new leap into space was another chapter in the same adventure. The gods above deal the cards, but we play them. My *patia* and my slingshot were on board, the first since Ahe, the other forever. In California, I would use the *patia* to clear some peaceful space where Iléana and Stephan could flourish, safe from the lean cows. Then I would leave the *patia* with them and continue alone into the Great Forest with the Child and the village all warm in my heart. And then the real game of *yin* and *yang* would begin, united by the breath the old monk in the Cave of Coins had told me about . . . When I was face to face with myself deep in the Great Forest writing my book, the magic slingshot would be essential . . . Hey, will you stop dreaming! There's a time for everything. Let's get to America to make some money first!

God, it felt good to be at sea again, amid the peaceful rhythm of sails and sheets, lounging like some sun-blessed animal, filling my eyes with the thousands and thousands of miles in front of the bowsprit, alone with my boat, alone with the wind and the waves, alone with the horizon and all my memories! I listened to the rustling of water on the hull as I leafed through the big picture album, carefully pasting in the images from these last years. They unrolled in the bow wave like a slow-motion film . . . Poro Poro and the *faré* we had built with our own hands . . . The patient compost pile in the shade of the *kaaia* tree near the tide flats . . . The white sand made fertile by the *taata nai-nai* laboring day and night under their blanket of palm fronds . . . Our papaya trees heavy with fruit, our giant watermelons . . . The quiet sounds of the village, where everything happened in the present tense . . . Neti, Tepuku, Raumati, and the Tamata Gang, who tried to turn the future into reality . . . The prodigious affair of the cats drowned in *aita péa-péa* . . . Meeting PHOBOS around the Suvorov campfire . . . Returning to Ahe because it wasn't yet time for us to leave Polynesia . . . JOSHUA sailing through the pass for the third and last time, low in the water, her cabin and forepeak crammed with fruit trees: twelve mango, twelve avocado, and twelve citrus trees (lemons and grapefruits). They would be our farewell present to the village.

Yet even as we were choosing the trees at the Tahiti Agriculture Service, hauling them down to the dock in six or seven trips in an old 2 CV Citroën, and stowing them on board, Iléana and I felt pretty sure that this final attempt would end in failure, too. But we also knew that we had to try to strike a spark for the Tuamotus' future one last time. It was something much closer to love than to logic. Maybe it was our way of completing the work we had started with the cats. And putting the question to the villagers fair and square: either they would watch the young trees die of thirst in their plastic tubs, or they would care for them. It was up to them to choose between *aita péa-péa* and the shovel.

Neti, Tepuku, and Raumati met us at Poro Poro. We talked things over, and all agreed on what to do. The next day, Mayor Toa agreed to share the trees among the twelve *farés*. He would wait for Friday evening, when everybody would be back from copra work. But the Tamata Gang set one condition: if each family hadn't planted its three trees by Monday morning, we would plant the remaining ones in front of the village hall.

Laughing, Papa Toa pointed toward the cemetery.

"It's all the same to me whether they go in the village or in front of the village hall. I'm seventy-five, and I'll soon be over there. I hope they understand before I go. In any case, it's up to them."

And this time, they chose the shovel! All the trees were planted the Saturday after our arrival. Planted in real holes, with chopped banana-tree trunks to feed the roots, with a mulch of dry fronds around the young saplings to hold moisture and give the taata nainai a chance to take over. I walked from one *faré* to the next as if in a dream. *Mai-tai tera*? (Is this good?) Each time, I answered without a second's hesitation: *Mai-tai roa* (Very good). And Sunday was a holiday in the village, which had turned into an orchard.

The six months of our last stay passed quickly. Stephan was growing up; soon he would need a more advanced school, in Tahiti or Moorea. After three years, during which we had devoted our souls to Ahe, it would soon be time to say goodbye and turn the page. In a subtle blend of joy and sadness, our excursions to the magic forest at the far end of the lagoon gradually became longer; we sometimes stayed there two weeks at a time. Raumati and Tepuku left their fish pen and moved to nearby Manihi atoll.

Neti passed his commercial sailing exam and would soon become a second officer on a copra schooner. Our relations with the village reminded us of two lovers walking hand in hand, who knew that they would soon part forever with a beautiful, friendly smile.

Each night, Cassiopeia and the Big Dipper were higher in the sky before the bow, the Southern Cross lower astern. And on the great Pacific chart, distant Polynesia appeared like a star twinkling deep within me. The southeast trade wind was starting to weaken; the northeasterlies would soon take its place. A few more days, and we will have quietly changed hemispheres. But changing tacks this last time hadn't been easy . . .

From Ahe, we had moved to Moorea, Tahiti's sister island. JOSHUA rode safely at anchor at the end of Cook's Bay, four hundred yards from our house. Stephan's school buzzed like a beehive, full of new classmates. We lived in a *faré* surrounded by greenery, which a friend let us have for a song—which was just as well, since my royalties, which had once flowed in a steady stream, had begun to dry up over the years.

Once we made ourselves at home under our tin roof, it warmed my heart to see Iléana organize her paint-box. She lined up her bottles of dye on a shelf and took out her bolts of fabric. She was getting her bearings, and the light had returned to her eyes. So things were working out for her, too. Because the tally of our three years in the Tuamotus reminded me of a boat that had been battered by the fortunes of the sea, its rudder loose, its lines frayed. Lost in the fog on the great expanse of the ocean, we hadn't known which way to head. Just then, this island of Rest and Reflection had appeared before our anxious sails. Like in a story from mythology, we would remain in this providential refuge and watch the auguries while awaiting a message from the gods to show us our next destination. Life had led us along its mysterious byways, in fair winds with all canvas set, in endless calms that tried our patience, in squalls taken while sailing triple-reefed as the bow sailed through time. And it had brought us here without our knowing quite why or how.

We gradually settled into a routine. After some initial hesitation, things began to come together. As gleeful as a kid finding Easter eggs in the bushes, Iléana got her first customers and sold five *pareus* one after another! Encouraged by that promising start, she visited the tourist boutiques, sold off her Ahe stock, took new orders.

I was getting my bearings, too: my pickaxe and shovel. I started a garden, crumbling its wonderful soil, rich with the promise of fertility, between my fingers. I rose before sunrise to delight in the intoxicating smell of humus blended with that of the morning dew. A desert dweller who came to a land of singing streams would be just as dazzled every morning.

Ahe's isolation had left us hungry to rediscover our cultural roots. My old friend Bernard Calvet lived next door with his wife Kristine and daughter Sabrina, who was two years younger than Stephan. Their *faré* was just off the little bumpy road that climbed the hill to the pineapple fields overlooking Cook's Bay. Around us, within a few minutes by bicycle, lived a doctor, three restaurateurs, an insurance agent, an architect, two importers, three talented painters, a wood sculptor, a chemist who worked for the pineapple-juice plant, a pharmacist, a cartoon artist, a gifted clarinet player, a journalist who wanted to start a bookstore at the end of Cook's Bay, three teachers, and Jean-Marie Dallet, the author of the most evocative book on Gauguin I knew. All had been drawn here by the call of Melville, Slocum, Gerbault, Pidgeon, Eric de Bisschop . . . the chart of the vast ocean with its innumerable, dreaming islands . . . the adventure of the great departure in which you jettison the junk of the past . . .

They had sailed here, some of them decades earlier, others more recently, and none seemed to regret choosing a new life far from the land of their ancestors. Several had kept their boats, but most lived on land or were looking to settle here. All told, a total of eight nationalities: French, German, Italian, Swedish, Belgian, American, Swiss, Mauritian. More than a third of these *popaas* had married Tahitian women. Tahiti's immigration service still maintained its traditionally easygoing ways, and patience or sentiment usually yielded permanent resident visas. Bursts of friendship were frequent within the Polynesian bureaucracy, and smiles and niceness on both sides nearly always softened the rigor of administrative regulations. That state of affairs might change in the future, but here in 1978–1980, things weren't too difficult. We felt in harmony with this friendly community of sailors and travelers who had adopted Polynesia and put down roots.

Lord, this island was beautiful, with its ring of mountains etched against the sky, lush valleys, and blue lagoons! Moorea would be the place to get me started writing the book I had been carrying, ever since Indochina, like a seed waiting for rain. I thought about starting it in Ahe, but that had been impossible. Our life there had been full to overflowing, dense and rich. Mere existence had required enormous effort just to put a few greens in the pot with our rice and fish. Physically, we were constantly on the edge, caught up in a kind of perpetual motion that reminded me of old Suvorov Tom. Not to mention our "great work" of raising the villagers' consciousness.

Sweat and Faith were the two breasts that had fed us on the atoll, but our intense commitment of body and soul left no room for even the simplest writing project.

Moorea was the flip side of the coin. Everything here was simple, right at hand; you could kick back and let go. Fish, chicken, and eggs could all be bought at the store a five-minute round trip away. The abundance was a bit expensive, but the house fairy was doing well with her *pareus*. Her sales began to cover our daily needs, and we didn't have to dip into the ship's cash-box too much. As for the rest, we were living in the Garden of Eden. Our neighbors Bernard and Kristine had a profusion of bananas, four mango trees, about a hundred pineapple bushes, and two jujube trees covered with fruit. Three wild avocados flourished alongside the road. And our garden produced more lettuce, bok choy, radishes, cucumbers, and green beans than our two families could ever eat.

As for trying to raise consciousness in the Pacific islands, I'd had enough of that for a good long time!

Shadows were lengthening on Cook's Bay and its ring of mountains. A delicious smell of roast chicken came from the oven. The cat purred in Iléana's lap, his favorite spot. Stephan and Sabrina were giving little kisses to their guinea pigs, who squealed with delight. Kristine came over with a pineapple tart. Joel House and Bernard Calvet rolled cigarettes. In the center of the circle, Moea sang Tahitian songs while accompanying herself on the guitar. We were waiting for P'tit Louis to show up with the sample comic book he had been slaving at for the past three months.

Now Moea started "Jeux interdits". She played the guitar so well I could listen to her forever. She played with all her soul. I thought of our friends from PHOBOS and Suvorov, where we watched the dancing red and yellow flower. Ugo had chosen an evening like this to describe the chaos theory, using images as pure as those of Moea's "Jeux interdits."

"At the moment of the Big Bang, chaos was total. It became less and less dense during the considerable time it took for the universe to become organized. Then the first embryos appeared with the gift of reproducing themselves on our hesitant earth. In a colossal struggle of infinite patience and fierce combat, life began to emerge, until it finally achieved consciousness. And with that consciousness, life gave us the choice of building the future instead of merely experiencing it. But we don't exist in a state of grace. Both science and philosophy recognize that chaos lives on within everything in existence, without exception. Fire and breaking waves contain chaos in its pure form, but the human brain still bears the indelible marks of that same chaos within its folds."

Moea's guitar was singing in the night. And I had dusted off my writing materials. Chaos or not, nothing would stand in my way from now on. Clear sky, calm sea, force four wind on a reach . . . all the conditions were right for me to set sail toward that fabulous archipelago where I would bring together present, past, and future in the same breath!

The island of Rest and Reflection . . . Never in my life had I taken it easy for such a long period of time: nearly two years spent watching the days go by in *la dolce vita*. I became a *tupa* again, with *tupa* reflexes, *tupa* behavior, a *tupa* hole. Tapping my skull produced only a hollow echo. When, out of curiosity, I tested it with a depth gauge to see what was happening in there, it showed a nearly total vacuum—or else an extremely subtle form of chaos.

My schedule wasn't too demanding. I nursed my compost pile and put a drop of sweat or two into our garden—which was plenty, since it grew all by itself. Once in a great while, I scratched at the rust that was eating away at JOSHUA. But I spent the better part of my days taking bike rides to see friends.

So what about the writing? Uh-oh . . . taboo subject; don't push me. You get ready to write a book—especially this one—as carefully as you prepare for a landfall in the fog after an uncertain crossing. And since there was no wind here, much less a crossing or a landfall, there was no point in wearing out my brain cells on a problem that didn't exist. The sun was shining, that was the main thing: let's take advantage of it.

Weeks passed that way, then months, somehow evaporating into nothingness. The book was far away. Whenever I started to feel a bit ill at ease, I dropped everything—family, garden, and friends—slapped a coat of fast-drying paint on JOSHUA, and sailed off on one of my solo pilgrimages to Suvorov. I threw everything over that way four times in eighteen months.

Suvorov . . . the peace of the great depths . . . nothing but deep blue all around . . . not a ripple on the water . . . I busied myself around the Bird Island well, planting my sprouted coconuts while thinking about PHOBOS and chaos theory. And I can attest that Suvorov's chaos is the gentlest chaos in the world.

And then after five or six weeks I would come home again, only to slip back into the lazy pace of an existence ruled by the laws of chance—while the rust slowly ate away at the fittings on my long-neglected boat.

At Ein Kerem, Philip used to say that *routine* is our worst enemy, because it approaches on velvet paws, without making the slightest sound, the better to trap us in its coils. Iléana could hardly recognize me. She had always seen me as a bundle of nerves, moving in a maelstrom where action and creative thought lent me wings. Whereas in two years of *farniente* here in Moorea, I had accomplished practically nothing, not a single worthwhile project. Yet it was here that the fundamental link appeared which joined the apparently empty period in Moorea with the one I had lived through in the Indian Ocean during the long way.

I had just rounded the Cape of Good Hope, my back bent under the three months of accumulated fatigue and nervous tension since leaving Plymouth. Shortly after Good Hope, a gale knocked me on my beam ends that left me on the point of quitting. But then the gods gave me two weeks of sparkling flat calm, a platinum mirror crisscrossed by albatrosses. A total calm, which gave me time to regain my equilibrium before the beautiful westerlies returned. And when the wind rose again on that immense, peaceful sea, my boat and I were ready to go on together as far as the final dangers off New Zealand. There, the porpoises were waiting to show us the opening to the Pacific, with mythical Cape Horn at the very end of the path, where I would regain the Alliance.

Thus, ten years apart, our time at Ahe began to resemble

rounding the Cape of Good Hope, and life in Moorea the healing calm of the Indian Ocean.

But Iléana was fed up. She felt I should have started my book a long time ago, instead of spinning excuse-stories full of gods and lifesaving porpoises while she busted her hump to earn enough money with her *pareus* to keep the household going. Whereas I had finally discovered the art of long-distance gliding, carried by the gentle thermals of Polynesia. I was working out a new existence—and how restful it was!

Still, in the midst of my torpor, a gust of wind from afar would occasionally come to briefly fill my sails. I would then come out of my hole for a lightning sortie, the way a sailor stuck in the Doldrums uses the slightest riffle to help him escape the Sargasso realm, where his willpower is in danger of dissolving if he stays becalmed too long.

The idea behind the first sortie had been on my mind since Ahe: *Chinese characters*. Stephan, who would soon be eight, could reproduce from memory the thirty ideograms from Rose Quong's book. We were sorry that her little manual didn't go farther. In a letter written as simply and clearly as possible, I wrote to the Chinese government, suggesting that it publish a book in the same spirit as Rose Quong's, but covering the hundred and fifty essential characters our school children could easily learn between kindergarten and the other grades. They would be more than enough for basic communication, of a sort: "You come house mine, sleep, eat, tomorrow go fishing." Or: "Next week I come house yours, help plant rice." It was baby-talk, but people don't need complicated sentences to understand each other. At Toboali, Deshumeurs and I knew fewer than a hundred words of Indonesian, but they were enough to get us all the friends we wanted.

Besides, Chinese ideograms let you formulate *concepts* by joining common words for things you can touch or see: "roof" and "woman" become "peace." "Sun" and "moon" together make "brilliant." And "brilliant" together with "clear" become "to understand." The other aspect of this writing's genius lies in the fact that it uses both sides of the brain, the logical and the intuitive. Teaching its fundamentals could only open the minds of future generations. And I think there would be nothing to lose if we searched the horizon and put our faith in building a bridge of cultural exchange between two great civilizations: China, full of sub-tle nuances, and our Cartesian West, often mesmerized by its own knowledge. This may seem like a naive dream. But dreams, like messages in bottles or specks of pollen carried by the wind, have always helped the world to evolve.

The second lightning sortie was sparked by some long talks I had with Joel House, an American who had been living in Polynesia for the past five or six years. Fascinated by oceanogra-phy since he was a child, Joel had learned a great deal about this vast subject and had many contacts in scientific circles. And he was worried, among other things, about the killing of tuna.

In the old days, tuna were caught on lines, so entire schools couldn't be wiped out. Whereas today, with increasingly efficient technologies—sonar, spotting helicopters, and factory ships—when a school of tuna is caught, nothing is left to let it rebuild it-self. Even the porpoises that coexist with the tuna are killed and canned along with them. No international agreements exist to reg-ulate the operations' size or fishing methods. The ocean appar-ently belongs to everybody, so everybody follows his most urgent short-term interest. No laws, no enforcement, no cops; it was catch as catch can, so why not go all the way? We wiped out the buffalo, so why not the sea—if "progress" demands it?

Joel explained that fish farming involves two main stages. The first is easy to master, because it's simple, quick, and cheap. The second stage, on the other hand, is extremely complicated, long, and uncertain.

The first stage consists in having a female fish lay eggs in a pool. A single tuna will lay about three million eggs, and caring for them involves proven techniques which have been around for decades. All the eggs in the pool will survive, protected from predator zooplankton and other hungry little animals that infest the sea. The eggs hatch undisturbed, giving birth to larvae which become fry (baby fish) and are then moved to a larger pool. For tuna, this first stage (eggs-larvae-fry) takes only a few weeks.

Then the second stage begins. But here, the difficulties multi-ply. The fry need more and more room as they grow. They have to be well fed and protected from disease, all of which involves large investments, delicate technology, huge pools, and know-how that has yet to be developed. It takes between eighteen months and two years for a tuna fry to become adult, so the final cost is astronomical. And while this method works in raising trout, salmon, and catfish, Joel said it has never worked properly with tuna, or at least not in a financially viable way. In any case, he added, farm fish are full of antibiotics and other chemicals that can only lead to genetic mutations while harming the environment, the way herbicides and nitrates do in agriculture.

To come back to open-ocean tuna, Joel had an idea that fascinated me. It consisted in bypassing the second stage in industrial fish farming. Instead of transferring the baby tuna produced in the first stage into expensive pools (and caring for them for two years, with all the uncertainty and expense that entails), they could be raised on special ships and simply *released at sea*. They would certainly encounter predators, but far fewer than if they began as eggs or larvae. Once released together in carefully selected ocean zones, the many fry born of a single tuna would quickly and instinctively gather in a school that would be fed and sheltered by the sea. We could restock the oceans with young tuna that way.

If a thing is worth trying once, it's worth trying a thousand times until it works; that's how the first plane got into the air. But Joel laughed, adding that the tuna project didn't raise questions only of technology. The real headache would be figuring out *whom the tuna belonged to*! That was a philosophical question, and science isn't very good at resolving questions of philosophy.

I put everything Joel told me into a letter I sent to my old friend, the oceanographer Alain Bombard. Perhaps he could get other scientists interested in the question. I was tossing another message in a bottle into the sea. It would wash up somewhere sooner or later, tomorrow, or in ten or twenty years. The length of the journey wasn't important. Someday, the message would reach the hands of a person with planetary consciousness.

My third sortie took place six or eight months later, after a trip to Suvorov. It involved an old score I wanted to settle with the French national anthem, the "Marseillaise." In a letter to the president (with copies to a few French journalists), I gave my opinion of that war-like song that glorifies pride and hate. "The day of glory is at hand . . . The bloody standard raised . . . May impure blood flow in our furrows . . ." Two centuries after the Revolution, we had to invent a new era, in which we reached out *a generous hand to our neighbor*. To face the challenges of the future, our anxious world needed *moral* values, not cannons and banners. The fact that we hadn't yet rewritten the bloodthirsty lyrics of the "Marseillaise" made me ashamed of a France that considers itself a beacon for other peoples.

Here in Moorea, life went along at its usual slow, nonchalant pace. Stephan's grades were catastrophic; except for Chinese characters and shooting his slingshot, nothing interested him. Iléana, in turn, was losing heart; paintbrush in hand and eyes in the distance, she waited desperately for inspiration, but it didn't come. Her mainspring had snapped. Few customers were buying her *pareus*, and she could see the lean cows closing in. As for me, I spent weeks sprawled in a corner of the *faré*, reading myself into a stupor. Things had come to a dead stop. The fine enthusiasm we had felt at the beginning had long since fled.

It can be hard to see the dividing line between routine and waiting. In *Wind, Sand, and Stars*, Saint-Exupéry writes that, from the greatest monarch to the humblest shepherd, we are all "sentinels of the State." I was waiting for something. And then one evening while I was watering my cucumbers and beans, the Child came to sit next to me. I was glad to see him again. He gave me his marvelous smile before transmitting his message: "It's high time you thought seriously about the only strategy that will someday let you write your book. Without it, you're going to go adrift."

It was true; since our arrival, I had been acting like an ostrich with its head in the sand. And here I was, in front of the mirror with myself.

During dinner, Iléana found me thoughtful. Thoughtful and depressed.

We had been in Moorea for nearly two years. I'd been sure I would be able to write here; after all, Jean-Marie Dallet managed just fine. But I hadn't begun the first page, and didn't even have a coherent outline in mind. I didn't know where I was, like a boat lost in the fog with reefs all around.

Iléana gently stroked my face, took my hands in hers, and looked deep into my eyes.

"I did a lot of thinking while I was alone with Stephan during your escapades to Suvorov. Especially the last time. I feel like I'm surrounded by reefs, too. School is a disaster for Stephan. And you're becoming a has-been. Look at me; you've got to wake up. JOSHUA is an extension of yourself. You know very well that you'll never be able to start your book until her fittings are taken care of. It will cost a lot, but we'll manage. We've always managed before."

"It wasn't hard then, we had money. Now we're almost broke."

"The money will come later. What you most need is peace of mind so you can write, and your boat won't let you have it if you let her fall apart a second time. You already learned a hard lesson with *The Long Way*. This time, it'll be a lot worse. First, JOSHUA has to become what she was in her glory days. That'll be the first step. Then we'll take off for America . . ."

"Are you out of your mind? Can you imagine us arriving there without a nickel, stumbling around a country where the dollar is king and you have to pay cash on the barrel for even a banana? Are you crazy?"

"Listen to me, please! Even with JOSHUA back in shape, not a single line is going to come out of your pen here in Moorea—or anywhere else in Polynesia. In Tahiti, *The Long Way* was born of a powerful impulse because you were holding all the cards, with some terrific trumps: you had arrived in great shape from your ten months at sea, your morale was high, and you had enough money to see you through the writing. You don't have those trump cards anymore, but you can get them back. Start with JOSHUA; that's the heart of the problem, the essential first stage."

"But getting JOSHUA back in shape means replacing everything on deck that is rusted: stanchions, handrails, pulpits, cleats, mooring bitts, and more. You have no idea what's involved. It's a job that's far beyond me. And this isn't monkey-work, it's a job for real professionals, with all the tools. In Tahiti, any job you can't do yourself takes forever—*aita péa-péa*. And when it's all done, you get an enormous bill that would put us flat on our backs."

"If you don't want Polynesia to be our elephant graveyard, you have to give JOSHUA back her wings, whatever the cost. But let's look at what follows. At Suvorov, Ugo and Isabella often talked about California. From north to south, the whole coast is dotted with yacht clubs—and you're famous there. Wait, don't get uptight, hear me out. You have the movie you shot during the long way, and its images are just breathtaking. With you there to introduce it at screenings, you'll pack the halls. The movie will be your *patia*. It will let you not only straighten out our finances, but also really communicate with all kinds of people. Remember Ugo and Isabella's thinking about the arms race? They sowed some precious seeds in us, and you can spread those seeds during your talks with the film. And it won't keep you from fattening our bank account while you're at it. Then you'll be free to devote yourself completely to your book. The United States will be the final key which will at last open the door to your writing. But the first key is JOSHUA."

It was past midnight, time to go to bed! But we didn't sleep. We talked until dawn, going over all sorts of things in our heads and hearts. Iléana is really a terrific woman. She was the one to get me back on track at that crucial moment when I hesitated to take the great leap into space with the last chapter of *The Long Way*. She too, sent me to see Philip at Ein Kerem when everything in me was collapsing. And again, she discovered Ahe. Each time I felt lost in the darkness, her calm intuition guided me toward the light. The only time I ever turned her down flat was when she had wanted us to go heave-to off Mururoa to protest against the Bomb after my return from New Zealand. I just didn't have faith, I was so disgusted by the media's and the public's incredible lack of interest in the FRI attempt. But in everything else, Iléana had always been right. Last night, I had been stumbling in the dark. Then the sky gradually brightened. And at dawn, everything was clear before the bow.

You can be becalmed for a long time on an glassy sea . . . and then whoosh! the wind starts to blow again, and the sea changes from one horizon to the other. Why? Simply because you set your sights high. The United States would be our next big project, and I would have to plan it carefully. Stephan and Iléana would stay in Moorea until I finished working on the boat in Tahiti. I didn't even want to think of the months that would take. In any case, it would be long, hard, and financially devastating.

A forest of masts stood between me and the Papeete quay. Not a single free space; what a mess! Finally, I spotted a mouse-hole between a blue ketch and a sloop. The guys aboard the ketch waved me in and eased off on their lines. I anchored, they caught my mooring lines. We would have to squeeze a bit. Soon, we were tied up side by side.

The guys on the ketch were Bruno, Claude, Daniel, and Michel. Added up, their four ages were about twice mine. We visited each other's boats, immediately feeling an incredible wave of friendship for each other. They had built KIM with their own hands, without a boatyard or professional welders. She was thirty-eight feet of nice work, all steel, including her deck. I admired the job they had done. Everything was functional, strong and simple; nothing fancy, and not a speck of rust. They weren't staying long, a month at the most. Then they were heading for Australia to earn some money, returning to France by way of Cape Horn—with maybe a winter in Adelie Land, like DAMIEN.

"What about you?"

"California. But first I have to get my boat back in shape. You saw the deck; it's going to be a hell of a job."

"It may not be as bad as you think. We'd be happy to lend you a hand. If you can arrange to get your boat hauled out at the navy shipyard, we can do the job in a week. For free, of course. The head of the metal-working shop is a buddy. Once there, we'll have everything we need to do good, fast work: steel scraps, pipes, and a complete set of tools, with torches, sanders, welding equipment. You get the picture."

I stood rooted to the spot; it was a standing knockout. I recognized the hand of the gods. And when the gods are involved, you have to move fast. Within two minutes, I was in the office of my old friend Jean-Roland de Marigny. He was the head of a large import company and had lots of contacts. The navy shipyard was Ali Baba's cave all over again. Problem was, you couldn't just stroll into it playing the harmonica and making slingshots for the kids, the way we had at Toboali with SNARK. In the old days, it was still possible; the shipyard used to accept yachts in transit. But Tahiti had more skilled workers now, and they complained that the yard was taking work away from them. The politicians got involved, with the result that the door to the Holy of Holies was closed to civilians—unless you happened to have some real pull.

Jean-Roland picked up his phone, dialed the yard chief's direct number, and in forty-five seconds, it was all settled!

"The hoist will take you tomorrow morning at eight o'clock sharp. You'll be put back in the water ten days later, at the latest. And your friends from KIM will be given passes for the duration of the job."

My mind was blown. With just a touch of their magic wand, the fairies had opened the gate between two separate realities, the old and the new. It was *baraka*, the balance point, a breathtaking ride on the white crest of a wave sparkling with life that left my last doubts far behind.

When I sailed back to Moorea two weeks later, Iléana couldn't believe her eyes. I had set sail for Tahiti facing an ordeal that I figured would take a very long time and wipe out our bank account. And here I was back again, so happy I could burst. Not only were all the fittings new, but also the bowsprit, rudder stock, and all the chainplates. Incredible, how much work four competent, determined guys can knock off in barely eight days!

I loaded six months of food aboard. Gleaming with fresh paint that wasn't hiding the slightest defect, JOSHUA was ready for the departure for San Francisco, where Ugo and Isabella awaited. Stephan and Iléana had their plane tickets. Thanks to the miracle created by the KIM guys and the shipyard boss, we had a fair amount of money left, even after these expenses.

Before we bid farewell to Polynesia, we decided to put into action my fruit-tree letter to France's mayors and town councillors, which I had written a few years earlier at Ahe and put away in a locker in the cabin. Iléana and I re-read it together. The last paragraph stood up well:

People have built cathedrals, and I think that a country whose roads, paths, and streets were lined with fruit trees would be more lovely than the most beautiful cathedral imaginable.

Yes, it would be beautiful. But for now, these were just words on paper, a vague murmur in the distance. If we wanted the words to become action, if we really wanted to see this letter hit the target we were aiming at, we had to add something besides mere words.

A check for fifteen thousand francs will be sent by return mail to the first town hall that agrees to use the entire sum to plant fruit trees in its community's public spaces.

There, that did it. We had added the missing paragraph. Now the whole letter could stand on its own.

Photocopies. Covering letters to newspapers and magazines in France. A big job.

We waited. Nothing happened.

I alerted the press again. The waiting stretched on. Still nothing in our mail box.

A few editors replied, saying they weren't interested in this business of "fruit trees that belonged to everyone (including the bees and the birds) without being anyone's private property." That was discouraging, since I had hoped to reach public opinion through the press.

I sent a complete file to my old journalist friend Dominique

Charnay, who had seen the beginnings of the affair at Ahe; he was there when the whole village started planting fruit trees. Dominique had also been aboard JOSHUA when I brought those same trees from Tahiti to the atoll.

Then one fine day the first telegram showed up in our mail box. It was signed by the mayor of Lachelle, and said that a letter of confirmation was on its way. The newspaper *Le Figaro* had finally broken the story!

The big project gathered steam. *Le Nouvel Observateur* followed *Le Figaro*'s lead. Alain Hervé's *Le Sauvage* joined the game in turn, followed by *Voiles et Voiliers*. The affair was snowballing. Dominique published a long article in *Les Cahiers du Yachting*, then in *V.S.D.* magazine. Thanks to Antoine, whom we had met two years earlier at Suvorov, Antenne 2's television newsmagazine picked up the ball. A series of radio broadcasts on France Inter followed, hosted by Antoine and Charnay, and that kicked off an avalanche. Soon I was buried under a wave of letters from sixty-three mayors scattered across France. Many of these letters were beautiful, full of feeling and sensitivity. One of the most instructive came from the mayor of Roumagne:

I am very interested in your proposal, which relates to some ideas I got during a recent visit to Czechoslovakia. In that country, streets are lined with fruit trees, in particular cherry and apricot trees. I would therefore like to be a candidate to receive your check.

Sixty-three mayors! When I launched this crusade, I never thought I'd have to devote so much time and energy to it. I expected a sprint of a few weeks; it had become a veritable marathon. It took me four months of hard work, pounds of photocopies, a huge correspondence. By the time I was done, the hand-written and typed pages stacked on my chart table were as thick as a book. I'd had to write a personal letter to each mayor, accompanied by a complete file. I put them all in contact with each other. Georges Lambert, the mayor of Lachelle (population 300) received the promised check, since he had answered first. And my reply to the other sixty-two candidates could be summed up this way:

Since you want to plant fruit trees in your community's public spaces, nothing is stopping you from devoting a small part of your budget to that hopeful, symbolic act.

I listened as the water flowed along the hull. I could spend entire days sitting at my chart table, listening to the music of the sea. Especially in good weather. And the weather had stayed fine since Polynesia and its scattering of islands had disappeared astern.

The Southern Cross had bid me farewell many days before. I didn't need my sextant to tell me that Polaris was thirty-two degrees above the horizon; the sun had given me my latitude at noon. On the chart of this huge ocean, I gazed at the three thousand miles I had already covered since Moorea.

The night was beautiful, with all the northern-hemisphere stars sparkling in the sky. Up there, the gods had made sure our journey was taking place under the best possible auspices. Since our departure, JOSHUA had been able to steer an almost direct course for San Francisco. But last week, a hurricane showed its ugly snout five hundred miles to the east. According to weather reports on station WWV, it was gathering strength and would cross our path in forty-eight hours to give us a serious pounding.

Curled up in my berth, I slept badly that night, trying to convince myself I wasn't really worried. The rigging was solid; six shrouds held the mast on either side, and both backstays were ready for the triple-reefed main to simplify sail handling in heavy weather. But a hurricane is still a hurricane, a big beast that no sailor in the world wants to find on his path.

The next day's dawn was a vision of hell. The trade wind was blowing every which way over an abnormal swell from the northwest. The barometer hadn't started falling yet, but I knew the filthy beast had spotted us for sure and was getting ready to pounce. I broke out the storm jib and put a reef in the main and the staysail as a precaution. After spending a long time watching the angry sea, I was about to go below to the calm of the cabin when a fish suddenly hit my trolling line. I quickly hauled it on deck: a beautiful dorado! And that's when the Child took things in hand, without wasting a second. "Quick, put it back in the water! I'll tell it to go tell the hurricane about the miracle. I bet that will calm it down."

Well, why not? When the weather looks bad, when worry is eating at you and you don't know quite which way to turn, a can of corned beef is a lot easier to cook than a dorado. And it worked! The next WWV bulletin reported that the tropical depression had moderated slightly and changed course: instead of hitting us, it would pass astern of us. I wished my dorado a long and happy life, shook out my precautionary reefs, and raised the genoa. Two days later we were far away, driven by a moderate southeast wind right in the middle of a northeast trade-wind area!

The southeast wind was holding at an ideal force four. JOSHUA was on a starboard tack, flying along on a reach. Then the wind went to the southwest. Unbelievable! San Francisco was just three hundred miles away. I sat at the chart table dreaming about the United States and the bundles of dollars I would scoop up there.

But dollars alone wouldn't satisfy me. I had given a lot of thought to what Ugo and Isabella had said at Suvorov: "For the first time in human history, a country can be less 'powerful' than a potential adversary without putting its own security at risk."

It was so obvious, anyone could see it. I had to get the Americans to understand how crazy the atomic arms race was, tell them the story of the two neighbors, John and Popov, and explain to John why he wasn't taking any risk by starting a unilateral nuclear de-escalation. And that was what I planned to do, while harvesting dollars by showing my film. A double hit with one throw of my *patia*—it would be terrific.

Another hundred and thirty-two miles and we would reach port, without a single day of really bad weather since leaving. Just the same, a squall did in first the genoa, then the jib. They were both shot; I salvaged their boltropes, which I could use as mooring lines. The anchor was ready to go, with sixty feet of chain and a hundred and seventy feet of nylon line neatly coiled at the foot of the mainmast. Everything was in order on deck and in the cabin. We would soon be in port again . . . I would have to get used to sounds different from those of the sea and the wind.

One of the real joys of blue-water cruising is that it lets you look far off in the distance. The day before, I had copied a page from *L'Appel aux Vivants*, by Roger Garaudy (Le Seuil, Paris, 1979), a page whose impact had practically sent me into orbit. I wanted to have those divinely inspired lines in my log so Stephan could think about them when he was grown.

The creative act is the fundamental experience and the revelation of the divine within us.

*Opening that crack of transcendence in us requires that we oc-
cupy that unique place of epiphany where faith, poetic creation, and
revolutionary action become one and the same.*

*Great art offers us the most obvious model of that transcen-
dence. What I call great art (by which I mean mainly non-Western
art, or Western art before the Renaissance) is the opposite of indi-
vidualistic art, which seeks singularity at all cost, because it is
aimed at the marketplace and competition, and because it merely
reflects a fragmented, hopeless world.*

*Great art is not a reflection, but a projection, an exploration and
experience of possible worlds. Beyond its creators, the work engen-
ders not passive spectators or consumers, but people who celebrate
this life as it is being born, joint creators in its creation. And not only
artistic creation, but creation itself.*

*That imagination has prophetic and subversive value because it
hints at possibilities whose conditions are not contained in what already exists. It suggests that the world is not a ready-made reality,
but a work to be created.*

*From that perspective, education consists not in preparing chil-
dren to adapt to the existing order or to its technical or political demands, stuffing them with knowledge or respect, but in showing
them that path to transcendence, that is, the invention of the future.
To make transcendence emerge despite all that conditioning.*

*True education isn't dogmatic, but prophetic. It is subversive be-
cause it teaches us to live creatively, even in the midst of chaos, to
not put our hopes in the shifting sands of nature or history, but to become aware that it is possible to live in other ways.*

*The concrete, practical consequences of this unshakable affir-
mation of transcendence are essentially revolutionary.*

*The only possible revolutions are those which don't exclude
mankind's transcendent dimension; which don't exclude the divine;
which are founded on this article of faith: that the basic foundation
of reality is an act of the creative freedom which is called God.*

*To be a revolutionary is to be a creator of that reality, to partic-
ipate in divine life.*

Thoughtfully, I closed my log. This morning I had re-read
Garaudy's page a dozen times while thinking about Stephan and
his love of slingshots. I didn't know where life would lead him, but
I hoped that he would someday understand that with his sling-

shot and his faith, David had toppled fierce Goliath, who believed only in the virtues of his sword, his armor, and his gold.

After thirty-eight days of wide horizons, the sun was rising behind the San Francisco hills. A crossing without any problems or damage, except for the genoa and the jib. The staysail would arrive worn out but intact for the final push. Before the bowsprit lay the first buoys of the long funnel-shaped channel that leads to the Golden Gate Bridge soaring across the entrance to the bay.

JOSHUA and I were entering the New World together, sailing on a wide expanse of water that was protected from every direction. Hundreds of sails crisscrossed the bay. I anchored in a quiet cove between two marinas. End of maneuver. No, not quite. An outboard was cruising slowly nearby. I invited the people aboard for a cup of coffee, which we drank quietly in the cabin. I wrote Ugo and Isabella's telephone number on a sheet of notepaper, and they promised to phone them within an hour.

Ugo and Isabella! Being at sea was great . . . but so was California. I checked out the terrain and found it solid. Soon, we would get to work. I cabled Iléana to take the first plane heading for San Francisco with Stephan. And all of life was great!

CHAPTER 23

I was deeply impressed by my first encounter with California. I found the place open to new ideas, contacts were direct and easy, and people had a highly developed civic sense. They were friendly and helpful, and listened to each other with respect. Speeding, whether in town or on the freeways, was severely punished; cars were for getting around, not blowing off steam. Administrative services seemed remarkably efficient. There were problems, of course, and rich and poor, but I found a great desire for justice in all social classes.

Where food was concerned, the choice was enormous: in every town where I showed my film, I found stores stocked with health foods and organically grown fruits and vegetables that cost little more than their commercial equivalents.

The towns also had second-hand stores—the salvation of thin wallets—which sold clothes that still had a lot of use in them. Once, before I gave a talk, Isabella thought I really looked too shabby, and took me to one. I came out with a good pair of shoes, two pairs of wool socks, a nearly new pair of corduroy pants, two shirts, and a handsome down vest, all for less than twenty dollars!

Still, the United States is a place where you have to paddle hard to keep your nose above water. Mary Crowley helped me draft the letters I fired off in all directions to promote my talks and film screenings. She was the founder of Ocean Voyages, a charter company located close to where JOSHUA was moored. She thought it wonderful that I was using my screenings also to talk about fruit trees and unilateral nuclear de-escalation. She put her copying machine at my complete disposal and often got on the phone to get me better terms from yacht clubs and universities.

But after a blazing start with my film screenings, the pace slowed as I scooped off the cream of the California coast. By year's end, it was all I could do to get through the last days of the month, what with exorbitant mooring fees, the telephone I needed on board, Stephan's tuition, and other expenses. I found myself fighting at knife-point to get decent honoraria for my screenings. Meanwhile, JOSHUA had neither jib nor genoa; and I could forget about the staysail; it was shot. With no way to escape under these conditions, the trap was slowly closing again.

That's when Sam, a building contractor with a boat in a nearby marina, stepped in to give me a terrific boost. One day, without anything in the back of my mind, I was telling him about my financial difficulties. Sam said, "Do you want a job on my construction site?" Though I was fifty-seven, he hired me on the spot.

For six months, with a shovel in my hand or pushing wheelbarrows of gravel, I worked a couple of days a week on Sam's projects. I made ten dollars an hour, like the rest of the crew. Just a couple of days a week because at fifty-seven, you aren't as strong as a man of thirty. I spent the rest of the time giving talks and screenings when I could, and teaching celestial navigation aboard JOSHUA on weekends. By putting all that together, the level of the ship's cash-box began to climb again. But it was really Sam who helped get us out of the hole. And by working side by side with my pals on the job, seeing how seriously they took their work, I came to understand why the United States would always pull through—regardless of the trials caused by Reagan's blind policies. (This was in 1982, in the middle of the arms race and big military budgets.)

Sam had a civil engineering degree, but that didn't keep him from working as hard as his fifteen workers. He had also been to journalism school and had worked as a reporter, among other things, for several years. All my sweat-and-shovel comrades on his construction crew had other talents as well. It made for wonderful flexibility where everyone was free to master work skills beyond some narrow specialty.

This was something I often discussed with Mary, Sam, Ugo, and Isabella. The United States' best quality lay in the aptitude Americans have for doing different kinds of work, whether they were handling a pen, a shovel, or a slide rule.

In the United States, people weren't afraid to shift their sights, to search for new horizons; they took a good hard look, then forged ahead. They weren't afraid of anything. It was a tough country, but it wasn't a country of slackers.

Two years after reaching California, JOSHUA headed out to sea again, with new sails. The genoa, jib, and staysail were a gift from Giulio Frezza and Franco, generous friends we had made along the way. We met on the marina dock, then had dinner together on board. "We're flying to Italy tomorrow," they said. "Give us a quick sketch of the sails you need, and we'll send them to you by air, as a present." And three weeks later, the sails arrived.

Stephan and Iléana stayed in San Francisco. She was working at a job where she was paid under-the-table, and Stephan was doing very well in school.

Aboard JOSHUA with me was the actor Klaus Kinski. He had dreamed of sailing around the world and was paying me a generous sum to take him sailing for a week; sort of a personal cruising school. I would drop him off in Mexico, then continue on to Costa Rica, where life isn't expensive. That important detail would finally give me the freedom to start writing. Besides, Costa Rica isn't that far from California. My family could join me later on, and I could take a plane to San Francisco from time to time in the meanwhile. It was a sensible plan, and life had taught me not to ask for the moon.

Life is a fascinating adventure, full of unexpected twists. You decide to do this or that . . . and then Chaos intervenes with its inescapable Law. Destiny needs to have its say, too, and it can be friendly—or otherwise. And when Destiny rushes at us with big sharp teeth, the entire sky comes crashing down on our poor carcasses, the unthinkable becomes reality, and we wind up naked on the beach.

It happened during my brief stop in the wonderful natural harbor at Cabo San Lucas, where Kinski was leaving me. The short stopover lasted twelve hours too long—because I let my guard down. On the morning of our third day there, heavy clouds with dark bat wings warned me that the neighborhood was getting unhealthy. Early that same afternoon, the sea, too, sent me a warning message, in the form of an unusual swell. If I had been at sea, twenty miles offshore, with a storm jib and triple-reefed mainsail, I would have come through without a scratch. But really bad weather is extremely rare in Baja in December; records show that severe storms have hit only twice in the last hundred years. So I didn't pay attention to the warning signs that the sky and the sea were giving me, and I stayed at that quiet anchorage instead of quickly getting out while I still had the time.

The hurricane struck during the night.

By dawn, the beautiful beach, whose sand had felt so soft the night before, had become a graveyard pounded by monstrous waves and sprinkled with our tears. Twenty-five boats were destroyed that night, with no mercy shown. JOSHUA lost her masts, her rudder stock was broken in two places, stanchions were flattened on the deck, hatch and pulpits ripped off, portholes shattered, cabin and forepeak full of sand, gravel, and horror.

And I was staggering along the shore, my spring broken and eyes dead, like the ghost of my boat. We had both died.

Bill and Laura Cutter, who had a house on the dunes facing the sea, took me in, helped me to heal. And they saw hope coming to life again, like a trembling flame. But their hearts were there to see that the little flame didn't flicker out for good.

Together, we started salvaging a few things by digging in the sand and gravel that filled the hull. Alerted by telephone, Ugo hopped on a plane and arrived the same evening. With him there, things really started to move. Then two young guys, Joe and Reto, came to give us a hand. They were crewing on a boat whose anchors had held, out beyond the area of the fiercest waves.

It took the six of us two days to recover all the material buried under the mass of sand: anchors, chains, hawsers, rolls of line, sets of charts, spare sails from the forepeak, tools, blocks, parts of the rigging, turnbuckles, mast gooseneck and fittings, and personal things. Amazing, how much stuff a cruising boat carries. Then we tackled the sand—tons and tons of sand. And the Child next to me said not to ask any questions, just work and work and work, don't look beyond the present . . . haul the sand, haul the sand, haul the sand, deny the fatigue in muscles that begged for relief, haul the sand, haul the sand, work like tireless automatons . . . haul the sand, haul the sand, even if you don't know why . . . haul the sand, haul the sand, work with all your might to lighten the boat, haul the sand, lighten the boat, haul the sand, haul the sand, lighten the boat, yell no to exhaustion a thousand times . . . haul the sand, haul the sand, haul the sand . . . The keel began to

appear and the Child shouted that we were working like gods because we had to save JOSHUA, who was carrying all the immensity
of the long way in her guts.

In a week of incredible effort, we freed the boat of its tons of
sand, then cleaned everything inside. Though severely battered
in places, the hull wasn't cracked anywhere. It had held! And the
high tide of the full moon was just three days away.

If we managed to get JOSHUA afloat, she would be heading for
new horizons with Joe and Reto aboard, once they had fixed her
up. They had offered to buy the wreck, but selling JOSHUA would
have been like selling my soul. On the other hand, I could *give* her
to them; that was not only my right, but my duty. I had neither the
financial means nor the strength to rebuild everything myself in
this out-of-the-way part of Mexico. And even if by some miraculous effort I could, I would be stuck there, completely exhausted,
without a penny to help me reach the *only* goal that could still
give meaning to my life: the book. In other words, I would be on
the beach at age fifty-eight and starting from scratch, with nothing in my hands and nothing in my pockets. Whereas Joe and Reto
were young and full of enthusiasm, and they loved JOSHUA. I loved
her too; I loved her with every fiber of my body, I loved her with
all my soul. But the die was cast . . . A page was turning on the
most beautiful chapter of my life, a love story that had lasted
twenty-one years, a great love story between a man and a boat.

We ran to the port captain's office to transfer the title, but the
official there refused to register it as a gift; you needed to state a
purchase price for everything to be legal. How about twenty dollars? We signed the bill of sale.

The great high tide of the full moon came right on schedule.
We had spent the entire day carefully preparing the salvage attempt. The sea was calm. Little wavelets lapped at the sand, coming closer and closer. The trench a bulldozer had dug between the
wreck and the sea at low tide was beginning to fill with water. A
strong hawser and a steel cable ran from JOSHUA's bow to a trawler
offshore. It was now or never. If we failed, the local authorities
would chop up the wreck with cutting torches to clear the beach
. . . and I would never get over it.

High tide . . . the bulldozer pushed with all its might . . . the
trawler pulled as hard as it could . . . we heard the first crunch of
sand under the hull . . . already, JOSHUA wasn't a wreck anymore

. . . very slowly, she began to slide toward life . . . a great cheer rose from the crowd that had gathered to see the miracle . . . and two minutes later, the magic boat was riding at anchor.

And my heart was bursting with joy!

From then on, everything happened so fast I felt I was moving in a dream. And yet I wasn't dreaming. Three months after the hurricane, there I was, painting the hull of my new boat in Rick Wood's boatyard in Richmond, on San Francisco Bay. It's true; life is a fascinating adventure. Especially when you're lucky enough to be beloved by the gods. I have that luck, that's all.

I had met Rick in Polynesia after he sailed around the Horn aboard his sturdy steel ketch SEA LION. He then went to California, where he set up a boatyard in Richmond. That's where my new boat was born, attended by many friends' good wishes.

But without John Hutton and his wife Ned, I would never have gotten the boat. I had known them well in Polynesia some ten years earlier, when they arrived aboard their big wooden cutter. We'd liked each other right away, felt a strong connection. When JOSHUA was in Papeete harbor, they looked her over from top to bottom and got a first-hand sense of the advantages of steel construction. They later built FAIRY TERN and an impressive number of hard-chine steel boats of their own design at various ports of call. It was their passion, and they had already been at it for the past seventeen years. And when the gods took JOSHUA away from me, Fate, which sometimes causes things to work out so well—coupled with Chaos—arranged it that John and Ned were finishing their eighteenth hull for one of Rick Wood's customers. Barely two days after Ugo's return to San Francisco, John telephoned me at the Cutters' house in Cabo San Lucas:

"Ned and I are going to build you a new boat in Rick's boatyard. Needless to say, our work is free; we owe you at least that much. And Ned says she absolutely agrees. Here, I'll let you talk to Rick . . . Wait a minute, Ugo wants to talk to you first; he's in Rick's office with us."

Ugo's voice, from a thousand miles away:

"I've given Rick a check so he can order the sheet steel. That's Isabella's and my contribution. And no arguments, please. You'll never be able to write your book if you don't have a boat underfoot. Here's Rick, he'll explain the rest."

At the other end, Rick came on the line:

"I can have the steel delivered tomorrow afternoon. There's room in the yard for your boat. John and Ned can use all our tools. And I'm not charging you a cent; it's my present. Here's John again."

There, the discussion became intense. John and Ned wanted me to get off to a good start with a 40-foot boat, the same size as JOSHUA. I absolutely refused. What I needed was a small boat: minimum gear, minimum maintenance, minimum complications. Just big enough for a chart table where I could write, but not so small that I'd have to crawl around the cabin on my hands and knees. Twenty-eight feet, say, or thirty, tops. But that raised a problem: they didn't have plans available for a boat of that size, or the time to draw them.

"We have a decent 36-foot design. What do you say?"

"Thirty-six or forty feet is about the same thing, it belongs to the big-boat category. I'll get stuck with lots of problems, I know how it goes. What I need is something really small and simple so I can write, otherwise I'll never manage."

"Listen, we'll feel bad if we can't do this for you. We might be able to reduce the 36-foot plans to thirty-two feet, but not less. If we went below that, the waterlines wouldn't work right; she'd be a cow. And Ned and I aren't about to get involved in anything that's less than the best. Thirty-two feet is our final offer. Take it or leave it."

"Okay, let's go with thirty-two feet. You guys are terrific, both of you. Give your wife Ned a big kiss for me!"

Meanwhile, my friends—Mary Crowley in the United States, Jean-Michel Barrault in France, Jeannot Rey in Tahiti—launched a fundraising campaign in the press among boat people. A flurry of checks poured in to help refill the ship's cash-box. To all you generous, anonymous contributors, thank you from the bottom of my heart.

So there I was, three months after the Cabo San Lucas drama, standing in front of my new boat, dreaming that I wasn't dreaming. The Wichard company, which makes stainless-steel fittings, gave me all the shackles and turnbuckles I needed. Sam gave me a big bundle of cable clamps for the shrouds. A guy who had taken my celestial navigation class the year before found me a terrific telephone pole for a mast. Next day, a man I didn't know came to see me.

"My name's Scott Wood, and I'm a shipwright. Your goddamned books got me so high, I want to give you a week of my life to shape your mast."

Using a chain saw, Scott cut the huge telephone pole into a

perfect eight-sided mast in three days. He finished the job with an electric plane, then screwed the sail track on. Meanwhile, I built the boom and spreaders, John Hutton fabricated the masthead fitting, and bingo! The mast was stepped before the end of the weekend, and all the shrouds tightened. And Peter Sutter, a master sailmaker in Sausalito, gave me a brand-new mainsail!

With the ship's cash-box in good shape again, I was in a position to buy an engine, and I was seriously considering it. But even a very small engine would put a huge dent in my finances. If I wanted to get by for a good long time while writing the book, it might be smart to avoid a big expense that wasn't absolutely necessary.

But the gods above held a meeting—and yet another miracle occurred. It came in the form of a man named Cliff, who ran an insurance agency in Oregon. He drove down as soon as he could, and took me to a nearby cafe to tell me what was on his mind. "I've been thinking about getting a boat, but I need to know more about the sea before I make a decision. Sailing with you would be ideal. If you agree to take me to Hawaii, I'll give you a brand-new engine of your choice." The deal was done in thirty seconds; two days later, John was installing my 12-horsepower diesel engine. It was an air-cooled, hand-cranked model, so I didn't have to worry about a water pump or starter batteries. And the exhaust pipe discharged on deck, inside the cockpit coaming, so there was no danger of seawater getting into it; a totally reliable setup. Besides, an air-cooled motor makes a hell of a racket and makes the cabin so hot so you tend to use the "iron spinnaker" as little as possible, so you don't wear it out.

Things kept happening at breakneck speed.

For ballast, Cliff and I loaded two tons of lead ingots aboard, stowed them in the hollow keel, then bolted a steel sheet on top of them, sealing it with a gasket cut from my inner tube supply.

John and Ned had already fabricated the pulpits, stanchions, and bowsprit.

We mounted the rudder and attached the trim tab for the self-steering rig.

And Cliff located a big tractor inner tube, which we immediately dubbed the "Bombard Dinghy."

Soon it would be time to baptize the boat itself. I was leaning toward *Iléana*, but she wouldn't hear of it, and suggested *Tamata* instead. I hesitated a little, but she was right; *Tamata* suited the boat perfectly. And while Iléana was painting the name on the cockpit coaming, the Child whispered in my ear: "Add the Chinese ideogram for 'heart-spirit;' that way, your pretty boat will have a symbolic name, too." It was a stroke of pure genius!

We hadn't started on the interior when Jacques Toujan showed up. He's got a heart the size of a mountain, and he travels around the world lending a hand to everyone he meets. He knows how to see things and people in all three dimensions at first glance.

In ten days spent working side by side with Jacques, we had the interior done. Nothing the least bit fancy, everything kept absolutely simple: three berths, a Primus stove on gimbals, a sink, no bulkheads or lockers—lots of open space. In this cabin, you felt you had some elbow-room. Food and heavy gear would go under the berths and the floorboards. Five shock cords ran fore and aft between the ribs to hold all the little things you want to get at quickly without having to rummage everywhere. And we built a huge chart table where I would be able to write in peace when the time came to start my book.

In a nearby dumpster we found several almost new foam-rubber mattresses. Iléana cut and glued them to fit, and sewed covers and cushions with her magic fingers. The place was starting to look really nice.

Ugo brought me the sextant, whose mirrors he'd had replaced.

Cliff stored the cans under the floorboards.

The rigging was tuned, the mainsail furled on the boom, genoa and staysail hanked on, sheets and halyards neatly coiled. Jacques and I quickly built a windvane for the self-steering rig. I was already starting to smell the sea and the freedom of the wide horizon; and God, it smelled good!

"Hey, Jacques. What would you say to taking a little hop from San Francisco to Hawaii with Cliff and me? TAMATA's a pretty boat, and we can see how she sails."

It took Jacques about a tenth of a second to make up his mind; he answered with a smile as warm as the sun. So the three of us would be sailing to Hawaii! I would then go on alone to Polynesia, instead of Costa Rica.

Polynesia, because it made sense for me to tie up in a place where I could stay as long as I pleased without being hassled by immigration officers.

Alone, because Stephan and Iléana were staying behind in San Francisco. She had made good friends and found the stimulation she needed. As for Stephan, he was finally doing well in school, which was a big consideration. As far I was concerned, I was sure of one thing: though the pace of life in the United States had given me a lot in certain intellectual areas, it was a tempo that didn't suit my writing at all. For me, settling here would mean abandoning the book—and winding up a wreck.

The barometer was high, the wind favorable; everything on board was ready. TAMATA was eager to point her bow toward the big adventure. Iléana and I already knew that separating had become inevitable, and probably final. Because the gods so willed it. That's the way it is. That's life. But it wasn't a parting in the usual sense; far from it. Iléana knew she would always be in my heart, whatever happened. And I knew I would always be in hers, whatever the future brought. We both knew that the bond connecting us would live on without losing its strength. Because that bond was sacred, the result of all that was strong and beautiful in what we had done together.

CHAPTER 24

Deep in the silence of the undergrowth and giant trees of the Great Forest, I walked and walked, seeking the pieces of the puzzle one after another. It reminded me of the fishermen of the Gulf of Siam recovering their long-line floats after storms and unpredictable currents had scattered them to the four winds.

And Time started to change dimension, as during an astral trip to the edge of beyond. With part of me here, part there, I was no longer quite sure which boat I was on, crossing the waves toward the Unknown . . . one of my two MARIE-THÉRÈSES . . . JOSHUA . . . TAMATA . . . SNARK . . . or Phuoc's father's little junk with its pretty latania-leaf sail . . . the heavy wire that the village men bent into strong fishhooks . . . the women singing under the big *badamier* tree as they twisted the fiber into lines . . . Hao's father entering the crack with the *cai tram* bark which Xai and I had gone deep into the distant forest to get . . . or Bai Ma taking us to the Cave of Coins where the old monk had gone through the three schools of "seeing," "doing," and "transmitting."

Lord, how far in my wake the Great Forest was . . . and yet so close. At first, I had wandered in a freezing country, arid and stony, without shadows or light. No seed could ever have sprouted in such a barren place. There, I almost lost the sacred fire, set down the burden that was too heavy for me, raised anchor to go anywhere at all, so long as it was as far away as possible.

After I had spent six or eight months of dull grayness turning in circles in front of the blank page, the gods really started to get concerned. So they sent me a Fairy. She put her warm hand in mine, our two hearts melted together, and together we left the terrible Desert of Solitude.

After that, having checked every detail of the rigging, I was able to cross unscathed through two Swamps of Shifting Sands full of three-headed crocodiles. It took me a long time to get my bearings, to cautiously adjust my aim, to avoid infuriating the nests of double-stinger wasps that lived in symbiosis with the crocs. But my magic slingshot's incredible accuracy worked wonders. I retrieved some pieces of the puzzle by reaching right into the throats of rabid dogs. It was a terrific game, dangerous at times, but very exciting to the Child, whose joy beat in the warmth of my heart.

Beyond the swamps, things got tough. No more fooling around. I wrestled constantly with the mirage-throwing dragon, the great neuron-eating drone, and the little thought-scrambling lizard. Those three evil genies harassed me ceaselessly, putting mountains of obstacles in my way. They spread Doubt, Fatigue, and Despair underfoot, wiped out the path, enveloped me in total darkness broken by dazzling flashes in which I couldn't tell stem from stern. And my magic slingshot nearly lost its power, because the three turned into puffs of air as soon as I glimpsed them through the fog. They constantly blocked my progress, preventing me from picking up the thousand pieces of the puzzle which the winds of Fate had scattered in the depths of my soul.

Then Hao's father could come to see how I was doing, and I rediscovered my two old allies, Patience and Tenacity.

The quest for that Holy Grail took eight long years of terrible battles. Against the ghosts of the past. Against those of the present. Against those I could make out here and there among the shadows of the future. And against myself, unmasking the tiniest ways in which Compromise tried to sneak into my writing. I won all those fights, one after another, often several in the same engagement. But each one left me broken with fatigue, and sometimes close to despair.

Once in a great while, a clearing enlivened by bird song would bring respite. Then I would find my center in the village sunshine, voluptuously spreading my toes with Xai in the frog pond near Xian's hut, sharpening my ragged neurons, reactivating my failing or lazy electrons with the help of the Great Breath. But I continued to avoid Bai Ma's grave . . . it was still too soon.

And I returned to the path through the Great Forest, which seemed endless. The path was uncertain, difficult, and full of traps, but the Child carried me along. At each new dawn, he would say, "When you start a job, you finish it, period."

To enter the crack like Hao's father—the only way to join the old monk's *yin* and *yang* with the Breath of the Alliance and thereby complete the puzzle in all three of its dimensions.

To see only the Essential.

To listen to the messages sent to me by voices from far away.

Never to forget, as Dominique Charnay used to say, that "words are there to show you, not to show off."

On one particularly tough day, as I was stumbling through a snarl of creepers, tangled roots, and carnivorous plants, a very nasty Beast pounced on me. The attack happened in the very depths of the Great Forest.

The Beast is something that can't be apprehended. The chiaroscuro of science calls it "an anarchic proliferation of giant cells." In ordinary language, it's called "cancer."

As soon as it sniffed out my trail, the Beast vomited a nightmarish bird that flapped around in my head on pincer-like wings. I recognized it immediately . . . I had encountered it before, during the war, on the banks of the Mekong . . . It was Fear . . . But not ordinary fear, or even terror. This was real Fear with big, big teeth, Fear that paralyzes, overwhelms our defenses, casts us dazed into emptiness.

When he saw what was happening, the Child handed me one of the best stones in our collection and said, "Start by shooting down that Bird of Evil!" And one shot from my magic slingshot broke its wing, sent it spiraling down into a red-ant nest. Then the Child went to get a stone that was as heavy as uranium, ten times harder than diamond, and as acute as an electron microscope.

This time, I shot the Beast right between the eyes, a master shot that should have dropped it at my feet, dead as a doornail. But the Beast only gave a laugh as powerful as the thunder of a dozen tropical storms, and jumped onto my shoulders to rip away ten pounds of solid muscle . . . and I was the one to fall to the ground in an immense lassitude, my faith shredded to tatters.

So the Child quickly rushed to high Heaven to ask the gods for advice. And when he came back, he said, "Tame the Beast!"

A stroke of genius! Why not?

Taming the Beast . . . It felt like rounding Cape Horn from east to west, tacking through a pea-soup fog, with rocks dripping foam on one side, icebergs hidden level with the waves on the other, and breaking waves sweeping over the boat, as I wondered whether the rigging would hold and how long this would go on. It was exhilarating sailing just the same, even if it wasn't much fun to sail triple-reefed through these tumultuous seas to the other side of the Great Forest.

But I found all the pieces of the puzzle!

In this way, eight years of my life passed between the day I entered the Great Forest and the day I emerged, my sails full of patches, but the book nearly finished.

Around the boat, the sea sparkled with pleasure. The sun was shining, soft and warm. And to my dazzled eyes, the world no longer looked the way it once did. I would even say the planet was astonished by something unimaginable.

Seeking peace, the East had opened up.

The Berlin Wall no longer existed.

The beginnings of a true de-escalation of nuclear missiles had replaced the Cold War, where one spark a little hotter than the rest could have blown everything up.

Now reconciled, Popov and John had thrown their grenades into the garbage can of History and were tending their garden, fixing the gutters, and cleaning the well. So what if the new consciousness, in the midst of such upheaval, at times still limped on its crutches? It would stand on its own two feet someday, after the innumerable stumbling steps that accompany creation.

In my opinion, it was absolutely clear that consciousness was progressing. But it took a real beating in the cynicism and lies orchestrated by the Gulf War in the name of a "new world order." Actually, it was nothing but an attempt by the iron fist to hold onto the old order established by the law of the strong and the greed of an unworthy West, the giant with feet of clay that walks hand in hand with its accomplice, the Golden Calf.

Alas, hate, stupidity, violence, and cowardice are still growing pretty much all over our shared planet, like poisonous plants grown by the Dragon.

The massacre of entire populations.

Massive deportations.

Legalized torture.

The dictatorship of guns sold by wealthy countries to the bloodthirsty leaders of underdeveloped ones where tanks outnumber plows!

The exodus of millions of hopeless refugees.

War is the worst monster mankind has ever created. The most hideous, stupid way imaginable to settle a problem. All wars are fratricidal, whatever they are called and regardless of the "good conscience" with which they are launched.

I've met plenty of idiots who think that space flight would never have happened if Hitler's rockets hadn't existed to show the way. That without the war in the Pacific and its mountains of dead, antibiotics wouldn't have been perfected. And also, among other absurdities, that wars are essential to control overpopulation. People who think that way have never heard machine-gun bullets hitting home, or seen bombs falling from the sky.

The East has collapsed. The West is crumbling in turn. Politics is clinging to the branches, but they are rotten. Economics is also desperately trying to cling to the branches; they're just as rotten. The vast majority of people refuse to understand that we aren't in a political or economic crisis, but a crisis of *moral* values. We aren't used to sailing on those waters, so they scare us, for the simple reason that it isn't easy to open our eyes and unclog our brains. But in the end, we're going to have to choose between dazzling advances in automatic weapons or raising our individual and collective consciousness.

The Step of Intelligence that Isabella Conti spoke of beside our Suvorov campfire still seems far off below the horizon. But in my gut, I'm certain that mankind will be ready to take that next, major step in its evolution the moment it puts all of its physical, mental, and spiritual resources into the scales to make Peace *first*.

Life has taught me that mankind holds the Choice in its hands. It therefore has the Power to shape its destiny instead of submitting to it. Not only the power, but also the *Responsibility*.

When we have made Peace, when we have strengthened it by taking a big sponge and wiping out old quarrels and forgiving past offenses, then Spirit and Heart will walk side by side on the Higher Path. And it doesn't take fancy formulas to see that this path will lead us to an incredible *possibility:* that of together creating a world that is at last worthy of humanity. A world no longer ruled by Injustice, Blood, Misery, or Shame.

But I won't see that better world to which we all aspire, not in this lifetime. The Fairy Tern has come to brush me with its light wings, carrying a message from the gods: "Little Brother, there isn't much water ahead for you to cross before you reach your final anchorage."

It's true; I hadn't really succeeded in taming the Beast, nor in changing its carnivorous nature. Each time it awakens and sinks its teeth into my tired carcass, Time shrinks a little more in front of the bowsprit. And the gods whose friendship has always accompanied me have no power over Time.

The wake is stretching out very slowly behind the sternpost now. What little wind has been pushing me has dropped to a light breeze. I think of the bright morning when I first raised my sails in the fresh monsoon wind to discover the world with MARIE-THÉRÈSE. In those days, my horizon had no limits; all the islands in my life's adventure were new ones.

Now twilight is approaching, the picture album is full, and I've put the entire puzzle together. Only one last piece refuses to fit . . . that of Bai Ma. Despite the half-century that has lapped at the blood near his grave year after year, his eyes still speak of war.

Flat calm. I'm very much afraid I've come too late. I watch the horizon and look to Heaven. I know that man can do nothing without the breath of Your spirit. And that You can do nothing without our hands. You and we humans are partners: Architect and builders. Partners through the fabulous Alliance, which we are free to accept or not. Free, because you put Choice in our hands when a branch of the primate family took the Step of Thought, millions of years ago.

All during my ephemeral existence, I've never asked You for anything for myself. You had enough to worry about, with our shaky humanity. I didn't want to bother You with my ridiculous little problems. But the anchorage isn't far off; soon I will have completed the circle of my life. And I need a bit of help. Stretch time out a little for me, so I can take care of some very old business. Otherwise the last piece will never take its place in the puzzle. I must talk with Bai Ma, in front of his grave, in the village of his childhood and mine. Maybe he'll listen then . . . and pick up the

Big Sponge. In the entire universe, only Bai Ma has the power to erase the stain of blood that still stands between us.

Suspended between dream and reality, the foam of the wake spins out in long tresses whitened by the sea, whitened by the years. A steady northeast monsoon wind brings me the smell of the forests and the rice paddies of the land of my childhood, the Indochina of my youth, the land of my roots.

As soon as the wind picks up, I very carefully round Ca Mau Point, the southern tip of Vietnam, with its treacherous mudbanks laid down by the Mekong. Then I sail toward Tamassou. Lord, the island looks beautiful in the rising sun! But I leave it some distance to starboard, so as not to make my route too much longer.

My eyes full of Tamassou, I trim the sails a bit to continue close-hauled, heading between Hon Chong and Hon Heo Island. I don't know if I can squeeze past Hon Chong without tacking. But suddenly the wind shifts thirty degrees, without slackening, something that never, ever happens during the northeast monsoon. Normally, the slightest wind shift is almost immediately followed by calm. Today, nothing of the sort: wind, wind, and more wind! I recognize the hand of the gods. And, to my astonishment, I see that the boat taking me to my final anchorage . . . is MARIE-THÉRÈSE! An inexpressible joy floods my heart. MARIE-THÉRÈSE, the beautiful junk of my first love, my beautiful junk with its aroma of pitch and distant forests.

Hon Heo is passing by to port, Hon Chong to starboard. My village is only a dozen miles away. I see the little jar of the Cave of Coins appear, shining in the sky. And also the parade of ghosts from my first departure toward the wide horizon . . . all those brothers immolated on the altar of War, all those wandering souls to whom I had promised I would someday return and bear witness.

My rigging is in order, sheets and halyards clear, mooring lines neatly coiled, two anchors on the deck. Ready to drop anchor. And there is the village . . . the sea and the forest . . . its sandy beach, where a wave comes to die after its long voyage . . . the soft dirt road that so many bare feet have walked . . . the huts protected by the altars to the ancestors . . . the monks' pagoda where the drum sounds to drive off the *ma qui*. . . . the incense sticks perfuming each grave.

Bai Ma is there, among the old ones who left the world of the living long ago, and also among the new ones, born in my absence. But Bai Ma is still speaking to them in the language of war and eternal rancor.

When he becomes aware of my presence, Bai Ma is speechless for a moment. Then he roars:

"Look at this scum who has dared to come back! This son of a she-dog can go croak among the *ma qui*! Always remember that his kind coldly considered using an atomic bomb to wipe us out at Dien Bien Phu! And the only reason they didn't use it was that they couldn't get one!"

And then the Child hurls the lightning bolt, shouting to all of us, the living and the dead:

"It is never a mistake to forgive!"

Bai Ma looks at the lightning bolt . . . hesitates, like a sailboat rolled keel upward by a terrific breaking wave . . . we watch as the boat slowly rights itself . . . Bai Ma picks up the Big Sponge . . . he erases the bloodstain in front of the grave.

And the last piece of the puzzle falls into place.

CHRONOLOGY

April 10, 1925. Born in Hanoi. A few months later, my family settles in Saigon.

August 15, 1945. End of the Second World War.

September 1945. Start of the Indochinese War.

1946. Drafted for French military service in Indochina.

1947. Coastal shipping aboard a junk in the Gulf of Siam. Bankrupt after six months, I return to Saigon to work in my father's business.

1948. Eight months' leave in Europe, then again work with my father.

1951. Departure aboard SNARK with Pierre Deshumeurs. We return to Saigon six months later.

1952. Solo departure from Kampot, Cambodia aboard MARIE-THÉRÈSE. Shipwrecked in the Chagos Bank the same year. A Royal Navy ship takes me to Mauritius, where I try various professions until 1955. MARIE-THÉRÈSE II is built in three months.

1958. Shipwreck in the Caribbean.

1960. I write *Vagabond des Mers du Sud [Sailing to the Reefs]*.

1961. Marriage to Françoise. Construction of JOSHUA, followed by two seasons of cruising school.

1963. Françoise and I set sail for Polynesia.

1966. Return to Europe. I write *Cap Horn à la Voile [Cape Horn: The Logical Route]*.

1968-1969. Solo sail from Plymouth to Tahiti.

1969-1971. I write *La Longue Route [The Long Way]*.

1970. I meet Iléana.

October 3, 1971. Stephan is born.

1973. To New Zealand, by way of Suvorov.

1974. Visit to Israel.

October 1975-August 1978. Ahe.

1978-80. Moorea for two years.

August 25, 1980. Departure for San Francisco.

December 8, 1982. JOSHUA is shipwrecked at Cabo San Lucas, Mexico.

1983. Construction of TAMATA and departure for Hawaii. I spend ten months there, writing 600 letters to 600 American publications, promoting the benefits of a unilateral nuclear de-escalation. At the time, I wrote in my log: *We may as well admit that the human species is led by men who are half crazy.*

Let's hope that women will some day rouse themselves to preserve Life while waiting for Intelligence to awaken within the bosom of humanity.

May 1984. Departure for Tahiti, by way of Suvorov. Reaching Papeete in early October, I start to write. But I find myself blocked, and spend six months scribbling unreadable pages.

1985. I meet Véronique. I take her to Suvorov. Big flash. I join her a few months later in Paris.

1986-1992. Writing *Tamata et l'Alliance* in France. TAMATA remains hauled out with some good friends at Raiatea, near Bora Bora. Véronique introduces me to southern Brittany. What a beautiful country—a land of light! From time to time we return to Raiatea to sail a bit under the tropical sun. The interruptions do my writing no harm; quite the contrary.

July, 1993. At Raiatea, I finish *Tamata et l'Alliance [Tamata and the Alliance]*.

Author's afterword

After being shipwrecked in Mexico and restored by Joe and Reto, JOSHUA sails again, this time to Seattle. Sold, a few years later, to a young American woman, she sails along the West coast of the United States. In 1990, she is acquired by the maritime museum of La Rochelle, not to be turned into an exhibit like a ship in a bottle, but free on the ocean with a new set of sails! As of the publication date of *Tamata et l'Alliance*, the magic boat is still soaking up spray in a cruising school under the command of a good skipper from the maritime museum. As for the Old Monkey, he is still on his feet, in spite of the Beast, which seems to have become a little tamer, since it hasn't sent me any metastases since our first contact four and a half years ago.

So along with the Child who holds lightning bolts in his hand, I say to all of you: greetings and fraternity!

Translator's afterword

Bernard Moitessier died in France on June 16, 1994. He is buried in the small Breton town of Le Bono, among sailors and fishermen.-W.R.

AN OVERVIEW OF CRUISING

Because of my various books, I've received many letters from people of all ages who were feeling the call of the open sea. Depending on their temperaments, they asked more or less directly for my advice on getting ready for the great departure. Here are my answers. Don't needlessly complicate your life. Give top priority to what is essential. Firmly leave the superfluous aside. If faced with a choice between the simple and the complicated, choose the simple without hesitation; sooner or later, what is complicated will almost always lead to problems—needless expense, loss of precious time, and waste of energy.

This "philosophy of simplicity" has guided me like a guardian angel ever since I first set sail. Make do with what you have. Don't have eyes bigger than your stomach. The fundamental question is, do I really want to live and travel on a sailboat? Once you've faced and answered that question honestly, everything will become clear, because you won't be kidding yourself.

The following pages don't pretend to be the way to do things, just the way I see and do them.

Theory

Unless you have a solid basis in theory and practice, I think it wisest to start very modestly at the beginning. Learn from other people's experience by reading books. For French readers, I think the book published by the Glénans sailing school offers a very solid foundation; you can find it in most nautical bookstores; I also like Antoine's book, *Mettre les Voiles* (Arthaud) very much. Those two books will help clear the way for you. I also know of an excellent American book, written by Larry and Lin Pardey, *The Self-Sufficient Sailor* (Norton).

First practical steps

Together with what you learn in books, don't hesitate to get your feet wet in an Optimist. You'll learn a tremendous amount. You may think, "Me, in an Optimist? That's a kid's boat! People will make fun of me!" To that, I would say, "Beware of pride!"

A few years ago in Tahiti, my friends René and Jocelyne had acquired a 27-foot sloop. He was 33 and a real athlete: martial arts, parachute-jumping, body surfing, and some diving, among other things. At 25, Jocelyne wasn't the least bit interested in sport, but she had good common sense. Neither had ever done any sailing—except for a trip to Moorea with a bunch of friends aboard a 60-foot ketch—and they asked me to show them the ropes.

The Arue yacht club agreed to lend us a Caravelle. At first glance, this big dry-sailing centerboard boat seemed ideal. But when we got to the yacht club, we were greeted by a swarm of children between 10 and 12 who were about to go out on Optimists. While waiting for the harbor area to clear, we watched them take off. One of the children, though obviously in way over his head, managed to get out into the channel amid the crowding and taunts of his friends. The children returned an hour later, like a swarm of bees. And we saw something that opened our eyes: the hapless kid of an hour before had been transformed. He was doing as well as the others, yelling "starboard" to any challengers, deftly handling the cross-winds in the narrow channel before raising his centerboard and sailing up to the ramp.

We helped him stow his gear and asked, "How long have you been sailing an Optimist?" Answer: "It's my first time." In a blinding flash, we were struck by the obvious. So René, Jocelyne, and I immediately set sail, each on one of those marvelous dinghies. Close reach, reach, beam reach, coming about, jibing, backing with reverse rudder. We checked to see how well the boats hove-to with the sail backed and the tiller down at 45 degrees. The wind rose and we watched for gusts, learned to anticipate shifts as a force four wind began to raise little whitecaps on the lagoon. René and Jocelyne were starting to take control of their boats. For the heck of it, we started racing. It was great fun; we were in seventh heaven!

And when we headed back a couple of hours later, nobody could have said which one of us had sailed the most miles in his life. It was extraordinary: *in a single outing, they had grasped the essentials!* Because each person was responsible for everything. When you're sailing alone, your boat punishes the slightest mistake or lapse of attention. But an Optimist is a forgiving boat, and it gives you fair warning; you really have to work to turn one over. Whereas a 14-foot 420 wouldn't behave at all the same way: it's a temperamental racing dinghy that I feel is much too fast and unpredictable for a beginner. If you don't have anything else available, of course sailing a 420 is a lot better than staying on the yacht club terrace. But as soon as the wind rises a notch, a 420 will dump you without giving you the time to understand why or how. So I don't think it's the best way to learn quickly and well at the same time.

As for learning in a group aboard a Caravelle, a number of things can make this inconvenient and a waste of time. You have a skipper, the helmsman—who is more or less competent, who is more or less of a teacher—and a crew, the people who do the work. The two most eager ones usually grab the jib sheets and the others become "moveable ballast": they aren't very motivated, and their attention wanders as soon as they start getting bored or cold. Meanwhile, the two people at the sheets start thinking it's high time they took a turn at the tiller. But you don't get the tiller just like that; you have to earn it, you have to deserve it. "Trim your jib a little better," says the skipper. "No, not like that! Are you asleep, or what? How did I ever get such a crew? And you want to take the helm, too?"

All right, I'm exaggerating a little. But still, that's the heart of the problem. On an Optimist, you get to take the tiller right away and you catch on very fast. I know of no better basic training. I consider this modest cockleshell the royal road to blue-water cruising. Aboard an Optimist, your senses sharpen naturally. The only voices you hear are whispered by the hull, sail, wind, and rocks. Through those instantly understandable messages, an Optimist will teach you the fundamental reflexes that will be needed aboard any other craft, small or big. Whether you're on the poop deck of a 2,000-ton three-master, in the cockpit of a 30-foot cutter, or on a 420 or a Caravelle, the basics are absolutely the same, the only difference being a matter of extrapolation depending on tonnage. And a beginner will learn the basics much better and faster aboard a sailing dinghy.

Of course I've met excellent sailors who had never set foot in a sailing dinghy or even tried their hand at crewing on a day sail before setting off for the great adventure aboard 25- to 45-foot boats. They've learned on their own, and I salute them. But how many others have given up because they tried to move up too fast? The sea and the gods don't like excessive haste, lack of preparation, or a casual or careless attitude—especially concerning the really important things.

A few final words on this subject. During her three cruising-school seasons, some 350 people crewed aboard JOSHUA. About 30% of these were complete novices. The other 70% had had some experience: they had taken sailing-school classes at Les Glénans or owned cruising boats. And I noticed a distinct difference between the two categories of non-beginners. The ones who had gone through the Glénans school—even if they had only sailed on a 16-foot Vaurien—very quickly got the hang of handling 15-ton JOSHUA. Whereas the cruising-boat owners, if they hadn't ever sailed dinghies, were almost always overwhelmed by events—to the point where I often wondered whether they ever used the sails on their boats, or mainly their motors. And I hope that despite the passage of time and the onrush of technology, Les Glénans still maintains its grand 1960s tradition, when sailing was the rule.

Choosing a type of boat

This is the second stage in preparing for the great departure. But be careful; take it easy. Here too, I think it's prudent not to rush ahead if you have any alternatives. Beware of falling in love; it blinds you at first, only to leave you unhappy and at a loss aboard a boat that doesn't in the least match your real hopes. Before you decide on this or that kind of boat, it's best to get a general idea of what would best suit you. The smart thing is to do some sailing on several types of boats. Hang around marinas during your vacations and weekends with only a small sea-bag, a good dose of nerve, and *enormous determination*. This is something the gods love. The more you sail on different kind of boats—cruising and racing, summer and winter—the clearer your thinking will become. It may take several seasons, but the effort won't be wasted. This attitude is particularly desirable because it lets you reach three goals at the same time: you'll get to know different kinds of boats; learn all

358   Bernard Moitessier

sorts of things about sailing (reefing, sail-trimming tricks, tidal currents, marine charts, buoyage systems, *Sailing Directions*, charts, etc.); and clear up many mysteries at little cost. It may seem hard to get that first "Yes" which will let you—with no other references than your smiling face—crew on a boat that is preparing to put out. But, as my old friend René Tournouer used to say: "You already have the 'No.' So you really aren't risking anything by insisting, to get yourself a 'Yes.'"

Choosing the boat's material

If you want to go far and keep your boat for a long time, nothing beats metal construction. During the night of the Cabo San Lucas hurricane [*December 8, 1982—Tr.*], 25 boats, almost all of them production fiberglass models, wound up on the beach. At dawn, the beach looked like a huge public dump: half-boats, quarter-boats, big sheets of fiberglass, debris everywhere—a total disaster. During that night, JOSHUA went aground at low tide and a 50-foot fiberglass ketch was driven on top of her. The big boat was destroyed in a couple of hours, whereas mine came through with some serious bumps but not a single crack. Two other boats, beached at high tide, survived the disaster. The first was a 40-foot ultra-light racer made of molded plywood; her keel was knocked askew, but wasn't beyond repair. The second was a sturdy 30-foot cutter of traditional plank construction on laminated ribs; she took some bad knocks, but no fatal ones. If they had gone aground at low- or mid-tide, they would have been destroyed like the others. Several fiberglass boats went on the beach at high tide, and stayed there, hopelessly wrecked.

Metal, fiberglass, molded wood, plywood, traditional planking

Steel:
I'm familiar with six or seven steel boats which were all very well built by competent amateurs whose main tools were a torch and welding gear. This type of construction is especially fast compared to wood or fiberglass. And maintenance is easy, provided no angle irons or T-irons are used. Floor plates, ribs, and rails must all be flat bar. That way, a paintbrush can reach everywhere—which is essential if you don't want to face major problems of interior corrosion that can't be remedied. Waterproof the corners that can't be reached (the junctions of the keel and the bow and sternpost, and under the mast) by welding a sheet of steel over them. On wooden boats, the frames always have limber holes, so any seawater that leaks in can flow freely the length of the keel, avoiding the risk of rot. A metal boat should not have limber holes; when a wave splashes through the companionway, which happens fairly often, you will only have a small section of the bilge to sponge out and rinse with fresh water, instead of the whole length of the keel. Don't screw or bolt any wood onto the deck and cabin top, regardless of the quality of the putty you use between the two materials. Using wood for bulwarks, hand rails, or hatch rails will almost always create corrosion sites. A pretty varnished hand rail may tempt you, but a length of galvanized (or stainless steel) pipe is much more sensible. And never use stainless steel for the

chainplates on a steel boat; stainless steel can crystallize over time, and your mast will someday fall on the deck.

It's true that I used Wichard stainless steel shackles aboard JOSHUA for 15 years without the slightest problem. And when she was built, TAMATA was also rigged with Wichard turnbuckles and shackles. But all that stainless steel gear was oversized (12-millimeter shackles and turnbuckles, where 10 or even 8 millimeters might theoretically be enough). Best to not play Russian roulette with your mast. It could be argued that production fiberglass boats are fitted with stainless steel chainplates, and do just fine. That's true, but the alloys and technology that produced those vital parts are the result of lengthy research. Moreover, the chainplates are bolted to the hull (or cast in the fiberglass), not welded. Any metallurgist will tell you that welding stainless steel can cause molecular changes in the alloy. When stainless is used for a cabin hatch cover slide or a hand rail, there's no danger; but chainplates are subjected to considerable strain during the life of a blue-water cruising boat.

When protected from electrolysis by zinc anodes, the wetted surfaces of a steel boat will remain in perfect condition. Normally, these anodes should be welded to the hull using their mounting brackets. But I've often seen hulls in perfect condition with anodes that were bolted on, to make it easier to replace them when they corrode; you can dive and do it underwater. In any case, it's best to set out with a good supply of anodes in the hold; you can't find them everywhere in the world.

Ideally, you should sand-blast the hull and deck before applying the first coat of paint. If you can also sand-blast the interior, so much the better. By far the best anticorrosion paint I know is *Dox Anode*, a zinc silicate paint that is just terrific. It must be applied to the plates immediately after sand-blasting. *Dox Anode* is sold commercially by the Meta shipyard (at Tarare, Rhone, in France) as *Metagrip*, and is also used on the hulls of all the aluminum boats built there. In addition to its remarkable anti-corrosion properties, it is also somewhat antifouling. JOSHUA sailed her first seven years with nothing but zinc silicate paint on her bottom, though I had to dive often to scrape barnacles.

As far as finish paints go, I used a good old glyceryl-phtallate resin-based alkyd paint on JOSHUA's hull, deck, and interior for 21 years. But paints have improved dramatically during the last ten or fifteen years. On TAMATA I used two-part epoxy for the exterior. It produced an extremely strong surface, and while it chalked a bit over time because of the sun, this didn't seem to affect its incredible protective quality.

Remember that epoxies give off highly toxic fumes while being applied, until they cure completely. I would never use them in an enclosed space like the cabin, even with very good ventilation. Polyurethanes (which don't chalk) are just as dangerous when applied in an enclosed space. It is worth noting that fresh-water tanks can be painted with epoxy; once completely cured, there is no risk of toxicity. This isn't true for all paints, so check them out.

Alkyd paint, which is much less resistant than epoxy or polyurethane, is perfectly adequate for a boat's interior. Originally, JOSHUA's interior was painted with two coats of a very good quality zinc chromate paint made by

Galia Color (in Lyons, France, I think), then two white finish coats, also from Galia Color. After that, I seem to recall a couple of maintenance coats for the interior every four or five years. As on all metal boats, you have to pay extra attention to the galley, head, and the area where Plexiglas is bolted to the hull around the port holes. For the exterior (hull and deck), the broad, flat surfaces were never a problem aboard JOSHUA: with one or two coats of good alkyd paint once or twice a year, I rested easy. During the first three or four years following JOSHUA's construction, I built up the layers of paint on the topsides to obtain a good protective layer on the hull and deck. After that, a coat or two every year. One word about epoxies and polyurethanes: whether for "industrial" or "marine" use, for a given quality, they are exactly the same... except in their effect on your wallet.

Naturally, the parts of the deck fittings that are often abraded (in particular the sheet and halyard cleats and the mooring bitts) have to be watched carefully and touched up fairly often if you want to avoid rust stains on the deck—and more serious problems later on. Ideally, all the fittings would be stainless steel, provided you painted them carefully where they were welded to the hull to avoid any danger of electrolysis. Lacking stainless steel, galvanized iron (or at least hot-dip galvanized) will greatly reduce the time spent maintaining the boat.

At the beginning of this section, I said that maintaining a steel boat is simple. For someone living aboard, that's true. But I wouldn't recommend this type of construction to a doctor or lawyer who can only go sailing for a few weeks a year. Such busy people might wind up spending most of their vacations in port, doing basic maintenance chores.

Aluminum alloy:

Steel construction is more than a century old; aluminum construction is still fairly recent. "If you want an aluminum boat without taking too many chances," a friend once told me, "it's best to buy one second-hand from a real expert; if everything is in good shape, you'll improve your chances of finding a really decent boat."

From what I've been able to learn here and there, aluminum won't cause serious electrolysis problems *if the electrical circuit is completely shielded* and you avoid long stays in industrial ports where stray currents are everywhere. My friend Antoine told me how afraid Americans are of aluminum: "They talk about aluminum sailboats that had spent two or three years at their moorage and were so corroded that it looked as if a giant can opener had split them along their waterlines." Was this the result of stray currents or inadequate (or non-existent) cathodic protection on the hull? Antoine thinks the problem was caused by the two factors combined. It's worth noting that Antoine's VOYAGE and BANANA SPLIT were built by the Meta shipyard using the "Strongall" procedure: extremely heavy aluminum sheets, without ribs; the thicker the aluminum, the stronger the welds.

One final point. As recently as 1993, several owners of aluminum boats told me that they could no longer find antifouling paint that was really compatible with aluminum from an electrolysis standpoint because international laws now forbid the use of tin in antifouling paints, to protect the environment. I don't know if that's rumor or reality; better check it out. Antoine, since launching his first aluminum boat, prefers to stick with *Dox Anode* (*Metagrip*), which, as noted earlier, is somewhat antifouling. He has to dive to brush off his hull a little more often, but figures that he is minimizing the risk of electrolysis by only using *Metagrip*.

Fiberglass:

Yards turn out production boats very quickly, and for reasons of profit margin, they're almost always lightweight. Even things as basic as the rigging, the chainplates, and the strength of the rudder have left me shaking my head. Do they just enjoy playing Russian roulette? I have far more confidence in good amateur construction. I have seen some excellent examples: heavy, carefully reinforced hulls; numerous chainplates of really respectable size; indestructible mast steps, pillars, and rudder blades, with fittings to match; wide, relatively long keels well attached to the hull. These are real boats, made to last. They can face heavy weather with confidence, handle an occasional scrape on a coral reef without splitting open, and require virtually no maintenance.

But how well would such a heavily built fiberglass boat sail? Jean-François Coste once told me something very interesting. On a sail around the world by the three capes (starting and finishing in Europe), the average speed difference between an ultra-light boat and another one exactly similar, but much heavier, would be about 2%. In other words, when the ultra-light covered 200 miles in 24 hours, her robust cousin would cover "only" 196.

Molded wood:

Cold-molded construction produces a boat that is very rigid, light, and watertight, if certain joints (cabin roof to deck, deck to hull, and keel to stem and sternpost) are made with great care. But construction takes much longer than one might first expect.

You often see hulls of molded wood or plywood covered with a coat of fiberglass and polyester resin to protect them against shipworms. I think that is *very dangerous*: if the layer cracks—and it will, sooner or later—shipworms will get in without your realizing it. And from then on, they will chew their way through the planking (which is thin, remember) faster and faster. You may not always realize what is going on, and after a few years the damage is irreparable. In my opinion, a fiberglass sheath is absolutely illusory protection and can turn a good boat into an abandoned hulk. If you're lucky enough to notice the presence of shipworms, there must be a way of dealing with them. I imagine that under those circumstances, the best thing to do would be to haul the boat out for several months to be sure no shipworms or their larvae remain alive and that the water in their tunnels is completely evaporated (you can hasten this by drilling small holes, to be plugged later). I would let everything dry out completely; three or four months wouldn't be too long. Once that's done, I would inject a very fluid epoxy (*Everdur*, for example), which is usually used to "vitrify" wood that has become spongy. But these are just suggestions. The problem is a tough one, and others who are more experienced than I will be better able to help you solve it.

Plywood:
Much faster to build with than molded wood, but not as rigid, obviously, since you're making a hard-chine boat; also, it is subject to the same ship-worm problem. I've often heard it said that the layers of glue in plywood or molded wood are barriers to shipworms. That's absolutely false; I've seen some disasters.

Traditional plank construction:
Absolutely solid, and capable of sailing for decades without major problems if the construction is well done, using first-class materials. But unless you are very skilled, it's best to leave the work to a reputable shipyard. Or to find a skilled craftsman and work together as much as possible, to learn as many useful things as you can. Either way, you have to be financially very secure to build a good boat using classic plank construction. Before World War II, and even for a time afterward, those boats were superbly built. The logs would spend eight to twelve years buried in mud (and out of reach of ship-worms, which are found in all climates) to draw out the sap. Then the log was allowed to dry very slowly, in the shade. It was cut into sheets and planks which were stored in a dry, well-ventilated warehouse to cure for several more years. The shipyards had a large supply, and the wood was really ready, without a trace of sapwood. The humblest fishing boat was built with the same love as a cathedral, because the builders had the time. Those days are gone.

A modern framework made of glued laminated wood (bow and stern pieces, bulkheads, floor timbers, ribs, side stringers, struts, deck- and cabin-top beams) will be terrifically strong if you don't skimp on fittings. Unless you're a millionaire, though, I doubt you'll ever find those wonderful long planks from our grandfathers' day to cover that great framework.

Contrary to a widely held belief, shipworms aren't a problem for a traditional planked boat. During the year I spent at Durban with MARIE-THÉRÈSE II, I worked in a shipyard that repaired and caulked wooden boats. The work fascinated me, so I observed and learned a great deal. At my other ports of call, I would always visit haul-out slips, either to lend friends a hand or just because I was drawn to them, like most boating people. And I met a number of young people who were replacing planking they said had been "devoured" by shipworms. *It was never necessary.* I repeat: *never.* The problem wasn't shipworms, but the almost superstitious fear they inspire.

Let's look at things calmly. The planking on a 30-foot Tahiti Ketch is between 1" and 1¼" thick. That's much more than is needed for strength, but the heavy thickness allows for a good caulk job. A few shipworm tunnels won't really reduce the hull's solidity, or even that of the plank in question. But they certainly need to be dealt with.

And now, to work. The boat is hauled out as usual. The hull, well brushed and rinsed, dries quickly. If a small damp spot appears on the hull—but outside of the caulk lines—and the damp spot is circular (an inch or so across), it's almost certainly the sign of a shipworm. Circle it with chalk. With a sharp chisel, cut horizontally across the wet spot to remove a thin sliver of wood, as if you were planing it. A tiny hole will appear; that's the opening to the tunnel. As you dig deeper with the chisel, the hole gets bigger. Stop as soon as you can poke a red-hot wire into it. To increase your chances of getting the shipworm, heat the area *as much as possible* with a blowtorch. Keep at it for a while, to be on the safe side. Don't worry if the paint burns; better to scorch two or three feet of wood than to risk missing the culprit. (In the Gulf of Siam, every time the junks were hauled out, their hulls were heated to the maximum with torches made of woven palm fronds.)

After the heat treatment, squirt some Xylene with a syringe into the tunnels, then paint and repaint all the stripped wood with a brush. After using the Xylene, plug everything with epoxy before the first coat of primer. Life is tenacious, so stay in dry dock for two or three days more, so you can check everything and avoid unexpected developments. For example, while you're looking for damp spots on the first day after hauling out, remember to inspect the planks above the waterline that aren't treated with antifouling paint; I've often seen shipworm damage four or six inches *above the waterline*. It was probably due to heel during a crossing, where larvae managed to dig their way in. Nothing mysterious about it. When you reach port after an ocean passage, there is almost always some seaweed clinging to the topsides that will continue to live out of water, hoping for a splash of water to give it something to eat and drink. A shipworm does the same thing: it adapts while awaiting better days. Painting with antifouling a good foot above the waterline will avoid these kinds of surprises. It's less elegant than a pretty band of shiny enamel at the waterline, but much more prudent.

If you discover shipworms in the keel, bow, or sternpost, that's more serious, but still no cause for alarm or despair. First, it's worth remembering that shipworms can survive out of water for a month or more in a large piece of wood. I'm absolutely convinced of that, because I've seen it with my own eyes. So I would leave my boat out of water for two or three months before injecting a few squirts of Xylene or some other more effective product from time to time. Then, epoxy.

To my knowledge, there aren't any books on the life cycle of shipworms. But I expect the owner of a wooden boat could find useful information on them in a library. I can also state that a copper bottom is no protection against shipworms. While I was a shipwright in Durban, the yard's customers were mainly big, 60- to 100-ton fishing boats which had all been copper-bottomed ten years or so before, and were leaking. So they were hauled out, and my crew removed the copper plating to caulk them. And what we saw was worth noting: all of those boats, *without exception*, had been seriously attacked by shipworms at the sternpost, keel, and garboard strake. I saw a dozen of them like that. Their owners were baffled. The yard's best workers repaired the damage as well they could (but very quickly, because it was the middle of the fishing season) while the rest of us caulked like maniacs, sometimes for 72 hours straight with just an occasional nap at the job site. And the boat went out to fish again, its owner swearing that two good coats of antifouling paint every six months were worth any amount of copper sheathing.

Leaving a wooden boat out of water for a long time isn't generally recommended, because the seams between the planks running the length of the boat begin to spread as the wood dries out. But all will return to normal a few days after the boat is back in the water, and a long spell in dry dock provides an excellent opportunity to check the hull's caulking and to work on any suspicious areas.

This isn't the place for a course in caulking, so here are just a few essential points:

1) Putty, good though it may be, *only* protects the wicking. Caulking compound (even those "miracle" products that ship chandlers try to sell you) won't keep water out if the strands of oakum or cotton aren't properly packed between the planks.

2) I've often heard it said that oakum or cotton packed very tightly between the planks can burst them, because oakum swells under water, and that it's therefore better to caulk "light." The truth is that a "light" caulk is much faster than a decent job where the fiber is packed properly. People who sincerely believe that "light" is better than "well-packed," may be right if the boat in question is a very old 18-foot J.I. with very thin planking, used for racing around the buoys, but certainly not for a cruising boat with normal planking.

3) Good caulking cotton produces a more watertight joint than tarred-hemp oakum. Cotton probably doesn't last as long as oakum, but it serves very well; when I have a choice, I don't hesitate to use it. But there are two kinds of caulking cotton: one looks a bit like string, off-white, and fairly rough to the touch. The other is almost pure white, woolly, and very soft. Use the soft kind; you won't regret it.

In closing, a boat that is hauled regularly, every six or eight months in the tropics, say, won't have shipworm problems. But don't forget that shipworms and other wood-eating worms also exist in the Atlantic and the Mediterranean.

Another major problem faced by a wooden boat during its lifetime is rot. If this occurs, it has to be dealt with, but—as with shipworms—without panicking. Without worrying too much, either. Calm down and think it over. Rot doesn't spread like wildfire; it goes very slowly. And everything in a wooden boat is oversized. A little rotten section of a rib, or anywhere else, isn't going to weaken the whole boat. And once you start replacing ribs, there's no end to it. It means being stuck in port with a big expenditure of money and energy. It may even spell the end of a dream that at the beginning had every chance of turning into a life of long ocean passages and new friendships in ports of call.

Here is the story of Peter, an American I met some fifteen years ago in Polynesia. He had fallen in love with and bought a good used boat in the Caribbean; it was about 30 feet, with classic planking. And one day Peter discovered a large area of rot in the inner side of the stem. Once he recovered from the shock, he started thinking. The bow's intrinsic strength hadn't been compromised, obviously. And even if the stem were half rotten (which it wasn't, as he discovered by carefully sounding the entire stem, after his disturbing discovery), the piece was so thick, it wouldn't be a problem. The trick was to stop the rot and keep it from spreading. His reasoning was sound, and so was what he did next.

Peter hauled out in Panama and spent two months there. 1) He started by drilling tiny holes in the affected area, the width of a large syringe needle, to let the humidity out. 2) He then heated the area with a blowtorch several times a day for three weeks or a month while airing out the boat. 3) For several days running, he then injected acetone into the tiny holes he had drilled at the start. Acetone is extremely volatile; as it evaporates, it draws out the last traces of humidity. 4) Finally, massive injections of *Everdur*, totally impregnating the entire rotten area, which was now perfectly dry. *Everdur* is a very fluid two-part epoxy which acts as a fungicide as it vitrifies the rotten area. If you soaked a dry sponge with *Everdur*, it would become as hard as a brick. I've successfully used *Everdur* for a small area of rot at the ends of JOSHUA's spreaders. Three years later, it was still holding, and I considered the repair permanent.

Size of the boat

Careful now—not too big! If you get greedy, you always wind up paying for it in time and worry. A 25- to 30-foot boat can spin out a wonderful wake; here are a few examples among many. LEGH II: around the world by the three capes. SUHAILI: around the world by the three capes, nonstop. DAMIEN: Greenland, the Amazon, the three capes, and the Adelie Coast. Many smaller boats have sailed around the world by following the trades and rounding the Cape of Good Hope. Naturally, a 45-footer is much faster and more comfortable than a 30- or 35-foot boat, but the difference in purchase price (or construction cost, if you build it yourself) and maintenance expenses is enormous.

Short of building your own boat, I think it's wisest to order a bare hull— hull, deck, cabin top, and rudder—from a good boatyard. The advantage of going this route is that you will have the basics in two or three months. If you choose a metal boat (and I hope you do) and the yard owner lets you work there, fabricate all your own topside fittings: stanchions, bow pulpit, sheet cleats, mooring bitts, handrails, etc. You can't imagine how much time those many pieces represent. Not only will you get exactly what you want, but it will also cost much less. And working alongside professionals has two further benefits: you will learn plenty of things that will come in handy later, and you'll get to know your boat backwards and forwards.

With the bulk of the job finished in just a few months, you might be tempted to think everything is done. But you're on a roll, so stick with it. Get your mast, rigging, sails (perhaps second-hand), a few rolls of line, three anchors, chain, a fresh-water tank (or jerry cans), a few pots and pans, a kerosene or propane stove, a bare-bones interior—and it's home sweet home! Not very comfortable? A mere detail, for the moment. You have the essentials. You can fiddle with interior arrangements little by little in ports of call. The advantage of doing things in increments is that you will know exactly what you need. It also gives you time to really think and figure how to go about doing things, avoiding costly mistakes. Better to raise anchor with plenty of money in the cash-box than to struggle under a ton of stuff you can live without. During her first five or six years, JOSHUA sailed for miles with a strictly "bed of nails" decor—and no winches on deck. I'm not saying that a more comfortable cabin and winches wouldn't have been preferable, but we had to choose between hoisting sail before winter started or shivering in the port of Marseille while we ate up our savings. Once the bow is pointed toward the open sea, you always manage. Twenty years later, TAMATA left San Francisco with only a few boxes of candles for light. Kerosene lamps, then a solar panel and batteries, came later.

Sail area and choice of rig

As far as I'm concerned, I always bear two principles in mind: maximum sail area, and divided sails. Being able to carry a lot of canvas in gentle to moderate airs means you can go quite a bit faster. And a divided rig is easier to handle when you're alone or in heavy weather. A six-foot bowsprit will allow a boat to carry much more sail than a similar boat without one. And if a boat has both a bowsprit and a mast that is three feet taller, the difference in the amount of sail it can carry in light or moderate wind will be enormous—and so will the difference in speed.

In light airs, a boat's speed isn't only a function of the pressure of the wind on the sails, but how regular that pressure is. Let's take a specific example. 1) The wind is fresh and two boats are sailing between a beam and a broad reach under somewhat reduced sail toward the same destination. 2) The wind begins to slacken, then drops considerably. Both boats raise all canvas, but the swells are big and the sea fairly choppy. This is when a large total sail surface will make all the difference. The boat with more sail (the one with a bowsprit and taller mast) will move much faster than the other one, not only because of the greater pressure of the wind, but also because the boat won't pound into the waves as much at all points of sail between a close reach and running. Moreover, the airflow is much more efficient on sails that are well filled. With a lot of sail in light or moderate wind on a choppy sea, the boat pounds less and the sails remain more stable, which is all to the good. On the other hand, it will be at a disadvantage vis-a-vis the other boat when close-hauled in a fresh wind, because of its extra windage aloft. So it's a matter of choice. I made mine long ago.

As for the choice of divided rigs, I also made my choice long ago. But I've come to prefer a cutter over a ketch rig. It means less weight and windage aloft; a more open deck; better performance close-hauled; the possibility of sailing into a strong wind under staysail alone; and of being maneuverable (including coming about) under staysail or mainsail alone when making an anchorage in light airs and flat sea. If I were to re-rig JOSHUA, she would be a cutter.

Not that a ketch rig doesn't have some advantages. One, it lets you set a mizzen staysail, which adds considerably to the total sail area and reduces rolling, making all the sails work better. Second, you can jibe comfortably even in a fresh breeze. Here is how I do it: 1) first, sheet in the mainsail completely; 2) set the self-steering windvane for a wind from full astern; 3) ease the mizzen sheet so the mizzen blankets the main; 4) set the windvane for the jibe; the mainsail will go to the other side smoothly since it is blanketed by the mizzen and is still sheeted in; 5) bring the mizzen over (no problem, given its relatively moderate area); 6) then bring over the jib and staysail (which were backwinded following the jibe) and sheet out the main for the new tack.

Thus described, the maneuver sounds complicated, and you may wonder why I haven't yet gotten around to buying one of those automatic vangs that ship chandlers carry. For one thing, the procedure isn't that complicated. For another, those devices are expensive and I find them cumbersome. I prefer an open, uncluttered deck. That way, I'm really at ease on my boat, free to go anywhere fast under all circumstances, without fear of tripping on anything.

The rudder: on the keel or on the transom?

I much prefer a rudder hung on the transom. First, this lets you rig a self-steering device that is extremely simple and strong, not to say indestructible, and which you can make yourself for next to nothing. When I see the prices of sophisticated and often fragile self-steering rigs, it really makes me wonder, especially since you then have to install them. That takes time and money better spent on more useful things: rolls of line, extra stores, or a few good spare anchors, for example. I'm not looking to earn extra royalties, but you can save a lot of money by carefully studying the appendix to *The Long Way*. It has very clear diagrams showing how to assemble an excellent self-steering rig that will take you far without any problems (naturally, I'm talking cruising, not racing).

Second, a transom-mounted rudder is a model of strength and simplicity and will never cause problems, whereas a keel-hung rudder might someday jam on its shaft.

Finally, I think having a keel-hung rudder on a wooden boat is really asking for trouble. Despite every precaution, shipworms will sooner or later burrow into the sternpost throat, and—which is far more serious—into the rudder trunk.

Blue-water cruising

This is an inexhaustible subject. You could write pages and pages, and it would remain like the horizon, which retreats as you go toward it. In any case, I've already shared my opinions on a number of problems in the technical appendices of my three previous books. And it is high time I wrapped this one up. So here, very briefly, are a few other thoughts that might be useful.

Sail and mast strength

In the appendix to *The Long Way*, I wrote a dozen pages on this important subject, illustrated with detailed diagrams. So I'll just summarize the main points here.

Sails:
1) Many observations have proved to me that sails sewn with very heavy thread are much stronger and more durable than ones sewn with the finer thread that lofts commonly use. But making sails that way takes more time (and is therefore more expensive), since the sailmakers have to change their bobbins more often. I've often heard it said that thin thread is less subject to

chafe, since it sinks into the fabric rather than sitting on the surface. That argument makes no sense at all. Whether the thread is heavy or thin, it necessarily stays on the surface. Only in the cotton sails of old did the thread sink into the fabric (assuming the sail was hand-sewn, and not zigzag stitched on a sewing machine).

2) Small triangular (not rectangular) patches sewn at the leech cringles can strengthen sails considerably, by reducing the risk of tearing during violent flapping, for example when you have to strike a sail fast in a big squall.

3) Rectangular patches sewn along the seams where they chafe against the spreaders and the lower shrouds can limit wear on the stitching at those critical points.

Taken together, these three points will produce sails that are much stronger and longer-lasting for cruising. (But probably not for racing, where the slightest unevenness on a sail's surface will hurt performance close-hauled.)

Masts:

Numerous chainplates, many shrouds, and oversized turnbuckles are the best combination I know to give you peace of mind in bad weather. JOSHUA's main mast survived six or seven serious knockdowns, plus a collision with a freighter. It was supported by six shrouds on each side, plus the backstays. Needless to say, TAMATA is rigged the same way. Of course that rigging represents extra weight and windage where you want it least when close-hauled, but to each his own.

One more thing I consider vital: being able to climb easily to the top of the mast under any condition (to replace a halyard, free a jammed sail slide, take a look from above to pick up a buoy, see a low shore or a reef, etc.). I found *Seabird Mast Steps* excellent. The halyards can't foul or chafe on them, and the stainless steel steps can be adapted to any shape mast, whether wood or aluminum.

Anchors and anchoring

I covered this topic at length in the appendix to *Cape Horn: The Logical Route*. For my part, I can't recall the least problem anchoring in sand or mud bottoms with the CQR plow, Fob, Britannia, or Trigrip anchors. For rocky bottoms, I prefer to use my good old stocked Herreshoff anchor; it has the great advantage of not fouling the anchor line too often, thanks to its diamond-shaped flukes. When the boat swings more than 180 degrees, the chain tends to slide along the exposed fluke, rather than catch on it.

I try as much as possible to avoid anchoring in water deeper than I can dive, in case I need to go down to free an anchor. And with extremely few exceptions, I always choose a big anchor over a smaller one. Whether an anchor weighs, say, 50 pounds instead of 35 doesn't make much difference in terms of muscular effort when you're getting underway. But the extra holding power on the bottom will be welcome in case the wind rises while you're still at anchor.

Some people prefer "all chain." Others prefer a combination: 45 to 75 feet of chain shackled to a nylon line. For several reasons (light weight, ease of handling, "give" in the anchor line) I belong to the latter group. But beware of the line's chafing at the bow and *especially on a rocky or coral bottom.* Remedying the problem is simple. (See diagrams A and B. As shown on Diagram B, note that the float must be big enough to keep the end of the chain well above the coral heads.)

When using "all chain" in shallow water, you no longer have the natural dampening effect caused by the weight and the curve of the chain. A violent jerk can snap it, especially if the chain is caught under a coral head. Remedy: a few yards of strong line between the mooring bitt and the chain, with a well-secured marline hitch. (Diagram C).

Propeller drag

JOSHUA had a very small two-bladed propeller, but it still cost me a dozen miles every 24 hours. So I used to remove it (by diving, with a wheel puller) before a long crossing. To avoid that annoyance, TAMATA's propeller is a folding model; it is much less efficient, but it doesn't slow the boat.

Heaving-to in fair weather

This is exactly the same technique as heaving-to in general: staysail backed, mainsail sheeted flat, helm down. (There are variations, such as using jib and mizzen instead of staysail and mainsail). Needless to say, you usually heave-to under shortened sail, since it's a heavy-weather tactic which I have already covered elsewhere in detail. I'm speaking here of heaving-to in fair weather. In general, to heave-to, you sheet all the sails flat, then come about (or jibe, if you prefer) without touching the sheets, and lash the tiller down when you have finished coming about. The boat will then drift very slowly, and the sea will seem to have completely calmed. This gives me time to rest or think, without risking a hasty or stupid decision. A few examples:

A) After a crossing during which I had been slammed around for three days, I finally sighted land. I was hungry and exhausted, having not picked up a single lighthouse before dawn. I felt drained, sailing like a blind man feeling his way, my frozen neurons dead and useless. What could I do? Simple: heave-to! Suddenly the boat quieted down, my neurons started firing again (jump-started by a hot cup of coffee and some soup and crackers). A twenty-minute nap did the rest. After that, a good breakfast and all was well again.

B) I was making for an atoll. It came into view. Terrific! The boat sped on, approaching the pass. I was so happy to reach the atoll after a week at sea, I was hypnotized. But be careful now... It might be a good idea to make sure the outgoing current isn't too strong, and to coil my halyards a bit better so as not to risk a last-minute tangle. I hove-to, which gave me all the time I needed to straighten everything on deck and to calmly decide the best way to take the pass.

C) I was crossing the Tuamotu Archipelago at night, in bad weather. Even with a Global Positioning System (GPS) I wouldn't have been sure of my position since the atolls aren't perfectly charted. So I hove-to from time to time, croquis A

VENT

MOUILLAGE MIXTE

B
calme plat

Le flotteur doit être assez
volumineux pour maintenir le bout
de la chaîne à bonne distance
des coraux.

C: "TOUT chaîné" par faible profondeur

cablot

nœud de
bosse

donner du mou
à la chaîne

La chaîne s'est prise
sous une roche ou un corail

listening to be sure I didn't hear swells breaking on some barrier reef hidden in the darkness.

Heaving-to is especially valuable for listening. Here's the perfect illustration. On a beautiful, full-moon night, I was sailing along, about a half mile off Bora Bora's barrier reef. I was in the lee of the island, on a broad reach. The wind was light, force two at the most; the boat was making about three knots. The sea was absolutely calm with a long southwesterly swell which I could distinctly see pounding on the reef in huge breakers. And yet, try as I might, the only thing I could hear was the rustle of water at the bow. So I closed to within a quarter-mile and continued to sail along the reef, struck by the beauty of the terrific breakers in the light of the full moon. And I still couldn't hear anything! I wanted to make sure, once and for all, so I hove-to. And then I heard real rolling thunder! I could even hear it in the cabin when I went below to light the stove for a cup of coffee. From that experience, I can say at least one thing with certainty: when your boat is sailing, even very slowly, you won't be warned by the sound of even a very large swell breaking on a reef, much less a gentle one. In every case, the only way to have the slightest chance of hearing the sea breaking on a reef is to heave-to. (Needless to say, you can't have any lights at all on deck—or even in the cabin—if you expect to see anything at night.

Radar

Let me say at the outset that radar can play some nasty tricks in the Tuamotus if you forget that it doesn't pick up breaking waves. On the screen, you might see land two miles away, for example. But it might be a small island well inside the barrier reef; the reef itself won't necessarily give you an echo. But radar can be an invaluable aid on many occasions: watching out for ships and fishing fleets, setting a pre-set alarm, making port at night... The list would be a long one, but I'm hardly one to talk, since I have no personal experience with radar units. If I were planning a long cruise, however, I wouldn't hesitate to install one. Their cost, size, and current drain have all dropped over the years, while their sensitivity and usefulness as an auditory alarm have increased. Some day, radar units will be as small as cracker boxes and be sold in every supermarket.

Global Positioning System (GPS)

This too, is amazing. You can find your position to within 450 or 600 feet in the middle of the ocean! But remember that nautical charts can be off by several miles in rarely traveled areas. Remember too, that a broken GPS unit can't normally be fixed with what you have on board. I wouldn't hesitate to buy one, but not before I had outfitted my boat with all the basics. And if I could treat myself to a GPS, it would primarily be to help me completely master my sextant. I should note that the HO 249 tables can be truly dangerous if you rely on them blindly when taking star sights, because they offer a very limited choice of stars for any given hour. The tables were created for use by airplanes, which fly at altitudes where all stars are visible at the same time. That's not the case for a sailor in overcast weather, with only fleeting clearings between clouds. After getting into real trouble with the HO 249 tables, I've switched for good to the NO 229 tables; they are slightly slower to use for star sights but trustworthy under all circumstances. They are published by the Defense Mapping Agency, Hydrographic/Topographic Center, Washington, D.C. 20315. I imagine you can find the same tables in the United Kingdom.

Solar panels

Another marvel! And their cost continues to fall in response to demand and new manufacturing techniques. TAMATA does perfectly well with a solar panel that charges her single 70-ampere battery, which in turn powers a ceiling and fluorescent light in the cabin and a white masthead light. The panel is movable, instead of fixed, which allows me to set it up wherever I like. That way, it's always in full sunlight and correctly oriented so it charges the battery at top efficiency from morning till night. At sea, in bad weather or when getting close to an anchorage, I stow the panel below to keep the deck clear for maneuvering.

Masthead light

In the old days, fish were abundant and there were far fewer fishing boats than today. But times have changed. Fishermen now seek their catches in the most unexpected places, and you can find them almost anywhere on the open ocean. I carry a white masthead light, visible over 360 degrees. It isn't "regulation," but I prefer to be spotted a long way off while I'm asleep. I also prefer to sail with all lights out when I'm on deck, and, out of caution, change course to cross behind any passing ships I encounter. When entering a port, I use little portable red and green lights, powered by ordinary 1.5 volt batteries. That lets me keep outside electrical lines to a minimum and avoid chances of failure and electrical problems in general.

Before ending this section, it's worth noting that I was twice nearly rammed in broad daylight, the first time aboard MARIE-THÉRÈSE II between Cape Town and Saint Helena, the second time in the Atlantic aboard JOSHUA, half a day's sail from Gibraltar. The era of Slocum, Voss, and Gerbault is past; you must be vigilant under all circumstances. This is when a radar alarm, carefully set both night and day, can give you valuable peace of mind.

Essential nautical documents

Pilot charts:
Absolutely ingenious. I can't imagine setting out without them. A few inexpensive sets cover all the oceans, providing many kinds of information for each month or quarter, depending on the ocean. The data is statistical, and reliable for a dozen years. With a complete set of Pilot Charts, you can easily plan a trip around the world without really having to dig into any other documents. At a glance, you can get useful information for an overview that will make choosing reasonable alternatives much simpler. Pilot Charts are published by the Defense Mapping Agency in Washington, D.C

Light List:

An essential aid. Each volume covers extensive areas of coast and ocean islands.

Ephemeris:

Miniature electronic calculators are very handy and fast, but a few drops of seawater can do them in. I would never sail without an ephemeris, which is a table of star positions. I find the American editions handier—more rugged and compact—than the French ones. Moreover, they cost much less; in 1993, Los Angeles ship chandlers were selling them for about $15. English ephemerides are laid out like the American ones, and probably cost about the same.

Star Finder:

A set of little plastic disks that let you very quickly figure the approximate altitudes and azimuths of the stars used in celestial navigation in advance and at any hour of the night. The Star Finder is invaluable under overcast skies, when a brief break in the clouds can give you just enough time to take a sextant sight on an observable star.

Tides in the Tuamotus

Logic to the contrary notwithstanding, the tide is high when the moon rises and sets, and low when the moon passes the meridian (upper and lower). I've often confirmed this information from late-19th century *Sailing Directions* (whose data is laid out much more clearly than in our modern ones).

Nautical charts

They are quite expensive, but many merchant ships (especially tankers) carry sets of out-of-date charts that they haven't disposed of yet. They are useless for ships drawing 15 to 30 feet, but valuable for us. You can sometimes walk down a gangplank with a big roll of charts under your arm just for the asking.

Sextant

I use the "no lens, both eyes open" method. The difference when taking a sun sight isn't usually more than a quarter-mile in calm seas. And in swells, you're sure to have brought the sun down to the horizon, and not to the top of some wave (a sextant lens considerably narrows your field of vision). Moreover, you can take a sight much faster with both eyes open. That's valuable in overcast weather, when the sun is playing hide and seek among the clouds. And for star sights, there's no comparison. Through the sextant lens you can see the star, but the horizon is completely blurry; you can't even tell if you're looking at the horizon or the sky. Without the lens and with both eyes open, you can see the star perfectly, but also make out the horizon clearly enough to bring the star down to it. On a clear night, you can get a remarkably accurate star fix. When the night isn't so clear, you can still get a fix by "dunking" the star—that is, by bringing it a little below the apparent horizon (more or less, depending on how unsure you are of the horizon). Thanks to a GPS's extreme precision, you can become a real star-juggler, in intimate contact with the sky; you can then use the electronics as an ally in case of emergency.

Weather reports

I heartily recommend Alan Watts' little book *Instant Weather Forecasting* (Adlard Coles, 1968), which taught me how to predict weather changes in a few minutes. It's terrific: all you do is compare the surface wind direction (cumulus) with the high-altitude direction (cirrus) and apply the "cross-wind rule;" a very clear diagram in Watts' book shows how to do it. On land, you can always find a fixed point (a tree, post, house roof) to observe the slow movement of cirrus. At sea, when the moon is up, you can easily see the cirrus moving across the lunar disk. And for the sun, I use the sextant's filters (dark glasses aren't enough to cut the sun's brightness).

The gods...

In closing, let me pass on a tip I think is invaluable, provided you take it the right way: it's worth making friends with the gods. They enjoy it, and occasionally lead us into the third dimension, where things become clear and the obvious effective. You think maybe the Old Monkey is starting to lose it at the end of his journey? Nothing could be further from the truth. I know what I'm talking about, and I've often enjoyed the gods' company—both here and beyond. Again, let me repeat: good luck to all of you!

GLOSSARY

This glossary is written for people who don't sail, to help them follow this story more easily. I have therefore written it as simply as I could. Sailors won't need it, and I hope they will forgive me if my explanations at times seem somewhat superfluous, or not always written in strictly nautical language.

Anchor winch. A kind of capstan used to pull up the anchor chain. The smaller the boat, the less necessary an anchor winch is, since you can raise the anchor by pulling up the chain by hand. Many racing boats, even large ones, prefer not to have an anchor winch, since they have large crews and an anchor winch is heavy and could get in the way when handling sails. In cruising, the opposite is true.

Beat. A boat is beating (or sailing close hauled) when she is sailing into the wind at an angle of about 45 degrees. As the angle increases, she is successively on a reach (60 degrees), a beam reach (wind at 90 degrees to the boat's axis), a broad reach, and a run (wind directly astern). A boat performs better on a reach than on a beat; she pitches less, pounds in the seas less, and goes faster.

Block and tackle. A set of pulleys rigged to increase tension when pulling on a line. A block and tackle can generate tremendous power. Long ago, one of Tahiti's mountains was pulled across to Pao Pao Bay on the neighboring

island of Moorea with a block and tackle rig which the locals had carved from mother of pearl from the lagoon. (They had first looped a rope woven from the bark of *burao* trees from the west coast around the mountain.) Many people today refuse to believe this true story, perhaps because they have forgotten that in olden days, people believed in something.

Bobstay. A kind of *stay* used to steady the bowsprit vertically. Most bobstays are made of steel cable (like the stays), but I prefer to use chain, which doesn't corrode as quickly.

Bonnet. An extra fair-weather sail that can be placed (or set) below another sail, to increase the sail area.

Boom. The horizontal piece of wood (or aluminum) to which the bottom edge of the sail (called the *foot*) is attached. Like a mast, a boom may be wood or aluminum alloy. JOSHUA's booms are wood, as are her masts.

Bottom. The submerged part of a boat's hull, from the keel to the waterline. This is in contrast to the *topsides*, the part of the hull from the waterline to the *gunwales* (where the hull meets the deck).

Bowsprit. A piece of wood (or iron, on JOSHUA and most steel boats) that extends forward of the bow. Few boats have bowsprits today, but I find one very handy, because it lets you set extra sails. On the other hand, a bowsprit can get in the way when you are in port.

Chainplates. Metal plates bolted or welded to the boat's sides to anchor the shrouds.

Coaming. The vertical part of the cabin above the deck which serves to protect the person at the helm against wind and spray.

Cockpit. A protective open compartment on deck behind the cabin. You normally steer from the cockpit.

Deadeye. A round block of wood threaded with a line, used to tighten a boat's shrouds. Today, deadeyes have been replaced with turnbuckles.

Fall off. To steer the boat away from the direction the wind is blowing from. Falling off is the opposite of luffing up.

Forestay (jibstay). A steel cable running from the bow to (usually) two thirds of the way up the mainmast. This helps steady the mast and also allows you to set the *staysail.* (See also *topmast stay.*)

Furl. To tie a sail down along its boom, after lowering the sail. Even without a boom, you can furl a sail anyway. You tie the bundle of sail with tie-downs (also called gaskets), which are short lengths of line or cloth.

Gaff. A strong pole, two to three yards long, with a rounded hook at the end. It is used to pick up an object that has fallen into the water, to push off a dock while maneuvering in port, etc.

Genoa. A large jib. You set a genoa when the wind isn't too strong; otherwise, the mast could break. A *storm jib* is a very small jib, used when the wind is blowing very hard.

Gunwale. The board or railing running along the top edge of the hull (usually where it meets the deck).

Halyard. A line (or very flexible, small-diameter steel cable) that runs through a pulley (or *block*) at the top of the mast and is used to hoist the sails. Each sail has its own halyard.

Heave-to. This is hard to explain in a few lines. This is a maneuver used in stormy weather which lets your boat fend for itself when the sea is very rough. There are several ways to heave-to. For example, you can take down (drop, or strike) all the sails, then use shock cords to tie the rudder tiller to leeward (i.e., to starboard if the wind is coming from port), and go take a nap. The boat will then float like a cork without making any headway, while you wait for the weather to clear. But it can sometimes be dangerous to heave-to without any sails up. So you can put up part of the mainsail and leave the jib aback (or backed, meaning it is fastened to the side the wind is coming from), with the tiller again tied to leeward. The boat will then drift slowly and create a kind of protective wake to windward, which prevents waves from breaking. But since the first boats started sailing, volumes have been written on how to heave-to, none of which have kept boats from sometimes being turned over by breaking waves. If the boat has a weighted keel, however, it will come back upright before it fills with water, which is the main thing.

Jib. A triangular sail at the front of the boat. In descending order of size, jibs include the big genoa, small genoa, working jib, small jib, smallest jib, and storm jib. You can even have storm jibs of different sizes, one small, another tiny. All these sails, from the genoa to the storm jib, and including the staysail, make up the headsails, i.e. the sails located forward of the main mast.

Jibe. To bring the sails (deliberately or by accident) from one side of the boat to the other, with the wind blowing from behind the boat. In a strong wind, an accidental jibe can snap the mast, if the boat is carrying too much canvas.

Landing (or making land). To come within sight of land, a lighthouse, or an island. Sailors are often nervous before a landing, for fear of having made a mistake in their navigation.

Mizzen. The mizzen mast is the rear mast on a two-masted boat, and the mizzen sail is the one attached to that mast. For short, we say "mizzen" to refer to that sail.

Patent log. A device used to measure the distance covered which works similarly to an odometer in a car. With a patent log, a small propeller towed on a line turns the register, which is attached to the rear of the boat. In racing, a much smaller and more sophisticated log is used, attached to the hull, whose propeller is only an inch or so in diameter, and therefore doesn't slow the boat. Most cruising boats have this second kind of log, which gives both the speed and distance covered.

Pitchpole. To capsize forward, stern over bow.

Reef. To make a sail's area smaller by lowering the sail part way, and tying the lower part in a bundle (usually on the boom). Used in strong wind.

Reef bands. Horizontal rows of little holes in the sails, reinforced (like buttonholes) by eyelets or grommets. Small lines called reef points are attached to the holes, and are used to tie down the bundled sail when it is reefed. The third reef

band is usually the highest, that is, the one used to reduce sail area the most. So sailing "triple-reefed" means sailing with a minimum of canvas.

Shackle. A U-shaped metal fitting with a pin or a bolt across the open end, used to connect stays, anchor chains, etc.

Sheet. A line used to orient the sails relative to the wind, and attached to the lower corner (or *clew*) of the sail. You sheet in (or harden) the sheet when you pull it toward the inside of the boat. You ease the sheet when you loosen it and let it run toward the outside of the boat. It's much easier to ease a sheet than to harden it, since to ease it, you can just release the tension on the sheet, and the strength of the wind does the rest. To harden a sheet, you need to use your muscles or a winch (or a block and tackle).

Shroud. A steel cable used to steady the mast from side to side. They are anchored to chainplates on the hull.

Spar. Any long piece of wood, such as a boom, bowsprit, etc.

Stay. A steel cable used to steady the mast, running parallel with the axis of the boat.

Staysail. A headsail carried between the mainsail and the jib. Small boats usually carry only a jib and no staysail. But cruising sailors often prefer a "split rig," that is, jib and staysail, which makes adjustments simpler, since the individual sails are smaller and easier to handle. Naturally, the dinghies you see sailing in sheltered water have no staysail; it would be useless and cumbersome on such small boats.

Storm jib. A very small, strong jib used in heavy weather.

Tack. (n.): A boat is said to be sailing on a port tack when the wind is coming from the port side, and on a starboard tack when it comes from starboard. Port is the left side of a boat when facing forward, starboard the right. As a noun, tack also has another meaning. It means the corner of the mainsail where the boom meets the mast. On a jib, it's the corner where the headstay meets the deck.

Tack. (v.) To change the boat's direction vis-a-vis the wind when the boat is sailing into the wind. It has the effect of changing you from a port to starboard tack, or starboard to port. Tacking (or coming about) is the opposite of jibing.

Topping lift. A line used to hold up the end of the boom when the mainsail or mizzen is not raised. Jibs and staysails don't usually have booms, and therefore no topping lifts.

Topmast stay. About the same as the forestay, except that the topmast stay runs from the bow (or the end of the bowsprit) to the top of the main mast. The topmast stay helps to steady the mast and lets you set the jib, storm jib, and genoa.

Topsides. The part of the hull from the waterline to the gunwales.

Turnbuckle. A threaded link that is used to pull together the eyes of two lines (usually used on the boat's rigging).

Whisker stay. A stay that steadies the bowsprit horizontally. (See also *bobstay*).

Winch. A little revolving drum with a crank handle, used to tighten the sheets and also for precise sail trimming. This is why winches are found even on fairly small boats. You can use a block and tackle instead of a winch, but it's slower and much more complicated.